# Latino Literature

## Voices in a Tradition

**HOLT, RINEHART AND WINSTON**

A Harcourt Education Company

Orlando • **Austin** • New York • San Diego • London

**Consultant and Reviewer**

**Rosa Fonseca**
**Franklin High School**
**El Paso, Texas**

Cover / *Family Couch* (2003) by Jose Ramirez
© Jose Ramirez. Collection of Dr. Alfonso Barba.

Copyright © by Holt, Rinehart and Winston

All rights reserved. No part of this publication may be reproduced or transmitted in any form or by any means, electronic or mechanical, including photocopy, recording, or any information storage and retrieval system, without permission in writing from the publisher.

Requests for permission to make copies of any part of the work should be mailed to the following address: Permissions Department, Holt, Rinehart and Winston, 10801 N. MoPac Expressway, Building 3, Austin, Texas 78759.

Acknowledgments appear on page 353, which is an extension of the copyright page.

**Holt, HRW,** and the **"Owl Design,"** are trademarks licensed to Holt, Rinehart and Winston, registered in the United States of America and/or other jurisdictions.

Printed in the United States of America

If you have received these materials as examination copies free of charge, Holt, Rinehart and Winston retains title to the materials and they may not be resold. Resale of examination copies is strictly prohibited.

Possession of this publication in print format does into entitle users to convert this publication, or any portion of it, into electronic format.

ISBN 0-03-078964-8

1 2 3 4 5 018 10 09 08 07 06 05

# Contents

**Voices in a Tradition** .................................................. 1

## PART 1
## ENCOUNTERS: A MEETING OF TWO WORLDS

|  |  |  |
|---|---|---|
| | **Introduction** ................................. | 3 |
| Álvar Núñez Cabeza de Vaca (Spain) | *from* **The Journey of Álvar Núñez Cabeza de Vaca (1542)** ............ TRAVEL JOURNAL *translated by* Fanny Bandelier | 11 |
| Fray Bartolomé de las Casas (Spain) | **Plague of Ants** ...................... HISTORY *translated by* Sandra Ferdman | 23 |
| *from the* Popol Vuh (Quiché Maya) | **The Creation of Humans** ........... SACRED TEXT *translated by* Dennis Tedlock | 28 |
| Sor Juana Inés de la Cruz (Mexico) | **Disillusionment** ....................... POEMS **Fabio, what pretty women covet most** **Speaking to you, belovèd, this afternoon** **These lying pigments . . .** **If men weighed the hazards of the sea** *from* **Reply to Sor Philothea** ............... LETTER *translated by* Alan S. Trueblood | 34 38 |
| | **Introduction: The Latino Oral Tradition** .......... | 40 |
| Anonymous (Latino Traditional) | **The Force of Luck** ................... FOLK TALE *retold by* Rudolfo A. Anaya | 42 |
| Anonymous (Mexico/Southwest U.S.) | **La Llorona, the Weeping Woman** ........ LEGEND *translated and retold by* Joe Hayes | 49 |
| Anonymous (Mexico) | **La Ofrenda (The Offering)** ............. FOLK TALE *retold by* Francisco González Sol | 52 |
| Anonymous (Mexico/South Texas) | **The Ballad of Gregorio Cortez** ............ BALLAD **El corrido de Gregorio Cortez** ........... CORRIDO | 56 56 |

# PART 2
# LATIN AMERICAN WRITING COMES OF AGE: MODERNISM AND THE BOOM

|  |  |  |
|---|---|---|
|  | **Introduction** | 61 |
| Joaquim Maria Machado de Assis (Brazil) | **A Canary's Ideas** ........ SHORT STORY<br>*translated by* Lorie Ishimatsu and Jack Schmitt | 68 |
| José Martí<br>(Cuba) | **Los dos principes** ................ POEMA<br>**The Two Princes** ................. POEM<br>*translated by* Elinor Randall | 73<br>73 |
| Rubén Darío<br>(Nicaragua) | **Lo fatal** ........................ POEMA<br>**What Gets You** .................. POEM<br>*translated by* Alberto Acereda and Will Derusha<br>**Versos de otoño** ................ POEMA<br>**Autumn Verses** .................. POEM<br>*translated by* Alberto Acereda and Will Derusha | 76<br>77<br>78<br>79 |
| Horacio Quiroga<br>(Uruguay) | **The Alligator War** ........ SHORT STORY<br>*translated by* Arthur Livingston | 82 |
| Gabriela Mistral<br>(Chile) | **Serene Words** ................... POEM<br>*translated by* Doris Dana | 90 |
| Jorge Luis Borges<br>(Argentina) | **The Other** ............... SHORT STORY<br>*translated by* Andrew Hurley | 94 |
| Pablo Neruda<br>(Chile) | **Ode to My Suit** .................. ODE<br>*translated by* Margaret Sayers Peden<br>**Horses** .......................... POEM<br>*translated by* Alastair Reid<br>**The Turtle** ...................... POEM<br>*translated by* Dennis Maloney | 102<br>104<br>106 |
| Octavio Paz<br>(Mexico) | **The Face and the Wind** ........... POEM<br>*translated by* Eliot Weinberger | 109 |
| Julio Cortázar<br>(Argentina) | **Continuity of Parks** ...... SHORT STORY<br>*translated by* Paul Blackburn<br>**House Taken Over** ......... SHORT STORY<br>*translated by* Paul Blackburn | 112<br>114 |
| Juan José Arreola<br>(Mexico) | **A Pact with the Devil** ..... SHORT STORY<br>*translated by* George D. Schade | 119 |

| | | |
|---|---|---|
| Sergio Vodánovic (Chile) | **The White Uniform** . . . . . . . . . . . . . . . . . . DRAMA<br>*translated by* William I. Oliver | 124 |
| Gabriel García Márquez (Colombia) | **The Handsomest Drowned Man in the World** . . . . . . . . . . . . . . . . . . . . . . SHORT STORY<br>*translated by* Gregory Rabassa | 133 |
| Luisa Valenzuela (Argentina) | **Up Among the Eagles** . . . . . . . . . . . . . . SHORT STORY<br>*translated by* Margaret Sayers Peden | 139 |
| Isabel Allende (Chile) | **Two Words** . . . . . . . . . . . . . . . . . . . . . SHORT STORY<br>*translated by* Margaret Sayers Peden | 145 |
| María Elena Llano (Cuba) | **In the Family** . . . . . . . . . . . . . . . . . . . SHORT STORY<br>*translated by* Beatriz Teleki | 152 |

# PART 3
# PANORAMA: LATINO WRITING IN THE UNITED STATES

| | | |
|---|---|---|
| | **Introduction** . . . . . . . . . . . . . . . . . . . . . . . . . . . . . . . . . . | 157 |
| Jesús Colón (Puerto Rican American) | **Easy Job, Good Wages** *from* **A Puerto Rican in New York and Other Sketches** . . . . . . . . . . . . . . . . . . . . . . . ESSAY | 164 |
| Fray Angélico Chávez (Mexican American) | **Hunchback Madonna** . . . . . . . . . . . . . SHORT STORY | 167 |
| Josephina Niggli (Mexican American) | **The Ring of General Macías** . . . . . . . . . . . . . . DRAMA | 174 |
| Américo Paredes (Mexican American) | **The Hammon and the Bean**s . . . . . . . . . SHORT STORY | 187 |
| Sabine Ulibarrí (Mexican American) | **My Wonder Horse** . . . . . . . . . . . . . . . . . SHORT STORY | 192 |
| Rolando Hinojosa-Smith (Mexican American) | **Words and Palabras** . . . . . . . . . . . . . . . . . . . . . . ESSAY | 197 |
| Nicholasa Mohr (Puerto Rican American) | **Mr. Mendelsohn** *from* **El Bronx Remembered** . . . . . . . . . . . . . . . NOVEL | 203 |
| Tomás Rivera (Mexican American) | **The Harvest** . . . . . . . . . . . . . . . . . . . . . SHORT STORY | 214 |

| Author | Title | Type | Page |
|---|---|---|---|
| Rudolfo Anaya (Mexican American) | Message from the Inca | SHORT STORY | 218 |
| | A New Mexico Christmas | ESSAY | 224 |
| Luis Omar Salinas (Mexican American) | Olivia | POEM | 230 |
| | This Is What I Said | POEM | 231 |
| | Coming Back from It | POEM | 232 |
| José Antonio Burciaga (Mexican American) | La Puerta | SHORT STORY | 234 |
| Gloria Anzaldúa (Mexican American) | To live in the Borderlands means you | POEM | 239 |
| Pat Mora (Mexican American) | Mi Madre | POEM | 243 |
| | Peruvian Child | POEM | 244 |
| | Graduation Morning | POEM | 245 |
| | Arte Popular | POEM | 246 |
| Alma Luz Villanueva (Mexican American) | Golden Glass | SHORT STORY | 248 |
| Lucha Corpi (Mexican American) | México | POEMA | 252 |
| | Mexico | POEM | 252 |
| | Emily Dickinson | POEMA | 253 |
| | Emily Dickinson | POEM | 253 |
| Esmeralda Santiago (Puerto Rican American) | A Shot at It from When I Was Puerto Rican | AUTOBIOGRAPHY | 255 |
| Mark Smith-Soto (Costa Rican American) | What I Mean | POEM | 263 |
| Victor Hernández Cruz (Puerto Rican American) | Problems with Hurricanes | POEM | 265 |
| Julia Alvarez (Dominican American) | El Doctor from Something to Declare | MEMOIR | 268 |
| | My English | ESSAY | 273 |
| | Washing the Windows | POEM | 277 |
| | Woman's Work | POEM | 278 |
| | Audition | POEM | 279 |
| Dagoberto Gilb (Mexican American) | Birthday | SHORT STORY | 282 |
| Margarita Engle (Cuban American) | Niña | SHORT STORY | 286 |
| Carmen Tafolla (Mexican American) | marked | POEM | 290 |

| Author | Work | Type | Page |
|---|---|---|---|
| Jimmy Santiago Baca (Mexican American/ Native American) | It Started | POEM | 293 |
| | Tomás Lucero | POEM | 295 |
| | Accountability | POEM | 297 |
| Judith Ortiz Cofer (Puerto Rican American) | An Hour with Abuelo from **An Island Like You** | SHORT STORY | 300 |
| | Picture of Whoopee from **Call Me Maria** | POEM | 304 |
| | Confessions of a Non-Native Speaker from **Call Me Maria** | POEM | 307 |
| Alberto Ríos (Mexican American) | Breaking Piñatas | MEMOIR | 311 |
| | On January 5, 1984, El Santo the Wrestler Died, Possibly | POEM | 313 |
| | The Lesson of Walls | POEM | 316 |
| Gary Soto (Mexican American) | The Mechanical Mind from **Local News** | SHORT STORY | 320 |
| | Black Hair | POEM | 324 |
| | History from **The Elements of San Joaquin** | POEM | 325 |
| Lorna Dee Cervantes (Mexican American) | Freeway 280 | POEM | 328 |
| | Refugee Ship | POEM | 330 |
| | Poem for the Young White Man... | POEM | 331 |
| Sandra Cisneros (Chicana) | Six Brothers | POEM | 335 |
| | Traficante | POEM | 337 |
| Rosario Morales and Aurora Levins Morales (Puerto Rican American) | Ending Poem | POEM | 339 |
| Martín Espada (Puerto Rican American) | Pegao | POEM | 342 |
| | Who Burns for the Perfection of Paper | POEM | 342 |
| | My Native Costume | POEM | 344 |
| | Colibrí | POEM | 345 |
| Diana García (Mexican American) | The Flat of the Land | SHORT STORY | 347 |

# Voices in a Tradition

The kaleidoscope that is Latino literature encompasses many points of view, many subjects, many themes—many voices. It includes loud voices of anger and protest, and soft voices of love and reconciliation. It deals in the harshest realism, yet reaches to flights of fancy unparalleled in modern literature. It opens to us the specific hopes, dreams, aspirations, struggles, and triumphs of Latino peoples throughout the Americas, yet it also deals with timeless and universal subjects and themes. It is a literature that touches on cultural and personal issues relevant to contemporary Americans—North, Central, and South—and yet is equally relevant to people all over the globe, no matter what their culture of origin.

The Latino literary tradition is a vast tradition and a very old one. It includes, of course, popular, bestselling Chicano writers like Sandra Cisneros and Gary Soto, but it also includes great writers of the past, such as the seventeenth-century Mexican nun Sor Juana Inés de la Cruz and the early Spanish explorer Cabeza de Vaca. The Latino literary tradition includes the still-thriving oral tradition of folk tales, legends, and *corridos,* but it also encompasses the imaginative, intellectually challenging works of great Latin American writers like Jorge Luis Borges and Octavio Paz. It is vast enough to house the magic realism of Gabriel García Márquez and Julio Cortázar, the gentle lyrics of Gabriela Mistral, the politically charged poetry of Lorna Dee Cervantes, and the deeply personal expressions of poets like Jimmy Santiago Baca, Pat Mora, and Pablo Neruda. In this book, you will learn the historical, cultural, and personal contexts for understanding and appreciating this great body of literature, in which Julia Alvarez and Rudolfo Anaya are cousins to Isabel Allende and Horacio Quiroga.

The Latino literary tradition is one of the richest, most diverse literary traditions in the world today, and it is the aim of this book to serve as a lens through which the reader can view and appreciate the colorful, varied, surprising, and imaginative landscape that is Latino literature.

# Part I

# Encounters: A Meeting of Two Worlds

Long before Columbus reached the Western Hemisphere in 1492, civilizations in the Americas had reached a high level of development. Contrary to earlier notions that the Americas were populated by primitive peoples spread out across a great wilderness, we now know from archaeological evidence—impressive cities, pyramid temples, sculptures, manuscripts, roads, and irrigation systems—that there had been sophisticated and technologically advanced cultures in the Americas for hundreds of years. Several of these cultures had flourished into great empires—the Maya, the Aztec, the Inca. Yet much of the life of the ancient Americas collapsed after the Europeans arrived, for the Spaniards brought not only gunpowder and horses but also a more insidious weapon—disease. Some historians believe that it was the spread of diseases previously unknown in the Americas—like smallpox—that wiped out most of the indigenous, or native, people.

> *"One fact in all this is widely known and beyond dispute: . . . the indigenous peoples never did the Europeans any harm whatever; on the contrary, they believed them to have descended from the heavens, at least until they or their fellow-citizens had tasted, at the hands of these oppressors, a diet of robbery, murder, violence, and all other manner of trials and tribulations."*
>
> —Bartolomé de las Casas (1474–1566)

The Spaniards brought their European literary traditions to the new land, but the native peoples already had their own rich store of literature, both written and oral. When enslaved Africans were brought to the Americas, their literary traditions were absorbed into the mix. The convergence of these diverse literary sources ultimately led to the development of a rich and unique Hispanic American literature.

## Visions of Wealth: The Lure of the Americas

The arrival of Christopher Columbus in the Americas marked the beginning of an ongoing collision between two worlds. Some Europeans were drawn to the Americas by their desire to convert native peoples to Christianity; others saw the new land as a place where they could seek escape from prosecution for crimes committed in their own countries. Most Europeans, however, were spurred on by one thing: the desire to become wealthy and powerful.

The natives of the Caribbean islands on which Columbus and his men had first landed spun tales of great wealth, telling the Europeans

what they wanted to hear: that gold, precious stones, and rich spices could be found in lands farther to the west. Perhaps the island natives told the Europeans this in order to get their unexpected and unwelcome visitors to leave them alone. We will never know, but what is important is that Columbus and his men returned to Spain determined to set forth on new voyages, and that he and the other explorers who followed him created among their fellow Europeans an obsession to discover wealth in the Americas. As one conquistador later said, "We came here to serve God and the King, and also to get rich."

## Hernán Cortés and the Conquest of Mexico

Under the leadership of Hernán Cortés, a small Spanish military expedition landed on Mexico's gulf coast in 1519. The coastal dwellers that Cortés and his men encountered told the Spaniards about the Aztecs, a fabulously prosperous people whose empire radiated out from its capital in central Mexico for hundreds of miles in all directions.

The Aztec religion had predicted that a bearded stranger would arrive in their land at about the same time that Cortés, who had an impressive full beard, appeared with his guns and horses—two things that were unknown in the Americas until this time. Cortés convinced the Aztec leader, Montezuma, to allow him and his men to cross over into the Aztec capital city of Tenochtitlán, which was strategically built upon a series of islands in the middle of a large lake. Once inside the city, Cortés's small band of soldiers, along with the Indian enemies of the Aztecs, succeeded in totally defeating the mighty Aztec armies. Cortés and his fellow Spaniards soon brought the Aztecs and other Mexican natives under military control, and the Spanish Crown established a system of viceroyalties in the Americas. These governing bodies were similar to the individual states in the United States today, but they were much larger, and each was governed by a viceroy, or official representative of the Spanish Crown. Much of present-day Mexico became the viceroyalty of New Spain, with its capital in Mexico City—the new name for what had been, until 1521, the capital of the Aztec empire.

The natives of Mexico suffered greatly under Spanish rule, and within a hundred years of Cortés's arrival, several million had died from disease and exposure, as well as from undergoing physical abuse in Spanish mines and on plantations. Yet, at the same time, many Spaniards mixed and intermarried with the native population to form a new race of *mestizos*—from a Latin word meaning "mixed." Today's Mexicans and Mexican Americans trace their ancestry to the vital combination of races, languages, and cultures that came about from this collision of two worlds—a collision that reverberates to this day.

## Narratives of the Early Colonial Period

The earliest Spanish American literature includes accounts written by explorers, settlers, and missionaries in the Americas. This literature consists of letters, such as those Columbus addressed to Ferdinand and Isabella of Spain; histories, such as the destruction of the Indies recounted by Bartolomé de las Casas; stories of expedition, such as the narrative by Álvar Núñez Cabeza de Vaca; and descriptions of the land and customs, such as the accounts of Juan Rodríguez Freile and José Gumilla.

Perhaps the most arresting of these early works is *La relación* (*The Relation*) by Cabeza de Vaca, published in 1542. Cabeza de Vaca had been with the Narváez expedition to Florida, which began in 1528. Of the four hundred men that set out, only four remained to reach Mexico in 1536. Cabeza de Vaca describes in rich detail extraordinary plant and animal life and various Indian peoples, providing a treasury of reliable information for future explorers. To some scholars of U.S. Latino literature, Cabeza de Vaca's account is the first example of Mexican American literature.

Cabeza de Vaca and his men never saw any of the fabled wealth they had heard so much about. Nevertheless, the tales they brought back to Mexico City fired the imagination of other explorers. In his account of the colony of New Granada in Colombia, Juan Rodríguez Freile describes the Indian ceremony that led to the legend of El Dorado, believed to be a land of fabulous wealth.

## Native Literature: The Popol Vuh

At the time of the Spanish conquest, in 1524, the Quiché (kee CHAY) Maya, one of the most influential peoples descended from the original Maya, occupied the Guatemalan highlands. Around 1550, a book known as the Popol Vuh was written in the Quiché language by a Quiché who had learned to read and write Spanish. Instead of being written in the hieroglyphics that were used by the Indians, this Quiché text was transcribed into Latin characters. The Popol Vuh, sometimes referred to as the Mayan Bible, was based on oral traditions that had been handed down through generations; it brings together Quiché myths, traditions, customs, and historical narratives.

Early in the eighteenth century, a Dominican priest named Father Francisco Ximénez, who knew the Quiché language, was shown the book. He made a translation of the Quiché into Spanish. The original version in Quiché has disappeared, but Ximénez's transcription and translation still exist. The Popol Vuh is considered one of the most important examples of native literature in the Americas.

## The Tenth Muse: Sor Juana

Many of the writers who produced imaginative literature such as poetry and plays during the Spanish colonial period wrote for an audience of both European and American readers. They followed the conventions of Spanish literature. During the seventeenth century, for example, poets were strongly indebted to the work of Luis de Góngora, a Spanish baroque writer with a mannered literary style.

The title "Tenth Muse" was given to a seventeenth-century Mexican poet, scholar, and nun: Sor Juana Inés de la Cruz. During her lifetime she produced enough poetry, prose, and plays to fill three volumes. When her work was published in Spain, she became known as the "Tenth Muse" in acknowledgment of her gifts. In Greek mythology the Muses were nine goddesses who exercised authority over the arts and sciences, inspiring human beings in these pursuits.

Sor (Sister) Juana, as she is generally known, wrote in the traditions of Spain's Golden Age. She uses all the poetic models of European writers and draws on classical, biblical, and mythological sources that her contemporaries use. She is considered the greatest lyric poet of the colonial period in Mexico. A rise of interest in feminism and women's writing has led to a new appreciation of her work in modern times.

## The Oral Tradition: Folk Tales and *Corridos*

Many of the oral forms of literature that flourished in Spain during the sixteenth and seventeenth centuries took root in Spain's new lands. Brought to the Americas by the first Spanish explorers and settlers, these forms evolved into an oral tradition that continues to thrive in Hispanic communities. In many cases, the Spanish forms and traditions blended with native Indian elements.

A synthesis of Spanish and Indian traditions is seen in the legend of La Llorona, the Weeping Woman. La Llorona is the subject of numerous folk tales, especially in the American Southwest. Stories about her first appeared around 1550 in Mexico City. Over hundreds of years, La Llorona has become an important cultural symbol in Mexican and Mexican American literature.

The Spaniards brought their *romances* with them. These were a form of ballad sung by troubadours. The *corrido* is a popular musical form that evolved in the mid-nineteenth century from these Spanish ballads. The name *corrido* comes from the verb *correr*—to run—and indicates that the narrative is fast paced. *Corridos* usually deal with adventure, heroism, or tragedy. Tensions in the borderlands of Texas created the right conditions for a *corrido* tradition and the creation of folklore like "The Ballad of Gregorio Cortez," inspired by a true story.

> *"When the natives of the mainland saw the ship approaching on the sea, they were astounded because they were seeing something they had never seen or heard about before.... They were quite astonished, believing that such people were sent by God's hand and that it would be proper to give them a warm reception. Then ten or twelve balsas were prepared—replete with food and fruit.... The Indians went to the ship with all this without any guile or malice, but rather with joy and pleasure to see such people."*
>
> **—Cieza de Leon**

The literature of the early period of Spanish colonization deals with encounters between the people of two different worlds. As more than one historian has noted, the discovery was mutual. If the indigenous peoples of the Americas were amazed by the strange people who appeared from across the sea—strange white men mounted on unknown beasts and bearing weapons that flashed with fire and explosions—then the Europeans were equally astonished by the things they found: the mighty Aztec cities; the lush landscapes; the unfamiliar sights, sounds, and smells. It was inevitable that there would be a great mixture of cultures as Spain expanded its settlements in the new land and that this often uneasy mixture would lead to both tragic and triumphant outcomes.

# Álvar Núñez Cabeza de Vaca

c. 1490–1558 (Spain)

## Meet the Writer

The call to high adventure quickened the pulse of many sixteenth-century Spaniards, among them **Álvar Núñez Cabeza de Vaca** (AHL vahr NOO nyes kah BEH sah deh VAH kah). Cabeza de Vaca, which means "cow's head," was the surname of Álvar Núñez's mother. The name was a title of honor dating back to a thirteenth-century battle in which an ancestor's stratagem of marking an unguarded mountain pass with a cow's skull led to a major military victory against the Moors. The king gratefully rewarded the hero with the title Cabeza de Vaca.

Cabeza de Vaca grew up in Andalusia, a region in southern Spain on the Mediterranean. He very likely witnessed the sailing of the renowned explorer Ferdinand Magellan and others who embarked from Cadiz upon sea voyages that were destined to change the face of the world known to Europeans at that time. In his teens he chose a military career, saw action in several battles, and eventually gained the attention of his superior officers. In 1527, he received a royal appointment to serve as second in command to Pánfilo de Narváez in an expedition to explore and claim for Spain the area that is now Florida.

Dazzled by the wealth that fellow Spaniards had begun amassing in Mexico, expedition commander Narváez and his men set out with grand dreams—dreams that were quickly dashed when they met fierce opposition from the native Indians. After many misfortunes, Narváez, a weak leader with whom Cabeza de Vaca often clashed, abandoned more than two hundred of his men—including his second in command. Cabeza de Vaca's narrative account *The Journey of Álvar Núñez Cabeza de Vaca* reveals the terrible hardships he and his companions endured as they walked across what is now Texas, New Mexico, and Arizona before reaching Mexico.

After reaching Mexico City, Cabeza de Vaca returned to Spain, where he completed his first narrative. In 1540, he was appointed governor of the territory in southern South America. The colonists in Río de la Plata had him removed from office and sent back to Spain in 1545.

# Background

To many, the Hispanic American literary tradition begins in what is now the southwestern United States with the arrival of the earliest Spanish explorers, missionaries, and soldiers. Cabeza de Vaca's account of his years among the Indians of the southwest, *La relación* (*The Relation*), is one of the most gripping of the "explorer narratives." It was first published in 1542. The first full translation of his work did not appear in English until 1851.

Cabeza de Vaca's narrative opens with the sailing of the armada under Governor Pánfilo Narváez in June 1527. The expedition consisted of five ships with about 600 men. Among the officers, Cabeza de Vaca was treasurer and provost marshal. After arriving on the island of Santo Domingo in September and gathering provisions, more than 140 men deserted. The expedition continued on to Cuba, where a hurricane destroyed two of the ships. After the expedition became stranded in Florida, the men were forced to build barges in order to retreat to the sea. Narváez abandoned his crew, but he did not survive his ignoble and cowardly flight. His ship was lost at sea.

The survivors sailed their rafts around the Gulf Coast. A violent storm wrecked their vessels off the coast of Texas. Only four men were left: Cabeza de Vaca, two Spaniards, and Estevánico, an enslaved black man from Morocco. For two years Cabeza de Vaca was a prisoner and slave of some Indian clans. As he traveled west and north, however, he gradually gained renown for his healing skills. By 1535, he reached what is now New Mexico and then headed southwest into Mexico. By then he had become the leader of a following of native Indians. In western Mexico he ran into a group of Spanish slave hunters under Diego de Alcarez. When Cabeza de Vaca became critical of the "Christian slavers," Alcarez had him arrested and seized the 600 Indians in his company as slaves.

Cabeza de Vaca left for Spain in 1537 and protested against the cruel practices of Alcarez. Although he had suffered greatly during his years in the Americas, Cabeza de Vaca had grown to love the land and to care for its native peoples. When he returned to the Americas as governor of Río de la Plata in southern South America, he hoped to deal humanely with its natives. Because he prohibited mistreatment of the Indians, however, Cabeza de Vaca's men had him deposed and returned to Spain in chains. He was never allowed to return to the Americas. Sent into exile in Africa for eight years, he was later pardoned, and he died an honored man in 1558.

**Before You Read** *According to Indian legend, somewhere in the northern territory (today the southwestern United States) stood seven cities rumored to have streets paved with gold and royal buildings filled with precious metals and jewels. This vision of untold wealth lured many Spanish adventurers to the Americas. For Cabeza de Vaca, dreams of triumph and fortune never materialized. Instead, he spent eight years wandering roughly six thousand miles over long stretches of North America on foot. The grueling odyssey is recorded in a report to King Charles V of Spain.*

*Cabeza de Vaca's journal served as a valuable source of information about the continent's people, animals, and vegetation. He eagerly shared his adventures with any who were willing to listen, including the Spanish viceroy in Mexico City and, upon his return to Spain, powerful Spanish royalty.*

*What are some elements of Cabeza de Vaca's account that make it not just a historical account but also an exciting adventure narrative?*

# *from* The Journey of Álvar Núñez Cabeza de Vaca

Álvar Núñez Cabeza de Vaca
*translated by* Fanny Bandelier

It being winter and the cold very great, and as we had been suffering so many days from hunger and from the injuries we received from the waves, that the next day people began to break down, so that when the sun set all those aboard of my barge had fallen in a heap and were so near dying that few remained conscious, and not five men kept on their feet.

When night came the skipper and I were the only ones able to manage the barge. Two hours after nightfall the skipper told me to steer the craft alone, since he felt that he would die that same night. Thereupon I stood at the helm, and after midnight went to see if the skipper was dead, but he said that, on the contrary, he felt better and would steer till daybreak. On that occasion I would have hailed death with delight rather than to see so many people around me in such a condition. After the skipper had taken the barge under his control I went to rest, very much without resting, for I thought of anything else but sleep.

Near daybreak I fancied to hear the sound of breakers, for as the coast was low, their noise was greater. Surprised at it, I called to the skipper, who said he thought we were near the shore. Sounding, we found seven fathoms, and he was of the opinion that we should keep off shore till dawn. So I took the oar and rowed along the coast, from which we were one league away, and turned the stern to seaward.

Close to shore a wave took us and hurled the barge a horse's length out of water. With the violent shock nearly all the people who lay in the

boat like dead came to themselves, and, seeing we were close to land, began to crawl out on all fours. As they took to some rocks, we built a fire and toasted some of our maize. We found rain water, and with the warmth of the fire people revived and began to cheer up. The day we arrived there was the sixth of the month of November.

After the people had eaten I sent Lope de Oviedo, who was the strongest and heartiest of all, to go to some trees nearby and climb to the top of one, examine the surroundings and the country in which we were. He did so and found we were on an island, and that the ground was hollowed out, as if cattle had gone over it, from which it seemed to him that the land belonged to Christians, and so he told us. I sent him again to look and examine more closely if there were any worn trails, and not to go too far so as not to run into danger. He went, found a footpath, followed it for about one-half league, and saw several Indian huts which stood empty because the Indians had gone out into the field.

He took away a cooking pot, a little dag and a few ruffs and turned back, but as he seemed to delay I sent two other Christians to look for him and find out what had happened.

They met him nearby and saw that three Indians, with bows and arrows, were following and calling to him, while he did the same to them by signs. So he came to where we were, the Indians remaining behind, seated on the beach. Half an hour after a hundred Indian archers joined them, and our fright was such that, whether tall or little, it made them appear giants to us. They stood still close to the first ones, near where we were.

We could not defend ourselves, as there were scarcely three of us who could stand on their feet. The inspector and I stepped forward and called them. They came, and we tried to quiet them the best we could and save ourselves, giving them beads and bells. Each one of them gave me an arrow in token of friendship, and by signs they gave us to understand that on the following morning they would come back with food, as then they had none.

The next day, at sunrise, which was the hour the Indians had given us to understand, they came as promised and brought us plenty of fish and some roots which they eat that taste like nuts, some bigger, some smaller, most of which are taken out of the water with much trouble.

In the evening they returned and brought us more fish and some of the same roots, and they brought their women and children to look at us. They thought themselves very rich with the little bells and beads we gave them, and thereafter visited us daily with the same things as before. As we saw ourselves provided with fish, roots, water and the other things we had asked for, we concluded to embark again and continue our voyage.

We lifted the barge out of the sand into which it had sunk (for which purpose we all had to take off our clothes) and had great work to set her afloat, as our condition was such that much lighter things would have given us trouble.

Then we embarked. Two crossbow shots from shore a wave swept over us, we all got wet, and being naked and the cold very great, the oars dropped out of our hands. The next wave overturned the barge. The inspector and two others clung to her to save themselves, but the contrary happened; they got underneath the barge and were drowned.

The shore being very rough, the sea took the others and thrust them, half dead, on the beach of the same island again, less the three that had perished underneath the barge.

The rest of us, as naked as we had been born, had lost everything, and while it was not worth much, to us it meant a great deal. It was in November, bitterly cold, and we in such a state that every bone could easily be counted, and we looked like death itself. Of myself I can say that since the month of May I had not tasted anything but toasted maize, and even sometimes had been obliged to eat it raw. Although the horses were killed during the time the barges were built, I never could eat of them, and not ten times did I taste fish. This I say in order to explain and that any one might guess how we were off. On top of all this, a north wind arose, so that we were nearer death than life. It pleased Our Lord that, searching for the remnants of our former fire, we found wood with which we built big fires and then with many tears begged Our Lord for mercy and forgiveness of our sins. Every one of us pitied not only himself, but all the others whom he saw in the same condition.

At sunset the Indians, thinking we had not left, came to bring us food, but when they saw us in such a different attire from before and so strange-looking, they were so frightened as to turn back. I went to call them, and in great fear they came. I then gave them to understand by signs how we had lost a barge and three of our men had been drowned, while before them there lay two of our men dead, with the others about to go the same way.

Upon seeing the disaster we had suffered, our misery and distress, the Indians sat down with us and all began to weep out of compassion for our misfortune, and for more than half an hour they wept so loud and so sincerely that it could be heard far away.

Verily, to see beings so devoid of reason, untutored, so like unto brutes, yet so deeply moved by pity for us, it increased my feelings and those of others in my company for our own misfortune. When the lament was over, I spoke to the Christians and asked them if they would like me to beg the Indians to take us to their homes. Some of the men, who had been to New Spain, answered that it would be unwise, as, once at their abode, they might sacrifice us to their idols.

Still, seeing there was no remedy and that in any other way death was surer and nearer, I did not mind what they said, but begged the Indians to take us to their dwellings, at which they showed great pleasure, telling us to tarry yet a little, but that they would do what we wished. Soon thirty of them loaded themselves with firewood and went to their lodges, which were far away, while we stayed with the others until it was almost dark. Then they took hold of us and carried us along hurriedly to where they lived.

Against the cold, and lest on the way some one of us might faint or die, they had provided four or five big fires on the road, at each one of which they warmed us. As soon as they saw we had regained a little warmth and strength they would carry us to the next fire with such haste that our feet barely touched the ground.

So we got to their dwellings, where we saw they had built a hut for us with many fires in it. About one hour after our arrival, they began to dance and to make a great celebration (which lasted the whole night), although there was neither pleasure, feast nor sleep in it for us, since we expected to be sacrificed. In the morning they again gave us fish and roots, and treated us so well that we became reassured, losing somewhat our apprehension of being butchered.

That same day I saw on one of the Indians a trinket he had not gotten from us, and asking from where they had obtained it they answered, by signs, that other men like ourselves and who were still in our rear, had given it to them. Hearing this, I sent two Christians with two Indians to guide them to those people. Very near by they met them, and they also were looking for us, as the Indians had told them of our presence in the neighborhood. These were the Captains Andres Dorantes and Alonso del Castillo, with all of their crew. When they came near us they were much frightened at our appearance and grieved at being unable to give us anything, since they had nothing but their clothes. And they stayed with us there, telling how, on the fifth of that same month, their barge stranded a league and a half from there, and they escaped without anything being lost.

All together, we agreed upon repairing their barge, and that those who had strength and inclination should proceed in it, while the others should remain until completely restored and then go as best they could along the coast, following it till God would be pleased to get us all together to a land of Christians.

So we set to work, but ere the barge was afloat Tavera, a gentleman in our company, died, while the barge proved not to be seaworthy and soon sank. Now, being in the condition which I have stated—that is, most of us naked and the weather so unfavorable for walking and for swimming across rivers and coves, and we had neither food nor any way to carry it, we determined upon submitting to necessity and upon wintering there, and we also agreed that four men, who were the most able-bodied, should go to Panuco, which we believed to be nearby, and that, if it was God, Our Lord's will to take them there, they should tell of our remaining on the island and of our distress. One of them was a Portuguese, called Alvaro Fernandez, a carpenter and sailor; the second was Mendez; the third, Figueroa, a native of Toledo; the fourth, Astudillo, from Zafra. They were all good swimmers and took with them an Indian from the island.

A few days after these four Christians had left, the weather became so cold and tempestuous that the Indians could no longer pull roots, and the canebrake in which they used to fish yielded

The arrival of Álvar Núñez Cabeza de Vaca and his companions, the sole survivors of Panfilo de Narváez's 1528 Florida expedition, at the Gulf of California after an eight-year trek: American engraving, 19th century.
The Granger Collection, New York

nothing more. As the lodges afforded so little shelter, people began to die, and five Christians, quartered on the coast, were driven to such an extremity that they ate each other up until but one remained, who being left alone, there was nobody to eat him. Their names are: Sierra, Diego, Lopez, Corral, Palacios and Gonzalo Ruiz. At this the Indians were so startled, and there was such an uproar among them, that I verily believe if they had seen this at the beginning they would have killed them, and we all would have been in great danger. After a very short time, out of eighty men who had come there in our two parties only fifteen remained alive.

Then the natives fell sick from the stomach, so that one-half of them died also, and they, believing we had killed them, and holding it to be certain, they agreed among themselves to kill those of us who survived.

But when they came to execute it an Indian who kept me told them not to believe we were the cause of their dying, for if we had so much power we would not have suffered so many of our own people to perish without being able to remedy it ourselves. He also told them there remained but very few of us, and none of them did any harm or injury, so that the best was to let us alone. It pleased Our Lord they should

*from* The Journey of Álvar Núñez Cabeza de Vaca

listen to his advice and counsel and give up their idea.

To this island we gave the name of the Island of Ill-Fate. The people on it are tall and well formed; they have no other weapons than bows and arrows with which they are most dexterous. The men have one of their nipples perforated from side to side and sometimes both; through this hole is thrust a reed as long as two and a half hands and as thick as two fingers; they also have the under lip perforated and a piece of cane in it as thin as the half of a finger. The women do the hard work. People stay on this island from October till the end of February, feeding on the roots I have mentioned, taken from under the water in November and December. They have channels made of reeds and get fish only during that time; afterwards they subsist on roots. At the end of February they remove to other parts in search of food, because the roots begin to sprout and are not good any more.

Of all the people in the world, they are those who most love their children and treat them best, and should the child of one of them happen to die, parents and relatives bewail it, and the whole settlement, the lament lasting a full year, day after day. Before sunrise the parents begin to weep, after them the tribe, and the same they do at noon and at dawn. At the end of the year of mourning they celebrate the anniversary and wash and cleanse themselves of all their paint. They mourn all their dead in this manner, old people excepted, to whom they do not pay any attention, saying that these have had their time and are no longer of any use, but only take space, and food from the children.

Their custom is to bury the dead, except those who are medicine men among them, whom they burn, and while the fire is burning, all dance and make a big festival, grinding the bones to powder. At the end of the year, when they celebrate the anniversary, they scarify themselves and give to the relatives the pulverized bones to drink in water. Every man has a recognized wife, but the medicine men enjoy greater privileges, since they may have two or three, and among these wives there is great friendship and harmony.

When one takes a woman for his wife, from the day he marries her, whatever he may hunt or fish, she has to fetch it to the home of her father, without daring to touch or eat of it, and from the home of the father-in-law they bring the food to the husband. All the while neither the wife's father nor her mother enter his abode, nor is he allowed to go to theirs, or to the homes of his brothers-in-law, and should they happen to meet they go out of each other's way a crossbow's shot or so, with bowed heads and eyes cast to the ground, holding it to be an evil thing to look at each other or speak. The women are free to communicate with their parents-in-law or relatives and speak to them. This custom prevails from that island as far as about fifty leagues inland.

There is another custom, that when a son or brother dies, no food is gathered by those of his household for three months, preferring rather to starve, but the relatives and neighbors provide them with victuals. Now, as during the time we were there so many of them died, there was great starvation in most of the lodges, due to their customs and ceremonials, as well as to the weather, which was so rough that such as could go out after food brought in but very little, withal working hard for it. Therefore the Indians by whom I was kept forsook the island and in several canoes went over to the mainland to some bays where there were a great many oysters and during three months of the year they do not eat anything else and drink very bad water. There is lack of firewood, but great abundance of mosquitoes. Their lodges are made of matting and built on oyster shells, upon which they sleep in hides, which they only get by chance. There we remained to the end of April, when we went to the seashore, where we ate blackberries for a whole month, during which time they danced and celebrated incessantly.

On the island I have spoken of they wanted to make medicine men of us without any examination or asking for our diplomas, because they cure diseases by breathing on the sick, and with that breath and their hands they drive the ailment away. So they summoned us to do the same in order to be at least of some use. We laughed, taking it for a jest, and said that we did not understand how to cure.

Thereupon they withheld our food to compel us to do what they wanted. Seeing our obstinacy, an Indian told me that I did not know what I said by claiming that what he knew was useless, because stones and things growing out in the field have their virtues, and he, with a heated stone, placing it on the stomach, could cure and take away pain, so that we, who were wiser men, surely had greater power and virtue.

At last we found ourselves in such stress as to have to do it, without risking any punishment. Their manner of curing is as follows: When one is ill they call in a medicine man, and after they are well again not only do they give him all they have, but even things they strive to obtain from their relatives. All the medicine man does is to make a few cuts where the pain is located and then suck the skin around the incisions. They cauterize with fire, thinking it very effective, and I found it to be so by my own experience. Then they breathe on the spot where the pain is and believe that with this the disease goes away.

The way we treated the sick was to make over them the sign of the cross while breathing on them, recite a Pater Noster[1] and Ave Maria,[2] and pray to God, Our Lord, as best we could to give them good health and inspire them to do us some favors. Thanks to His will and the mercy He had upon us, all those for whom we prayed, as soon as we crossed them, told the others that they were cured and felt well again. For this they gave us good cheer, and would rather be without food themselves so as to give it to us, and they gave us hides and other small things. So great was the lack of food then that I often remained without eating anything whatsoever for three days, and they were in the same plight, so that it seemed to me impossible for life to last, although I afterwards suffered still greater privations and much more distress, as I shall tell further on.

The Indians that kept Alonso del Castillo, Andres Dorantes and the others, who were still alive, being of another language and stock, had gone to feed on oysters at another point of the mainland, where they remained until the first day of the month of April. Then they came back to the island, which was from there nearly two leagues off, where the channel is broadest. The island is half a league wide and five long.

All the people of this country go naked; only the women cover part of their bodies with a kind of wool that grows on trees. The girls go about in deer skins. They are very liberal towards each other with what they have. There is no ruler among them. All who are of the same descendancy cluster together. There are two distinct languages spoken on the island; those of one language are called Capoques, those of the other Han. They have the custom, when they know each other and meet from time to time, before they speak, to weep for half an hour. After they have wept the one who receives the visit rises and gives to the other all he has. The other takes it, and in a little while goes away with everything. Even sometimes, after having given and obtained all, they part without having uttered a word. There are other very queer customs, but having told the principal ones and the most striking, I

---

1. **Pater Noster:** prayer to God, beginning with "Our Father, who art in heaven . . ."
2. **Ave Maria:** prayer to the Virgin Mary, beginning with "Hail, Mary . . ."

must now proceed to relate what further happened to us.

After Dorantes and Castillo had come back to the island, they gathered together all the Christians, who were somewhat scattered, and there were in all fourteen. I, as told, was in another place, on the mainland, whither my Indians had taken me and where I suffered from such a severe illness that, although I might otherwise have entertained some hope for life, this was enough to take it away from me completely. When the Christians learned of it they gave an Indian the robe of marten we had taken from the cacique, as stated, in order that he should guide them to where I was, to see me, and so twelve of them came, two having become so feeble that they did not dare to take them along.

The names of those who came are: Alonso del Castillo, Andres Dorantes and Diego Dorantes, Valdivieso, Estrada, Tostado, Chaves, Gutierrez, an Asturian priest; Diego de Huelva, Estevanico, the negro Benitez, and as they reached the mainland they found still another of our men named Francisco de Leon, and the thirteen went along the coast. After they had gone by, the Indians with whom I was told me of it, and how Hieronimo de Alaniz and Lope de Oviedo had been left on the island.

Cabeza de Vaca Expedition: Álvar Núñez Cabeza de Vaca and his men during their eight-year trek between the Gulf of Mexico and Mexico City, 1528–36.
The Granger Collection, New York

My sickness prevented me from following or seeing them. I had to remain with those same Indians of the island for more than one year, and as they made me work so much and treated me so badly I determined to flee and go to those who live in the woods on the mainland, and who are called those from (of) Charruco.[3]

I could no longer stand the life I was compelled to lead. Among many other troubles I had to pull the eatable roots out of the water and from among the canes where they were buried in the ground, and from this my fingers had become so tender that the mere touch of a straw caused them to bleed. The reeds would cut me in many places, because many were broken and I had to go in among them with the clothing I had on, of which I have told. This is why I went to work and joined the other Indians. Among these I improved my condition a little by becoming a trader, doing the best in it I could, and they gave me food and treated me well.

They entreated me to go about from one part to another to get the things they needed, as on account of constant warfare there is neither travel nor barter in the land.

So, trading along with my wares I penetrated inland as far as I cared to go and along the coast as much as forty or fifty leagues. My stock consisted mainly of pieces of seashells and cockles, and shells with which they cut a fruit which is like a bean, used by them for healing and in their dances and feasts. This is of greatest value among them, besides shell-beads and other objects. These things I carried inland, and in exchange brought back hides and red ochre with which they rub and dye their faces and hair; flint for arrow points, glue and hard canes wherewith to make them, and tassels made of the hair of deer, which they dye red. This trade suited me well because it gave me liberty to go wherever I pleased; I was not bound to do anything and no longer a slave. Wherever I went they treated me well, and gave me to eat for the sake of my wares. My principal object in doing it, however, was to find out in what manner I might get further away. I became well known among them; they rejoiced greatly when seeing me and I would bring them what they needed, and those who did not know me would desire and endeavor to meet me for the sake of my fame.

My sufferings, while trading thus, it would take long to tell; danger, hunger, storms and frost overtaking me often in the open field and alone, and from which through the mercy of God, Our Lord, I escaped. For this reason I did not go out trading in winter, it being the time when the Indians themselves remain in their huts and abodes, unable to go out or assist each other.

Nearly six years I spent thus in the country, alone among them and naked, as they all were themselves. . . .

*Cabeza de Vaca stays in the coastal region for six years, four of them as a trader much respected by the Native Americans, but all the while he keeps looking for a way to escape to "the land of the Christians." He delays his escape in order to find another Spaniard, Oviedo, who later disappears. Cabeza de Vaca and the other survivors of the expedition—Dorantes, Castillo, and Estevánico—become enslaved by Indians from different tribes, who meet when they end up gathering at the same spot during prickly pear season. The Spaniards' planned escape is delayed by a year because each one ends up being forced to travel with the tribe he is enslaved by. When the tribes meet up again during the next prickly pear season, the Spaniards renew their plans for escape. The narrative continues with a recounting of the escape.*

---

3. **Charruco:** group of Indians, possibly Karankawan, that lived on the Texas mainland near Matagorda Bay. (Also spelled Chorruco.)

Two days after moving we recommended ourselves to God, Our Lord, and fled, hoping that, although it was late in the season and the fruits of the tunas[4] were giving out, by remaining in the field we might still get over a good portion of the land. As we proceeded that day, in great fear lest the Indians would follow us, we descried smoke, and, going towards it, reached the place after sundown, where we found an Indian who, when he saw us coming, did not wait, but ran away. We sent the negro[4] after him, and as the Indian saw him approach alone he waited. The negro told him that we were going in search of the people that had raised the smoke. He answered that the dwellings were nearby and that he would guide us, and we followed. He hurried ahead to tell of our coming. At sunset we came in sight of the lodges, and two crossbow shots before reaching them met four Indians waiting for us, and they received us well. We told them in the language of the Mariames that we had come to see them. They appeared to be pleased with our company and took us to their homes. They lodged Dorantes and the negro at the house of a medicine man, and me and Castillo at that of another. These Indians speak another language and are called Avavares. [They were those who used to fetch bows to ours and barter with them, and, although of another nation and speech, they understand the idiom of those with whom we formerly were and had arrived there on that very day with their lodges.] Forthwith they offered us many tunas, because they had heard of us and of how we cured and of the miracles Our Lord worked through us. And surely, even if there had been no other tokens, it was wonderful how He prepared the way for us through a country so scantily inhabited, causing us to meet people where for a long time there had been none, saving us from so many dangers, not permitting us to be killed, maintaining us through starvation and distress and moving the hearts of the people to treat us well, as we shall tell further on.

On the night we arrived there some Indians came to Castillo complaining that their heads felt very sore and begging him for relief. As soon as he had made the sign of the cross over them and recommended them to God, at that very moment the Indians said that all the pain was gone. They went back to their abodes and brought us many tunas and a piece of venison, something we did not know any more what it was, and as the news spread that same night there came many other sick people for him to cure, and each brought a piece of venison, and so many there were that we did not know where to store the meat. We thanked God for His daily increasing mercy and kindness, and after they were all well they began to dance and celebrate and feast until sunrise of the day following. . . .

Early the next day many Indians came and brought five people who were paralyzed and very ill, and they came for Castillo to cure them. Every one of the patients offered him his bow and arrows, which he accepted, and by sunset he made the sign of the cross over each of the sick, recommending them to God, Our Lord, and we all prayed to Him as well as we could to restore them to health. And He, seeing there was no other way of getting those people to help us so that we might be saved from our miserable existence, had mercy upon us, and in the morning all woke up well and hearty and went away in such good health as if they never had had any ailment whatever. This caused them great admiration and moved us to thanks to Our Lord and to greater faith in His goodness and the hope that He would save us, guiding us to where we could

---

4. **tunas:** the fleshy fruit of the prickly pear cactus.
5. **negro:** a term for a person of African descent, seldom used today; refers to Estevánico, the enslaved Moor who is a member of the Cabeza de Vaca expedition.

serve Him. For myself I may say that I always had full faith in His mercy and in that He would liberate me from captivity, and always told my companions so. . . .

Nothing was talked about in this whole country but of the wonderful cures which God, Our Lord, performed through us, and so they came from many places to be cured, and after having been with us two days some Indians of the Susolas begged Castillo to go and attend to a man who had been wounded, as well as to others that were sick and among whom, they said, was one on the point of death. Castillo was very timid, especially in difficult and dangerous cases, and always afraid that his sins might interfere and prevent the cures from being effective. Therefore the Indians told me to go and perform the cure. They liked me, remembering that I had relieved them while they were out gathering nuts, for which they had given us nuts and hides. This had happened at the time I was coming to join the Christians. So I had to go, and Dorantes and Estevanico went with me.

When I came close to their ranches I saw that the dying man we had been called to cure was dead, for there were many people around him weeping and his lodge was torn down, which is a sign that the owner has died. I found the Indian with eyes up turned, without pulse and with all the marks of lifelessness. At least so it seemed to me, and Dorantes said the same. I removed a mat with which he was covered, and as best I could prayed to Our Lord to restore his health, as well as that of all the others who might be in need of it, and after having made the sign of the cross and breathed on him many times they brought his bow and presented it to me, and a basket of ground tunas, and took me to many others who were suffering from vertigo. They gave me two more baskets of tunas, which I left to the Indians that had come with us. Then we returned to our quarters.

Our Indians to whom I had given the tunas remained there, and at night returned telling that the dead man whom I attended to in their presence had resuscitated, rising from his bed, had walked about, eaten and talked to them, and that all those treated by me were well and in very good spirits. This caused great surprise and awe, and all over the land nothing else was spoken of. All who heard it came to us that we might cure them and bless their children, and when the Indians in our company (who were the Cultalchulches) had to return to their country, before parting they offered us all the tunas they had for their journey, not keeping a single one, and gave us flint stones as long as one and a half palms, with which they cut and that are greatly prized among them. They begged us to remember them and pray to God to keep them always healthy, which we promised to do, and so they left, the happiest people upon earth, having given us the very best they had.

We remained with the Avavares Indians for eight months, according to our reckoning of the moons. During that time they came for us from many places and said that verily we were children of the sun. Until then Dorantes and the negro had not made any cures, but we found ourselves so pressed by the Indians coming from all sides, that all of us had to become medicine men. I was the most daring and reckless of all in undertaking cures. We never treated anyone that did not afterwards say he was well, and they had such confidence in our skill as to believe that none of them would die as long as we were among them.

# Bartolomé de las Casas
**1474–1566** (Spain)

## Meet the Writer

The writings of **Bartolomé de las Casas** (bahr toh loh MAY day lahs KAH sahs) are among the most notable documents dealing with the early years of the Spanish colonization of the Americas. Like Cabeza de Vaca, las Casas came to view the Spaniards' treatment of Indians as inhumane and tyrannical. However, he did not begin his career as a reformer. He was born in Seville, Spain. His father and three uncles had traveled with Columbus on the second voyage to the Americas in 1493. (Las Casas later became the editor of Columbus's published journal.) In 1502, las Casas sailed to the West Indies to seek his fortune. He received a land grant, which included slaves as part of his property. In 1513, he traveled to Cuba, was awarded more land, and became a successful farmer.

After witnessing an Indian massacre by the Spaniards, las Casas underwent a moral conversion and began a lifelong crusade for reform. In 1523, he became a Dominican friar—a Catholic monk—and was sent to a Dominican monastery in Hispaniola. In 1527, he started writing his *Historia de las Indias* (*History of the Indies*), which was completed in 1561.

## Background

Under the *encomienda* (ihn koh mee EHN dah) system, Spanish colonists received a parcel of land as well as a certain number of Indians, who were enslaved and forced to work in fields or gold mines. In 1537, the pope prohibited further enslavement of the Indians. Charles V, king of Spain, issued new laws in 1542 that abolished the *encomienda* system.

Reform was short-lived. Las Casas tried to enact the new laws, but the colonists rebelled and forced King Charles to revoke the new laws. Las Casas became so unpopular that he was accused of treason. He retreated to Spain in 1547 and for the remainder of his life was an advocate for native Americans. He became known as "Protector of the Indians."

**Before You Read** One of the greatest tragedies caused by European colonization of the Americas was the devastating spread of diseases previously unknown in that part of the world. The beginning of this section of las Casas's account describes the ravages of the most destructive of these diseases: smallpox. Las Casas then goes on to describe how, in 1518, the Spanish settlements on the island of Hispaniola in the West Indies were devastated by an invasive species of ants. Las Casas describes vividly the afflictions of this plague and the various remedies that were used to destroy the ants. More than four centuries later, las Casas's narrative is still engrossing. As you read, note examples of las Casas's religious beliefs. How do they influence his perspective on events?

# Plague of Ants
*from* History of the Indies
## Fray Bartolomé de las Casas
*translated by* Sandra Ferdman

Around this time, in the year 1518 or 1519, something else happened on this island.[1] By the will or consent of God, to relieve them of the anguished and tortured lives they endured toiling in all sorts of labor, but mostly in the mines, and to punish those who oppressed them by making them suffer their absence, there came a terrible plague in which nearly all the few Indians left perished, with only a small number surviving. The epidemic was smallpox, brought over by someone from Castile,[2] and which attacked the poor Indians. The pox, which burns like fire, grew out of the earth's heat. The Indians, whose custom it was to wash themselves in the rivers at every opportunity, took to washing themselves even more in their anguish. As a result the smallpox was locked inside their bodies, and, as in a devastating pestilence, all died in a short time. Added to these causes were the thinness and meager substance of their bodies from lack of food, their nakedness, their sleeping on the ground, the excessive labor, and the little or no care for their health and preservation they received from those whom they served. Finally, seeing that the Indians were dying, the Spaniards began to understand the need they had and would continue to have of them, which moved them to make some effort to cure them, but this was of little help to most, for it ought to have begun many years earlier. I do not believe that 1,000 souls were left alive or escaped this misery, from the infinite number of people who had lived on this island and whom we saw with our own eyes, as is explained in book I. No Christian can doubt that, although God by his secret judgments might have permitted afflicting these peoples in this way and with such inhumanity, and, in short, putting an end to them, that on the day

---
1. **this island:** Hispaniola, in the West Indies.
2. **Castile:** a region in Spain, formerly a kingdom. Queen Isabella of Spain was from Castile.

of final judgment, and on the day of universal judgment, those who were ministers of such harshness and caused the loss of so many souls, will be severely punished by divine justice. If they did not repent while still alive they will pay for their greed and cruelty, for taking lives before their time, before their conversion, and so for the loss of so many souls (because all others on this island and on the neighboring ones believe, and I do not doubt it because I saw much of it myself, that they died without faith and without sacraments in their simple paganism). No Christian doubts this.

And because they realized that the Indians were dying, they began to slacken off and leave the mines, for they had no one left to send there to die or even to kill, and so they looked instead for other profits and new ways to acquire wealth, one of which was to plant cassia trees, which grew so quickly and in such numbers that it seemed as if this soil had not been created for any other tree, nor these trees for any other soil but this one, so ordered by Divine Providence and nature. In a very few days, many great estates were established of these cassia trees, from which the entire populated world could have been supplied. Their stalks were very big and thick, full of pulp, very honey-sweet. Ask the doctors and pharmacists if their virtue is lesser or greater than that of Alexandria.[3]

The citizens of this island, that is to say, the Spaniards, because there is nothing left to say about the Indians, were not just a little proud, promising themselves many riches by putting all their hopes in the cassia tree. It would be good to believe that they might have attributed to God a part of this prospect, but they were already beginning to enjoy the fruits of their labors and to fulfill their expectations when God sent over this whole island and over the island of Saint John,[4] principally, a plague. One might have feared, if it continued to grow, that the plague would totally depopulate them.

This plague was an infinite number of ants that were on this island and on the other and that could not be stopped in any way nor by any human means because of the sheer number of them. The ants bred on this island had an advantage over the ones on Saint John in the amount of damage done to the trees they destroyed, and the ants of the other island had an advantage over these in their fierceness, as they bit and caused greater pain than wasps that bite and hurt men. They could not defend themselves from these ants at night in their beds, nor could they survive if the beds were not placed on four small troughs filled with water. The ants on this island began to eat the trees from the root up, and as though fire had fallen from the sky and burned them, they stood all scorched and dried out.[5] They also attacked the orange and pomegranate trees, of which there were many groves, very pretty and full on this island, and they left none without burning them out completely. To see it was a great pity. Many groves were destroyed in the city of Santo Domingo, and among them a very important one belonging to the Dominicans' monastery (of pomegranate trees and sweet, dry, and bitter orange trees), and in a place called La Vega another one, quite notable, belonging to the Franciscans.[6] These trees stood behind the cassia trees, and, as they were sweeter, they destroyed

---

3. **Alexandria:** a seaport in Egypt, founded by Alexander the Great. It was a center of culture and learning in the ancient world, and scholars came from many countries to study at its library and museum.
4. **Saint John:** one of the Virgin Islands, in the West Indies.
5. **fire had fallen ... dried out:** Edward O. Wilson, an expert on ants, has concluded that the most likely species of ant described by las Casas is the tropical fire ant, *Solenopsis geminata*.
6. **Dominicans' ... Franciscans:** religious orders.

them even more quickly and burned them out. I believe that they devastated over one hundred million trees that were planted for profit. It was, certainly, a great shame to see so many properties, so rich, annihilated by such a relentless plague. The grove of Saint Francis in La Vega, already mentioned, was full of orange trees that gave sweet, dry, and bitter fruit. There I saw very beautiful pomegranate trees and cassia trees, and great stalks of cassia, nearly four hands in length. And just a short time later I saw all of it charred out. I saw the same thing in many other cassia tree estates that were in that area. The spreads of cassia trees on that land, and those that could have been planted, would without doubt have been enough, alone, to provide for all of Europe and Asia, even if they had been eaten as one eats bread, because of the great fertility of that land and its size. It extends for 80 leagues from sea to sea, full of rivers and happiness, and as flat as the palm of one's hand. We have talked about this at great length in our *Apologética historia*.[7]

Some looked for remedies to extirpate[8] this plague of ants. They dug around the trees as deeply as they could and killed the ants by drowning them in water. Other times they burnt them with fire. They found, inside the earth, three and four and more hands deep, their seedbeds and eggs, as white as snow, and they would burn one and two measures[9] of them every day, and by dawn, they would find an even greater quantity of live ants. The priests from Saint Francis of La Vega placed a mercury chloride[10] stone, which must have weighed three or four pounds, on a roof railing. All the ants of the house rushed there, and after eating from the stone they all fell dead. As if they had sent messengers to those who were within one and a half leagues, inviting them to the banquet of mercury chloride, not one ant, I believe, failed to come. One could see the roads filled with those coming to the monastery. They finally climbed up on the roof and ate from the mercury chloride and then fell dead, so that the roof was black as if they had sprayed it with charcoal dust. This lasted as long as the stone of mercury chloride did. The stone was like two great fists and like a ball; I saw it as large as I said it was when they first put it there, and a few days later I saw it again, only now the size of a hen's egg or a little bigger.

Once the priests saw that the mercury chloride was of no use, except to soil their home, they decided to take it away. They marveled at two things, which were worthy of admiration. First, at the natural instinct and the strength with which it endows sensitive and insensitive creatures, as is apparent in the case of these ants, who from such a distance could feel the mercury chloride, if one may put it this way, and how the same instinct guided them and brought them to it. Second, how a little animal so tiny and small (like these ants, which were very tiny) could have such strength as to be able to bite the mercury chloride, and, finally, to diminish it and finish it off, the mercury chloride in stone form, before it is ground, being as hard as a stone of alum, if not more so, and almost like a small rock.

As the citizens of Santo Domingo saw the affliction of this plague grow, doing such damage to them, and as they could not end it by any human means, they agreed to ask for help from the Highest Tribunal. They made great processions begging Our Father to free them from such a plague so harmful to their worldly goods. In order to receive divine blessing more quickly, they thought of taking a saint as a lawyer, whichever one by chance Our Lord should

---

7. **Apologética historia:** This is a collection of data about the Indians, intended to show that the Indians met Aristotle's requirements of a good life.
8. **extirpate:** remove; destroy.
9. **measures:** A dry measure consisted of 4,625 liters.
10. **mercury chloride:** poisonous compound used as an insecticide.

declare best suited. Thus, with the procession over one day, the bishop, and clergy, and the whole city cast lots over which of the litany's saints Divine Providence would see fit to give them as a lawyer. Fortune fell on Saint Saturnin,[11] and receiving him with happiness and joy as their patron, they celebrated him with a feast of great solemnity, as they have each year since then, by vow, as I believe. I do not know if they even fast on the eve. From that day on one saw by plain sight that the plague was diminishing, and if it did not end altogether, it was because of their sins. I now believe that it no longer exists, because they have again restored some of the cassia trees, and orange and pomegranate trees. I say restore referring not to what the ants burned out, but to the new trees that were planted. Some believed and said that the ants originated with the importation and cultivation of banana trees. Petrarch recounts in his *Trionfi*[12] that in the realm of Pisa a certain city was depopulated by a plague of ants that came over it like this one. Nicolaus Leonicus,[13] book II, chapter 71 of *Varia Historia,* refers to two very great cities, one named Miunte and the other Atarnense, which were depopulated by a multitude of mosquitos that at a certain time came upon them. Thus it is that, when God wishes to punish lands or the men who live in them for their sins, he does not lack the means to afflict them, and can even do so with the tiniest little creatures. So it was with the plagues of Egypt.

---

11. **Saint Saturnin:** one of the apostles sent out to Christianize Gaul in the third century. He was martyred when he refused to sacrifice to pagan images.
12. **Petrarch . . . Trionfi:** Francesco Petrarca (1304–1374), Italian poet. *Trionfi* (*The Triumphs*) was an unfinished allegory.
13. **Nicolaus Leonicus** (1428–1524): author of a scholarly treatise on disease that was published in Venice in 1497.

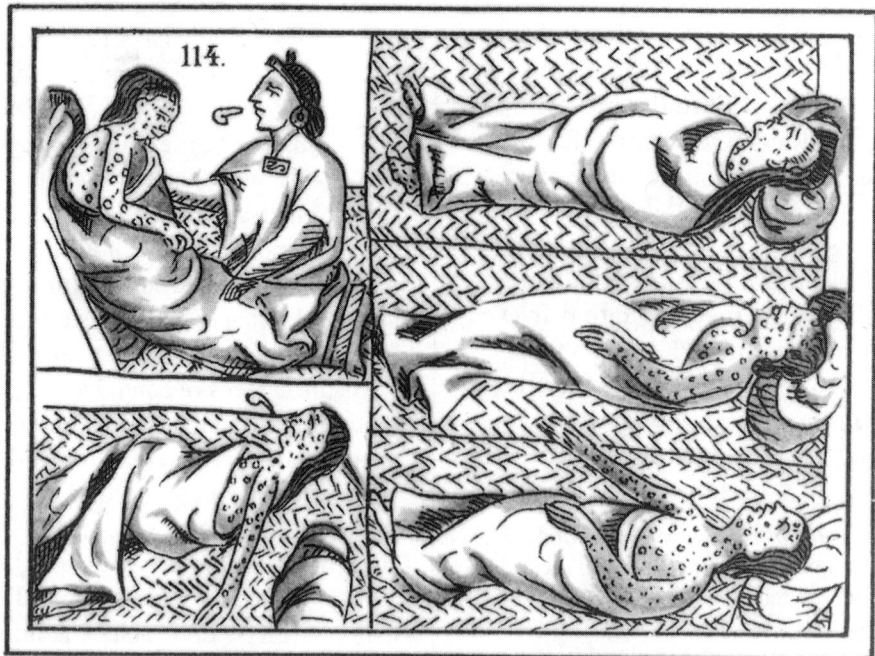

This page from the Florentine Codex depicts adults covered with smallpox pustules during an epidemic in Tenochtitlán, Mexico, in 1520.

# Popol Vuh

### c. 1554–1558 (Guatemala)

## Background

> *This is the beginning of the Ancient Word, here in this place called Quiché. Here we shall inscribe, we shall implant the Ancient Word, the potential and source for everything done in the citadel of Quiché, in the nation of Quiché people.*
> —Opening lines of the Popol Vuh

The Popol Vuh is considered the most important book in the native languages of the Americas. It is also a literary masterpiece. The title *Popol Vuh* literally means "book of the mat." Mats, or *petates,* were used by the ruling lords when they sat in council; thus, the Popol Vuh is sometimes referred to as the "Book of the Council." It has also been called the Bible of the Quiché Mayas, the indigenous, or native, people of Guatemala.

The name Quiché (kee CHAY) comes from Indian words meaning "land of many trees." The Quiché were one of the most numerous and influential peoples that had descended from the ancient Mayas. According to one estimate, fourteen generations of Quiché kings ruled the largest Mayan kingdom for nearly five hundred years.

The Popol Vuh tells the story of the origins and destiny of the Quiché people. It contains narratives dealing with the myths, traditions, and history of the Mayas, from the ancient past until 1550. The original sixteenth-century text has been lost. We know only that it was written in Quiché, using the Spanish alphabet. There may have been an earlier Popol Vuh written in Mayan hieroglyphs, but it has never been discovered. The Quiché Mayas believed that the Popol Vuh was a gift from the gods.

At the beginning of the eighteenth century, a Dominican friar named Francisco Ximénez translated the sixteenth-century Quiché manuscript into Spanish. His work is the oldest version of the Popol Vuh in existence.

The Popol Vuh brings together the myths and historical narratives that had been the oral heritage of the Quiché people. It begins with an account of the creation of the world. Later sections of the Popol Vuh deal with the origins of the Quiché kingdom, the migration to Guatemala's highlands, conquests, the founding of the citadel, and the history of the Quiché kings.

**Before You Read** In the Popol Vuh the group of gods identified as Bearer, Begetter; Maker, Modeler; and Sovereign Plumed Serpent do not succeed at first in creating human life when they fashion the earth and its plants and animals. They fail in their attempt to form people who will be able to talk and to honor the gods. Using a process called "sowing" and "dawning," the gods first create beings who lack arms and who make sounds but cannot speak. The gods determine that these beings shall be the animals that serve for food.

On the second attempt, the gods make a creature of mud that is unable to walk or to reproduce; it dissolves in water. During the third try, the gods make beings out of wood who can talk and reproduce but who have empty hearts and minds and who do not honor the gods. These wooden men, or manikins, are destroyed by a great flood. On their fourth and final attempt, the gods use yellow corn and white corn for the human body and model the first people from corn dough.

What can you infer about Quiché Mayan values from this account?

# The Creation of Humans
*from the* **Popol Vuh**
*translated by* Dennis Tedlock

And here is the beginning of the conception of humans, and of the search for the ingredients of the human body. So they spoke, the Bearer, Begetter, the Makers, Modelers named Sovereign Plumed Serpent:

"The dawn has approached, preparations have been made, and morning has come for the provider, nurturer, born in the light, begotten in the light. Morning has come for humankind, for the people of the face of the earth," they said. It all came together as they went on thinking in the darkness, in the night, as they searched and they sifted, they thought and they wondered.

And here their thoughts came out in clear light. They sought and discovered what was needed for human flesh. It was only a short while before the sun, moon, and stars were to appear above the Makers and Modelers. Split Place, Bitter Water Place[1] is the name: the yellow corn, white corn came from there.

And these are the names of the animals who brought the food: fox, coyote, parrot, crow. There were four animals who brought the news of the ears of yellow corn and white corn. They were coming from over there at Split Place, they showed the way to the split.

And this was when they found the staple foods.

And these were the ingredients for the flesh of the human work, the human design, and the water was for the blood. It became human

---

1. **Split Place, Bitter Water Place:** According to the translator, Dennis Tedlock, this place is a high mountain near the Guatemalan border with Mexico.

blood, and corn was also used by the Bearer, Begetter.

And so they were happy over the provisions of the good mountain, filled with sweet things, thick with yellow corn, white corn, and thick with pataxte and cacao, countless zapotes, anonas, jocotes, nances, matasanos, sweets—the rich foods filling up the citadel named Split Place, Bitter Water Place. All the edible fruits were there: small staples, great staples, small plants, great plants. The way was shown by the animals.

And then the yellow corn and white corn were ground, and Xmucane[2] did the grinding nine times. Food was used, along with the water she rinsed her hands with, for the creation of grease; it became human fat when it was worked by the Bearer, Begetter, Sovereign Plumed Serpent, as they are called.

After that, they put it into words:

the making, the modeling of our first mother-
    father,[3]
with yellow corn, white corn alone for the
    flesh,
food alone for the human legs and arms,
for our first fathers, the four human works.

It was staples alone that made up their flesh.

These are the names of the first people who were made and modeled.

This is the first person: Jaguar Quitze.[4]

And now the second: Jaguar Night.[5]
And now the third: Not Right Now.[6]
And the fourth: Dark Jaguar.[7]

And these are the names of our first mother-fathers. They were simply made and modeled, it is said; they had no mother and no father. We have named the men by themselves. No woman gave birth to them, nor were they begotten by the builder, sculptor, Bearer, Begetter. By sacrifice alone, by genius alone they were made, they were modeled by the Maker, Modeler, Bearer, Begetter, Sovereign Plumed Serpent. And when they came to fruition, they came out human:

They talked and they made words.
They looked and they listened.
They walked, they worked.

They were good people, handsome, with looks of the male kind. Thoughts came into existence and they gazed; their vision came all at once. Perfectly they saw, perfectly they knew everything under the sky, whenever they looked. The moment they turned around and looked around in the sky, on the earth, everything was seen without any obstruction. They didn't have to walk around before they could see what was under the sky; they just stayed where they were.

As they looked, their knowledge became intense. Their sight passed through trees, through rocks, through lakes, through seas, through mountains, through plains. Jaguar Quitze, Jaguar Night, Not Right Now, and Dark Jaguar were truly gifted people.

And then they were asked by the builder and mason:

"What do you know about your being? Don't you look, don't you listen? Isn't your speech good, and your walk? So you must look, to see

---

2. **Xmucane:** She and her husband, Xpiyacoc, are parents of the twins One Hunahpu and Seven Hunahpu, and grandparents of a second generation of twins, the heroes Hunahpu and Xbalanque. Xpiyacoc is a matchmaker and Xmucane is a midwife.
3. **mother-father:** According to Tedlock, the men serve symbolically as parents to everyone in their line.
4. **Jaguar Quitze:** founder of the Cauec line.
5. **Jaguar Night:** founder of the Greathouse line.
6. **Not Right Now:** founder of the Lord Quiché line.
7. **Dark Jaguar:** He and his wife have no male children.

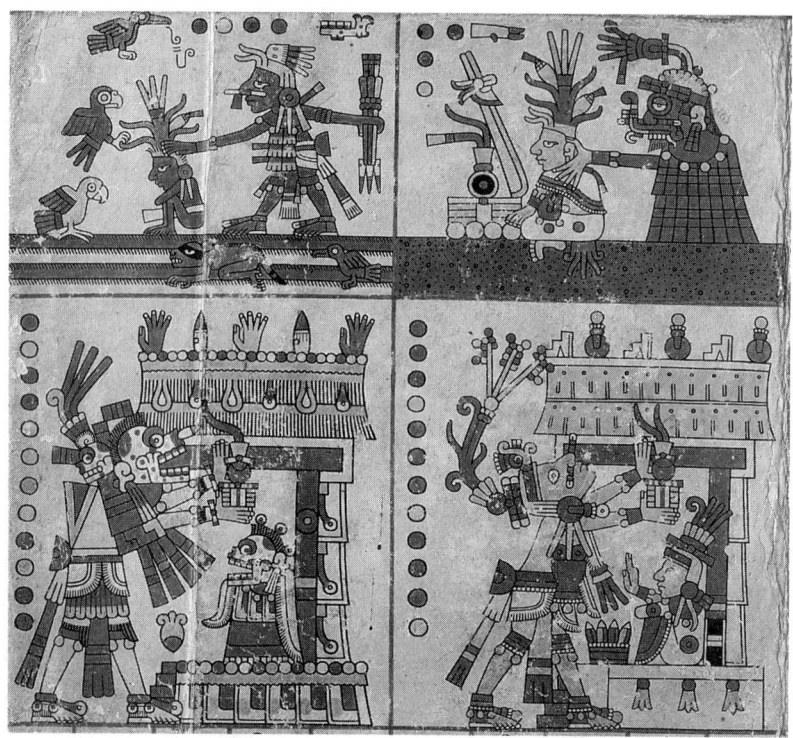

out under the sky. Don't you see the mountain-plain clearly? So try it," they were told.

And then they saw everything under the sky perfectly. After that, they thanked the Maker, Modeler:

> "Truly now,
> double thanks, triple thanks
> that we've been formed, we've been given
> our mouths, our faces,
> we speak, we listen,
> we wonder, we move,
> our knowledge is good, we've understood
> what is far and near,
> and we've seen what is great and small
> under the sky, on the earth.
> Thanks to you we've been formed,
> we've come to be made and modeled,
> our grandmother, our grandfather,"

they said when they gave thanks for having been made and modeled. They understood everything perfectly, they sighted the four sides, the four corners in the sky, on the earth, and this didn't sound good to the builder and sculptor:

"What our works and designs have said is no good:

'We have understood everything, great and small,' they say." And so the Bearer, Begetter took back their knowledge:

"What should we do with them now? Their vision should at least reach nearby, they should see at least a small part of the face of the earth, but what they're saying isn't good. Aren't they merely 'works' and 'designs' in their very names? Yet they'll become as great as gods, unless they procreate, proliferate at the sowing, the dawning, unless they increase."

"Let it be this way: now we'll take them apart

just a little, that's what we need. What we've found out isn't good. Their deeds would become equal to ours, just because their knowledge reaches so far. They see everything," so said

> the Heart of Sky, Hurricane,
> Newborn Thunderbolt, Sudden Thunderbolt,[8]
> Sovereign Plumed Serpent,
> Bearer, Begetter,
> Xpiyacoc, Xmucane,
> Maker, Modeler,

as they are called. And when they changed the nature of their works, their designs, it was enough that the eyes be marred by the Heart of Sky. They were blinded as the face of a mirror is breathed upon. Their vision flickered. Now it was only from close up that they could see what was there with any clarity.

And such was the loss of the means of understanding, along with the means of knowing everything, by the four humans. The root was implanted.

---

8. **Heart ... Thunderbolt:** At the beginning of the narrative, these gods are identified as gods from the primordial sky, who engage in a dialogue with the other gods, who are from the primordial sea.

And such was the making, modeling of our first grandfather, our father, by the Heart of Sky, Heart of Earth.

And then their wives and women came into being. Again, the same gods thought of it. It was as if they were asleep when they received them, truly beautiful women were there with Jaguar Quitze, Jaguar Night, Not Right Now, and Dark Jaguar. With their women there they really came alive. Right away they were happy at heart again, because of their wives.

Red Sea Turtle is the name of the wife of Jaguar Quitze.

Prawn House is the name of the wife of Jaguar Night.

Water Hummingbird is the name of the wife of Not Right Now.

Macaw House is the name of the wife of Dark Jaguar.

So these are the names of their wives, who became ladies of rank, giving birth to the people of the tribes, small and great.

And this is our root, we who are the Quiché people.

# Sor Juana Inés de la Cruz

c. 1648–1695 (Mexico)

## Meet the Writer

**Sor Juana Inés de la Cruz** (sohr hoo AH nah day lah kroos) is widely considered to be the greatest lyric poet of Mexico's colonial period. She became known in Spain as the "Tenth Muse," a reference to the nine Muses of Greek mythology—goddesses who presided over the arts and sciences, inspiring humans in their creative endeavors. Her beginnings, however, were far more humble than this comparison suggests. She was born to a poor family on the farmstead of San Miguel de Nepantla in Mexico and was baptized Juana Ramírez de Asbaje. She took the name Juana Inés de la Cruz in 1669, when she permanently entered the convent of Santa Paula. She is referred to by her ecclesiastical, or religious, name: Sor Juana (Sister Juana).

According to her own account in the famous *Reply to Sor Philothea*, Sor Juana learned to read when she was three. She devoured all the books in her grandfather's library and was largely self-taught. She begged her mother to let her dress as a man so she could study in the university, which did not admit women.

When she was about eight, Juana went to live in Mexico City with her maternal aunt and the aunt's husband, Juan de Mata. Juana became known as a child prodigy. The Matas arranged for her to be presented to the new viceroy, and she came to court when she was sixteen as a lady-in-waiting to the wife of the viceroy (who is called Laura in Sor Juana's poems). Juana was highly admired for her beauty, learning, and poetic talent. Because her background was humble, she would have been denied the opportunity to marry within court circles, had she possessed that desire. She always claimed that she never sought marriage.

Before she was twenty, Juana entered the convent, where she was to remain for the rest of her life. At first, she enjoyed an open and liberal—and surprisingly affluent—lifestyle, effectively having her own apartment, with living quarters, a bathroom, and kitchen facilities. She maintained her own library and was permitted to receive visitors—even male visitors. She held *tertulias,* or informal social meetings, with men of learning and soon became the center of a thriving intellectual community. She composed music, wrote poems and plays, and continued her studies. Sor Juana wrote her masterpiece, *Primero sueño* (*First Dream*), a philosophical poem that was daringly ahead of its time, during this early period of artistic freedom and intellectual growth.

A new viceroy arrived in 1680, and Sor Juana became friendly with the viceroy's wife, María Luisa, who is called Lisi or Lísida in the poems. When the viceroy and his wife returned to Spain in 1688, they took Sor Juana's writings with them for publication. Their departure, however, left Sor Juana without the protection of patrons. The Catholic Church, already critical of her worldly lifestyle, closed in on the now-vulnerable nun. In 1690, she was attacked for criticizing a sermon by a Jesuit priest. Using the feminine pseudonym of Sor Filotea, the Bishop of Puebla accused her of neglecting her religious duties for world affairs. Sor Juana defended her search for knowledge in the famous *Respuesta a sor Filotea* (*Reply to Sor Philothea*), which some readers consider the first feminist declaration. In fact, in 1974 Sor Juana was awarded the title "First Feminist of the Americas" at a ceremony in Mexico City.

Ultimately, however, Sor Juana was forced by the Church to renounce her books. She eventually sold her library of four thousand books as well as other personal possessions: her musical instruments, scientific equipment, and other accoutrements of the Renaissance scholar. In April 1695, the convent was stricken with plague. Sor Juana contracted the disease while caring for her sister nuns and died on April 17. She remains one of Mexico's most important literary figures, studied by schoolchildren and university scholars. Today, the interest in this remarkable woman is greater than ever before, with books, plays, films, Web sites, and countless scholarly articles dedicated to explorations of her achievements and contributions.

## Background

Octavio Paz, a Nobel Prize–winning contemporary Mexican poet, has called Sor Juana "the greatest versifier of the Spanish Language," adding, "Few poets in our language equal her, and those who can surpass her can be counted on the fingers of one hand." Sor Juana's poetry represents the range of forms and themes characteristic of the writers of Spain's Golden Age. Like other Spanish seventeenth-century writers, she uses wit and wordplay and draws on classical, biblical, and mythological sources. Among her compositions are *villancicos* (carols) to be sung on religious holidays. Her most significant poem is *Primero sueño*, a philosophical poem that tells of the soul's quest for knowledge. But her lyric poems, especially her sonnets, several of which are reprinted here, are among her most lasting and popular works.

**Before You Read**  Sor Juana wrote many love poems, some as passionate as any penned by secular writers. These translations are numbered following an organizational pattern suggested by Octavio Paz. (The Spanish originals use different numbering.) Here, the first line of each poem provides the title. The lines in italics at the beginning of each poem were written by an early editor of Sor Juana's works; they serve as brief, if not always accurate, summaries of each poem's theme.

Paz placed Sor Juana's lyric poems into such categories as "The Convent and the Court," "Divine Love," and "The Self, the World." Sor Juana's poems exhibit many of the characteristics of courtly Renaissance poetry: elaborate conceits, or comparisons; meditations on the fleeting nature of life and beauty (the "carpe diem" or "seize the day" theme); direct addresses to an absent lover; and concluding lines that sum up the point or moral of the poem in a witty, memorable way. Where do you find examples of these literary devices in the poems that follow?

# 7

# Disillusionment

## Sor Juana Inés de la Cruz
*translated by* Alan S. Trueblood

*Sure consolation in disillusion*

        Disillusionment,
this is the bitter end,
this proves you're rightly called
the end of illusion.
5        You've made me lose all,
yet no, losing all
is not paying too dear
for being undeceived.
        No more will you envy
10  the allurements of love,
for one undeceived
has no risk left to run.
        It's some consolation
to be expecting none:
15  there's relief to be found
in seeking no cure.

        In loss itself
I find assuagement:[1]
having lost the treasure,
20  I've nothing to fear.
        Having nothing to lose
brings peace of mind:
one traveling without funds
need not fear thieves.
25        Liberty itself
for me is no boon:
if I hold it such,
it will soon be my bane.
        No more worries for me
30  over boons so uncertain:
I will own my very soul
as if it were not mine.

---

1. **assuagement**: relief.

# 15
# Fabio, what pretty women covet most

**Sor Juana Inés de la Cruz**
*translated by* Alan S. Trueblood

*She demonstrates that in love a single attachment is reasonable and desirable*

   Fabio, what pretty women covet most
is worship from every man who comes along.
Altars are strictly useless in their eyes
unless the weight of victims makes them groan.
5    Therefore, should one man only pay them court,
they'll protest to Fortune they've been cheated,
convinced the gist of being a deity
lies not in beauty but in being entreated.[2]
   Yet, prizing moderation in such matters,
10 for throngs of suitors I've a strong distaste.
I only wish to grant my love's increase
   to one who feels it cannot be replaced.
Love's delicacy consists in being loved;
one pinch too much or little spoils love's taste.

---

2. **entreated:** begged.

# 22
# Speaking to you, belovèd, this afternoon

**Sor Juana Inés de la Cruz**
*translated by* Alan S. Trueblood

*In which she allays misgivings with the rhetoric[3] of tears*

   Speaking to you, belovèd, this afternoon,
I could see by your gestures and doubting air
that words were unavailing to convince you,
and I longed to have you see my heart laid bare.

---

3. **rhetoric:** eloquence; art of persuasion.

  5          Then Love, reading my mind, came to my aid
and achieved what I thought no one could do:
he distilled my broken heart until it flowed
and swelled the stream of tears wept over you.
          So, beloved, put an end to harshness now,
10  jealous torments will cease if you command,
and doubts no longer trouble your peace of mind
          with needless gloom, with insubstantial shams,
since, in that flood of tears, you saw and touched
my broken heart within your very hands.

# 27
# These lying pigments…

## Sor Juana Inés de la Cruz
*translated by* Alan S. Trueblood

*She disavows[4] the flattery visible in a portrait of herself, which she calls bias*

          These lying pigments facing you,
with every charm brush can supply
set up false premises of color
to lead astray the unwary eye.
5         Here, against ghastly tolls of time,
bland flattery has staked a claim,
defying the power of passing years
to wipe out memory and name.
          And here, in this hollow artifice—
10  frail blossom hanging on the wind,
vain pleading in a foolish cause,
          poor shield against what fate has wrought—
all efforts fail and in the end
a body goes to dust, to shade, to nought.

---

4. **disavows:** denies; disclaims.

# 29
# If men weighed the hazards of the sea

**Sor Juana Inés de la Cruz**

*translated by* Alan S. Trueblood

*She ponders the choice of a way of life binding until death*

        If men weighed the hazards of the sea,
none would embark. If they foresaw
the dangers of the ring,[5] rather than taunt
the savage bull, they'd cautiously withdraw.
5        If the horseman should prudently reflect
on the headlong fury of the steed's wild dash,
he'd never undertake to rein him in
adroitly, or to wield the cracking lash.
        But were there one of such temerity
10 that, facing undoubted peril, he still planned
to drive the fiery chariot and subdue
        the steeds of Apollo[6] himself with daring hand,
he'd stop at nothing, would not meekly choose
a way of life binding a whole life through.

---

5. **ring:** bullring.
6. **Apollo:** in some versions of Greek mythology, the sun god, who rode his chariot across the heavens.

**Before You Read**  When the second viceroy and his wife, María Luisa, left for Spain in 1688, Sor Juana lost her powerful protectors. Her intellectual and artistic accomplishments brought disapproval from Church officials. In November 1690, Manuel Fernández de Santa Cruz, the bishop of Puebla, published (without her permission) a critique Sor Juana had written of a forty-year-old sermon by a Portuguese Jesuit priest. The bishop rebuked her for her interest in secular (nonreligious) studies. In 1691, Sor Juana wrote the Respuesta a sor Filotea de la Cruz, *an articulate self-defense as well as a defense of women's right to knowledge. The excerpt reprinted here is from the autobiographical section of the reply, in which Sor Juana describes her love of learning. What qualities in Sor Juana do you most admire or identify with?*

# *from* Reply to Sor Philothea
## Sor Juana Inés de la Cruz
*translated by* Alan S. Trueblood

To go on with the account of this strong bent of mine, about which I want you to be fully informed, let me say that when I was not yet three, my mother sent a sister of mine, older than I, to learn to read in one of those establishments called Amigas [girls' elementary schools], at which point affection and mischievousness on my part led me to follow her. Seeing that she was being given lessons, I became so inflamed with the desire to learn to read, that I tricked the mistress—or so I thought—by telling her that my mother had directed her to give me lessons. This was not believable and she did not believe me, but falling in with my little trick, she did give me lessons. I continued attending and she went on teaching me, no longer as a joke, since the event opened her eyes. I learned to read in so short a time that I already knew how when my mother found out, for the mistress kept it from her in order to give her a pleasant surprise and receive her recompense all at one time. I kept still, since I thought I would be whipped for having acted on my own initiative. The person who taught me is still alive (may God preserve her) and can attest to this.

I remember that at this period, though I loved to eat, as children do at that age, I refrained from eating cheese, because someone had told me it made you stupid, and my urge to learn was stronger than my wish to eat, powerful as this is in children. Afterward, when I was six or seven and already knew how to read and write, along with all the sewing skills and needlework that women learn, I discovered that in the City of Mexico there was a university with schools where the different branches of learning could be studied, and as soon as I learned this I began to deluge my mother with urgent and insistent pleas to change my manner of dress and send me to stay with relatives in the City of Mexico so that I might study and take courses at the university. She refused, and rightly so; nevertheless, I found a way to read many different books my grandfather owned, notwithstanding the punishments and reproofs this entailed, so that when I went to the City of Mexico people were astonished, not so much at my intelligence as at the memory and store of knowledge I had at an age at which it would seem I had scarcely had time to learn to speak.

I began to study Latin, in which I do not believe I had twenty lessons in all, and I was so intensely studious that despite the natural concern of women—especially in the flower of their youth—with dressing their hair, I used to cut four or five fingers' width from mine, keeping track of how far it had formerly reached, and making it my rule that if by the time it grew back to that point, I did not know such-and-such a thing which I had set out to learn as it grew, I would cut it again as a penalty for my dullness. Thus it would happen that it would grow back and I still would not know what I had set myself to learn, because my hair grew rapidly, whereas I was a slow learner, and I did indeed cut it as a punishment for my slowness, for I did not consider it right that a head so bare of knowledge should be dressed with hair, knowledge being the more desirable ornament. I became a nun because, although I knew that that way of life involved much that was repellent to my nature—I refer to its incidental, not its central aspects—nevertheless, given my total disinclination to marriage, it was the least unreasonable and most becoming choice I could make to assure my ardently desired salvation. To which first consideration, as most important, all the other small frivolities of my nature yielded and gave way, such as my wish to live alone, to have no fixed occupation which might curtail my freedom to study, nor the noise of a community to interfere with the tranquil stillness of my books. This made me hesitate a little before making up my mind, until, enlightened by learned persons that hesitation was temptation, I overcame it by the grace of God and entered upon the life I now pursue so unworthily. I thought I was escaping from myself, but, alas for me, I had brought myself along. In this propensity I brought my greatest enemy, given me by Heaven whether as a boon or a punishment I cannot decide, for, far from dying out or being hindered by all the exercises religion entails, it exploded like gunpowder. *Privatio est causa appetitus* [Privation arouses the appetite] had its confirmation in me.

I went back (I misspeak: I had never stopped); I went on with the studious pursuit (in which I found relaxation during all the free time remaining from my obligations) of reading and more reading, study and more study, with no other teacher than books themselves. One can readily imagine how hard it is to study from those lifeless letters, lacking a teacher's live voice and explanations. Still I happily put up with all those drawbacks, for the sheer love of learning. Oh, if it had only been for the love of God, which would have been the sound way, what merit would have been mine! I *will* say that I tried to uplift my study as much as I could and direct it to serving Him, since the goal I aspired to was the study of theology, it seeming to me a mean sort of ineptitude for a Catholic not to know all that can be found out in this life through natural means concerning divine mysteries. I also felt that being a nun and not a lay person, I should, because of my ecclesiastical status, make a profession of letters—and furthermore that, as a daughter of Saint Jerome and Saint Paula, it would be a great disservice for the daughter of such learned parents to be a fool. This is what I took upon myself, and it seemed right to do so, unless of course—and this is probably the case—it was simply a way of flattering and applauding my own natural tendency, proposing its own pleasure to it as an obligation.

In this way I went on, continually directing the course of my study, as I have said, toward the eminence of sacred theology. To reach this goal, I considered it necessary to ascend the steps of human arts and sciences, for how can one who has not mastered the style of the ancillary branches of learning hope to understand that of the queen of them all?

# The Latino Oral Tradition

The blending of Spanish and native oral literary traditions in the sixteenth and seventeenth centuries created a rich body of folk tales, poetry, and folk music, much of which reflects characteristics of European folk literature even as it presents Latino subjects and concerns. Among the features of Latino folk literature that would be familiar to students of European folklore are the following:

- the triumph of the weak or poor over the strong or wealthy (or of the uneducated over the educated)
- a humorous or satirical view of human weakness or folly
- a hero or heroine who must pass a test or answer a perplexing riddle in order to receive a reward, such as marriage to a desirable partner
- animals that speak and act like people
- a fiendish villain who goes about playing cruel practical jokes
- ghostly apparitions that frighten wayward people into reforming their lives
- magic and enchantment
- events, characters, or objects appearing in threes
- a lesson or moral in which virtue is rewarded

Like all folk literature, folk tales offer a record of the beliefs, values, and concerns of the culture in which they are rooted. For example, the tale of La Llorona focuses on a legend unique to Mexican American culture. The figure that appears in this traditional tale also appears in works of contemporary writers, suggesting the importance that the story holds in the hearts of the people within that culture.

Folk ballads such as "The Ballad of Gregorio Cortez" draw on the traditional *corrido* form to immortalize legendary figures, historical events, political issues, and other important topics. Usually set to music, *corridos* highlight the inherent musicality of the Spanish language.

From the mountain villages of northern New Mexico and southern Colorado to the urban areas of Texas and California, the Latino oral tradition remains a vital, evolving presence, as seen in the arts of storytelling, poetry, and musical performance. As the Spanish language thrives, so does the oral tradition of Latino literature.

# The Force of Luck
## A Mexican American Folk Tale

## Background

Passed down from generation to generation, folk tales represent a vital part of the Latino literary tradition. Folk tales take a variety of different forms from region to region and from storyteller to storyteller. The characters in folk tales tend to be ordinary and flat—that is, uncomplicated. Often they don't have names; they may be identified only by their occupation: the Priest, the Mayor, the Baker. Folk tales deal with basic, recurring themes: A poor person becomes rich; an ignorant person outsmarts an educated person; an overlooked youngest child is really a prince. Like fables, folk tales often present a lesson or moral, and they may take a humorous or satirical view of human weaknesses and follies.

Apart from characters' names, settings, and regional details, what is Latino about Latino folk tales? In his important 1970 collection *Folktales of México*, the renowned Mexican American scholar and folklorist Américo Paredes identified five major categories of Mexican and Mexican American folk tale: animal tales, ordinary tales, jokes and anecdotes, formula tales, and legendary tales.

Latino folk tales often feature religious motifs—most of them derived from Catholic belief. Priests, angels, saints, and the devil are commonly occurring characters. Satan is often the fiendish villain in Latino folk tales, though sometimes he is "brought down to size" as a trickster figure. Death is treated matter-of-factly; characters may pass between heaven, hell, and earth as easily as they might pass from one town to another, and the dead may visit the living.

Latino folk tales erase the distinctions between fantasy and reality in unexpected and creative ways, always with an eye to exposing truths about the human condition. Yet they are often as practical and sensible as they are magical, focusing on the earthy realities that give everyday life its meaning and substance.

"The Force of Luck" is a Mexican American folk tale retold by Rudolfo A. Anaya from his collection *Cuentos: Tales from the Hispanic Southwest*. With its generic, timeless setting, as well as its one-dimensional characters and uncomplicated plot, "The Force of Luck" is truly a universal tale, exhibiting features found not only in Latino but also in other world oral traditions.

**Before You Read**  *The following folk tale, retold by the famous Mexican American writer Rudolfo A. Anaya, deals with an argument and the manner in which it is resolved. At what point in the story does the miller's "luck" change? How many of the story's events are attributable to luck or chance, and how many to other factors?*

# The Force of Luck

*retold by* Rudolfo A. Anaya

Once two wealthy friends got into a heated argument. One said that it was money which made a man prosperous, and the other maintained that it wasn't money, but luck, which made the man. They argued for some time and finally decided that if only they could find an honorable man then perhaps they could prove their respective points of view.

One day while they were passing through a small village they came upon a miller who was grinding corn and wheat. They paused to ask the man how he ran his business. The miller replied that he worked for a master and that he earned only four bits° a day, and with that he had to support a family of five.

The friends were surprised. "Do you mean to tell us you can maintain a family of five on only fifteen dollars a month?" one asked.

"I live modestly to make ends meet," the humble miller replied.

The two friends privately agreed that if they put this man to a test perhaps they could resolve their argument.

"I am going to make you an offer," one of them said to the miller. "I will give you two hundred dollars and you may do whatever you want with the money."

"But why would you give me this money when you've just met me?" the miller asked.

"Well, my good man, my friend and I have a long standing argument. He contends that it is luck which elevates a man to high position, and I say it is money. By giving you this money perhaps we can settle our argument. Here, take it, and do with it what you want!"

So the poor miller took the money and spent the rest of the day thinking about the strange meeting which had presented him with more money than he had ever seen. What could he possibly do with all this money? Be that as it may, he had the money in his pocket and he could do with it whatever he wanted.

When the day's work was done, the miller decided the first thing he would do would be to buy food for his family. He took out ten dollars and wrapped the rest of the money in a cloth and put the bundle in his bag. Then he went to the market and bought supplies and a good piece of meat to take home.

On the way home he was attacked by a hawk that had smelled the meat which the miller carried. The miller fought off the bird but in the struggle he lost the bundle of money. Before the miller knew what was happening the hawk grabbed the bag and flew away with it. When he realized what had happened he fell into deep thought.

"Ah," he moaned, "wouldn't it have been better to let that hungry bird have the meat! I could have bought a lot more meat with the money he

---

° **four bits:** fifty cents (informal).

took. Alas, now I'm in the same poverty as before! And worse, because now those two men will say I am a thief! I should have thought carefully and bought nothing. Yes, I should have gone straight home and this wouldn't have happened!"

So he gathered what was left of his provisions and continued home, and when he arrived he told his family the entire story.

When he was finished telling his story his wife said, "It has been our lot to be poor, but have faith in God and maybe someday our luck will change."

The next day the miller got up and went to work as usual. He wondered what the two men would say about his story. But since he had never been a man of money he soon forgot the entire matter.

Three months after he had lost the money to the hawk, it happened that the two wealthy men returned to the village. As soon as they saw the miller they approached him to ask if his luck had changed. When the miller saw them he felt ashamed and afraid that they would think that he had squandered the money on worthless things. But he decided to tell them the truth and as soon as they had greeted each other he told his story. The men believed him. In fact, the one who insisted that it was money and not luck which made a man prosper took out another two hundred dollars and gave it to the miller.

"Let's try again," he said, "and let's see what happens this time."

The miller didn't know what to think. "Kind sir, maybe it would be better if you put this money in the hands of another man," he said.

"No," the man insisted, "I want to give it to you because you are an honest man, and if we are going to settle our argument you have to take the money!"

The miller thanked them and promised to do his best. Then as soon as the two men left he began to think what to do with the money so that it wouldn't disappear as it had the first time. The thing to do was to take the money straight home. He took out ten dollars, wrapped the rest in a cloth, and headed home.

When he arrived his wife wasn't at home. At first he didn't know what to do with the money. He went to the pantry where he had stored a large earthenware jar filled with bran. That was as safe a place as any to hide the money, he thought, so he emptied out the grain and put the bundle of money at the bottom of the jar, then covered it up with the grain. Satisfied that the money was safe he returned to work.

That afternoon when he arrived home from work he was greeted by his wife.

"Look, my husband, today I bought some good clay with which to whitewash the entire house."

"And how did you buy the clay if we don't have any money?" he asked.

"Well, the man who was selling the clay was willing to trade for jewelry, money, or anything of value," she said. "The only thing we had of value was the jar full of bran, so I traded it for the clay. Isn't it wonderful, I think we have enough clay to whitewash these two rooms!"

The man groaned and pulled his hair.

"Oh, you crazy woman! What have you done? We're ruined again!"

"But why?" she asked, unable to understand his anguish.

"Today I met the same two friends who gave me the two hundred dollars three months ago," he explained. "And after I told them how I lost the money they gave me another two hundred. And I, to make sure the money was safe, came home and hid it inside the jar of bran—the same jar you have traded for dirt! Now we're as poor as we were before! And what am I going to tell the two men? They'll think I'm a liar and a thief for sure!"

"Let them think what they want," his wife said calmly. "We will only have in our lives what the good Lord wants us to have. It is our lot to be poor until God wills it otherwise."

**The Force of Luck**

So the miller was consoled and the next day he went to work as usual. Time came and went, and one day the two wealthy friends returned to ask the miller how he had done with the second two hundred dollars. When the poor miller saw them he was afraid they would accuse him of being a liar and a spendthrift. But he decided to be truthful and as soon as they had greeted each other he told them what had happened to the money.

"That is why poor men remain honest," the man who had given him the money said. "Because they don't have money they can't get into trouble. But I find your stories hard to believe. I think you gambled and lost the money. That's why you're telling us these wild stories."

"Either way," he continued, "I still believe that it is money and not luck which makes a man prosper."

"Well, you certainly didn't prove your point by giving the money to this poor miller," his friend reminded him. "Good evening, you luckless man," he said to the miller.

"Thank you, friends," the miller said.

"Oh, by the way, here is a worthless piece of lead I've been carrying around. Maybe you can use it for something," said the man who believed in luck. Then the two men left, still debating their points of view on life.

Since the lead was practically worthless, the miller thought nothing of it and put it in his jacket pocket. He forgot all about it until he arrived home. When he threw his jacket on a chair he heard a thump and he remembered the piece of lead. He took it out of the pocket and threw it under the table. Later that night after the family had eaten and gone to bed, they heard a knock at the door.

"Who is it? What do you want?" the miller asked.

"It's me, your neighbor," a voice answered. The miller recognized the fisherman's wife.

"My husband sent me to ask you if you have any lead you can spare. He is going fishing tomorrow and he needs the lead to weight down the nets."

The miller remembered the lead he had thrown under the table. He got up, found it, and gave it to the woman.

"Thank you very much, neighbor," the woman said. "I promise you the first fish my husband catches will be yours."

"Think nothing of it," the miller said and returned to bed. The next day he got up and went to work without thinking any more of the incident. But in the afternoon when he returned home he found his wife cooking a big fish for dinner.

"Since when are we so well off we can afford fish for supper?" he asked his wife.

"Don't you remember that our neighbor promised us the first fish her husband caught?" his wife reminded him. "Well this was the fish he caught the first time he threw his net. So it's ours, and it's a beauty. But you should have been here when I gutted him! I found a large piece of glass in his stomach!"

"And what did you do with it?"

"Oh, I gave it to the children to play with," she shrugged.

When the miller saw the piece of glass he noticed it shone so brightly it appeared to illuminate the room, but because he knew nothing about jewels he didn't realize its value and left it to the children. But the bright glass was such a novelty that the children were soon fighting over it and raising a terrible fuss.

Now it so happened that the miller and his wife had other neighbors who were jewelers. The following morning when the miller had gone to work the jeweler's wife visited the miller's wife to complain about all the noise her children had made.

"We couldn't get any sleep last night," she moaned.

"I know, and I'm sorry, but you know how it is with a large family," the miller's wife explained. "Yesterday we found a beautiful piece of glass and I gave it to my youngest one to play with and when the others tried to take it from him he raised a storm."

The jeweler's wife took interest. "Won't you show me that piece of glass?" she asked.

"But of course. Here it is."

"Ah, yes, it's a pretty piece of glass. Where did you find it?"

"Our neighbor gave us a fish yesterday and when I was cleaning it I found the glass in its stomach."

"Why don't you let me take it home for just a moment? You see, I have one just like it and I want to compare them."

"Yes, why not? Take it," answered the miller's wife.

So the jeweler's wife ran off with the glass to show it to her husband. When the jeweler saw the glass he instantly knew it was one of the finest diamonds he had ever seen.

"It's a diamond!" he exclaimed.

"I thought so," his wife nodded eagerly. "What shall we do?"

"Go tell the neighbor we'll give her fifty dollars for it, but don't tell her it's a diamond!"

"No, no," his wife chuckled, "of course not." She ran to her neighbor's house. "Ah yes, we have one exactly like this," she told the miller's wife. "My husband is willing to buy it for fifty dollars—only so we can have a pair, you understand."

"I can't sell it," the miller's wife answered. "You will have to wait until my husband returns from work."

That evening when the miller came home from work his wife told him about the offer the jeweler had made for the piece of glass.

"But why would they offer fifty dollars for a worthless piece of glass?" the miller wondered aloud. Before his wife could answer they were interrupted by the jeweler's wife.

"What do you say, neighbor, will you take fifty dollars for the glass?" she asked.

"No, that's not enough," the miller said cautiously. "Offer more."

"I'll give you fifty thousand!" the jeweler's wife blurted out.

"A little bit more," the miller replied.

"Impossible!" the jeweler's wife cried, "I can't offer any more without consulting my husband." She ran off to tell her husband how the bartering was going, and he told her he was prepared to pay a hundred thousand dollars to acquire the diamond.

He handed her seventy-five thousand dollars and said, "Take this and tell him that tomorrow, as soon as I open my shop, he'll have the rest."

When the miller heard the offer and saw the money he couldn't believe his eyes. He imagined the jeweler's wife was jesting with him, but it was a true offer and he received the hundred thousand dollars for the diamond. The miller had never seen so much money, but he still didn't quite trust the jeweler.

"I don't know about this money," he confided to his wife. "Maybe the jeweler plans to accuse us of robbing him and thus get it back."

"Oh, no," his wife assured him, "the money is ours. We sold the diamond fair and square—we didn't rob anyone."

"I think I'll still go to work tomorrow," the miller said. "Who knows, something might happen and the money will disappear, then we would be without money and work. Then how would we live?"

So he went to work the next day, and all day he thought about how he could use the money. When he returned home that afternoon his wife asked him what he had decided to do with their new fortune.

The Force of Luck

"I think I will start my own mill," he answered, "like the one I operate for my master. Once I set up my business we'll see how our luck changes."

The next day he set about buying everything he needed to establish his mill and to build a new home. Soon he had everything going.

Six months had passed, more or less, since he had seen the two men who had given him the four hundred dollars and the piece of lead. He was eager to see them again and to tell them how the piece of lead had changed his luck and made him wealthy.

Time passed and the miller prospered. His business grew and he even built a summer cottage where he could take his family on vacation. He had many employees who worked for him. One day while he was at his store he saw his two benefactors riding by. He rushed out into the street to greet them and ask them to come in. He was overjoyed to see them, and he was happy to see that they admired his store.

"Tell us the truth," the man who had given him the four hundred dollars said. "You used that money to set up this business."

The miller swore he hadn't, and he told them how he had given the piece of lead to his neighbor and how the fisherman had in return given him a fish with a very large diamond in its stomach. And he told them how he had sold the diamond.

"And that's how I acquired this business and many other things I want to show you," he said. "But it's time to eat. Let's eat first then I'll show you everything I have now."

The men agreed, but one of them still doubted the miller's story. So they ate and then the miller had three horses saddled and they rode out to see his summer home. The cabin was on the other side of the river where the mountains were cool and beautiful. When they arrived the men admired the place very much. It was such a peaceful place that they rode all afternoon through the forest. During their ride they came upon a tall pine tree.

"What is that on top of the tree?" one of them asked.

"That's the nest of a hawk," the miller replied.

"I have never seen one; I would like to take a closer look at it!"

"Of course," the miller said, and he ordered a servant to climb the tree and bring down the nest so his friend could see how it was built. When the hawk's nest was on the ground they examined it carefully. They noticed that there was a cloth bag at the bottom of the nest. When the miller saw the bag he immediately knew that it was the very same bag he had lost to the hawk which fought him for the piece of meat years ago.

"You won't believe me, friends, but this is the very same bag in which I put the first two hundred dollars you gave me," he told them.

"If it's the same bag," the man who had doubted him said, "then the money you said the hawk took should be there."

"No doubt about that," the miller said. "Let's see what we find."

The three of them examined the old, weather-beaten bag. Although it was full of holes and crumbling, when they tore it apart they found the money intact. The two men remembered what the miller had told them and they agreed he was an honest and honorable man. Still, the man who had given him the money wasn't satisfied. He wondered what had really happened to the second two hundred he had given the miller.

They spent the rest of the day riding in the mountains and returned very late to the house.

As he unsaddled their horses, the servant in charge of grooming and feeding the horses suddenly realized that he had no grain for them. He ran to the barn and checked, but there was no grain for the hungry horses. So he ran to the neighbor's granary and there he was able to buy a large clay jar of bran. He carried the jar home and emptied the bran into a bucket to wet it before he fed it to the horses. When he got to the bottom of the jar he noticed a large lump which turned out to be a rag covered package. He examined it and felt something inside. He immediately went to give it to his master who had been eating dinner.

"Master," he said, "look at this package which I found in an earthenware jar of grain which I just bought from our neighbor!"

The three men carefully unraveled the cloth and found the other one hundred and ninety dollars which the miller had told them he had lost. That is how the miller proved to his friends that he was truly an honest man.

And they had to decide for themselves whether it had been luck or money which had made the miller a wealthy man!

# La Llorona
## A Mexican American Folk Tale

## Background

Many cultures have legends of ghostly figures who inhabit the night. La Llorona (lah yoh ROH nah), the Weeping Woman, is one such figure. Stories about her appear throughout Mexico and the southwestern United States. The legend of La Llorona has been kept alive by oral tradition—people passing on the story by word of mouth.

The most common version of the story describes the origin of La Llorona in this way: An Indian woman is betrayed by her deceitful husband. Insane with rage and anguish, she drowns their children and soon afterward dies in remorse. Her restless spirit takes human form and appears to unsuspecting people, usually around the lake or river where the drowning is supposed to have taken place. She is often dressed in flowing white and is weeping or wailing, grieving the loss of her children. Many scholars have seen in the La Llorona story certain parallels with the ancient Greek myth of Medea, who, after being abandoned by her husband, Jason, murdered their children in a fit of grief and revenge.

According to some students of folklore, the legend of La Llorona has its roots in Aztec mythology and dates back to the time of the conquest of Mexico. The ancient legend says that the goddess Cihuacoatl appeared in the capital city of Tenochtitlán one night shortly before the invasion of Mexico by Hernán Cortés. She was dressed in white and weeping loudly, crying for her lost children—the Aztec people. Shortly after the Spaniards arrived, the Aztec Empire was conquered.

In other versions of the legend, La Llorona is identified with La Malinche (lah mah LEEN chay), one of the most famous figures in Mexican folklore. La Malinche is the name given to the Indian woman, sometimes called Doña Marina, who was an interpreter for Cortés and who was blamed by some for the ease with which the Spaniards conquered the Aztecs.

The forms La Llorona takes vary from locale to locale. In one part of New Mexico, she is seen as a beautiful woman on horseback, dressed in elegant riding clothes. In a part of rural southern Colorado, she is reported as emerging from a big black rock at night, enveloped in a white mist and growing taller and taller until she vanishes. In many parts of Mexico and the Southwest, she is a frightening, skeletal-faced or horse-faced figure of ill omen: If you run into her as she walks around crying out for her dead children, it means that you yourself are marked for death.

**Before You Read**   Like most tales of ghostly creatures, the legend of La Llorona is recounted in a variety of creative ways. The story's locale, its tone, and many of its specific details are within the storyteller's or writer's full control. This version is influenced by its author's childhood roots in Arizona. What examples of "local color" can you find?

# La Llorona, the Weeping Woman

*translated and retold by* Joe Hayes

This is a story that the old ones have been telling to children for hundreds of years. It is a sad tale, but it lives strong in the memories of the people, and there are many who swear that it is true.

Long years ago in a humble little village there lived a fine-looking girl named María. Some say she was the most beautiful girl in the world! And because she was so beautiful, María thought she was better than everyone else.

As María grew older, her beauty increased. And her pride in her beauty grew too. When she was a young woman, she would not even look at the young men from her village. They weren't good enough for her!

"When I marry," María would say, "I'll marry the most handsome man in the world."

And then one day, into María's village rode a man who seemed to be just the one she had been talking about. He was a dashing young ranchero—the son of a wealthy rancher from the southern plains.

He could ride like a Comanche! In fact, if he owned a horse, and it grew tame, he would give it away and go rope a wild horse from the plains. He thought it wasn't manly to ride a horse unless it was half wild.

He was handsome! And he could play the guitar and sing beautifully. María made up her mind—this was the man for her! She knew just the tricks to win his attention.

If the ranchero spoke when they met on the pathway, she would turn her head away. When he came to her house in the evening to play his guitar and serenade her, she wouldn't even come to the window. She refused all his costly gifts.

The young man fell for her tricks. "That haughty girl María," he said to himself. "I can win her heart. That's the girl I'll marry."

And so everything turned out just as María planned. Before long, she and the ranchero became engaged and soon they were married.

At first, things were fine. They had two children and they seemed to be a happy family together.

But after a few years, the ranchero went back to the wild life of the prairies. He would leave town and be gone for months at a time. And when he returned home, it was only to visit his children. He seemed to care nothing for the beautiful María. He even talked of setting María aside and marrying a woman of his own wealthy class.

As proud as María was, of course she became very angry with the ranchero. She also began to feel anger toward her children, because he paid attention to them, but just ignored her.

One evening, as María was strolling with her two children on the shady pathway near the river, the ranchero came by in a carriage. An elegant woman sat on the seat beside him. He stopped and spoke to his children, but didn't even look at María. He whipped the horses on up the street.

When she saw that, a terrible rage filled María, and it all turned against her children. And, although it is sad to tell, the story says that in her anger María seized her two children and threw them into the river!

But as they disappeared down the river, she realized what she had done! She ran down the bank of the river, reaching out her arms to them. But they were long gone.

On and on ran María, driven by the fear that filled her heart, until finally she sank to the ground and lay still.

The next morning, a traveler brought word to the villagers that a beautiful woman lay dead on the bank of the river. That is where they found María, and they laid her to rest where she had fallen.

But from the first night she was in the grave, the villagers heard the sound of crying down by the river. At first they thought it was only the wind they were hearing. But when they listened more carefully, they heard words. "A a a a a i i i i . . . my children," a voice sobbed pitifully. "Where are my children?"

And they saw a woman walking up and down the bank of the river, dressed in a long white robe, the way they had dressed María for burial.

On many a dark night, they saw her walk the river bank. But more often, they would hear her cry for her children. And so they no longer spoke of her as María. They called her La Llorona (lah yoh-RROH-nah)—the weeping woman. And by that name she is known to this day.

And they still warn the young ones, "When it grows dark, get inside the house. La Llorona may be about, looking for her children. Be careful! She might mistake you for one of her own children."

They tell of many children down through the years who have been chased by the crying ghost—and of some who have even been caught!

*La Llorona*
(The Crying Woman)
Carmen Lomas Garza
Gouache painting
18 x 26 inches
©1989 Carmen Lomas Garza.
Wolfgang Dietze. Collection
of Sonia Saldivar-Hull &
Felix Hull, Austin/Austin, TX.

# La Ofrenda
## A Mexican American Folk Tale

## Background

Many folk tales deal with the traditional celebration of *el Día de los Muertos*, the Day of the Dead, observed on November 2. Passed down from generation to generation by word of mouth, these tales serve to teach the traditions and beliefs surrounding *el Día de los Muertos* to new generations. The holiday is celebrated chiefly in Mexico and by communities of Mexican Americans in the United States.

**Early Roots.** In Mexico, before the arrival of the Spaniards in 1519, the Day of the Dead was a festival celebrated during the harvest in autumn. Crops were collected and offered to the Earth, which was seen as a mother. During this period, it was considered important to honor one's ancestors, who, it was believed, returned from the underworld to visit the living.

Unable to root out these ancient customs, the Catholic Church allowed *el Día de los Muertos* to continue, but it was to be observed on the first two days of November, which coincided with the Catholic holy days All Saints' Day and All Souls' Day. Thus, the cultural traditions of Europeans and indigenous peoples of the Americas were blended.

**Honoring the Dead.** Preparation for the Day of the Dead often begins several weeks in advance. People clean the cemeteries, paint the gravestones, and prepare special foods. Some people build altars in their houses, but most people visit the cemeteries and decorate the graves of relatives with *ofrendas*, or offerings. These include brilliant yellow-orange marigolds, the "flower of the dead"; white and cream-colored candles; clay and papier-mâché skull and skeleton figures; framed family photographs; toys and candies for children; food and drink; and even clothing. On the evening of October 31, families set out the offerings for the spirits of children who have died. The next day, they make offerings for adult souls, who are believed to arrive after midnight. Candles light the way back for the spirits, and marigold petals create a path so that the spirits can find their way back home. During the evening, families gather in cemeteries to remember deceased relatives and friends.

In some places, the holiday is celebrated with a candle-lit procession. In other places, the festival takes on a carnival-like atmosphere, complete with games and rides. A symbol associated with the holiday is the skull, called a *calavera*; sugar skulls and skull-shaped breads and cookies are often eaten by relatives or friends. Another custom is the writing of *calaveras*, short poems mocking the epitaphs of friends.

Most folk tales about *el Día de los Muertos* are set in the countryside, where the tales originated. The storytellers are usually family elders who pass along to children the customs that they must respect and carry on.

**Before you Read** *Values, beliefs, and cultural elements underlie all folk tales. Most folk tales, in fact, have a clear message, or moral—a lesson about proper conduct in life. What is the moral of this folk tale?*

# La Ofrenda (The Offering)

*retold by* Francisco González Sol

While many people uphold the customs of their ancestors, there are always those who refuse to follow the older ways. For instance, they refuse to believe that the souls of the departed return to visit during *el Día de los Muertos*.[1] They ignore that this is a special holiday, a time to clean up the family graves, cook traditional dishes, and prepare an *ofrenda* for the returning souls.

Among the nonbelievers was Don Nicacio. He lived in the pueblo of Chamilpa[2] and sold firewood. He was known throughout the town for his dependable service, especially during late October and early November, when much firewood was consumed.

Nicacio's wife, María del Rosario, was more inclined to follow the traditions of her people.

---

1. *el Día de los Muertos:* the Day of the Dead.

2. **Chamilpa:** town outside Cuernavaca, Mexico.

When November came, she tried in vain to convince Nicacio to prepare an *ofrenda* for *el Día de los Muertos*.

"It doesn't have to be grand. Even a small *ofrenda* will be fine, my husband. Just a few flowers, some candles, and a small offering of food. This is a special time. Have you forgotten Juanita?"

Nicacio shook his head. "Our daughter died only two years ago. How could I forget?"

"Then stay at home. Don't go to work. Can't you see that no one is working today? Help me build the *ofrenda*. Or at least give me some money to buy more food, flowers and candles."

"Ay, María, you're *loca*.[3] When we die, we die, and that's it. We don't come back ever again. All this about the *ofrenda* is just a story, a silly story. And you will have to get by with what we have. I'm not giving you more money for this superstition."

Nicacio ignored María's entreaties. He thought only of the opportunity to make some extra money. Grabbing his machete,[4] he headed for a heavily wooded area at the base of the mountain to search for firewood and *ocote*.[5] The place was far, but he knew he would find the best *ocote* there.

Following paths seldom traveled, Nicacio finally came upon a large, leafy oak tree that promised a good yield of *ocote*.

"I'll find a lot here and get a good price for it. *Ocote* is scarce these days, and no one else would venture this far from the pueblo for it."

Since dusk was fast approaching, Nicacio lost no time in tying the machete around his waist and climbing the tree. At the very top, he found a good joint formed by two sturdy branches. Leaning through the joint, he went to work.

Up in the tree, the wind was cool and brisk, and the birds seemed to sing more loudly. The bells of the small church in town chimed to announce the afternoon service. Pausing to rest, Nicacio could see Chamilpa in the distance.

Suddenly, the two branches supporting Nicacio snapped closed, trapping him at the waist. The woodsman struggled to free himself by wriggling and shoving. Frustrated and frightened, he called for help. But he knew that the chances of someone hearing him were very remote.

Hours passed and evening came. Nicacio resigned himself to the futility of further struggle, and fell limp with exhaustion. He recalled María pleading with him to stay home and give her money to buy flowers and candles for the *ofrenda*. He thought of Juanita, so sweet and innocent, who would never enjoy her eighth birthday.

Nicacio sighed, "Why would the dead return when they suffered so much during life? When I die, I don't ever want to come back."

Darkness brought a dampness that chilled the woodsman to his bones. The wind howled. Again Nicacio heard the church bells, this time announcing the midnight rosary service for the dead. As Nicacio glanced up, he noticed a lengthy procession heading in his direction. His heart quickened with the hope of rescue.

"When they're close enough, I'll yell. One of them is bound to hear me. I'm so tired and hungry . . . It'll be good to get out of this tree."

As they approached, he began to distinguish their features. He saw that each one held a flickering candle, though some candles were so short they burned the fingers of the bearer. Everyone seemed weary, their faces distorted as if by hunger or thirst. Silently they walked with their *morrales* (knapsacks) full of holes. Some were barefoot. Others wore sandals so shabby that their feet were barely protected.

"What a sad group of people. They seem so miserable," thought Nicacio.

As the procession passed under the tree, Nicacio began shouting, "Help me! Hey, you down there, help me! I'm up in the tree! Someone *please* help me!"

---

3. *loca:* crazy.
4. **machete:** large knife used to cut underbrush.
5. *ocote:* bark coated with resin.

But no one seemed to notice Nicacio. The procession continued its slow journey toward Chamilpa. Finally, Nicacio stopped yelling, realizing how useless his efforts were.

What a long procession this was! The line of people never seemed to end.

Nicacio's eyes widened. "There goes my *compadre*[6] Juan. But it can't be! He died three years ago. I attended his burial myself. And here comes my friend Hilario, and Beto, the son of my *comadre*[7] Anastasia. I must be hallucinating . . . these people are dead."

"Juan! Hilario! Beto! Can you hear me? I'm up in the tree! Help me get out!"

Nicacio shook his head. "My mind *must* be playing tricks on me."

Glancing down once more he saw his beloved daughter, Juanita, walking in the procession.

"Juanita, my sweet little one!" Nicacio wept as he watched her silently pass, wearing a tattered dress, her face drawn with hunger. Unlike the others, Juanita carried a piece of *ocote* instead of a candle.

On and on the procession continued into the pueblo. Nicacio was consumed by anguished thoughts of his wife, his daughter, and death.

Hours passed, and dawn approached. As Nicacio stirred, he saw the procession leaving Chamilpa, heading once again in his direction. As the people drew near, Nicacio tried calling to them one more time, but again he was ignored.

Discouraged, he slumped down and wearily watched as the people passed.

"Everyone looks different now. They seem more energetic. Why, many are even smiling and talking to each other."

Indeed, some wore new clothes, and their feet were covered with new sandals. Their *morrales* were filled with food.

Nicacio was happy to see the people so content. "Why, my *compadre* Juan has a bottle of tequila. And Hilario is smoking one of his favorite cigarettes. Oh, there's Beto eating a tamale. He always loved tamales!"

Nicacio eagerly looked for Juanita. When he found her, she was smiling, too. Nicacio waved wildly—but again, the girl did not notice her father.

"It doesn't matter that she can't see me," thought Nicacio. "My beloved Juanita looks happy, and that's the important thing. She's wearing a new dress and carrying a candle and plate of beans."

The procession passed and disappeared into the thick woods at the base of the mountain.

The sun rose, warming the chilled air. Suddenly, the branches opened, and Nicacio was free. He wasted no time scrambling down the tree, and he ran all the way home, eager to see María.

María, however, was not happy to see Nicacio. "I asked you to stay home and give me money for the *ofrenda*. You not only left, but you stayed out all night long! You probably got drunk and spent all the money. Thank God I had just enough from my laundry earnings to buy a dress and a candle for Juanita's *ofrenda*. For food, all I could afford was a small plate of beans."

Nicacio recalled seeing Juanita in her new dress, carrying the candle and the plate of beans. He wept with shame and asked María for forgiveness. He told her what he had seen.

Both knelt and asked Juanita to forgive them for the meager offering.

From that day on, Nicacio prepared an annual feast, brimming with food and candles, for Juanita and for all the dead of Chamilpa.

---

6. *compadre:* male friend or godfather.
7. *comadre:* female friend or godmother.

# The Ballad of Gregorio Cortez
## A Mexican American *Corrido*

## Background

The *corrido,* a form of anonymous folk poetry, is a descendant of the romance, a kind of ballad that developed during the Middle Ages. The conquistadors brought these ballad forms to America. The traditional *corrido* is a fast-paced ballad, usually set to music, which tells a story of tragedy, heroism, or adventure. It has been described as a form of folk history. *Corridos* have been composed about the death of a bullfighter, the deeds of a highwayman, a natural disaster, and the Mexican Revolution. In recent times, *corridos* have dealt with the struggles of immigrants crossing the border into the United States. The *corrido,* which is found in all Hispanic countries, has the greatest vitality in Mexico.

Cultural conflict in the border area of the lower Rio Grande and South Texas resulted in the popularity of border *corridos*. The border *corridos,* which developed after 1848 and reached their peak at the turn of the twentieth century, deal with a struggle against oppression—Mexicans defend their rights against the Anglos. The central figure in "The Ballad of Gregorio Cortez" is a representative border *corrido* hero.

**The Real Gregorio Cortez.** "The Ballad of Gregorio Cortez" is based on recorded historical events. In June 1901, the Karnes County sheriff went to the ranch where Gregorio and his brother Romaldo (Ramón in the poem) were tenant farmers. The sheriff was investigating a horse theft and heard that Gregorio had acquired a mare. A deputy's poor translation led to a misunderstanding, and the sheriff shot Romaldo. Then Gregorio shot and killed the sheriff. He was forced to become a fugitive.

According to some people, Gregorio Cortez was a peaceful, hard-working man who killed in self-defense and was unjustly pursued. According to others, he was a horse thief and a coldblooded murderer. By all accounts, however, the fugitive Cortez was clearly courageous and an exceedingly good shot. Although captured and tried for murder and horse theft, he eventually received a pardon. Shortly after his release, however, he died from undetermined causes.

The story of Gregorio Cortez was adapted as a film starring Edward James Olmos in 1982.

The Spanish text of the poem, reprinted alongside the English translation, shows the characteristics of *corrido* verse. The *corrido* uses a four-line stanza form with the rhyme pattern *abcb*. A line will be repeated occasionally, recalling the refrain tradition in typical ballads.

**Before You Read** Like many folk ballads, this *corrido* portrays its hero as a larger-than-life figure. In oral as well as written literature, the words artists choose reflect their feelings about the characters and events they describe. How does this *corrido*'s unnamed composer appear to feel about Cortez?

# El corrido de Gregorio Cortez

# The Ballad of Gregorio Cortez
Anonymous

1
En el condado del Carmen
la desgracia ha sucedido,
murió el Cherife Mayor
quedando Román herido.

2
En el condado del Carmen
la desgracia sucedió,
murió el Cherife Mayor,
no saben quién lo mató.

3
Salió con rumbo a Laredo
sin ninguna timidez:
—Síganme rinches cobardes,
yo soy Gregorio Cortez.

4
Decía Gregorio Cortez,
con su alma muy encendida:
—No siento haberlo matado,
la defensa es permitida.

1
In the county of El Carmen,
The misfortune has occurred;
The Major Sheriff[1] died,
Leaving Román badly wounded.

2
In the county of El Carmen,
The misfortune occurred;
The Major Sheriff died;
It is not known who killed him.

3
He went out toward Laredo[2]
Without showing any fear,
"Follow me, you cowardly rangers,[3]
I am Gregorio Cortez."

4
Then said Gregorio Cortez,
And his soul was all aflame,
"I don't regret that I killed him;
A man must defend himself."

---

1. **Sheriff:** W. T. "Brack" Morris.
2. **Laredo** (lah RAY doh): city and port of entry in South Texas.
3. **rangers:** Texas Rangers. The number of pursuers is sometimes 300; in other versions, as many as 600.

5
Decía Gregorio Cortez,
con su pistola en la mano:
—No corran rinches cobardes
con un puro mexicano.

6
Como a las ocho serían,
como tres horas después,
supieron que el malhechor
era Gregorio Cortez.

7
Iban los americanos
por el viento que volaban
porque se iban a ganar
dos mil pesos que les daban.

8
Decían los americanos:
—Si lo hallamos ¿qué le haremos?
Si le entramos por derecho
Muy poquitos volveremos.

9
Iban los americanos
iban siguiendo la huella,
porque alcanzar a Cortez
era alcanzar a una estrella.

10
Decía Gregorio Cortez:
—¿Pá qué se valen de planes?
No me pueden agarrar
ni con esos perros jaunes.

11
Gregorio le dice a Juan:
—Muy pronto lo vas a ver;
anda díles a los rinches
que me vengan a aprehender.

5
Then said Gregorio Cortez,
With his pistol in his hand,
"Don't run, you cowardly rangers,
From a real Mexican."

6
It must have been about eight o'clock,
About three hours afterward,
They found out that the wrongdoer
Had been Gregorio Cortez.

7
The Americans were riding
Through the air as if they flew;
Because they wanted to get
Two thousand dollars they were offered.

8
Then the Americans said,
"If we find him, what shall we do?
If we fight him man to man
Very few of us will return."

9
The Americans were riding,
They were following the trail;
Because trying to overtake Cortez
Was like overtaking a star.

10
Then said Gregorio Cortez,
"What is the use of your scheming?
You cannot catch me,
Even with those bloodhounds."

11
Gregorio says to Juan,[4]
"You will see it very soon;
Go tell the rangers
To come and arrest me."

---

4. **Juan:** who is at the Cypress Ranch, according to other versions.

12
Allá por El Encinal
lo alcanzaron a rodear,
poquitos más de trescientos
y allí les brincó el corral.

13
Salió Gregorio Cortez,
salió con rumbo a Laredo,
no lo quisieron seguir
porque le tuvieron miedo.

14
Venían todos los rinches,
venían buscando a Cortez,
les preguntaban a muchos:
—¿Dónde está el Rancho El Ciprés?

12
Over by El Encinal[5]
They succeeded in surrounding him;
Quite a few more than three hundred,
But there he jumped their corral.

13
Gregorio Cortez went out,
He went out toward Laredo,
They decided not to follow
Because they were afraid of him.

14
All the rangers were coming,
They were looking for Cortez;
They asked of many people,
"Where is the ranch of El Ciprés?"[6]

---

5. **El Encinal** (ehl ehn see NAHL): literally "The Woods"; the name of a village in South Texas.

6. **El Ciprés** (ehl see PREHS): literally "The Cypress"; the name of a ranch in South Texas.

15
Cuando llegaron los rinches
Gregorio se presentó:
—Por la buena sí me llevan,
porque de otro modo no.

16
Ya mataron a Cortez,
ya se acabó la cuestión,
la pobre de su familia,
lo lleva en el corazón.

17
Ya con ésta me despido
con las hojas del ciprés,
aquí termina el corrido
de don Gregorio Cortez.

15
When the rangers arrived,
Gregorio gave himself up,
"You will take me if I'm willing,
But not any other way."

16
Now they have killed Cortez,
Now matters are at an end;
His poor family
Are suffering in their hearts.

17
Now with this I say farewell,
With the leaves of the cypress,
This is the end of the ballad
Of Don Gregorio Cortez.

# Part 2

# Latin American Writing Comes of Age: Modernism and the Boom

## (1880s – 1970s)

Since the beginning of European colonization, Latin American literature has evolved as a complex synthesis, or combination, of diverse cultures. The traditions of both written and oral Spanish and Portuguese literature—the legacy of the conquistadors and missionaries—left their mark on the literary traditions of the native Indian populations of Central and South America. Other European cultures, such as the Dutch, French, and German, left their own legacies. The Europeans had brought with them many enslaved Africans from various cultures, such as the Yoruba from Nigeria, and these cultures, too, mingled with native Indian cultures. Thus, the rich tapestry of legends, tales, myths, and epic narratives left by the native Aztec, Mayan, and Incan cultures was interwoven with European and African influences.

### Nationalism, Regionalism, and the Romantic Movement

The vitality and diversity of Latin American literature that was only hinted at during the early colonial period grew steadily from its native, European, and African roots but would not fully flower until the late nineteenth century. By the early nineteenth century, wars of independence had ended the long colonial period in Latin America. Many countries and regions gained their independence from their European colonizers. Inevitably, the ideals of **nationalism**—an intense pride in and focus on one's own nation, almost to the exclusion of all others—grew during this period. As in other parts of the Western world at this time, nationalism and the desire for political independence went hand in hand with a literary and cultural movement called **Romanticism.** Romanticism celebrated a belief in freedom and individualism, acknowledged the wisdom of the common people, saw rural life as superior to industrialized city life, and advocated a focus on the native traditions—the folkways—of one's own nation or region.

A focus on **regionalism**—on depicting local physical and social details and customs—was a defining aspect of nineteenth-century Romantic literature the world over. Central and South American writers began to record their observations about local "types," such as the *gaucho*—the Argentine "cowboy"—and the Mexican Indians (*los Indios*). A literary form called the *cuadro de costumbres*—the local sketch—became a significant and distinctive creation in Latin America. According to some scholars, the modern short story (which did not fully develop into the form we know today until the late nineteenth century) is derived from such vignettes, or brief literary sketches.

## The Development of Modernism

During the nineteenth century, Latin American writers sought to create a distinctive, independent literature. Very few writers, however, were known outside their own countries. Latin American writers did not yet have the international reputation they have today, nor did their works tend to be translated into other languages. In the last decades of the nineteenth century, however, a movement known as *modernismo* (modernism) emerged. The modernist writers were influenced by innovations in European and American literature. They were particularly influenced by the French symbolist poets and the poets of the French Parnassian school—a group more interested in poetic form than content. Restless and hungry for new modes of expression, the Latin American modernists pored over the works of such American writers as Edgar Allan Poe and Walt Whitman and freely borrowed ideas from them.

Latin American modernism is often associated with the Cuban poet José Martí, but the writer usually credited with being the most influential early figure of modernism is Rubén Darío, from Nicaragua. The publication of his volume of poetry *Azul* (*Blue*) in 1888 was a watershed event that changed the face of Latin American writing and opened the door to the preeminence it enjoys today as one of the world's richest literary traditions. Darío became the leader of the new poets in Latin America. He transformed and expanded the limits of Spanish verse, and other writers adapted his experiments with meter and rhythm.

The modernist movement produced outstanding fiction as well as poetry. Especially notable in later Latin American modernist storytelling is the influence of **naturalism.** Naturalism, a bleak outgrowth of realism, seemingly stood against everything Romanticism represented. In naturalism, there are no heroes and no redemption; life is grim and stark and has no happy endings. Human beings are weak and ineffectual at best, brutal and evil at worst. Horacio Quiroga, a writer from Uruguay who set many of his stories in the jungles of Argentina, became a master of this new school of fiction, producing stories that are blood-chilling in their depictions of unforgiving nature and the dark side of human psychology. Even his lighter tales are darkly ironic rather than simply humorous, with a sharp edge of harsh realism.

## Jorge Luis Borges and the "New Narrative"

After 1914, the Latin American modernist movement began to wane. New movements were arising, along with concerns about the social and economic problems associated with World War I. From the 1920s until the 1940s, most Latin American literature was straightforward realism with a social message. The unadorned narratives attempted to illustrate the external realities of life in the Americas, without much interest in internal, or psychological, realities.

All of that changed in the 1940s with the groundbreaking contributions of one writer: Argentina's Jorge Luis Borges. Borges's *Ficciones,* a volume of short fiction published in 1944, has been called "the single most important collection of short fiction in the history of Spanish American literature." With the selections in this collection, Borges broke with every previous *–ism*—Romanticism, realism, naturalism, modernism—to create a new kind of fiction. He paved the way for later writers, such as Julio Cortázar and Gabriel García Márquez, who were practitioners of what some critics refer to as the "new narrative."

What were Borges's specific contributions? He was an intensely intellectual writer who created intricate puzzles in words. (Not surprisingly, one of the most-often repeated images in many of his works is that of the labyrinth, or maze, which he felt symbolized the mysterious and ungraspable nature of the universe.) He blurred the boundaries between fiction and nonfiction, creating what some critics have called "fictionalized essays," and he self-consciously wrote some stories with the ongoing acknowledgment (between himself and the reader) that they were fiction. He experimented with new narrative techniques, such as the "story within a story," that broke with traditional chronological structure. Above all, he played with complex philosophical ideas, such as the nature of time and the limits of human perception. He used himself as both character and narrator (sometimes simultaneously) and frequently explored the idea of the "double" who dreams—or is the dream of—the writer (Borges himself).

## The Latin American "Boom"

*Ficciones* was published in several languages. Probably more than any other work, it was the book that put Latin American literature "on the map" and on a par with anything else being written. Borges's work eventually drew the world's attention to other experimental Latin American writers, such as Argentina's Julio Cortázar, Colombia's Gabriel García Márquez, Mexico's Carlos Fuentes, and Peru's Mario Vargas Llosa. This was the beginning of *El boom* (the Boom)—the emergence of an outstanding body of Latin American fiction in the period following World War II. From the 1960s through the 1970s, Latin American fiction began to garner worldwide recognition and acclaim, and writers worked from a new sense that they were creating a Latin American cultural identity that would reach a large international audience.

According to some readers, the work that officially started the Boom was Julio Cortázar's novel *Hopscotch* (1963). *Hopscotch* was an experimental "puzzle" novel with 155 chapters that were to be read in an out-of-sequence order; the reader was advised to start in the middle and skip from chapter to chapter, as in a game of hopscotch.

**Characteristics of Magic Realism**

- A magical or supernatural element that is never explained but is accepted by the characters
- Inclusion of legend or folklore
- Time treated in cyclical rather than linear fashion; the present may repeat the past
- Events presented from multiple points of view
- Matter-of-fact tone in spite of the fantastic nature of the story

## Magic Realism: Strange New World

The literary style or movement that is most associated with literature of the Boom is **magic realism.** The term *magic realism* was first used by the German art critic Franz Roh to describe a school of European painters. In 1949, the Cuban writer Alejo Carpentier used the term *lo real maravilloso* (magic realism) to describe a type of Latin American fiction that combines ordinary events and characters with elements of myth and fantasy. Magical elements occur in a setting that is realistic, with recognizable descriptions of human beings and society. Though sometimes confused with science fiction and fantasy, magic realism is quite different. Whereas some technological or magical force is necessary to explain extraordinary actions and events in science fiction or fantasy, in magic realism the extraordinary elements are never questioned; they are, in fact, considered perfectly normal by the characters, who live in an ordinary world that is at times "invaded" by the strange, the mysterious, and the unexplainable. A blue-haired boy may appear in a garden, or the ghost of a nosy aunt may take up residence in a bathtub, but everything that happens in a magic realist story is considered natural to the characters in the story, no matter how illogical or bizarre the events appear to be.

Although magic realism is now a worldwide movement or style that appears in the literatures of Europe, Asia, North America, and Africa, it is best known as a Latin American phenomenon, and many of the greatest practitioners of magic realism have been, and remain, Latin American writers. Although magic realism once seemed exotic and offbeat, it has gained mainstream acceptance over the years. Many magic realist works have become enormous bestsellers: for example, Gabriel García Márquez's *One Hundred Years of Solitude* and *Love in the Time of Cholera;* Isabel Allende's *House of the Spirits;* and Laura Esquivel's *Like Water for Chocolate.*

## New Directions: Postmodernism and Beyond

A number of Latin American writers who emerged during the Boom continue to write: Mario Vargas Llosa; Carlos Fuentes; Gabriel García Márquez; and José Donoso. More recently, Isabel Allende, a Chilean writer who has moved to the United States, has become well known.

A new generation of writers has followed those who were made famous during the Latin American Boom. Sometimes identified as **postmodern,** these later authors have created a new kind of writing that tends to break down distinctions between prose and poetry, between popular and high culture, and between genres. Some of the experiments represent outgrowths of Jorge Luis Borges's work, which utilized postmodern elements even before the term *postmodern* came to be applied to writers' works.

### Latin American Writers Associated with Magic Realism

- **Isabel Allende** (Chile)
- **Jorge Luis Borges** (Argentina)
- **Julio Cortázar** (Argentina)
- **Carlos Fuentes** (Mexico)
- **Gabriel García Márquez** (Colombia)
- **Mario Vargas Llosa** (Peru)

The ongoing contributions of Latin American writers to world literature cannot be underestimated. But the legacy of the literature of the Americas does not end with Latin America. To the north, the United States—a nation of immigrants where all cultures converge—expands and continues the rich legacy of Latino literature.

> "... we writers within the tremendously far-flung American region ... are faced with the unavoidable task of critical communication within a world which is empty and is not less full of injustices, punishments and sufferings because it is empty—and we feel also the responsibility for reawakening the old dreams which sleep in statues of stone in the ruined ancient monuments, in the wide-stretching silence in planetary plains, in dense primeval forests, in rivers which roar like thunder. We must fill with words the most distant places in a dumb continent and we are intoxicated by this task of making fables and giving names."
>
> —Pablo Neruda
> *from* "Towards the Splendid City,"
> Nobel Lecture, December 13, 1971

**Latin American Winners of the Nobel Prize in Literature**

**Gabriela Mistral**
(Chile, 1945)

**Miguel Ángel Asturiás**
(Guatemala, 1967)

**Pablo Neruda**
(Chile, 1971)

**Gabriel García Márquez**
(Colombia, 1982)

**Octavio Paz**
(Mexico, 1990)

# Joaquim Maria Machado de Assis

**1838–1908** (Brazil)

## Meet the Writer

"Ahead of his time" is a particularly apt phrase when applied to the nineteenth-century Brazilian writer **Joaquim Maria Machado de Assis** (zhwah KEEM muh REE uh muh SHAH doo dih ah SEES). Long before early twentieth-century European writers like James Joyce and Marcel Proust began to reproduce the thoughts, emotions, associations, and memories of their characters in prose by using such techniques as stream of consciousness, Machado de Assis was creating his own literary examinations of the inner workings of the human mind. In combining psychological realism with dreamlike situations, he anticipated late twentieth-century Latin American magic realist writers such as Gabriel García Márquez and Julio Cortázar.

The son of a poor house painter and a laundry worker, Machado de Assis faced many obstacles early in his life. When he was a child, he suffered from epilepsy and stuttered. His mother died when he was ten years old, and his father died two years later. Shy and lonely, he began to spend much of his spare time at a local bookstore whose owner, Paula Brito, became his friend and advisor. By the time he was seventeen, Machado de Assis was working as a proofreader for Brito's publishing company and had begun writing his own poetry and fiction. Although it took some time for him to be recognized by the English-speaking world, he has always enjoyed respect in his native Brazil. When the Brazilian Academy of Letters was founded in the late 1890s, Machado de Assis was named its president for life. He has been called the greatest novelist of Brazil.

## Background

Most of Machado de Assis's early writings were in the Romantic tradition popular at that time. In the 1880s, however, he began writing the innovative style of fiction for which he is known today. He explored the psychological motivations of characters even before Sigmund Freud's work in psychoanalysis began the vogue for psychological realism in the early twentieth century.

**Before You Read** *A common theme in modern Latin American writing concerns the issue of perception. What is the nature of reality? How can we ever understand the world around us? Where does fantasy end and reality begin? Long before the magic realist writers came on the literary scene, Joaquim Maria Machado de Assis explored such questions in his novels and more than two hundred short stories. His ironic worldview—which more often than not tipped over into outright cynicism—is fully on display in this fanciful story. As you read, ask yourself, "Whose perceptions of the world are being ridiculed here? In what sense are a canary's ideas also human ideas?"*

# A Canary's Ideas

## Joaquim Maria Machado de Assis
*translated by* Lorie Ishimatsu and Jack Schmitt

A man by the name of Macedo,[1] who had a fancy for ornithology,[2] related to some friends an incident so extraordinary that no one took him seriously. Some came to believe he had lost his mind. Here is a summary of his narration.

At the beginning of last month, as I was walking down the street, a carriage darted past me and nearly knocked me to the ground. I escaped by quickly side-stepping into a secondhand shop. Neither the racket of the horse and carriage nor my entrance stirred the proprietor, dozing in a folding chair at the back of the shop. He was a man of shabby appearance: his beard was the color of dirty straw, and his head was covered by a tattered cap which probably had not found a buyer. One could not guess that there was any story behind him, as there could have been behind some of the objects he sold, nor could one sense in him that austere, disillusioned sadness inherent in the objects which were remnants of past lives.

The shop was dark and crowded with the sort of old, bent, broken, tarnished, rusted articles ordinarily found in secondhand shops, and everything was in that state of semidisorder befitting such an establishment. This assortment of articles, though banal, was interesting. Pots without lids, lids without pots, buttons, shoes, locks, a black skirt, straw hats, fur hats, picture frames, binoculars, dress coats, a fencing foil, a stuffed dog, a pair of slippers, gloves, nondescript vases, epaulets,[3] a velvet satchel, two hatracks, a slingshot, a thermometer, chairs, a lithographed portrait by the late Sisson,[4] a backgammon board, two wire masks for some future Carnival[5]—all this and more, which I either did not see or do not remember, filled the shop in the area around

---

1. **Macedo** (mah SAY doh)
2. **ornithology:** the study of birds.

3. **epaulets** (ehp uh LEHTS): shoulder ornaments worn on military and other uniforms.
4. **lithographed...Sisson:** relatively inexpensive print by a minor artist.
5. **Carnival:** period of feasting and merrymaking before the start of Lent; in Brazil, Carnival is a major festival similar to Mardi Gras in New Orleans.

the door, propped up, hung, or displayed in glass cases as old as the objects inside them. Further inside the shop were many objects of similar appearance. Predominant were the large objects—chests of drawers, chairs, and beds—some of which were stacked on top of others which were lost in the darkness.

I was about to leave, when I saw a cage hanging in the doorway. It was as old as everything else in the shop, and I expected it to be empty so it would fit in with the general appearance of desolation. However, it wasn't empty. Inside, a canary was hopping about. The bird's color, liveliness, and charm added a note of life and youth to that heap of wreckage. It was the last passenger of some wrecked ship, who had arrived in the shop as complete and happy as it had originally been. As soon as I looked at the bird, it began to hop up and down, from perch to perch, as if it meant to tell me that a ray of sunshine was frolicking in the midst of that cemetery. I'm using this image to describe the canary only because I'm speaking to rhetorical[6] people, but the truth is that the canary thought about neither cemetery nor sun, according to what it told me later. Along with the pleasure the sight of the bird brought me, I felt indignation regarding its destiny and softly murmured these bitter words:

"What detestable owner had the nerve to rid himself of this bird for a few cents? Or what indifferent soul, not wishing to keep his late master's pet, gave it away to some child, who sold it so he could make a bet on a soccer game?"

The canary, sitting on top of its perch, trilled this reply:

"Whoever you may be, you're certainly not in your right mind. I had no detestable owner, nor was I given to any child to sell. Those are the delusions of a sick person. Go and get yourself cured, my friend . . ."

---

6. **rhetorical** (rih TAWR ih kuhl): here, able to use and understand effective, eloquent language.

"What?" I interrupted, not having had time to become astonished. "So your master didn't sell you to this shop? It wasn't misery or laziness that brought you, like a ray of sunshine, to this cemetery?"

"I don't know what you mean by 'sunshine' or 'cemetery.' If the canaries you've seen use the first of those names, so much the better, because it sounds pretty, but really, I'm sure you're confused."

"Excuse me, but you couldn't have come here by chance, all alone. Has your master always been that man sitting over there?"

"What master? That man over there is my servant. He gives me food and water every day, so regularly that if I were to pay him for his services, it would be no small sum, but canaries don't pay their servants. In fact, since the world belongs to canaries, it would be extravagant for them to pay for what is already in the world."

Astonished by these answers, I didn't know what to marvel at more—the language or the ideas. The language, even though it entered my ears as human speech, was uttered by the bird in the form of charming trills. I looked all around me so I could determine if I were awake and saw that the street was the same, and the shop was the same dark, sad, musty place. The canary, moving from side to side, was waiting for me to speak. I then asked if it were lonely for the infinite blue space . . .

"But, my dear man," trilled the canary, "what does 'infinite blue space' mean?"

"But, pardon me, what do you think of this world? What is the world to you?"

"The world," retorted the canary, with a certain professorial air, "is a secondhand shop with a small rectangular bamboo cage hanging from a nail. The canary is lord of the cage it lives in and the shop that surrounds it. Beyond that, everything is illusion and deception."

With this, the old man woke up and approached me, dragging his feet. He asked me if I

wanted to buy the canary. I asked if he had acquired it in the same way he had acquired the rest of the objects he sold and learned that he had bought it from a barber, along with a set of razors.

"The razors are in very good condition," he said.

"I only want the canary."

I paid for it, ordered a huge, circular cage of wood and wire, and had it placed on the veranda of my house so the bird could see the garden, the fountain, and a bit of blue sky.

It was my intention to do a lengthy study of this phenomenon, without saying anything to anyone until I could astound the world with my extraordinary discovery. I began by alphabetizing the canary's language in order to study its structure, its relation to music, the bird's appreciation of aesthetics,[7] its ideas and recollections. When this philological[8] and psychological analysis was done, I entered specifically into the study of canaries: their origin, their early history, the geology and flora of the Canary Islands,[9] the bird's knowledge of navigation, and so forth. We conversed for hours while I took notes, and it waited, hopped about, and trilled.

As I have no family other than two servants, I ordered them not to interrupt me, even to deliver a letter or an urgent telegram or to inform me of an important visitor. Since they both knew about my scientific pursuits, they found my orders perfectly natural and did not suspect that the canary and I understood each other.

Needless to say, I slept little, woke up two or three times each night, wandered about aimlessly, and felt feverish. Finally, I returned to my work in order to reread, add, and emend. I corrected more than one observation, either because I had misunderstood something or because the bird had not expressed it clearly. The definition of the world was one of these. Three weeks after the canary's entrance into my home, I asked it to repeat to me its definition of the world.

"The world," it answered, "is a sufficiently broad garden with a fountain in the middle, flowers, shrubbery, some grass, clear air, and a bit of blue up above. The canary, lord of the world, lives in a spacious cage, white and circular, from which it looks out on the rest of the world. Everything else is illusion and deception."

The language of my treatise also suffered some modifications, and I saw that certain conclusions

---

7. **aesthetics** (ehs THEHT ihks): the study or theory of beauty, especially as captured in art.
8. **philological** (fihl oh LAHJ ih kuhl): here, relating to the study of language; linguistic.
9. **flora of the Canary Islands:** plant life of an island group in the Atlantic Ocean off Africa's northwestern coast; the birds known as canaries are native to these islands.

which had seemed simple were actually presumptuous. I still could not write the paper I was to send to the National Museum, the Historical Institute, and the German universities, not due to a lack of material but because I first had to put together all my observations and test their validity. During the last few days, I neither left the house, answered letters, nor wanted to hear from friends or relatives. The canary was everything to me. One of the servants had the job of cleaning the bird's cage and giving it food and water every morning. The bird said nothing to him, as if it knew the man was completely lacking in scientific background. Besides, the service was no more than cursory, as the servant was not a bird lover.

One Saturday I awoke ill, my head and back aching. The doctor ordered complete rest. I was suffering from an excess of studying and was not to read or even think, nor was I even to know what was going on in the city or the rest of the outside world. I remained in this condition for five days. On the sixth day I got up, and only then did I find out that the canary, while under the servant's care, had flown out of its cage. My first impulse was to strangle the servant—I was choking with indignation and collapsed into my chair, speechless and bewildered. The guilty man defended himself, swearing he had been careful, but the wily bird had nevertheless managed to escape.

"But didn't you search for it?"

"Yes, I did, sir. First it flew up to the roof, and I followed it. It flew to a tree, and then who knows where it hid itself? I've been asking around since yesterday. I asked the neighbors and the local farmers, but no one has seen the bird."

I suffered immensely. Fortunately, the fatigue left me within a few hours, and I was soon able to go out to the veranda and the garden. There was no sign of the canary. I ran everywhere, making inquiries and posting announcements, all to no avail. I had already gathered my notes together to write my paper, even though it would be disjointed and incomplete, when I happened to visit a friend who had one of the largest and most beautiful estates on the outskirts of town. We were taking a stroll before dinner when this question was trilled to me:

"Greetings, Senhor[10] Macedo, where have you been since you disappeared?"

It was the canary, perched on the branch of a tree. You can imagine how I reacted and what I said to the bird. My friend presumed I was mad, but the opinions of friends are of no importance to me. I spoke tenderly to the canary and asked it to come home and continue our conversations in that world of ours, composed of a garden, a fountain, a veranda, and a white circular cage.

"What garden? What fountain?"

"The world, my dear bird."

"What world? I see you haven't lost any of your annoying professorial habits. The world," it solemnly concluded, "is an infinite blue space, with the sun up above."

Indignant, I replied that if I were to believe what it said, the world could be anything—it had even been a secondhand shop . . .

"A secondhand shop?" it trilled to its heart's content. "But is there really such a thing as a secondhand shop?"

---

10. **Senhor** (sih NYAWR): "mister" (Portuguese).

# José Martí
## 1853–1895 (Cuba)

## Meet the Writer

Many people who have never heard of **José Martí** (hoh SAY mahr TEE) know the famous Cuban song "Guantanamera" ("The Girl from Guantánamo"), which is based on lyrics from Martí's *Versos sencillos* (*Simple Verses*). Although Martí is considered a major Latin American poet, he dedicated most of his life to political causes.

He was born in Havana in 1853, when Cuba was still a Spanish colony. He became committed to revolutionary political ideas early in his life. When he was sixteen, he got into trouble with the Spanish authorities and was sentenced to six years of hard labor in the quarries of San Lázaro. His sentence was commuted, and he was exiled to Spain, where he attended the Universities of Zaragoza and Madrid. A period of wandering took him to Mexico, Guatemala, Venezuela, France, and New York.

In 1892, Martí founded the Cuban Revolutionary Party. He returned to Cuba to take part in the invasion in 1895. His death in battle a month later made him a national hero.

In addition to his reputation as a remarkable poet, Martí is recognized as an original prose writer. He wrote a number of *crónicas* (chronicles) about contemporary events, including accounts of life in the United States. In New York he started a magazine dedicated to the children of South America: *La edad de oro* (*The Age of Gold*).

## Background

Martí was influenced by classic Spanish writers and by the French Parnassian poets and symbolists. He was associated with the literary movement known as *modernismo*, or modernism, which began in Latin America and flowered in the twenty years around the turn of the century.

José Martí produced three major books of poetry: *Ismaelillo* (*Little Ismael*, 1882); *Versos sencillos*; and *Versos libres* (*Free Verses*). Many of Martí's poems express a personal anguish. He once wrote, "Without profound pain, man never produced truly beautiful works."

**Before You Read**  The American writer Helen Hunt Jackson (1830–1885) is best known for her Romantic novel Ramona, which José Martí translated into Spanish. Martí admired Jackson's work; like him, she was both literary and political, with a definite social agenda. (Ramona, a bestseller in its day, attempted to bring about social reform by exposing wrongs done to Native Americans in the western United States.) While in New York, Martí published an adaptation of one of Jackson's works in his children's magazine La edad de oro (The Age of Gold).

# Los dos principes
## José Martí

*Idea de la poetisa norteamericana Helen Hunt Jackson*

    El palacio está de luto
    Y en el trono llora el rey,
    Y la reina está llorando
    Donde no la pueden ver:
5  En pañuelos de holán fino
    Lloran la reina y el rey:
    Los señores del palacio
    Están llorando también.
    Los caballos llevan negro
10 El penacho y el arnés:
    Los caballos no han comido,
    Porque no quieren comer:
    El laurel del patio grande
    Quedó sin hoja esta vez:
15 Todo el mundo fue al entierro
    Con coronas de laurel:
    —¡El hijo del rey se ha muerto!
    ¡Se le ha muerto el hijo al rey!

# The Two Princes
## José Martí
*translated by* Elinor Randall

*An idea of the North American poet Helen Hunt Jackson*

    The palace is draped in mourning,
    The king on his throne sheds tears
    And the queen is also crying,
    Where no one can see her cry.
5  The king and the queen are weeping
    Into kerchiefs of fine batiste,
    And the noblemen of the palace
    Are also shedding tears.
    The horses are harnessed in black,
10 The trappings and their panaches;
    The horses have eaten nothing
    For they had no wish to eat.
    These days the courtyard laurel
    Are shorn of all their leaves,
15 And everyone went to the funeral
    Bringing their laurel wreaths—
    The king has lost his son!
    The son of the king is dead!

|  |  |
|---|---|
| | En los álamos del monte |
| 20 | Tiene su casa el pastor: |
| | La pastora está diciendo |
| | "¿Por qué tiene luz el sol?" |
| | Las ovejas, cabizbajas, |
| | Vienen todas al portón: |
| 25 | ¡Una caja larga y honda |
| | Está forrando el pastor! |
| | Entra y sale un perro triste: |
| | Canta allá dentro una voz— |
| | "¡Pajarito, yo estoy loca, |
| 30 | Llévame donde él voló!": |
| | El pastor coge llorando |
| | La pala y el azadón: |
| | Abre en la tierra una fosa: |
| | Echa en la fosa una flor: |
| 35 | —¡Se quedó el pastor sin hijo! |
| | ¡Murió el hijo del pastor! |

|  |  |
|---|---|
| | The shepherd's house is set |
| 20 | Among the mountain poplars; |
| | The shepherd's wife is asking: |
| | "Why does the sun shed light?" |
| | The sheep, their heads bowed low, |
| | All come to the inner door |
| 25 | Where the shepherd is lining a coffin, |
| | A long and spacious coffin! |
| | A doleful dog is going |
| | Into and out of the house; |
| | Within a voice is singing: |
| 30 | "I am crazy, my little bird; |
| | Do take me to where he flew!" |
| | The weeping shepherd seizes |
| | His shovel and his hoe; |
| | He digs a grave in the ground |
| 35 | And tosses a flower within. |
| | The shepherd has no son left! |
| | The son of the shepherd is dead! |

# Rubén Darío
## 1867–1916 (Nicaragua)

## Meet the Writer

The central figure of Latin American *modernismo* is **Rubén Darío** (roo BEHN dah REE oh). He was only twenty-one when his volume of prose and poetry, *Azul* (*Blue*), was published in 1888. The book is considered a turning point in Latin American and Spanish literature.

Born Félix Rubén García Sarmiento in Metapa, Nicaragua, in 1867, he eventually changed his name to Darío, an old family name. He traveled widely and served as a diplomatic representative for several South American countries. During his life he had several complicated relationships with women, and after the death of his first wife, he became an immoderate drinker.

Darío began writing poetry when he was very young. He read European Romantic poets such as the French writer Victor Hugo, as well as classic Spanish writers. On a trip to Chile, he discovered Spanish American poets whose works were influenced by the French symbolists and by the North American writers Edgar Allan Poe and Walt Whitman. This literary discovery inspired and energized him.

*Azul,* issued in a second edition in 1890, blended the influences of Romantic, classic, and symbolist poetry to emerge as something quite new. Critics and poets acknowledged Darío's mastery of meters, the musicality of his language, and his superb use of irony.

In 1914, Darío was honored in New York with a medal from the Hispanic Society of America. He returned to Nicaragua in 1916 and died there the same year, before he was fifty. Although he is not as well known today as such Latin American poets as Pablo Neruda and Octavio Paz, he is still, to some, Latin America's greatest poet.

## Background

The Nobel Prize-winning Mexican poet and critic Octavio Paz once claimed that after the death of Sor Juana Inés de la Cruz in seventeenth-century Mexico, no major poetry was written in Spanish for two centuries. Modernism, which began in Latin America, signaled a revival:

...[It] smashed windows and broke doors so that the fresh air of the times could revive the dying language. Modernism was not merely a school of poetry: it was also a dancing class, a gymnasium, a circus, and masked ball. Ever since, Spanish has been able to put up with the most raucous noises, the most dangerous escapades. And the influence of Modernism has not ended: everything written in Spanish afterward has been affected in one way or another by that great renascence.

Rubén Darío and other modernists worked with a number of different metrical forms. Darío was unique for exhibiting an exceptionally wide command of verse forms. He brought a new flexibility to poetry and introduced the modern *vers libre,* or free verse. Darío was able to blend traditional patterns and rhythms with innovative rhythms, imagery, and symbols. The Argentine writer Jorge Luis Borges has said of him: "Darío's place is central. It is not a live influence but a reference point: a point of arrival and a point of departure, a limit that has to be reached or surpassed."

---

# Lo fatal
## Rubén Darío

*A René Pérez*

Dichoso el árbol que es apenas sensitivo,
y más la piedra dura porque ésa ya no siente,
pues no hay dolor más grande que el dolor de ser vivo,
ni mayor pesadumbre que la vida consciente.

5   Ser, y no saber nada, y ser sin rumbo cierto,
y el temor de haber sido y un futuro terror...
Y el espanto seguro de estar mañana muerto,
y sufrir por la vida y por la sombra y por

lo que no conocemos y apenas sospechamos,
10  y la carne que tienta con sus frescos racimos,
y la tumba que aguarda con sus fúnebres ramos,
y no saber a dónde vamos,
ni de dónde venimos...!

**Before You Read** *A literal translation of this poem's Spanish title (see page 76) would be "The Fatal Thing" or "Fatal."* Fatal *can mean "deadly," but it can also mean "fateful"—related to fate or destiny. Try to put this poem's message into your own words. What is the "fatal thing," and to whom is it fatal? Is the English title "What Gets You" equally suited to the poem? (Think about whether the English title can be interpreted in more than one way.)*

# What Gets You
## Rubén Darío
*translated by* Alberto Acereda and Will Derusha

*For René Pérez*

How fortunate the tree that is scarcely aware,
and more so the hard stone because it no longer feels,
since there is no greater pain than the pain of living,
nor deeper sorrow than conscious life.

5    Being, and knowing nothing, and being without a true course,
and the fear of having been, and a future terror . . .
And the certain dread of being dead tomorrow,
and suffering because of life, and because of shadow, and because of

what we don't know and scarcely suspect,
10   and the flesh that tempts with its fresh-picked bunches,
and the tomb that awaits with its funeral bouquets,
and not knowing where we are going,
nor from where we have come . . . !

# Versos de otoño
## Rubén Darío

Cuando mi pensamiento va hacia ti, se perfuma;
tu mirar es tan dulce, que se torna profundo.
Bajo tus pies desnudos aún hay blancor de espuma,
y en tus labios compendias la alegría del mundo.

5    El amor pasajero tiene el encanto breve,
y ofrece un igual término para el gozo y la pena.
Hace una hora que un nombre grabé sobre la nieve;
hace un minuto dije mi amor sobre la arena.

Las hojas amarillas caen en la alameda,
10   en donde vagan tantas parejas amorosas.
Y en la copa de Otoño un vago vino queda
en que han de deshojarse, Primavera, tus rosas.

**Before You Read** *Although the title of this poem is "Autumn Verses," what other seasons are directly or indirectly mentioned in this poem? To whom is the poem addressed, and how do you know?*

# Autumn Verses
**Rubén Darío**
*translated by* Alberto Acereda and Will Derusha

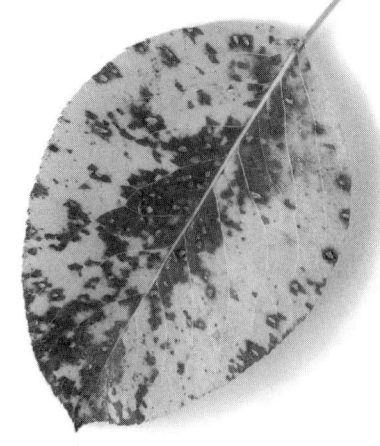

When my thought strays to you, it becomes perfumed;
your glance is so sweet, it turns profound.
Under your naked feet there is still the whiteness of foam,
and in your lips you epitomize the joy of the world.

5    Short-lived love has a brief charm
and offers the same end to delight and sorrow.
An hour ago I engraved a name in the snow;
a minute ago I expressed my love on the sand.

Yellow leaves fall on the boulevard
10  where so many loving couples stroll.
And in Autumn's cup there is a vague wine
into which your roses, Springtime, will drop their petals.

# Horacio Quiroga
1878–1937 (Uruguay)

## Meet the Writer

Considered one of Latin America's finest short story writers, **Horacio Quiroga** (oh RAY see oh kee ROH gah) was a master of two types of stories: macabre tales of horror and suspense and jungle fables with animals as characters.

Tragic events in Quiroga's own life no doubt contributed to his sense of the macabre. Shortly after Quiroga's birth in Uruguay, his father, an Argentine diplomat, was killed in a hunting accident. His mother soon remarried, but his stepfather committed suicide. When he was a young man, Quiroga accidentally shot and killed a friend. There were other personal tragedies: Quiroga's attempts to start a business failed, his first wife took her own life, and his second marriage ended unhappily in separation.

Quiroga's jungle tales were inspired by the periods of time Quiroga spent living in the jungle province of Misiones in Argentina, where he frequently struggled against harsh conditions to sustain his family. In fact, the difficult life there caused his first wife to commit suicide. Given Quiroga's life experiences, it is not surprising that so many of his stories focus on the conflict between people and nature, illustrating an uncompromising vision of life as an eternal, often brutal struggle for survival.

Unfortunately, Quiroga's life ended as tragically as it began. In 1937, he was diagnosed with cancer at a clinic in Buenos Aires; while still at the clinic he ended his own life by taking poison. Today, he is considered a unique and memorable voice in Latin American literature.

## Background

"The Alligator War" is an allegory, a type of story in which characters, places, or events stand for something other than themselves. In "The Alligator War," animals represent human characteristics. The old alligator is not simply the "wise man" of the group; he may also represent the human tendency to make generalizations based on limited experience or insufficient information. As in most allegories, however, the events of the story also make an important comment about the human condition.

**Before You Read**  The beast fable, in which animal characters speak and behave as humans do, is common to most cultures. Often, the stories are full of satire, poking fun at the follies or weaknesses of human beings.

As you read, consider that this story was first published in 1918. Think about what has happened to rain forests and jungles around the globe since that time. Does Quiroga's satire have as much meaning today as it had in his own time? How might the story be different if Quiroga had written it today?

# The Alligator War

## Horacio Quiroga
*translated by* Arthur Livingston

It was a very big river in a region of South America that had never been visited by white men; and in it lived many, many alligators—perhaps a hundred, perhaps a thousand. For dinner they ate fish, which they caught in the stream, and for supper they ate deer and other animals that came down to the waterside to drink. On hot afternoons in summer they stretched out and sunned themselves on the bank. But they liked nights when the moon was shining best of all. Then they swam out into the river and sported and played, lashing the water to foam with their tails, while the spray ran off their beautiful skins in all the colors of the rainbow.

These alligators had lived quite happy lives for a long, long time. But at last one afternoon, when they were all sleeping on the sand, snoring and snoring, one alligator woke up and cocked his ears—the way alligators cock their ears. He listened and listened, and, to be sure, faintly, and from a great distance, came a sound: *Chug! Chug! Chug!*

"Hey!" the alligator called to the alligator sleeping next to him, "Hey! Wake up! Danger!"

"Danger of what?" asked the other, opening his eyes sleepily and getting up.

"I don't know!" replied the first alligator. "That's a noise I never heard before. Listen!"

The other alligator listened: *Chug! Chug! Chug!*

In great alarm the two alligators went calling up and down the riverbank: "Danger! Danger!" And all their sisters and brothers and mothers and fathers and uncles and aunts woke up and began running this way and that with their tails curled up in the air. But the excitement did not serve to calm their fears. *Chug! Chug! Chug!* The noise was growing louder every moment; and at last, away off down the stream, they could see something moving along the surface of the river, leaving a trail of gray smoke behind it and beating the water on either side to foam: *Chush! Chush! Chush!*

The alligators looked at each other in the greatest astonishment: "What on earth is that?"

But there was one old alligator, the wisest and most experienced of them all. He was so old that only two sound teeth were left in his jaws—one in the upper jaw and one in the lower jaw. Once, also, when he was a boy, fond of adventure, he had made a trip down the river all the way to the sea.

"I know what it is," said he. "It's a whale. Whales are big fish, they shoot water up through their noses, and it falls down on them behind."

At this news, the little alligators began to scream at the top of their lungs, "It's a whale! It's a whale! It's a whale!" and they made for the water intending to duck out of sight.

But the big alligator cuffed with his tail a little alligator that was screaming nearby with his mouth open wide. "Dry up!" said he. "There's nothing to be afraid of! I know all about whales! Whales are the afraidest people there are!" And the little alligators stopped their noise.

But they grew frightened again a moment afterward. The gray smoke suddenly turned to an inky black, and the *Chush! Chush! Chush!* was now so loud that all the alligators took to the water, with only their eyes and the tips of their noses showing at the surface.

*Cho-ash-h-h! Cho-ash-h-h! Cho-ash-h-h!* The strange monster came rapidly up the stream. The alligators saw it go crashing past them, belching great clouds of smoke from the middle of its back and splashing into the water heavily with the big revolving things it had on either side.

It was a steamer, the first steamer that had ever made its way up to the Parana. *Chush! Chush! Chush!* It seemed to be getting farther away again. *Chug! Chug! Chug!* It had disappeared from view.

One by one, the alligators climbed up out of the water onto the bank again. They were all quite cross with the old alligator who had told them wrongly that it was a whale.

"It was not a whale!" they shouted in his ear—for he was rather hard of hearing. "Well, what was it that just went by?"

The old alligator then explained that it was a

**The Alligator War**    83

steamboat full of fire and that the alligators would all die if the boat continued to go up and down the river.

The other alligators only laughed, however. Why would the alligators die if the boat kept going up and down the river? It had passed by without so much as speaking to them! That old alligator didn't really know so much as he pretended to! And since they were very hungry they all went fishing in the stream. But alas! There was not a fish to be found! The steamboat had frightened every single one of them away.

"Well, what did I tell you?" said the old alligator. "You see, we haven't anything left to eat! All the fish have been frightened away! However—let's just wait till tomorrow. Perhaps the boat won't come back again. In that case, the fish will get over their fright and come back so that we can eat them." But the next day the steamboat came crashing by again on its way back down the river, spouting black smoke as it had done before, and setting the whole river boiling with its paddle wheels.

"Well!" exclaimed the alligators. "What do you think of that? The boat came yesterday. The boat came today. The boat will come tomorrow. The fish will stay away and nothing will come down here at night to drink. We are done for!"

But an idea occurred to one of the brighter alligators: "Let's dam the river!" he proposed. "The steamboat won't be able to climb a dam!"

"That's the talk! That's the talk! A dam. A dam! Let's build a dam!" And the alligators all made for the shore as fast as they could.

They went up into the woods along the bank and began to cut down trees of the hardest wood they could find—walnut and mahogany, mostly. They felled more than ten thousand of them altogether, sawing the trunks through with the kind of saw that alligators have on the tops of their tails. They dragged the trees down into the water and stood them up about a yard apart, all the way across the river, driving the pointed ends deep into the mud and weaving the branches together. No steamboat, big or little, would ever be able to pass that dam! No one would frighten the fish again! They would have a good dinner the following day and every day! And since it was late at night by the time the dam was done, they all fell sound asleep on the riverbank.

*Chug! Chug! Chug! Chush! Chush! Chush! Cho-ash-h-h-h-h! Cho-ash-h-h-h-h! Cho-ash-h-h-h-h!*

They were still asleep the next day when the boat came up; but the alligators barely opened their eyes and then tried to go to sleep again. What did they care about the boat? It could make all the noise it wanted but it would never get by the dam!

And that is what happened. Soon the noise from the boat stopped. The men who were steering on the bridge took out their spyglasses and began to study the strange obstruction that had been thrown up across the river. Finally a small boat was sent to look into it more closely. Only then did the alligators get up from where they were sleeping, run down into the water, and swim out behind the dam, where they lay floating and looking downstream between the piles. They could not help laughing, nevertheless, at the joke they had played on the steamboat!

The small boat came up, and the men in it saw how the alligators had made a dam across the river. They went back to the steamer but soon after came rowing up toward the dam again.

"Hey, you alligators!"

"What can we do for you?" answered the alligators, sticking their heads through between the piles in the dam.

"That dam is in our way!" said the men.

"Tell us something we don't know!" answered the alligators.

"But we can't get by!"

"I'll say so!"

"Well, take the old thing out of the way!"

"Nosireesir!"

The men in the boat talked it over for a while and then they called: "Alligators!"

"What can we do for you?"

"Will you take the dam away?"

"No!"

"No?"

"No!"

"Very well! See you later!"

"The later the better," said the alligators.

The rowboat went back to the steamer, while the alligators, as happy as could be, clapped their tails as loud as they could on the water. No boat could ever get by that dam and drive the fish away again!

But the next day the steamboat returned; and when the alligators looked at it, they could not say a word from their surprise: it was not the same boat at all but a larger one, painted gray like a mouse! How many steamboats were there, anyway? And this one probably would want to pass the dam! Well, just let it try! No, sir! No steamboat, little or big, would ever get through that dam!

"They shall not pass!" said the alligators, each taking up his station behind the piles in the dam.

The new boat, like the other one, stopped some distance below the dam; and again a little boat came rowing toward them. This time there were eight sailors in it, with one officer. The officer shouted: "Hey, you alligators!"

"What's the matter?" answered the alligators.

"Going to get that dam out of there?"

"No!"

"No?"

"No!"

"Very well!' said the officer. "In that case, we shall have to shoot it down!"

"Shoot it up if you want to!" said the alligators.

And the boat returned to the steamer.

But now, this mouse-gray steamboat was not an ordinary steamboat; it was a warship, with armor plate and terribly powerful guns. The old alligator who had made the trip to the river mouth suddenly remembered and just in time to shout to the other alligators, "Duck for your lives! Duck! She's going to shoot! Keep down deep under water."

The alligators dived all at the same time and headed for the shore, where they halted, keeping all their bodies out of sight except for their noses and their eyes. A great cloud of flame and smoke burst from the vessel's side, followed by a deafening report. An immense solid shot hurtled through the air and struck the dam exactly in the middle. Two or three tree trunks were cut away into splinters and drifted off downstream. Another shot, a third, and finally a fourth, each tearing a great hole in the dam. Finally the piles were entirely destroyed; not a tree, not a splinter, not a piece of bark was left; and the alligators, still sitting with their eyes and noses just out of water, saw the warship come steaming by and blowing its whistle in derision at them.

Then the alligators came out on the bank and held a council of war. "Our dam was not strong enough," said they; "we must make a new and much thicker one."

So they worked again all that afternoon and night, cutting down the very biggest trees they could find and making a much better dam than they had built before. When the gunboat appeared the next day, they were sleeping soundly and had to hurry to get behind the piles of the dam by the time the rowboat arrived there.

"Hey, alligators!" called the same officer.

"See who's here again!" said the alligators, jeeringly.

"Get that new dam out of there!"

"Never in the world!"

"Well, we'll blow it up, the way we did the other!"

"Blaze away, and good luck to you!"

You see, the alligators talked so big because they were sure the dam they had made this time would hold up against the most terrible cannon-balls in the world. And the sailors must have thought so, too; for after they had fired the first shot a tremendous explosion occurred in the dam. The gunboat was using shells, which burst among the timbers of the dam and broke the thickest trees into tiny, tiny bits. A second shell exploded right near the first, and a third near the second. So the shots went all along the dam, each tearing away a long strip of it till nothing, nothing, nothing was left. Again the warship came steaming by, closer in toward shore on this occasion, so that the sailors could make fun of the alligators by putting their hands to their mouths and holloing.

"So that's it!" said the alligators, climbing up out of the water. "We must all die, because the steamboats will keep coming and going, up and down, and leaving us not a fish in the world to eat!"

The littlest alligators were already whimpering, for they had had no dinner for three days; and it was a crowd of very sad alligators that gathered on the river shore to hear what the old alligator now had to say.

"We have only one hope left," he began. "We must go and see the Sturgeon! When I was a boy, I took that trip down to the sea along with him. He liked the salt water better than I did and went quite a way out into the ocean. There he saw a sea fight between two of these boats; and he brought home a torpedo that had failed to explode. Suppose we go and ask him to give it to us. It is true the Sturgeon has never liked us alligators; but I got along with him pretty well myself. He is a good fellow, at bottom, and surely he will not want to see us all starve!"

The fact was that some years before an alligator had eaten one of the Sturgeon's favorite grandchildren, and for that reason the Sturgeon had refused ever since to call on the alligators or receive visits from them. Nevertheless, the alligators now trouped off in a body to the big cave under the bank of the river where they knew the Sturgeon stayed, with his torpedo beside him. There are sturgeons as much as six feet long, you know, and this one with the torpedo was of that kind.

"Mr. Sturgeon! Mr. Sturgeon!" called the alligators at the entrance of the cave. No one of them dared go in, you see, on account of that matter of the Sturgeon's grandchild.

"Who is it?" answered the Sturgeon.

"We're the alligators," the latter replied in a chorus.

"I have nothing to do with alligators," grumbled the Sturgeon crossly.

But now the old alligator with the two teeth stepped forward and said, "Why, hello, Sturgy. Don't you remember Ally, your old friend that took that trip down the river when we were boys?"

"Well, well! Where have you been keeping yourself all these years?" said the Sturgeon, surprised and pleased to hear his old friend's voice. "Sorry I didn't know it was you! How goes it? What can I do for you?"

"We've come to ask you for that torpedo you found, remember? You see, there's a warship keeps coming up and down our river scaring all the fish away. She's a whopper, I'll tell you, armor plate, guns, the whole thing! We made one dam and she knocked it down. We made another and she blew it up. The fish have all gone away and we haven't had a bite to eat in near onto a week. Now you give us your torpedo and we'll do the rest!"

The Sturgeon sat thinking for a long time, scratching his chin with one of his fins. At last he answered: "As for the torpedo, all right! You can have it in spite of what you did to my eldest son's first-born. But there's one trouble: who knows how to work the thing?"

The alligators were all silent. Not one of them had ever seen a torpedo.

"Well," said the Sturgeon proudly, "I can see I'll have to go with you myself. I've lived next to that torpedo a long time. I know all about torpedoes."

The first task was to bring the torpedo down to the dam. The alligators got into line, the one behind taking in his mouth the tail of the one in front. When the line was formed it was fully a quarter of a mile long. The Sturgeon pushed the torpedo out into the current and got under it so as to hold it up near the top of the water on his back. Then he took the tail of the last alligator in his teeth and gave the signal to go ahead. The Sturgeon kept the torpedo afloat, while the alligators towed him along. In this way they went so fast that a wide wake followed on after the torpedo, and by the next morning they were back at the place where the dam was made.

As the little alligators who had stayed at home reported, the warship had already gone by upstream. But this pleased the others all the more. Now they would build a new dam, stronger than ever before, and catch the steamer in a trap, so that it would never get home again.

They worked all that day and all the next night, making a thick, almost solid dike, with barely enough room between the piles for the alligators to stick their heads through. They had just finished when the gunboat came into view.

Again the rowboat approached with the eight men and their officer. The alligators crowded behind the dam in great excitement, moving their paws to hold their own with the current, for this time they were downstream.

"Hey, alligators!" called the officer.

"Well?" answered the alligators.

"Still another dam?"

"If at first you don't succeed, try, try, again!"

"Get that dam out of there!"

"No, sir!"

"You won't?"

"We won't!"

"Very well! Now you alligators just listen! If you won't be reasonable, we are going to knock this dam down, too. But to save you the trouble of building a fourth, we are going to shoot every blessed alligator around here. Yes, every single last alligator, women and children, big ones, little ones, fat ones, lean ones, and even that old codger sitting there with only two teeth left in his jaws!"

The old alligator understood that the officer was trying to insult him with that reference to his two teeth, and he answered: "Young man, what you say is true. I have only two teeth left, not counting one or two others that are broken off. But do you know what those two teeth are going to eat for dinner?" As he said this the old alligator opened his mouth wide, wide, wide.

"Well, what are they going to eat?" asked one of the sailors.

"A little dude of a naval officer I see in a boat over there!"—and the old alligator dived under water and disappeared from view.

Meantime the Sturgeon had brought the torpedo to the very center of the dam, where four alligators were holding it fast to the river bottom waiting for orders to bring it up to the top of the water. The other alligators had gathered along the shore, with their noses and eyes alone in sight as usual.

The rowboat went back to the ship. When he saw the men climbing aboard, the Sturgeon went down to his torpedo.

Suddenly there was a loud detonation. The warship had begun firing, and the first shell struck and exploded in the middle of the dam. A great gap opened in it.

"Now! Now!" called the Sturgeon sharply, on seeing that there was room for the torpedo to go through, "Let her go! Let her go!"

As the torpedo came to the surface, the Sturgeon steered it to the opening in the dam, took aim hurriedly with one eye closed, and pulled at the trigger of the torpedo with his teeth. The propeller of the torpedo began to revolve, and it started off upstream toward the gunboat.

And it was high time. At that instant a second

shot exploded in the dam, tearing away another large section.

From the wake the torpedo left behind it in the water the men on the vessel saw the danger they were in, but it was too late to do anything about it. The torpedo struck the ship in the middle, and went off.

You can never guess the terrible noise that torpedo made. It blew the warship into fifteen thousand million pieces, tossing guns and smokestacks and shells and rowboats—everything—hundreds and hundreds of yards away.

The alligators all screamed with triumph and made as fast as they could for the dam. Down through the opening bits of wood came floating, with a number of sailors swimming as hard as they could for the shore. As the men passed through, the alligators put their paws to their mouths and holloed, as the men had done to them three days before. They decided not to eat a single one of the sailors, though some of them deserved it without a doubt. Except that when a man dressed in a blue uniform with gold braid came by, the old alligator jumped into the water off the dam and snap! snap! ate him in two mouthfuls.

"Who was that man?" asked an ignorant young alligator, who never learned his lessons in school and never knew what was going on.

"It's the officer of the boat," answered the Sturgeon. "My old friend, Ally, said he was going to eat him, and eaten him he has!"

The alligators tore down the rest of the dam, because they knew that no boats would be coming by that way again.

The Sturgeon, who had quite fallen in love with the gold lace of the officer, asked that it be given him in payment for the use of his torpedo. The alligators said he might have it for the trouble of picking it out of the old alligator's mouth, where it had caught on the two teeth. They also gave him the officer's belt and sword. The Sturgeon put the belt on just behind his front fins and buckled the sword to it. Thus togged out, he swam up and down for more than an hour in front of the assembled alligators, who admired his beautiful spotted skin as something almost as pretty as the coral snake's, and who opened their mouths wide at the splendor of his uniform. Finally they escorted him in honor back to his cave under the riverbank, thanking him over and over again and giving him three cheers as they went off.

When they returned to their usual place they found the fish had already returned. The next day another steamboat came by; but the alligators did not care, because the fish were getting used to it by this time and seemed not to be afraid. Since then the boats have been going back and forth all the time, carrying oranges. And the alligators open their eyes when they hear the *chug! chug! chug!* of a steamboat and laugh at the thought of how scared they were the first time and of how they sank the warship.

But no warship has ever gone up the river since the old alligator ate the officer.

# Gabriela Mistral
**1889–1957** (Chile)

## Meet the Writer

Writers in Latin America are frequently political activists. Chilean writer **Gabriela Mistral** (gah bree AY lah mees TRAHL) was not only a renowned poet but also an international cultural ambassador. She became Chile's delegate to the League of Nations and was her country's consul to France, Italy, Spain, Portugal, and Guatemala.

Mistral was christened Lucila Godoy y Alcayaga; she took her pen name from the names of two of her favorite poets, Gabriele D'Annunzio, of Italy, and Frédéric Mistral, of France. When Mistral was in her teens, she fell passionately in love with a railway worker; a few years later the young man took his own life. Death was already a subject in the poet's work; now she began to consider life and death more broadly, along with themes of childhood and motherhood. Her first recognition came with a collection of poems called *Sonetos de la muerte* (*Sonnets of Death*). Three other collections followed: *Desolación* (*Despair*), *Ternura* (*Tenderness*), and *Tala* (*Tree Fall*). The proceeds for *Tala* were devoted to children orphaned by the Spanish Civil War.

In 1945, Mistral became the first Latin American woman to receive the Nobel Prize in literature. When she died in 1957, the Chilean government declared three days of national mourning.

## Background

Mistral once said that the artist is to society what the soul is to the individual. Her life and writing reflect this sentiment. Her simple, straightforward verse reflects simple themes that anyone can relate to: love, nature, children, religion, and the cycles of life and death.

Much of Mistral's poetry is musical; in fact, she wrote children's songs, poems, and lullabies. The following poem, "Serene Words," has been set to music as part of a song cycle.

**Before You Read**  *The poet says that these words have come to her "in the middle of" her life. We know that the poet has faced many tragedies; despite that, she says here that she has learned a surprising "truth." We get a hint at the "truth" in the poem's title. What does the word* serene *suggest to you? What kinds of words would you use at this time in your own life to describe what you have learned?*

# Serene Words

## Gabriela Mistral
*translated by* Doris Dana

Now in the middle of my days I glean
this truth that has a flower's freshness:
life is the gold and sweetness of wheat,
hate is brief and love immense.

5  Let us exchange for a smiling verse
that verse scored with blood and gall.°
Heavenly violets open, and through the valley
the wind blows a honeyed breath.

°  **gall:** something that is very bitter to the taste; literally, bile, fluid secreted by the liver.

Now I understand not only the man who prays;
10  now I understand the man who breaks into song.
Thirst is long-lasting and the hillside twisting;
but a lily can ensnare our gaze.

Our eyes grow heavy with weeping,
yet a brook can make us smile.
15  A skylark's song bursting heavenward
makes us forget it is hard to die.

There is nothing now that can pierce my flesh.
With love, all turmoil ceased.
The gaze of my mother still brings me peace.
20  I feel that God is putting me to sleep.

# Jorge Luis Borges
**1899–1986** (Argentina)

## Meet the Writer

**Jorge Luis Borges** (HAWR heh loo EES BAWR hehs) may have done more to put Latin American literature "on the map" in terms of worldwide recognition than any other single Latin American writer. His short-fiction collections *Ficciones* (1944) and *El Aleph* (1949) had a profound influence on the growth and development of Latin American literature, paving the way for such renowned writers as Gabriel García Márquez, Carlos Fuentes, and Julio Cortázar.

Born in Buenos Aires, Argentina, Borges was steeped in literature from his earliest years. His grandmother was English, and he learned to read in English as well as in Spanish. His father had translated the Persian poet Omar Khayyám's *Rubáiyát* and had an impressive library of English books. By the time he was nine, Borges had read all of Charles Dickens, Rudyard Kipling, Mark Twain, and Edgar Allan Poe.

Between 1914 and 1918, Borges lived in Geneva, Switzerland, where he was educated. He quickly became multilingual, adding French, Latin, and German to his list of languages. Following World War I, he spent some years in Spain, where he associated with an avant-garde group of poets known as ultraists. Ultraism, an offshoot of French symbolism and surrealism, was highly intellectual and experimental, emphasizing free verse, complicated meters, and nontraditional symbols and imagery. In 1921, Borges returned to Argentina, where he founded three literary magazines to promote ultraist ideas. Before 1930, he had written four books of essays and three books of poetry.

In 1938, Borges had a serious accident that was a turning point in his life. The accident resulted in septicemia, or blood poisoning. While recovering, he began to write stories that were unconventional in narrative style and subject matter. He considered these short prose tales to be "fictions" instead of short stories, since they are usually unlike the traditional short story.

Borges's opposition to Argentine president Juan Perón, who came to power in 1946, cost him his job at the Buenos Aires library. Although offered a job as chicken inspector in the city market, he finally found a job teaching, but he was kept under surveillance. When Perón was overthrown in 1955, Borges became director of the National Library of Argentina and a member of the National Academy. He also taught at the University of Buenos Aires.

As a result of his 1938 accident, Borges's eyesight deteriorated until he finally became blind. After 1955, he turned to poetry. In 1961, when he was in his sixties, he finally achieved widespread international recognition when he shared the International Publishers Prize with the Irish absurdist writer Samuel Beckett. Borges died in 1986.

## Background

Borges has been called "one of the most bookish of writers." He had an extensive knowledge of world literature, and his work is full of allusions, or references, to other works of literature, from virtually all time periods and cultures. Borges made no attempt to appeal to the reader of "popular" fiction; his work is unabashedly intellectual. Although he was a noted poet and critic, his reputation rests chiefly on his stories. Some of his fictions are brief fantasies; others read like autobiographical sketches, essays, or philosophical parables; only a few, mostly written in his later years, seem like traditional short stories. Even the stories that seem more traditional have elements that set them apart: They may involve universal, or archetypal, characters in unidentified settings; they may have nontraditional narrative structures that play with chronology; they may be constructed like puzzles, such as "story-within-a-story" tales; or they may have intellectually ambiguous endings. Borges's fictions are often compared to the surrealistic stories of Franz Kafka.

One of Borges's recurring motifs, or ideas, is that of alternative realities. Personal identity is unreal; Borges invents his own reality. His fondness for detective stories comes out in his use of logical puzzles and paradoxes in many of his stories. Sometimes, he is the writer of the story even as he is the character in the story; he meets himself—or is it the other way around? One of his most identifiable recurring images is that of the labyrinth, or maze; his imaginative world is a huge labyrinth of alternative possibilities.

**Before You Read**  *In such stories as "Borges and Myself" and "The Other," Borges appears as a character along with his double. Some critics have suggested that this use of the double reflects a duality in Borges's own personality. In "The Other," Borges alludes to many events from his life, including memories of relatives, books that he read, and conversations from the past. What elements of a puzzle do you find in this story?*

# The Other

## Jorge Luis Borges
*translated by* Andrew Hurley

The incident occurred in February, 1969, in Cambridge, north of Boston. I didn't write about it then because my foremost objective at the time was to put it out of my mind, so as not to go insane. Now, in 1972, it strikes me that if I do write about what happened, people will read it as a story and in time I, too, may be able to see it as one.

I know that it was almost horrific while it lasted—and it grew worse yet through the sleepless nights that followed. That does not mean that anyone else will be stirred by my telling of it.

It was about ten o'clock in the morning. I was sitting comfortably on a bench beside the Charles River. Some five hundred yards to my right there was a tall building whose name I never learned. Large chunks of ice were floating down the gray current. Inevitably, the river made me think of time . . . Heraclitus' ancient image.[1] I had slept well; the class I'd given the previous evening had, I think, managed to interest my students. There was not a soul in sight.

Suddenly, I had the sense (which psychologists tell us is associated with states of fatigue) that I had lived this moment before. Someone had sat down on the other end of my bench. I'd have preferred to be alone, but I didn't want to get up immediately for fear of seeming rude. The other man had started whistling. At that moment there occurred the first of the many shocks that morning was to bring me. What the man was whistling—or *trying* to whistle (I have never been able to carry a tune)—was the popular Argentine milonga *La tapera*,[2] by Elías Regules. The tune carried me back to a patio that no longer exists and to the memory of Alvaro Melián Lafinur,[3] who died so many years ago. Then there came the words. They were the words of the *décima*[4] that begins the song. The voice was not Alvaro's but it tried to imitate Alvaro's. I recognized it with horror.

I turned to the man and spoke.

"Are you Uruguayan or Argentine?"

---

1. **Heraclitus' ancient image:** Heraclitus (hehr uh KLYT uhs) was a Greek philosopher who lived c. 500 B.C. He said, "You cannot step twice into the same river, for other waters are continually flowing on." He insisted that the world we see is constantly changing.
2. **milonga** *La tapera:* popular dance in Argentina and Bolivia.
3. **Alvaro Melián Lafinur:** Borges's cousin, a poet.
4. *décima:* Spanish stanza of ten eight-syllable lines. It has a rigid metrical structure.

"Argentine, but I've been living in Geneva since '14," came the reply.

There was a long silence. Then I asked a second question.

"At number seventeen Malagnou, across the street from the Russian Orthodox Church?"

He nodded.

"In that case," I resolutely said to him, "your name is Jorge Luis Borges. I too am Jorge Luis Borges. We are in 1969, in the city of Cambridge."

"No," he answered in my own, slightly distant, voice, "I am here in Geneva, on a bench, a few steps from the Rhône."

Then, after a moment, he went on:

"It *is* odd that we look so much alike, but you are much older than I, and you have gray hair."

"I can prove to you that I speak the truth," I answered. "I'll tell you things that a stranger couldn't know. In our house there's a silver maté[5] cup with a base of serpents that our great-grandfather brought from Peru. There's also a silver washbasin that was hung from the saddle. In the wardrobe closet in your room, there are two rows of books: the three volumes of Lane's translation of the *Thousand and One Nights*—which Lane called *The Arabian Nights Entertainment*—with steel engravings and notes in fine print between the chapters, Quicherat's Latin dictionary, Tacitus' *Germania* in Latin and in Gordon's English version, a *Quixote* in the Garnier edition, a copy of Rivera Indarte's *Tablas de sangre* signed by the author, Carlyle's *Sartor Resartus,* a biography of Amiel,[6] and, hidden behind the others, a paperbound volume detailing the sexual customs of the Balkans. Nor have I forgotten a certain afternoon in a second-floor apartment on the Plaza Dubourg."

"Dufour," he corrected me.

---

5. **maté:** a type of tea, popular all over South America.
6. **Thousand and One Nights ... Amiel:** books in Borges's home. Henri Frederic Amiel was a nineteenth-century French critic.

"All right, Dufour," I said. "Is that enough for you?"

"No, he replied. "Those 'proofs' of yours prove nothing. If I'm dreaming you, it's only natural that you would know what I know. That long-winded catalog of yours is perfectly unavailing."

His objection was a fair one.

"If this morning and this encounter are dreams," I replied, "then each of us does have to think that he alone is the dreamer. Perhaps our dream will end, perhaps it won't. Meanwhile, our clear obligation is to accept the dream, as we have accepted the universe and our having been brought into it and the fact that we see with our eyes and that we breathe."

"But what if the dream should last?" he asked anxiously.

In order to calm him—and calm myself, as well—I feigned a self-assurance I was far from truly feeling.

"My dream," I told him, "has already lasted for seventy years. And besides—when one wakes up, the person one meets is always oneself. That is what's happening to us now, except that we are two. Wouldn't you like to know something about my past, which is now the future that awaits you?"

He nodded wordlessly. I went on, a bit hesitatingly:

"Mother is well, living happily in her house in Buenos Aires, on the corner of Charcas and Maipú, but Father died some thirty years ago. It was his heart. He had had a stroke—that was what finally killed him. When he laid his left hand over his right, it was like a child's hand resting atop a giant's. He died impatient for death, but without a word of complaint. Our grandmother had died in the same house. Several days before the end, she called us all in and told us, 'I am an old, old woman, dying very slowly. I won't have anyone making a fuss over such a common, ordinary thing as that.' Norah, your sister, is married and has two children. By the way—at home, how is everyone?"

"Fine. Father still always making his jokes against religion. Last night he said Jesus was like the gauchos,[7] who'll never commit themselves, which is why He spoke in parables."

He thought for a moment, and then asked: "What about you?"

"I'm not sure exactly how many books you'll write, but I know there are too many. You'll write poetry that will give you a pleasure that others will not fully share, and stories of a fantastic turn. You will be a teacher—like your father, and like so many others of our blood."

I was glad he didn't ask me about the success or failure of the books. I then changed my tack.

"As for history . . . There was another war, with virtually the same antagonists. France soon capitulated; England and America battled a German dictator named Hitler—the cyclical Battle of Waterloo. Buenos Aires engendered another Rosas in 1946,[8] much like our kinsman in the first one. In '55, the province of Córdoba saved us, as Entre Ríos[9] had before. Things are bad now. Russia is taking over the planet; America, hobbled by the superstition of democracy, can't make up its mind to be an empire. Our own country is more provincial with every passing day—more provincial and more self-important, as though it had shut its eyes. I shouldn't be surprised if the teaching of Latin were replaced by the teaching of Guaraní."[10]

I realized that he was barely listening. The elemental fear of the impossible yet true had come over him, and he was daunted. I, who have never been a father, felt a wave of love for that poor young man who was dearer to me than a child of my own flesh and blood. I saw that his hands were clutching a book. I asked what he was reading.

"*The Possessed*—or, as I think would be better, *The Devils,* by Fyodor Dostoievsky," he answered without vanity.

"It's a bit hazy to me now. Is it any good?"

The words were hardly out of my mouth when I sensed that the question was blasphemous.

"The great Russian writer," he affirmed sententiously, "has penetrated more deeply than any other man into the labyrinths of the Slavic soul."

I took that rhetorical pronouncement as evidence that he had grown calmer.

I asked him what other works by Dostoievsky he had read.

He ticked off two or three, among them *The Double.*[11]

I asked him whether he could tell the difference between the characters when he read, as one could with Joseph Conrad, and whether he planned to read on through Dostoievsky's entire corpus.[12]

"The truth is, I don't," he answered with a slight note of surprise.

I asked him what he himself was writing, and he told me he was working on a book of poetry to be called *Red Anthems.* He'd also thought about calling it *Red Rhythms* or *Red Songs.*

"Why not?" I said. "You can cite good author-

---

7. **gauchos:** South American cowboys, generally of Indian and Spanish ancestry.
8. **another Rosas in 1946:** a reference to Argentina's Fascist dictator Juan Domingo Perón, who was forced to step down as vice president in 1945 but who came back and was elected president in 1946.
9. **Entre Ríos:** province in Argentina.
10. **Guaraní:** language spoken by the Guaraní Indians in Paraguay.

---

11. **The Double:** In this novel by the Russian writer Dostoievsky, an official named Golyadkin encounters his double, but the existence of the double is ambiguous. This, of course, echoes the situation of the story Borges is telling.
12. **corpus:** collection of writings.

ity for it—Rubén Darío's blue poetry and Verlaine's gray song."¹³

Ignoring this, he clarified what he'd meant—his book would be a hymn to the brotherhood of all mankind. The modern poet cannot turn his back on his age.

I thought about this for a while, and then asked if he really felt that he was brother to every living person—every undertaker, for example? every letter carrier? every undersea diver, everybody that lives on the even-numbered side of the street, all the people with laryngitis? (The list could go on.) He said his book would address the great oppressed and outcast masses.

"Your oppressed and outcast masses," I replied, "are nothing but an abstraction. Only individuals exist—if, in fact, anyone does. *Yesterday's man is not today's,* as some Greek said. We two, here on this bench in Geneva or in Cambridge, are perhaps the proof of that."

Except in the austere pages of history, memorable events go unaccompanied by memorable phrases. A man about to die tries to recall a print that he glimpsed in his childhood; soldiers about to go into battle talk about the mud or their sergeant. Our situation was unique and, frankly, we were unprepared. We talked, inevitably, about literature; I fear I said no more than I customarily say to journalists. My *alter ego*¹⁴ believed in the imagination, in creation—in the discovery of new metaphors; I myself believed in those that correspond to close and widely acknowledged likenesses, those our imagination has already accepted: old age and death, dreams and life, the flow of time and water. I informed the young man of this opinion, which he himself was to express in a book, years later.

But he was barely listening. Then suddenly he spoke.

"If you have been me, how can you explain the fact that you've forgotten that you once encountered an elderly gentleman who in 1918 told you that he, too was Borges?"

I hadn't thought of that difficulty. I answered with conviction.

"Perhaps the incident was so odd that I made an effort to forget it."

He ventured a timid question.

"How's your memory?"

I realized that for a mere boy not yet twenty, a man of seventy some-odd years was practically a corpse.

"It's often much like forgetfulness," I answered, "but it can still find what it's sent to find. I'm studying Anglo-Saxon, and I'm not at the foot of the class."

By this time our conversation had lasted too long to be conversation in a dream.

I was struck by a sudden idea.

"I can prove to you this minute," I said, "that you aren't dreaming me. Listen to this line of poetry. So far as I can recall, you've never heard it before."

I slowly intoned the famous line: *"L'hydre-univers tordant son corps écaillé d'astres."*¹⁵

I could sense his almost fear-stricken bafflement. He repeated the line softly, savoring each glowing word.

"It's true," he stammered, "I could never write a line like that."

Hugo had brought us together.

I now recall that shortly before this, he had fervently recited that short poem in which

---

13. **Rubén ... gray song:** a reference to Darío's volume of poetry *Azul* (*Blue*) and French symbolist poet Verlaine's verse "Nothing is more precious than that gray song, / Where indecision is joined to precision."

14. ***alter ego:*** a close friend; another side of oneself.

15. ***L'hydre-univers ... d'astres:*** a line from French writer Victor Hugo's poem "Ce que dit la bouche d'ombre." The Hydra, a mythological creature with nine heads, is also a constellation. The line can be translated as "The snakelike universe twisting its star-scaled body."

Whitman[16] recalls a night shared beside the sea—a night when Whitman had been truly happy.

"If Whitman sang of that night," I observed, "it's because he desired it but it never happened. The poem gains in greatness if we sense that it is the expression of a desire, a longing, rather than the narration of an event."

He stared at me.

"You don't know him," he exclaimed. "Whitman is incapable of falsehood."

A half century does not pass without leaving its mark. Beneath our conversation, the conversation of two men of miscellaneous readings and diverse tastes, I realized that we would not find common ground. We were too different, yet too alike. We could not deceive one another, and that makes conversation hard. Each of us was almost a caricature of the other. The situation was too unnatural to last much longer. There was no point in giving advice, no point in arguing, because the young man's inevitable fate was to be the man that I am now.

Suddenly I recalled a fantasy by Coleridge.[17] A man dreams that he is in paradise, and he is given a flower as proof. When he wakes up, there is the flower.

I hit upon an analogous stratagem.[18]

"Listen," I said, "do you have any money?"

"Yes," he replied. "About twenty francs. I invited Simón Jichlinski to have dinner with me at the Crocodile tonight."

"Tell Simón that he'll practice medicine in Carouge, and that he will do a great deal of good . . . now, give me one of your coins."

He took three silver pieces and several smaller coins out of his pocket. He held out one of the silver pieces to me; he didn't understand.

I handed him one of those ill-advised American bills that are all of the same size though of very different denominations. He examined it avidly.

"Impossible!" he cried. "It's dated 1964."

(Months later someone told me that banknotes are not dated.)

"This, all this, is a miracle," he managed to say. "And the miraculous inspires fear. Those who witnessed the resurrection of Lazarus[19] must have been terrified."

We haven't changed a bit, I thought. Always referring back to books.

He tore the bill to shreds and put the coin back in his pocket.

I had wanted to throw the coin he gave me in the river. The arc of the silver coin disappearing into the silver river would have lent my story a vivid image, but fate would not have it.

I replied that the supernatural, if it happens twice, is no longer terrifying; I suggested that we meet again the next day, on that same bench that existed in two times and two places.

He immediately agreed, then said, without looking at his watch, that it was getting late, he had to be going. Both of us were lying, and each of us knew that the other one was lying. I told him that someone was coming to fetch me.

"Fetch you?" he queried.

"Yes. When you reach my age, you'll have almost totally lost your eyesight. You'll be able to see the color yellow, and light and shadow. But don't worry. Gradual blindness is not tragic. It's like the slowly growing darkness of a summer evening."

---

16. **Whitman:** Walt Whitman (1819–1892), considered by some the greatest poet the United States has ever produced. He was much admired by Borges and many other Latin American writers for his innovative contributions to poetry.
17. **Coleridge:** Samuel Taylor Coleridge (1772–1834), an English Romantic poet.
18. **analogous stratagem:** comparable scheme or trick.
19. **Lazarus:** In the New Testament of the Christian Bible, the brother of Mary and Martha. He was raised from the dead (John 11–12).

We parted without having touched one another. The next day, I did not go to the bench. The other man probably didn't, either.

I have thought a great deal about this encounter, which I've never told anyone about. I believe I have discovered the key to it. The encounter was real, but the other man spoke to me in a dream, which was why he could forget me; I spoke to him while I was awake, and so I am still tormented by the memory.

The other man dreamed me, but did not dream me *rigorously*—he dreamed, I now realize, the impossible date on that dollar bill.

# Pablo Neruda
**1904–1973** (Chile)

## Meet the Writer

**Pablo Neruda** (PAH bloh neh ROO duh) once remarked, "If you ask what my poetry is, I must confess that I don't know, but if you'll ask my poetry, it will tell you who I am." Widely considered the greatest Latin American poet of the last century, Neruda is, according to one survey, "the most frequently translated poet on the globe." His vast output from the 1920s to the 1970s consists of more than forty books.

Neruda was born Neftalí Ricardo Reyes Basoalto in Parral, Chile, on July 12, 1904. His mother died a month after his birth. In 1906, his father moved the family to Temuco. When he was a child, Neruda enjoyed walking in the woods, an experience he later recalled in his memoirs. He also began writing his first poems.

Neruda left Temuco for Santiago in 1921 in order to study at the university. He never completed his studies but during these years began his career as a poet. He had taken the name Pablo Neruda, partly in homage to Jan Neruda, a Czech poet. *Veinte poemas de amor y una canción desesperada* (*Twenty Love Poems and a Song of Despair*), which appeared in 1924, was an immediate success. Its subject is the love Neruda felt for two women. Neruda later said, "I have never uttered insincere words of love. I could not have written a single line that departed from the truth." This collection of poetry has since been translated into many languages and has sold more than two million copies in Spanish. Neruda could not survive on the proceeds from his poetry, however, and in 1927 he accepted an appointment as consul to Rangoon (now Yangon) in Burma (now Myanmar).

Neruda remained in Asia for five years, where he felt isolated. Many of the poems written during this period reflect his despair and gloom. In 1932, he returned to Chile. His first volume of *Residencia en la tierra* (*Residence on Earth*) was published in 1933. Still unable to live on what he earned from his poetry, Neruda accepted other consular jobs, which took him to Argentina and then to Spain, where his friend, the poet Federico García Lorca, introduced him to Spanish writers and intellectuals.

In Spain in 1935, Neruda published the second edition *of Residence on*

*Earth* in two volumes. These poems had a powerful impact on his contemporaries. Neruda was using a new diction and antipoetic imagery to express a bleak vision of the world. It has been noted that Neruda, who admired the American poet Walt Whitman, adapts Whitman's technique of the catalog, stringing together long lists of various elements and unconnected metaphors. After the onset of the civil war in Spain in 1936, Neruda was drawn to Communism. When he returned to Chile in 1937, he remained active politically. As special consul in Paris in 1939, he helped thousands of Spanish émigrés reach Chile after Francisco Franco came to power.

In 1940, Neruda was named consul general to Mexico. He was elected a senator in 1945 and joined the Communist Party in Chile. After quarreling with the Chilean president, Neruda had to go into hiding to avoid arrest. Much of his next major work, *Canto general* (*General Song*), was written while he was seeking refuge. Although the book is marred by political propaganda, it contains the superb "The Heights of Machu Picchu," one of his greatest poems, which extols the glories of the Incan past.

In the early 1950s, Neruda married his third wife, Matilde Urrutia, who inspired his poetry during the final decades of his life. Neruda received the Nobel Prize in literature in 1971. Knowing that he was terminally ill, he returned from France to Chile, where he died in 1973.

Pablo Neruda's life has been a subject of interest to other writers. He has appeared as a character in the novel *Ardiente paciencia* (*Burning Patience*) by Antonio Skármata (1985), also known as *The Postman of Neruda*. The story was adapted as a film script in 1995. In the movie, Neruda, exiled on a small Italian island, befriends the unschooled postman who delivers his mail. Neruda teaches the young man, Mario, about poetry. When Mario falls in love, he asks Neruda to help him win the girl of his dreams.

## Background

Neruda's poetry continued to evolve throughout his career. In the 1950s, Neruda published a series of volumes of odes that praise "unpoetic" everyday things in simple language. The first book, *Odas elementales* (*Elementary Odes*), appeared in 1954. *Extravagaria* (a made-up word that means "vagaries") appeared in 1958. It is more personal and contemplative than Neruda's earlier poetry and uses unusual typography and word spacing. In 1959, he published *Cien sonetos de amor* (*One Hundred Love Sonnets*), dedicated to his beloved Matilde. *Las piedras de Chile* (*The Stones of Chile*), published in 1961, deals with the rock formations around Isla Negra.

**Before You Read**  In 1954, Neruda published the first of a series of books that marked a radical change in his poetry. He moved from the concern with social justice in Canto general to a simple joy in elemental, or basic, things. In the four volumes of odes, Neruda celebrates trivial things, which for him have dignity. He praises such concrete objects as scissors, spoons, vegetables, and socks and abstract concepts such as age, sadness, and laziness. The tone of these poems is generally light and optimistic. Neruda tends to use short lines, sometimes one or two syllables long. Some critics have called his technique in the odes "a spiraling pattern." He begins with something insignificant, such as a suit, and then creates an emotional link to the object.

The word ode comes from a Greek word meaning "song." An ode is generally a long, complex poem written in a formal style on some dignified or serious subject. By calling his poem an ode, what does Neruda imply about the importance of everyday things?

# Ode to My Suit
## Pablo Neruda
*translated by* Margaret Sayers Peden

Every morning, suit,
you are waiting on a chair
to be filled
by my vanity, my love,
5   my hope, my body.
Still
only half awake
I leave the shower
to shrug into your sleeves,
10  my legs seek
the hollow of your legs,
and thus embraced
by your unfailing loyalty
I take my morning walk,
15  work my way into my poetry;
from my windows I see
the things,
men, women,
events, and struggles
20  constantly shaping me,
constantly confronting me,
setting my hands to the task,
opening my eyes,
creasing my lips,
25  and in the same way,
suit,
I am shaping you,
poking out your elbows,
wearing you threadbare,
30  and so your life grows
in the image of my own.
In the wind
you flap and hum
as if you were my soul,
35  in bad moments
you cling

to my bones,
abandoned, at nighttime
darkness and dream
40  people with their phantoms
your wings and mine.
I wonder
whether someday
an enemy
45  bullet
will stain you with my blood,
for then
you would die with me,
but perhaps
50  it will be
less dramatic,
simple,
and you will grow ill,
suit,
55  with me,
grow older
with me, with my body,
and together
we will be lowered
60  into the earth.
That's why
every day
I greet you
with respect and then
65  you embrace me and I forget you,
because we are one being
and shall be always
in the wind, through the night,
the streets and the struggle,
70  one body,
maybe, maybe, one day, still.

**Before You Read**  The title Extravagaria, *in which this poem appears, is an invented word. It might be translated as "extravagant items" or "vagaries." Neruda considered this volume, published in 1958, his "most personal book." It was written after a period when he was engaged in writing social and political poetry. What techniques does the poet use to convey to the reader his emotional response to the horses?*

# Horses
## Pablo Neruda
*translated by* Alastair Reid

From the window I saw the horses.

I was in Berlin, in winter. The light
was without light, the sky skyless.

The air white like a moistened loaf.

5    From my window, I could see a deserted arena,
a circle bitten out by the teeth of winter.

All at once, led out by a single man,
ten horses were stepping, stepping into the snow.

          Scarcely had they rippled into existence
10     like flame, than they filled the whole world of my eyes,
          empty till now. Faultless, flaming,
          they stepped like ten gods on broad, clean hoofs,
          their manes recalling a dream of salt spray.

          Their rumps were globes, were oranges.

15     Their color was amber and honey, was on fire.

          Their necks were towers
          carved from the stone of pride,
          and in their furious eyes, sheer energy
          showed itself, a prisoner inside them.

20     And there, in the silence, at the mid-
          point of the day, in a dirty, disgruntled winter,
          the horses' intense presence was blood,
          was rhythm, was the beckoning light of all being.

          I saw, I saw, and seeing, I came to life.
25     There was the unwitting fountain, the dance of gold, the sky,
          the fire that sprang to life in beautiful things.

          I have obliterated that gloomy Berlin winter.

          I shall not forget the light from these horses.

**Before You Read**  In *The Stones of Chile,* published in 1961, Neruda examines the rock formations around Isla Negra, where he lived with his beloved wife Matilda Urrutia. In the stones visible from his home, Neruda imagined various forms, such as those of animals. In this poem the stones take on the form of an old turtle.

# The Turtle
**Pablo Neruda**
*translated by* Dennis Maloney

The turtle that
has walked
so long
and seen so much
5   with
his
ancient
eyes,
the turtle
10  that fed on
olives
of the deep
sea,
the turtle that has swum
15  for seven centuries
and known
seven
thousand
springs,
20  the turtle
shielded
against
the heat
and cold,
25  against
the rays and waves,
the turtle
of yellow
and silver,
30  with stern
lunar
amber
and rapine feet,
the turtle
35  remains
here
asleep,
and doesn't know it.

The old man
40  assumed
a hardness,
abandoned
the love of waves
and became rigid
45  as an iron plate.

Closing
the eyes that
have dared
so much
50  ocean, sky, time, and earth,
and now, he sleeps
among the other
rocks.

# Octavio Paz
## 1914–1998 (Mexico)

### Meet the Writer

**Octavio Paz** (ohk TAH vee oh pahs), born in Mexico City, said that writers in Spanish America and Brazil have felt a profound separation from writers in the United States and Europe. For Paz, that sense of separation began in childhood. In his acceptance of the Nobel Prize in literature in 1990, Paz described this feeling of being apart: "I lived in a town on the outskirts of Mexico City, in an old dilapidated house that had a jungle-like garden and a great room full of books. . . . The beyond was here, all was here. . . . When was the spell broken? . . . I must have been about six when one of my cousins . . . showed me . . . a photograph of soldiers marching along a huge avenue, probably in New York. 'They've returned from the war,' she said. This handful of words disturbed me. . . . I vaguely knew that somewhere far away, a war had ended a few years earlier and that the soldiers were marching to celebrate their victory. For me, that war had taken place in another time, not here and now. . . .

"For us, as Spanish Americans, the real present was not in our own countries: it was the time lived by others . . . . We had to go and look for it and bring it back home."

Paz's first volume of poetry was published in 1933, just after he graduated from the National University of Mexico. In a few years he was on his way to becoming an international literary celebrity. Diplomatic assignments for his country took him to Paris, Japan, and India. Academic teaching posts and fellowships took him to the United States.

In addition to poetry, Paz is well known for his nonfiction, especially his literary essays, such as those in *The Labyrinth of Solitude,* in which he analyzes the complex character of the Mexican people. He has also written a highly regarded biography/criticism of the Mexican poet Sor Juana Inés de la Cruz.

Paz often said that writing poems was his way of connecting himself not only to his own country but also to the modern world—that it was his way of bringing that wider world home.

# Background

Paz's poetry is challenging, incorporating many characteristics of modernism: elliptical, or obscure, imagery; surrealism; sophisticated allusions to philosophical or political concepts; and contrasting elements. Yet even as he explores difficult, abstract concepts, he bases much of his imagery on the Mexican landscape itself: its stones, sand, and soil, as well as its "mythical" landscape.

Octavio Paz was appointed Mexican ambassador to India in 1962—an important moment in the writer's life and work. From his experiences in India, he learned about that nation's great mythologies and religions. Buddhism became an influence on his work and thought, appealing to Paz's sense of the metaphysical—the deep, abstract, spiritual aspects of existence that cannot easily be put into words.

**Before You Read** According to tradition, sometime around 528 B.C. an Indian prince named Siddhartha Gautama (sihd DAHR tuh GOW tuh muh) went on a personal quest to search for the meaning of life. One fateful day, he rested under a fig tree. As he greeted the morning star, the meaning of life became clear to him, and he experienced what he called "enlightenment." He came to believe that all suffering in the world is caused by desire, and that to attain inner peace, he must practice self-denial. The name Buddha, meaning "enlightened one," was given to Gautama by his followers. All over Asia, a traveler can still find ancient stone monuments to the Buddha. Some of the monuments are mere remnants—a foot, a torso, or the gently smiling head of the Buddha.

We can easily see what the "face" in the poem's title is. What is the "wind"?

# The Face and the Wind

## Octavio Paz
*translated by* Eliot Weinberger

Beneath an unrelenting sun:
ocher[1] plains, lion-colored hills.
I struggled up a craggy slope of goats
to a place of rubble:
5   lopped columns, headless gods.
Surreptitious flashes of light:
a snake, or some small lizard.
Hidden in the rocks,
the color of toxic ink,
10  colonies of brittle beetles.
A circular courtyard, a wall full of cracks.
Clutching the earth—blind knot,
tree all roots—a pipal,[2] the religious fig.
Rain of light. A grey hulk: the Buddha,
15  its features a blurred mass.
Ants climbed and descended
the slopes of its face.
Still intact,
the smile, that smile:
20  a gulf of pacific[3] clarity.
And I was, for a moment, diaphanous,[4]
a wind that stops
turns on itself and is gone.

---

1. **ocher** (OH kuhr): usually yellow or yellowish brown.
2. **pipal** (PEE puhl): Indian fig tree. Siddhartha Gautama, the founder of Buddhism, is believed to have received his heavenly inspiration under a fig tree.
3. **pacific:** peaceful.
4. **diaphanous** (dy AF uh nuhs): transparent; airy.

# Julio Cortázar
**1914–1984** (Argentina/France)

## Meet the Writer

Like many Latin American writers, **Julio Cortázar** (HOO lee oh kohrt AH zahr) admired the macabre tales of nineteenth-century American writer Edgar Allan Poe. "I stole the book," Cortázar once explained, recounting his first acquaintance with Poe stories at the age of nine, ". . . because my mother didn't want me to read it; she thought I was too young and she was right. The book scared me and I was ill for three months because I believed in it." The fascination with Poe was far more than a passing childhood interest. As an adult, Cortázar translated four of Poe's books into Spanish. In his writing, he echoed Poe by producing nightmarish stories with unreliable narrators, narrative twists, and overtones of madness, in which it is not always possible to separate reality from fantasy.

Julio Cortázar was born in Brussels, Belgium, to Argentine parents. The family returned to their South American homeland when Cortázar was about six, and he was educated in Argentina. As an adult, he first supported his writing career by teaching high school and university courses; later, he managed a publishing association. Ultimately, he became a translator, working for the United Nations in Paris after moving to France in 1951 because of a clash with Juan Perón's fascist political regime in Argentina. Cortázar eventually became a French citizen, but he retained his Argentine citizenship and always thought of himself as both South American and European. His experiences as an exile from his own homeland led him to become more politically involved over the years, and in the 1970s he became a member of a group that investigated human rights violations in Latin America. He died of a blood disease in Paris in 1984.

## Background

Cortázar is mentioned in the same breath as Jorge Luis Borges and Gabriel García Márquez as one of Latin America's greatest practitioners of magic realism. Cortázar, though, is closer to the intellectual surrealism of Borges than to the more accessible magic realism of García Márquez, whose works are usually rooted in the earthy reality of Latin American life. Cortázar's stories, like those of Borges, are often ambiguous; they play with narrative structure and with concepts like time, perception, madness, and the nature of reality. Cortázar's fiction, though, has a unique and distinctive energy that may have something to do with his lifelong love of jazz music; he seems to infuse many of his tales with the kind of improvisation and playfulness associated with jazz.

Like nightmares that begin with ordinary scenes that slowly distort into something bizarre, Cortázar's stories move seamlessly from reality to fantasy. As the critic Alexander Coleman once observed, "Cortázar's stories start in a disarmingly conversational way, with plenty of local touches. . . . But something always seems to go awry just when we least expect it."

**Before You Read** *"Continuity of Parks" is one of Cortázar's most famous stories. It is also one of his most puzzling. Pay attention to what happens in this narrative. At what point does the boundary between the reader of the novel and the characters in the novel begin to blur? How do you interpret the ending of this very short story?*

# Continuity of Parks
## Julio Cortázar
*translated by* Paul Blackburn

He had begun to read the novel a few days before. He had put it down because of some urgent business conferences, opened it again on his way back to the estate by train; he permitted himself a slowly growing interest in the plot, in the characterizations. That afternoon, after writing a letter giving his power of attorney and discussing a matter of joint ownership with the manager of his estate, he returned to the book in the tranquillity of his study which looked out upon the park with its oaks. Sprawled in his favorite armchair, its back toward the door—even the possibility of an intrusion would have irritated him, had he thought of it—he let his left hand caress repeatedly the green velvet upholstery and set to reading the final chapters. He remembered effortlessly the names and his mental image of the characters; the novel spread its glamour over him almost at once. He tasted the almost perverse pleasure of disengaging himself line by line from the things around him, and at the same time feeling his head rest comfortably on the green velvet of the chair with its high back, sensing that the cigarettes rested within reach of his hand, that beyond the great windows the air of afternoon danced under the oak trees in the park. Word by word, licked up by the sordid dilemma of the hero and heroine, letting himself be absorbed to the point where the images settled down and took on color and movement, he was witness to the final encounter in the mountain cabin. The woman arrived first, apprehensive; now the lover came in, his face cut by the backlash of a branch. Admirably, she stanched the blood with her kisses, but he rebuffed her caresses, he had not come to perform again the ceremonies of a secret passion, protected by a world of dry leaves and furtive paths through the forest. The dagger warmed itself against his chest, and underneath liberty pounded, hidden close. A lustful, panting dialogue raced down the pages like a rivulet of snakes, and one felt it had all been decided from eternity. Even to those caresses which writhed about the lover's body, as though wishing to keep him there, to dissuade him from it; they sketched abominably the frame of that other body it was necessary to destroy. Nothing had been forgotten: alibis, unforeseen hazards, possible mistakes. From this hour on, each instant had its use minutely assigned. The cold-blooded, twice-gone-over reexamination of the details was barely broken off so that a hand could caress a cheek. It was beginning to get dark.

Not looking at one another now, rigidly fixed

upon the task which awaited them, they separated at the cabin door. She was to follow the trail that led north. On the path leading in the opposite direction, he turned for a moment to watch her running, her hair loosened and flying. He ran in turn, crouching among the trees and hedges until, in the yellowish fog of dusk, he could distinguish the avenue of trees which led up to the house. The dogs were not supposed to bark, they did not bark. The estate manager would not be there at this hour, and he was not there. He went up the three porch steps and entered. The woman's words reached him over the thudding of blood in his ears: first a blue chamber, then a hall, then a carpeted stairway. At the top, two doors. No one in the first room, no one in the second. The door of the salon, and then, the knife in hand, the light from the great windows, the high back of an armchair covered in green velvet, the head of the man in the chair reading a novel.

**Before You Read** *Julio Cortázar's link to Edgar Allan Poe is especially evident in this story, which has some interesting parallels to Poe's famous "The Fall of the House of Usher." Like "Usher," this story concerns the last members of a family line, a brother and sister living in a strange, too-large house that has its own secrets. The siblings have removed themselves from the normal flow of life and lead lives that are strangely stunted and limited. And then . . . they* appear. *Who might "they" be? What might the story's title mean?*

# House Taken Over

## Julio Cortázar
*translated by* Paul Blackburn

We liked the house because, apart from its being old and spacious (in a day when old houses go down for a profitable auction of their construction materials), it kept the memories of great-grandparents, our paternal grandfather, our parents and the whole of childhood.

Irene and I got used to staying in the house by ourselves, which was crazy, eight people could have lived in that place and not have gotten in each other's way. We rose at seven in the morning and got the cleaning done, and about eleven I left Irene to finish off whatever rooms and went to the kitchen. We lunched at noon precisely; then there was nothing left to do but a few dirty plates. It was pleasant to take lunch and commune with the great hollow, silent house, and it was enough for us just to keep it clean. We ended up thinking, at times, that that was what had kept us from marrying. Irene turned down two suitors for no particular reason, and María Esther went and died on me before we could manage to get engaged. We were easing into our forties with the unvoiced concept that the quiet, simple marriage of sister and brother was the indispensable end to a line established in this house by our grandparents. We would die here someday, obscure and distant cousins would inherit the place, have it torn down, sell the bricks and get rich on the building plot; or more justly and better yet, we would topple it ourselves before it was too late.

Irene never bothered anyone. Once the morning housework was finished, she spent the rest of the day on the sofa in her bedroom, knitting. I couldn't tell you why she knitted so much; I think women knit when they discover that it's a fat excuse to do nothing at all. But Irene was not like that, she always knitted necessities, sweaters for winter, socks for me, handy morning robes and bedjackets for herself. Sometimes she would do a jacket, then unravel it the next moment because there was something that didn't please her; it was pleasant to see a pile of tangled wool in her knitting basket fighting a losing battle for a few hours to retain its shape. Saturdays I went downtown to buy wool; Irene had faith in my good taste, was pleased with the colors and never a skein[1] had to be returned. I took advantage of

---

1. **skein** (skayn): coiled length of thread or yarn.

these trips to make the rounds of the bookstores, uselessly asking if they had anything new in French literature. Nothing worthwhile had arrived in Argentina since 1939.

But it's the house I want to talk about, the house and Irene, I'm not very important. I wonder what Irene would have done without her knitting. One can reread a book, but once a pullover is finished you can't do it over again, it's some kind of disgrace. One day I found that the drawer at the bottom of the chiffonier,² replete with mothballs, was filled with shawls, white, green, lilac. Stacked amid a great smell of camphor³—it was like a shop; I didn't have the nerve to ask her what she planned to do with them. We didn't have to earn our living, there was plenty coming in from the farms each month, even piling up. But Irene was only interested in the knitting and showed a wonderful dexterity, and for me the hours slipped away watching her, her hands like silver sea-urchins, needles flashing, and one or two knitting baskets on the floor, the balls of yarn jumping about. It was lovely.

How not to remember the layout of that house. The dining room, a living room with tapestries, the library and three large bedrooms in the section most recessed, the one that faced toward Rodríguez Peña.⁴ Only a corridor with its massive oak door separated that part from the front wing, where there was a bath, the kitchen, our bedrooms and the hall. One entered the house through a vestibule⁵ with enameled tiles, and a wrought-iron grated door opened onto the living room. You had to come in through the vestibule and open the gate to go into the living room; the doors to our bedrooms were on either side of this, and opposite it was the corridor leading to the back section; going down the passage, one swung open the oak door beyond which was the other part of the house; or just before the door, one could turn to the left and go down a narrower passageway which led to the kitchen and the bath. When the door was open, you became aware of the size of the house; when it was closed, you had the impression of an apartment, like the ones they build today, with barely enough room to move around in. Irene and I always lived in this part of the house and hardly ever went beyond the oak door except to do the cleaning. Incredible how much dust collected on the furniture. It may be Buenos Aires is a clean city, but she owes it to her population and nothing else. There's too much dust in the air, the slightest breeze and it's back on the marble console tops and in the diamond patterns of the tooled-leather desk set. It's a lot of work to get it off with a feather duster; the motes rise and hang in the air, and settle again a minute later on the pianos and the furniture.

I'll always have a clear memory of it because it happened so simply and without fuss. Irene was knitting in her bedroom, it was eight at night, and I suddenly decided to put the water up for *mate*.⁶ I went down the corridor as far as the oak door, which was ajar, then turned into the hall toward the kitchen, when I heard something in the library or the dining room. The sound came through muted and indistinct, a chair being knocked over onto the carpet or the muffled buzzing of a conversation. At the same time or a second later, I heard it at the end of the passage which led from those two rooms toward the door. I hurled myself against the door before it was too late and shut it, leaned on it with the

---

2. **chiffonier** (shihf uh NIHR): high, narrow chest of drawers, with or without a mirror.
3. **camphor:** chemical used as an insect repellent.
4. **Rodríguez Peña:** street in Buenos Aires, Argentina.
5. **vestibule:** small entrance hall.

6. ***mate*** (MAH tay): tealike beverage made from dried leaves of a South American evergreen tree.

weight of my body; luckily, the key was on our side; moreover, I ran the great bolt into place, just to be safe.

I went down to the kitchen, heated the kettle, and when I got back with the tray of *mate*, I told Irene:

"I had to shut the door to the passage. They've taken over the back part."

She let her knitting fall and looked at me with her tired, serious eyes.

"You're sure?"

I nodded.

"In that case," she said, picking up her needles again, "we'll have to live on this side."

I sipped at the *mate* very carefully, but she took her time starting her work again. I remember it was a grey vest she was knitting. I liked that vest.

The first few days were painful, since we'd both left so many things in the part that had been taken over. My collection of French literature, for example, was still in the library. Irene had left several folios of stationery and a pair of slippers that she used a lot in the winter. I missed my briar pipe, and Irene, I think, regretted the loss of an ancient bottle of Hesperidin.[7] It happened repeatedly (but only in the first few days) that we would close some drawer or cabinet and look at one another sadly.

"It's not here."

One thing more among the many lost on the other side of the house.

But there were advantages, too. The cleaning was so much simplified that, even when we got up late, nine thirty for instance, by eleven we were sitting around with our arms folded. Irene got into the habit of coming to the kitchen with me to help get lunch. We thought about it and decided on this: while I prepared the lunch, Irene would cook up dishes that could be eaten cold in the evening. We were happy with the arrangement because it was always such a bother to have to leave our bedrooms in the evening and start to cook. Now we made do with the table in Irene's room and platters of cold supper.

Since it left her more time for knitting, Irene was content. I was a little lost without my books, but so as not to inflict myself on my sister, I set about reordering papa's stamp collection; that killed some time. We amused ourselves sufficiently, each with his own thing, almost always getting together in Irene's bedroom, which was the more comfortable. Every once in a while, Irene might say:

"Look at this pattern I just figured out, doesn't it look like clover?"

After a bit it was I, pushing a small square of paper in front of her so that she could see the excellence of some stamp or another from Eupen-et-Malmédy.[8] We were fine, and little by little we stopped thinking. You can live without thinking.

(Whenever Irene talked in her sleep, I woke up immediately and stayed awake. I never could get used to this voice from a statue or a parrot, a voice that came out of the dreams, not from a throat. Irene said that in my sleep I flailed about enormously and shook the blankets off. We had the living room between us, but at night you could hear everything in the house. We heard each other breathing, coughing, could even feel each other reaching for the light switch when, as happened frequently, neither of us could fall asleep.

Aside from our nocturnal rumblings, everything was quiet in the house. During the day

---

7. **Hesperidin** (hehs PEHR ih dihn): liquid made from the rinds of citrus fruits and used for various medicinal purposes.

8. **Eupen-et-Malmédy** (uh PEHN ay MAHL may dee): district in eastern Belgium.

there were the household sounds, the metallic click of knitting needles, the rustle of stamp-album pages turning. The oak door was massive, I think I said that. In the kitchen or the bath, which adjoined the part that was taken over, we managed to talk loudly, or Irene sang lullabies. In a kitchen there's always too much noise, the plates and glasses, for there to be interruptions from other sounds. We seldom allowed ourselves silence there, but when we went back to our rooms or to the living room, then the house grew quiet, half-lit, we ended by stepping around more slowly so as not to disturb one another. I think it was because of this that I woke up irremediably and at once when Irene began to talk in her sleep.)

Except for the consequences, it's nearly a matter of repeating the same scene over again. I was thirsty that night, and before we went to sleep, I told Irene that I was going to the kitchen for a glass of water. From the door of the bedroom (she was knitting) I heard the noise in the kitchen; if not the kitchen, then the bath, the passage off at that angle dulled the sound. Irene noticed how brusquely I had paused, and came up beside me without a word. We stood listening to the noises, growing more and more sure that they were on our side of the oak door, if not the kitchen then the bath, or in the hall itself at the turn, almost next to us.

We didn't wait to look at one another. I took Irene's arm and forced her to run with me to the wrought-iron door, not waiting to look back. You could hear the noises, still muffled but louder, just behind us. I slammed the grating and we stopped in the vestibule. Now there was nothing to be heard.

"They've taken over our section," Irene said. The knitting had reeled off from her hands and the yarn ran back toward the door and disappeared under it. When she saw that the balls of yarn were on the other side, she dropped the knitting without looking at it.

"Did you have time to bring anything?" I asked hopelessly.

"No, nothing."

We had what we had on. I remembered fifteen thousand pesos in the wardrobe in my bedroom. Too late now. I still had my wrist watch on and saw that it was 11 P.M. I took Irene around the waist (I think she was crying) and that was how we went into the street. Before we left, I felt terrible; I locked the front door up tight and tossed the key down the sewer. It wouldn't do to have some poor devil decide to go in and rob the house, at that hour and with the house taken over.

# Juan José Arreola

**c. 1918–2001** (Mexico)

## Meet the Writer

The Mexican writer **Juan José Arreola** (hwahn hoh SAY ahr ree OHL ah) was never one to follow literary trends. He wrote "non-realistic," or fantastic, fiction at a time when Mexican writers were expected to write about political, national concerns; he focused on short fiction at a time when the novel was the preferred literary form in Mexico and other parts of Latin America; and he created odd, quirky little stories to explore serious subjects at a time when it was almost unthinkable to approach important issues with anything other than solemn realism. Nevertheless, he was a distinguished contributor to Mexican writing who remains a strong influence on many writers.

Arreola was born in Ciudad Guzmán, Mexico. One of fourteen children, he had to leave school at an early age to help support his family. He worked at many different jobs before discovering his real interests: acting and writing. Arreola studied acting in Mexico City and spent a year in France working as an extra for the Comédie Française, France's national theater. He then returned to Mexico City to work as an editor. His first stories were published in the early 1940s in the magazine *Pan*, which he later co-edited.

## Background

Although he experimented with many genres, Arreola is best known for his short fiction, including the satirical *Bestiaro*, in which he used animal characters to poke fun at human traits, and the collection *Confabulario*, which contains his most famous story, "The Switchman." Arreola's inventiveness extended to the title itself: He invented the word *Confabulario*, which suggests a collection of fables.

Characterized by a sense of the absurd, Arreola's prose defies traditional literary categories. Many of the stories in this collection lack conventional plot structure and character development; instead, Arreola sketches out a bizarre or fantastical situation and leaves the reader to wonder, "What does it all mean?"

**Before You Read** The narrator of this story hopes to escape his troubles for a while at the movies. Arriving late, he sits down next to a "distinguished" stranger who seems to have a special interest in the movie's plot: the story of a man who makes a pact with the devil. Soon, the impoverished narrator finds himself seriously considering whether endless wealth might be worth the cost of one's soul. Does he make the right decision?

# A Pact with the Devil

## Juan José Arreola
*translated by* George D. Schade

Although I hurried and broke into a run to get to the movie, the film had already started. In the dark hall I tried to find a seat. I sat down next to a distinguished looking man.

"Excuse me," I said to him, "but could you tell me briefly what has happened on the screen?"

"Yes. Daniel Brown, whom you see up there, has made a pact with the Devil."

"Thank you. Now I want to know what the conditions of the pact are. Could you explain them to me?"

"With pleasure. The Devil commits himself to making Daniel Brown rich for seven years. In exchange for his soul, naturally."

"Just seven?"

"The contract can't be renewed. Daniel Brown signed it with a little blood not long ago."

With this information I was able to fill in the film's plot. It was sufficient but I wanted to know something more. The helpful stranger seemed to be a man of judgment. While Daniel Brown was putting a large quantity of gold coins in his pocket, I asked him, "In your opinion, which of the two has compromised himself more?"

"The Devil—"

"How is that?" I replied in surprise.

"Daniel Brown's soul, believe me, wasn't worth much at the moment when he surrendered it."

"Then the Devil—"

"Is going to come out on the short end of the deal, because Daniel shows how greedy he is for money, you see."

Indeed, Brown was spending money hand over fist. His simple country soul was dazzled. With reproachful eyes my neighbor added, "Wait until you get to the seventh year pretty soon."

I shivered. I was sorry for Daniel Brown. I couldn't help asking, "Excuse me, but haven't you ever been poor?"

My neighbor's profile, blurred in the darkness, smiled weakly. He took his eyes from the screen where Daniel Brown was beginning to feel remorse and said without looking at me, "Do you know, I don't know what poverty is."

"If that's the case—"

"On the other hand, I know very well what seven years of being rich can accomplish."

I made an effort to understand what those years might be like, and I saw Paulina's image, smiling, in a new dress and surrounded by pretty things. This image led to other thoughts: "You said a while back that Daniel Brown's soul was worthless. How do you explain then that the Devil has given him so much?"

"That poor boy's soul can improve; remorse can make it grow," answered my neighbor philosophically, then adding maliciously, "The Devil will not have wasted his time then."

"And if Daniel repents?"

My interlocutor seemed disgusted by my pity. His mouth opened as if to speak, but there came out only a little guttural sound. I insisted: "Because Daniel Brown could repent and then—"

"It wouldn't be the first time things have gone badly for the Devil. Some men have slipped out of his hands in spite of the contract—"

"Really, that's not very honest," I said, without realizing.

"What did you say?"

"If the Devil keeps his word, all the more reason for the man to keep his," I said in explanation.

"For example—" and my neighbor made a significant pause.

"Take Daniel Brown," I answered. "He adores his wife. Look at the house he bought her. He has given his soul for love and he should keep his word."

My companion was quite disconcerted by this reasoning.

"Pardon me," he said, "a minute ago you were taking Daniel's part."

"I'm still on his side. But he should keep his word."

"Would you?"

I couldn't answer. On the screen Daniel Brown was in a gloomy state. Riches were not enough to make him forget his simple country life. His house was big and luxurious, but strangely sad. The finery and the jewels were not becoming to his wife. She seemed so changed.

The years sped by and the money poured rapidly from Daniel's hand just like seeds in former years during planting time, but now, instead of plants, sadness and remorse were growing.

I made an effort and said, "Daniel should keep his word. I would too. There's nothing worse than poverty. He has sacrificed himself for his wife and the rest doesn't matter."

"You are right. You understand because you have a wife too, don't you?"

"I would give anything so that Paulina could have everything she needed."

"Your soul?"

We were speaking in low voices. Nonetheless, the people near us seemed to be annoyed. Several times they had asked us to be quiet. My friend, who seemed very much interested in the conversation, said to me, "Why don't we go out into the lobby? We could see the film later."

I couldn't refuse and we went out. For the last time I looked at the screen: in tears Daniel Brown was confessing to his wife the pact he had made with the Devil.

I continued to think about Paulina, the desperate straits in which we lived, the poverty that she supported without complaint and which made me suffer the more. I certainly did not understand Daniel Brown, who was weeping with his pockets full of money.

"Are you poor?"

We had crossed the lobby and were entering a narrow, dark, slightly humid-smelling corridor. When he had pushed aside the worn curtain, my companion asked me again, "Are you poor?"

"Today," I answered, "the movie costs less than usual, but if you knew what a time I had deciding to spend that money. Paulina insisted that I come; arguing with her about it made me late."

"Then what do you think of a man who solves his problems like Daniel did?"

"It's worth considering. My affairs are in bad shape. People no longer dress with much care, but go about in any fashion. They mend their own clothes, clean and fix them up time and

*Diablo Rojo Mask* (mxm044)
Michoacan, Mexico, c. 1990
Wood painted with oil paints, 7 ½" w. × 5 ½" d. × 8 ½" h.
Anthony H. Fisher, Indigo Arts Gallery, Philadelphia

again. Paulina herself knows how to get along very well. By ingenious combinations, changes here and there, she improvises clothes; it's certainly true that she hasn't had a new dress for ages."

"I promise to be your customer," said my companion, taking pity on me. "This week I'll order a couple of suits."

"Thanks. Paulina was right when she asked me to go to the movies. When she finds this out she will be very happy."

"I could do something else for you," my new customer added, "for example, I'd like to propose a business deal to make a purchase from you—"

"Excuse me," I answered rapidly, "but we have nothing else to sell; the last things were some of Paulina's earrings—"

"Think carefully now, there is perhaps something that you are forgetting—"

I pretended to think a little. There was a pause which my benefactor interrupted with a strange voice, "Reflect now, look, there's Daniel Brown. A little before you arrived, he had nothing to sell, and nevertheless—"

Suddenly I noticed the man's face had grown sharper. The red light from a sign on the wall gave a strange, fiery brilliance to his eyes. He observed my anxiety and said with a clear, distinct voice, "My dear sir, after all this, an introduction seems unnecessary. I am completely at your service."

Instinctively I made the sign of the cross with my right hand, but without taking it from my pocket. This seemed to take away the sign's virtue, because the Devil, fixing a knot in his tie, said calmly, "Here in my wallet I have a document which—"

I was perplexed. I saw Paulina again standing at the threshold of our house in her faded, but becoming, dress just as she was when I left, her face bent and smiling, her hand hidden in the middle pocket of her apron.

Our fortune was in my hands, I thought. This evening we had scarcely anything to eat. Tomorrow there would be food on the table, and dresses and jewels and a big, beautiful house. My soul?

While I was plunged in such thoughts, the Devil had taken out a crackling sheet of paper and in his hand a needle shone. "I would give anything so that you could have everything you wanted," I had said to my wife many times. Anything. My soul? Now the one who could put my words into effect stood before me. But I kept on meditating. I was doubtful. I felt rather dizzy. Brusquely, I decided: "It's a deal. But on one condition."

The Devil, who was already trying to prick my arm with his needle, seemed disconcerted. "What condition?"

"I'd like to see the end of the film," I answered.

"But what do you care what happens to that imbecile of a Daniel Brown? Besides, that's only a story. Don't bother, just go ahead and sign. The document is all in order, all we need is your signature, here on this line."

The Devil's voice was insinuating, clever, like the sound of gold coins. He added, "If you like, I can give you an advance right now."

He seemed to be an astute businessman. I replied decisively, "I must see the end of the film. Then I'll sign."

"You give me your word?"

"Yes."

We went back to the movie. I couldn't see at all, but my guide knew how to find the two seats easily. On the screen, that is, in the life of Daniel Brown, a surprising change had come about, due to some unfathomable mysterious circumstances. There was a poor and shabby house in the country. Brown's wife was preparing the meal near the fire. It was twilight and Daniel was returning from the fields with his hoe on his shoulder. Tired, sweaty, his coarse clothing all dusty and dirty, he seemed happy, nonetheless. Leaning on his hoe, he stood near the door. His wife approached, smiling. The two of them watched the day that was gently ending, promising the peace and rest of night. Daniel looked gently at his wife, and then casting his eye over the clean poverty of the house, he asked, "But don't you miss our former riches? Don't you really need all the things we had?"

The woman answered slowly, "Your soul is worth more than all that, Daniel—"

The country fellow's face lit up, his smile seemed to spread, to fill the whole house, to come from the landscape. Music swelled up from that smile and seemed to dissolve the images little by little. Then, from Daniel Brown's poor and happy home three white letters appeared, getting bigger and bigger, until they filled the whole screen.

Suddenly I found myself without knowing how among the departing crowd, pushing, trampling, violently opening a path. Someone caught me by the arm and tried to hold me back. With a wrench I broke loose and soon was out on the street.

It was night. I started to walk fast, going faster and faster until I finally began running. I didn't turn around once or stop until I got home. I entered as calmly as I could and closed the door carefully.

Paulina was waiting for me. Throwing her arms around my neck, she said, "You seem upset."

"No, it's nothing—"

"Didn't you like the film?"

"Yes, but—"

I was upset. I put my hands over my eyes. Paulina stood there looking at me, and then, without being able to stop she began to laugh and laugh happily at me. I was confused and bewildered, not knowing what to say. In the middle of her laughter she exclaimed with a gay reproach, "Is it possible that you fell asleep?"

These words calmed me down. They pointed a way out for me. As if ashamed, I answered, "It's true. I did fall asleep."

And then, as an excuse, I added, "I had a dream and I'm going to tell it to you."

When I finished my story, Paulina told me that it was the best film that I could have told her about. She seemed happy and laughed a great deal. Nevertheless, when I was going to bed I saw how with a little bit of ashes she cautiously traced the sign of the cross over the threshold of our house.

# Sergio Vodánovic

**1926–2001** (Chile)

## Meet the Writer

One of Chile's leading playwrights was born not in Latin America but in the European nation of Croatia (formerly a part of Yugoslavia). **Sergio Vodánovic** (SAYR hee oh voh DAHN oh veek) spent most of his life in Santiago, Chile, although he studied in the United States at Yale and Columbia universities. At various times, Vodánovic worked as a journalist, a university professor, and a screenwriter; however, he is best known for his contributions to Chilean theater. By the 1960s he was well respected in the theatrical world, both as a playwright and as a critic. Two of his early works, *Deja que los perros ladren* (1959) and *Viña: Three Beach Plays* (1964), are still performed in Chile, the United States, and other countries. Vodánovic died in Santiago, Chile, in 2001.

## Background

The years between 1940 and 1970 were a highly significant, experimental time for Chilean theater. Playwrights began to turn away from classical and folkloric themes toward a stark examination of the problems of contemporary Chilean society. Politically and socially, tensions were growing in Chile among a wealthy, powerful aristocracy, an impoverished working class, and a middle class that largely bore the burden of economic instability. An old order—in which social class determined one's opportunities and fate—was falling apart, and the outcome was unknown.

Vodánovic's plays of the 1960s reflect the intense anxiety and uncertainty of this time. In the three one-act plays of *Viña,* an ocean resort in central Chile named Viña del Mar is the backdrop for three different scenes of social struggle. Seemingly ordinary encounters between people take bizarre turns that expose both the brutality and the absurdity of a vanishing way of life. With simple props and twists of circumstance, Vodánovic reveals the fragility of the aristocratic order and shows us how artificial the distinctions between "upper" and "lower" class are. At the same time, he hints at the potential dangers of the new way: a growing attitude of ruthless materialism among people of all classes.

**Before You Read** *"The White Uniform" is the first one-act play in Vodánovic's* Viña: Three Beach Plays. *In this play a haughty upper-class woman is vacationing at Viña del Mar with her spoiled little boy and her young maid. The mistress's casual cruelty toward her maid may seem shameful to us now, but it would not have been unusual at the time the play was written. As you read, think about the play's title and the importance of the white uniform. What does it represent to the maid, to her employer, and to society at large? In the end, what answer does it provide to the upper-class woman's sense of natural superiority and entitlement?*

# The White Uniform

## Sergio Vodánovic
*translated by* William I. Oliver

*Setting: the beach. Upstage, a canvas tent. Seated on the sand before the tent are the Lady and the Maid. The Lady is wearing a terry cloth robe over her swimming suit. She sports the tan of a long summer. The Maid wears a white uniform.*

THE LADY (*calling out to her little boy, who is supposedly playing by the seashore*): Alfie! Alfie! Don't throw sand at the little girl! Why don't you go swimming! The water's wonderful! No, Alfie, no! Don't kick the little girl's sand castle! Play with her . . . that's right, Alfie, play with her . . .
THE MAID: He's such a little . . . fighter.
THE LADY: He's his father's boy . . . there's just no holding him. He has such a strong personality, comes to him through his father, his grandfather, his grandmother, too . . . especially his grandmother!
THE MAID: Do you expect the master to come tomorrow?
THE LADY (*shrugging her shoulders*): I don't know. Here it is March already, all my friends have gone back, but Alfred keeps me couped up here at the beach. Tells me he wants the kid to get everything he can out of the vacation. If you ask me, he's the one who's getting everything out of it. (*She takes off her robe and stretches out to sunbathe.*) Sunshine! Sunshine! Three months of sunbathing. I'm drunk with sunshine. (*She looks intently at the Maid.*) How do you keep from burning?
THE MAID: I stay indoors . . .
THE LADY: Oh, well, what did you expect? You came for work and not a vacation. You're paid well enough, aren't you?
The Maid: Yes, Ma'am. I was just answering your question.
(*The Lady stretches out once more and resumes her sunbathing. The Maid picks up a bag and takes out an illustrated true romance magazine and begins to read.*)
THE LADY: What are you up to?
THE MAID: I'm reading.
THE LADY: Did you buy it?
THE MAID: Yes, Ma'am.
THE LADY: Well, you're not so bad off then if you can afford magazines, eh? (*The Maid makes no answer and resumes reading.*) Go on! Go right ahead! Go right on reading! Let Alfie blow up! Let him drown!

THE MAID: But he's playing with the little girl . . .
THE LADY: I didn't bring you to the beach to read. I brought you to watch Alfie. (*The Maid gets up and starts to go toward Alfie.*) Wait! You can see him well enough from here. I want you to stay with me, but keep an eye on him just the same. You know, I like coming to the beach with you.
THE MAID: Why?
THE LADY: Oh, I don't know. I suppose for the same reason that I like coming in the car even though the house is only a couple of blocks away. (*She chuckles.*) I like them to see the car. It never fails. Every day someone stops to look at it and admire it. Of course you wouldn't notice a thing like that. I suppose you're used to it . . . in a way. Tell me, what is your home like?
THE MAID: I have none.
THE LADY: Well, you weren't born a maid, were you? You must have been brought up somewhere. You must have had parents. Are you from the country?
THE MAID: Yes.
THE LADY: And you wanted to come to the city, eh?
THE MAID: No. I liked it in the country.
THE LADY: Then why did you come to the city?
THE MAID: My father couldn't make enough . . .
THE LADY: Oh, don't give me that. I know all about tenant farmers. They've got it easy. They're given their own little lots to farm, there's free food, they even have some left over to sell. Some of them even have their own little cows. Did your father have cows?
THE MAID: Yes, Ma'am. One.
THE LADY: You see? What more could you want? Alfie! Don't go so far out. Be careful of the waves. How old are you?
THE MAID: I?
THE LADY: I am talking to you, aren't I? You'd think I was crazy, talking to myself.

**The White Uniform** 125

THE MAID: I'm almost twenty-one . . .
THE LADY: Twenty-one! I was married when I was twenty-one. Have you ever thought of marriage? (*The Maid looks down but makes no answer.*) Oh, that was stupid of me. Why should you want to get married? You've got everything you want with us. Plenty of food, a good room, clean uniforms. Get married and then see what you've got. A raft of kids, that's what.
THE MAID (*almost to herself*): I would like to get married . . .
THE LADY: Oh, don't be silly! That's the kind of idea you get from those cheap true romance magazines. Just remember, there are no more true blue knights in shining armor. What matters is not the shine of the armor but the shine of their money. I used to be furious when my parents would turn down my boyfriends because they didn't have any money. But then along came Alfred with his industries and factories and estates, and my folks didn't rest until they married me to him. I didn't like him. He was fat and he had a disgusting habit of clearing his nose and then swallowing. But then, later, in marriage you get used to everything. And I suppose you have to come to the conclusion that it all adds up to the same thing, except for money. I have money, and you don't. That's the real difference between us. Don't you think?
THE MAID: Yes, but . . .
THE LADY: Oh! So you do agree? Well, it's a lie! There's something even more important than money: one's class. You can't buy that! Either one has it or one doesn't. Alfred has no class. I do. I could live in a pigsty, but people would still know that I was someone. Not just anyone, but someone! You see that, don't you?
THE MAID: Yes, Ma'am.
THE LADY: Here . . . let me look at your magazine. (*The Maid hands it to her and The Lady thumbs through it. She spies something and laughs out loud.*) So this is what you read?
THE MAID: I like it, Ma'am.
THE LADY: Ridiculous! Utterly ridiculous! Look at that clod dressed up in a dinner jacket. He looks as comfortable as a hippopotamus in a girdle. (*She returns to the magazine.*) And he's supposed to be . . . the Count of Lamarquina! The Count of Lamarquina! Well, let's see what the Count has to say for himself. (*She reads aloud.*) "My child, I will never permit you to marry Robert. He is a commoner. Remember that the blood that flows in our veins is blue." And this must be the Count's daughter?
THE MAID: Yes. She's called Mary. She's a simple girl, good and sweet. And she's in love with Robert, the gardener at the castle. The Count won't hear of it. But you know, I have a hunch it's going to come out all right in the end. Because in last month's issue, Robert told Mary that he had never known his parents, and when the parents aren't known you can just bet that they are rich and aristocratic, and that they lost their son when he was little or that the little boy was kidnapped . . .
THE LADY: And you believe all this?
THE MAID: It's nice, Ma'am.
THE LADY: What is?
THE MAID: That things like that should happen. That suddenly one day you discover you're someone else, that instead of being poor, you're rich, that instead of being no one, you're someone.
THE LADY: That just can't be, don't you understand? Look at the daughter. Did you ever see me wearing hoops like that? Have you ever seen one of my friends wearing something as ghastly as that? And her hair, it's hideous. Don't you realize that a woman like that can't be an aristocrat? Let's see . . . is there a picture of the gardener?
THE MAID: Yes. Near the end. (*She takes the magazine, finds the place, and shows it to The Lady, who laughs.*)
THE LADY: And so this is the man you think may

be the son of an aristocrat? With a nose like that? And hair like that? Look . . . just suppose that tomorrow someone should kidnap little Alfie. Do you think that for one minute he will lose his air of distinction?
THE MAID: Oh look, Ma'am! Alfie just kicked over the little girl's sand castle.
THE LADY: You see? He's only four years old, and already he knows how to give orders, how not to care about other people. You can't learn that. It's in the blood.
THE MAID (*getting up*): I'll fetch him.
THE LADY: Let him be. He's having fun. (*The Maid unbuttons the top button of her uniform and fans herself.*)
 Are you hot?
THE MAID: The sun has a sting to it.
THE LADY: Don't you have a swimming suit?
THE MAID: No.
THE LADY: Haven't you ever worn one?
THE MAID: Oh, yes.
THE LADY: When?
THE MAID: Before hiring out. Sometimes, on Sundays, we'd take a trip to the beach in a truck that belonged to the uncle of one of my friends.
THE LADY: You'd go swimming.
THE MAID: On the big beach at Cartagena. We'd rent swimming suits and spend the whole day at the beach. We'd take our lunch and . . .
THE LADY (*amused*): Rent swimming suits?
THE MAID: Yes. There's a woman who rents them right there at the beach.
THE LADY: We had to stop once at Cartagena for gas, so we got out to look at the beach. It was really funny! And those rented swimming suits, some of them were so big they hung like bags all over! Others were so tight, the women's breasts were nearly popping out! What kind did you rent? A loose one or a tight one? (*The Maid looks down, embarrassed.*) It must be strange seeing the world from a rented swimming suit or a cheap dress or a maid's uniform the way you do. Something like that must happen to those people who pose for the photographs in your magazine. When they put on a dinner jacket or an evening gown, I'm sure they must change inside. They must see people differently. When I put on my first pair of stockings the whole world changed. Everyone seemed different. I was different. And the only real change was that I had put on a pair of nylons. Tell me, what does the world look like from behind that white uniform?
THE MAID (*timidly*): The same . . . the sand has the same color . . . the clouds are the same . . . I guess . . .
THE LADY: But it isn't . . . it's different. Look. Wearing this swimming suit and this robe, stretched out here on the sand, I know that I am in "my place," all this belongs to me. On the other hand, you, dressed as a maid, you know the beach is not your place, and that alone must make you see things differently.
THE MAID: Maybe.
THE LADY: Listen. I've got an idea. Give me your uniform.
THE MAID: What?
THE LADY: Give me your uniform.
THE MAID: But . . . why?
THE LADY: Because I want to see what the world looks like. I want to see the beach from behind a white uniform.
THE MAID: Now?
THE LADY: Yes. Now.
THE MAID: But it's just that . . . I . . . I don't have anything on underneath.
THE LADY (*tossing her the terry cloth robe*): Here. Put this on.
THE MAID: But I'm only wearing panties . . .
THE LADY: The robe is long enough to cover you. At any rate, you'll be showing off less than you did in those suits you rented at the beach at Cartagena. (*She gets up and pulls The Maid to her feet.*) Come on, into the tent and change. (*She forces The Maid into the tent and later throws the*

robe into the tent. She walks downstage and calls to her son.) Alfie, why don't you go into the water? Wade a little . . . get your feet wet. Don't be such a stick-in-the-mud! That's right! Isn't the water nice? (*She returns to the tent and calls inside.*) Are you ready? (*She goes inside the tent.*)

(*After a moment, The Maid emerges, dressed in the terry cloth robe. She has put her hair up, and her whole manner has shifted from that of the timid girl we have seen. Delicately, she stretches out on the sand. The Lady comes out buttoning the top buttons of the uniform. She moves to sit down in front of The Maid, stops, turns back, and takes a place behind her.*)

THE LADY: No. Not in front. At the beach a maid always sits behind her mistress.

(*She sits down and looks about in all directions, highly amused. Delicately, The Maid changes her position. The Lady picks up The Maid's magazine and begins to read it. She smiles ironically, but the smile disappears as she becomes interested in the story. Quite naturally, The Maid reaches for the beach bag that belongs to The Lady. She takes out a bottle of suntan lotion and begins to apply it to her legs. The Lady sees her, starts to scold her, but cannot manage to say more than*) What are you doing?

(*The Maid does not answer. The Lady decides to continue reading, but from time to time she spies upon The Maid to see what she is doing. The Maid is now sitting up examining her fingernails.*) Why are you looking at your nails?

THE MAID: I need a manicure.

THE LADY: I never saw you look at your nails before.

THE MAID: It hadn't occurred to me.

THE LADY: The uniform is hot.

THE MAID: They're of the best. They never wear out.

THE LADY: I know. I bought them.

THE MAID: It fits you.

THE LADY (*amused*): You look pretty good yourself. (*She laughs*). It would be quite easy to mistake you. You'd catch the eye of any young boy. Oh, now wouldn't that be a wonderful story!

THE MAID: Alfie's going out a little far. Go look after him.

THE LADY (*jumping up and moving downstage rapidly*): Alfie! Alfie! Don't go in so far. Be careful of a wave. (*She catches herself suddenly and turns back to The Maid.*) Why didn't you go?

THE MAID: Where?

THE LADY: Why did you tell me to look after Alfie?

THE MAID (*quite naturally*): You're wearing the uniform.

THE LADY: So you like the game, eh?

(*The little boy playing nearby throws a rubber ball that rolls to the feet of The Maid. She looks at it but makes no movement to pick it up. The Maid looks at The Lady. Instinctively The Lady moves to the ball, picks it up, and throws it back in the direction from which it came. The Maid looks in The Lady's beach bag and finds a pair of sun glasses, which she then puts on.*)

(*Annoyed*) Who gave you permission to put on my glasses?

THE MAID: How does the beach look from behind a white uniform?

THE LADY: Oh, it's cute. And you? How do you see the beach now?

THE MAID: Oh, it's cute.

THE LADY: How so?

THE MAID: Because there's no difference.

THE LADY: What do you mean?

THE MAID: You with your white uniform are the maid; and I with this robe and these glasses am the lady.

THE LADY: How dare you? What do you mean?

THE MAID: Would you have bothered to pick up that ball if you hadn't been in a uniform?

THE LADY: We're playing a game.

THE MAID: When?

THE LADY: Now.

THE MAID: And before?

THE LADY: Before?
THE MAID: Yes. When I was dressed in the uniform . . .
THE LADY: That's no game. That's reality.
THE MAID: Why?
THE LADY: Because it is.
THE MAID: It's just a game . . . a longer game . . . like cops and robbers. Some have to be cops, and some have to be robbers.
THE LADY (*angry*): You're becoming insulting!
THE MAID: You're the one who's insulting. Don't scream at me.
THE LADY: What do you mean? How dare you talk to me like that?
THE MAID: And you don't talk to me that way, do you?
THE LADY: I?
THE MAID: Yes.
THE LADY: That's it! The game is over!
THE MAID: I like it!
THE LADY: It's finished! (*She advances threateningly on The Maid.*)
THE MAID (*quite definitely*): You get back!
THE LADY (*stopping short*): Are you going crazy?
THE MAID: I'm going to be a lady.
THE LADY: I can fire you whenever I want.
   (*The Maid bursts into laughter as though she had just heard the funniest joke in the world.*)
What are you laughing at?
THE MAID (*still laughing*): It's so ridiculous!
THE LADY: What? What's so ridiculous?
THE MAID: That you should fire me . . . dressed like that! Who ever heard of a maid firing her mistress?
THE LADY: Take off those glasses! Take off that robe! They're mine!
THE MAID: Go look after the baby!
THE LADY: The game is over. Give me back my things or I'll take them away from you.
THE MAID: Be careful! We're not alone on this beach.
THE LADY: And what of it? You think because I've got this white uniform on, they're not going to know the lady from the maid?
THE MAID (*calmly*): Don't raise your voice to me.
   (*The Lady lunges at The Maid and tries to tear the robe off of her.*)
THE LADY (*while struggling*): You slut! I'll show you who I am! I'll show you! I'll have you thrown in jail!
   (*The fight draws a group of bathers. The group is composed of two young men, one young girl, and an older gentleman of distinguished appearance. Before they can interfere, The Maid gets the better of things, pinning The Lady on the sand. The Lady continues screaming such things as:* "You tramp," "Wait till my husband gets hold of you," "I'm going to put you in jail," "This is what happens when one tries to be . . ." *et cetera.*)
FIRST YOUNG MAN: What's the matter?
SECOND YOUNG MAN: Is she having a fit?
YOUNG GIRL: She's gone crazy.
FIRST YOUNG MAN: They do sometimes. They're so lonely.
SECOND YOUNG MAN: May we help you?
THE MAID: Yes. Please. There's a comfort station nearby . . .
SECOND YOUNG MAN: I'm a medical student. I'll give her an injection so that she'll sleep for awhile.
THE LADY: Idiots! I am the mistress! My name is Patricia Hurtado. My husband is Alfred Jiménez, the politician . . .
YOUNG LADY (*laughing*): She thinks she's a lady.
FIRST YOUNG MAN: She's crazy.
SECOND YOUNG MAN: It's just an attack of hysterics.
FIRST YOUNG MAN: Let's take her away.
THE MAID: If you don't mind, I'll stay here . . . I have to look after my little boy. He's over there, wading.
THE LADY: That's a lie! We exchanged costumes just as a game! She isn't even wearing a swimming suit. All she's got on under that robe are panties! Look at her!

SECOND YOUNG MAN (*with a gesture to the first young man*): Come on! You take her feet and I'll take her arms.
YOUNG GIRL: Oh, how funny! She says the lady's naked . . .

(*The young men take The Lady and carry her off in spite of her kicking and screaming.*)

THE LADY: Let go of me! I'm not crazy! She's the one! Call Alfie! He'll recognize me!

(*The two men carry The Lady off. The Maid stretches out on the sand as though nothing had happened, making herself ready for a long sunbath.*)

THE GENTLEMAN: I suppose it's a sign of our times. No one seems to notice it, but every time you turn around something like this happens.
THE MAID: Like this?
THE GENTLEMAN: They're destroying the established order of things. Old people want to be young; young people want to be old; poor people want to be rich; and the rich people want to be poor. My daughter-in-law goes every week to weave with some women of the working classes. And she likes it! (*Slight pause.*) Has she been with you for a long time?
THE MAID: Who?
THE GENTLEMAN: Your maid.
THE MAID (*trying to remember*): A little over a year.
THE GENTLEMAN: And this is the way she pays you back! Pretending to pass for a lady! As though one couldn't tell a lady at a glance! (*Pause.*) Do you know why these things happen?
THE MAID (*very interested*): Why?
THE GENTLEMAN (*with a mysterious air*): Communism . . .
THE MAID: Ah!
THE GENTLEMAN (*reassuringly*): But we don't need to worry. Everything is back to normal again. Order is always re-established in the end. That's a fact. There's no doubt about it. And now if you'll excuse me, I must take my constitutional. I've got to, at my age. The circulation, you know. And don't you worry, the sun is the best sedative. At your service, ma'am. (*He starts out but then turns back.*) And don't be too hard on your maid. After all, maybe we're to blame for some of it . . . you can't tell.

(*The Distinguished Gentleman leaves. The Maid stretches out on her back to sunbathe. Suddenly she remembers Alfie, and sits up. She looks at Alfie tenderly and calls to him.*)

THE MAID: Alfie . . . if you're going to sit on that rock, be careful, you might get a scratch. Yes, that's better, run on the sand. That's right, Alfie, that's right, my son . . .

(*The Maid stares tenderly and maternally at Alfie as he plays on the seashore. The lights dim and the curtain closes.*)

# Gabriel García Márquez

b. 1928–   (Colombia)

## Meet the Writer

**Gabriel García Márquez** (gah bree EHL gahr SEE ah MAHR kehs), Latin America's best-known living writer, likes to joke that he was famous for a long time but nobody knew it. Although he had begun publishing short fiction in the late 1940s, it was his masterpiece *One Hundred Years of Solitude* that catapulted him into the international spotlight in 1970 and earned him the Nobel Prize for literature in 1982. This novel also brought worldwide attention to magic realism, a technique that combines incredible events with realistic details and relates them all in a matter-of-fact tone.

Although García Márquez acknowledges the influence of such writers as Franz Kafka and William Faulkner, he attributes the main source of his inspiration to his childhood in his grandparents' large, rambling house in the small village of Aracataca, just off Colombia's northern Caribbean coast. In Aracataca, thinly disguised as the village Macondo in much of his fiction, García Márquez's grandmother often told tales of ghosts, spirits, and dead ancestors. As she filled his imagination with supernatural elements, she narrated her stories in a matter-of-fact way, as if there were nothing extraordinary about the bizarre events she was recounting. His grandfather, whom García Márquez has called "the most important figure of my life," told him stories about the past, including his adventures in at least two civil wars. Thus, from an early age the future author of magic realist fiction had already begun to accept the possibility of fantastic events within the course of everyday life.

When García Márquez was almost eight years old, he moved to Sucre, a river port. Later, he won a scholarship to a high school near Bogotá, the capital of Colombia, and eventually enrolled in law school, which he disliked and never finished. From the time he was eighteen, he had known he wanted to be a journalist and a writer. His first job, in 1950, was with a newspaper, and eventually he became a well-known journalist.

During his years as a journalist, García Márquez began to write fiction.

He published stories locally and joined an informal group of writers who vigorously discussed the works of European and American authors as varied as James Joyce, Virginia Woolf, Ernest Hemingway, Sophocles, Kafka, and Faulkner. His first novella, or short novel, was called *Leaf Storm*, set in the fictional village of Macondo. Published in 1952, it was followed in 1961 by a second novella, *No One Writes to the Colonel*, and then by his first novel, *In Evil Hour*, in 1962.

According to García Márquez, the entire first chapter of *One Hundred Years of Solitude* suddenly came to him as he was driving from Mexico City to Acapulco in 1965. Warning his wife not to bother him about anything, especially about money, he worked feverishly for eighteen months to complete his novel. He says that his wife then asked him, "Did you really finish it? We owe twelve thousand dollars." She had borrowed from friends for a year and a half. But García Márquez's gamble paid off. *One Hundred Years of Solitude*, an epic masterpiece that tells the comic and tragic saga of seven generations of Macondo's founding family, has been one of the most popular novels in modern times, consistently making its way onto "Top 100 Books of the Twentieth Century" lists.

## Background

García Márquez says that he is amused by the fact that he is most often praised for his imagination, since everything he writes has a basis in reality. For example, *Love in the Time of Cholera* (1988) is based on his parents' relationship, and *The General in His Labyrinth* (1990) is a fictional novel about Simón Bolívar, "the liberator of South America." His novel *Of Love and Other Demons* (1996) was inspired by a true story he covered as a journalist. Assigned to watch the opening of a burial tomb at a convent in Cartagena, Colombia, García Márquez saw the remains of a young girl with twenty-two meters—over 72 feet—of hair attached to her skull. The girl, who had been buried for two centuries, became the basis for the novel's main character, Sierva Maria.

Latin American folklore, family tales of ghosts and ancestors, bizarre events of everyday life: All of these elements combine in García Márquez's fiction to create worlds in which the impossible is not only possible but expected. Comparing himself with the American writer William Faulkner, García Márquez says, "Faulkner was surprised at certain things that happened in life. . . . In Mexico, surrealism runs through the streets. Surrealism comes from the reality of Latin America."

Alejo Carpentier, the Cuban novelist who first used the term *lo real maravilloso* (magic realism), believed that by incorporating magic, myth, imagination, and religion into literature, we can expand our rigid concept of "reality."

**Before You Read** *García Márquez subtitles this story "A Tale for Children," even though it contains allusions to Greek mythology, Homer's* Odyssey, *and Latin American cultural history. As you read, think about the characteristics "The Handsomest Drowned Man in the World" shares with children's stories or fairy tales. In what sense must the reader become a child to accept and respond to the magic realism of the story?*

# The Handsomest Drowned Man in the World

## Gabriel García Márquez
*translated by* Gregory Rabassa

*A Tale for Children*

The first children who saw the dark and slinky bulge approaching through the sea let themselves think it was an enemy ship. Then they saw it had no flags or masts and they thought it was a whale. But when it was washed up on the beach, they removed the clumps of seaweed, the jellyfish tentacles, and the remains of fish and flotsam, and only then did they see that it was a drowned man.

They had been playing with him all afternoon, burying him in the sand and digging him up again, when someone chanced to see them and spread the alarm in the village. The men who carried him to the nearest house noticed that he weighed more than any dead man they had ever known, almost as much as a horse, and they said to each other that maybe he'd been floating too long and the water had got into his bones. When they laid him on the floor they said he'd been taller than all other men because there was barely enough room for him in the house, but they thought that maybe the ability to keep on growing after death was part of the nature of certain drowned men. He had the smell of the sea about him and only his shape gave one to suppose that it was the corpse of a human being, because the skin was covered with a crust of mud and scales.

They did not even have to clean off his face to know that the dead man was a stranger. The village was made up of only twenty-odd wooden houses that had stone courtyards with no flowers and which were spread about on the end of a desertlike cape. There was so little land that mothers always went about with the fear that the wind would carry off their children and the few dead that the years had caused among them had to be thrown off the cliffs. But the sea was calm and bountiful and all the men fit into seven boats. So when they found the drowned man they simply had to look at one another to see that they were all there.

That night they did not go out to work at sea. While the men went to find out if anyone was missing in neighboring villages, the women stayed behind to care for the drowned man. They took the mud off with grass swabs, they removed the underwater stones entangled in his hair, and they scraped the crust off with tools used for scaling fish. As they were doing that they noticed that the vegetation on him came from faraway oceans and deep water and that his clothes were in tatters, as if he had sailed through labyrinths of coral. They noticed too that he bore his death with pride, for he did not have the lonely look of other drowned men who came out of the sea or that haggard, needy look of men who drowned in rivers. But only when they finished cleaning him off did they become aware of the kind of man he was and it left them breathless. Not only was he the tallest, strongest, most virile, and best-built man they had ever seen, but even though they were looking at him there was no room for him in their imagination.

They could not find a bed in the village large enough to lay him on nor was there a table solid enough to use for his wake. The tallest men's holiday pants would not fit him, not the fattest ones' Sunday shirts, nor the shoes of the one with the biggest feet. Fascinated by his huge size and his beauty, the women then decided to make him some pants from a large piece of sail and a shirt from some bridal brabant linen[1] so that he could continue through his death with dignity. As they sewed, sitting in a circle and gazing at the corpse between stitches, it seemed to them that the wind had never been so steady nor the sea so restless as on that night and they supposed that the change had something to do with the dead man. They thought that if that magnificent man had lived in the village, his house would have had the widest doors, the highest ceiling, and the strongest floor, his bedstead would have been made from a midship frame held together by iron bolts, and his wife would have been the happiest woman. They thought that he would have had so much authority that he could have drawn fish out of the sea simply by calling their names and that he would have put so much work into his land that springs would have burst forth from among the rocks so that he would have been able to plant flowers on the cliffs. They secretly compared him to their own men, thinking that for all their lives theirs were incapable of doing what he could do in one night, and they ended up dismissing them deep in their hearts as the weakest, meanest, and most useless creatures on earth. They were wandering through that maze of fantasy when the oldest woman, who as the oldest had looked upon the drowned man with more compassion than passion, sighed:

"He has the face of someone called Esteban."[2]

It was true. Most of them had only to take another look at him to see that he could not have any other name. The more stubborn among them, who were the youngest, still lived for a few hours with the illusion that when they put his clothes on and he lay among the flowers in patent leather shoes his name might be Lautaro.[3] But it was a vain illusion. There had not been enough canvas, the poorly cut and worse sewn pants were too tight, and the hidden strength of his heart popped the buttons on his shirt. After midnight the whistling of the wind died down and the sea fell into its Wednesday drowsiness.[4] The silence put an end to any last doubts: he was Esteban. The women who had dressed him, who had combed his hair, had cut his nails and shaved him were unable to hold back a shudder of pity when they had to resign themselves to his

---

1. **brabant** (bruh BANT) **linen:** linen from Brabant, a province of Belgium known for its fine lace and cloth.
2. **Esteban** (ehs TEH bahn): Spanish equivalent of "Stephen." In Christian tradition, Stephen was the first martyr. He was stoned to death because of his beliefs.
3. **Lautaro** (low TAH roh): leader of the Araucanian Indian people who resisted the Spanish conquistadors entering their land, in what is now Chile, during the sixteenth century. Lautaro is now seen as a Chilean national hero.
4. **Wednesday drowsiness** (and later **Wednesday meat** and **Wednesday dead body**): *Wednesday* is a colloquial expression for "tiresome." In many fishing villages, fishers returned from the sea on Thursday, so by Wednesday, people began running out of food and were generally weary and bored.

*Carpa en Movimiento*, by Sergió Bustamante
©www.sergiobustamante.com.mx

being dragged along the ground. It was then that they understood how unhappy he must have been with that huge body since it bothered him even after death. They could see him in life, condemned to going through doors sideways, cracking his head on crossbeams, remaining on his feet during visits, not knowing what to do with his soft, pink, sea lion hands while the lady of the house looked for her most resistant chair and begged him, frightened to death, sit here, Esteban, please, and he, leaning against the wall, smiling, don't bother, ma'am, I'm fine where I am, his heels raw and his back roasted from having done the same thing so many times whenever he paid a visit, don't bother, ma'am, I'm fine where I am, just to avoid the embarrassment of breaking up the chair, and never knowing perhaps that the ones who said don't go, Esteban, at least wait till the coffee's ready, were the ones who later on would whisper the big boob finally left, how nice, the handsome fool has gone. That was what the women were thinking beside the body a little before dawn. Later, when they covered his face with a handkerchief so that the light would not bother him, he looked so forever dead, so defenseless, so much like their men that the first furrows of tears opened in their hearts. It was one of the younger ones who began the weeping. The others, coming to, went from sighs to wails, and the more they sobbed the more they felt like weeping, because the drowned man was becoming all the more Esteban for them, and so they wept so much, for he was the most destitute, most peaceful, and most obliging man on earth, poor Esteban. So when the men returned with the news that the drowned man was not from the neighboring villages either, the women felt an opening of jubilation in the midst of their tears.

"Praise the Lord," they sighed, "he's ours!"

The men thought the fuss was only womanish frivolity. Fatigued because of the difficult nighttime inquiries, all they wanted was to get rid of the bother of the newcomer once and for all before the sun grew strong on that arid, windless day. They improvised a litter with the remains of foremasts and gaffs,[5] tying it together with rigging so that it would bear the weight of the body until they reached the cliffs. They wanted to tie the anchor from a cargo ship to him so that he would sink easily into the deepest waves, where fish are blind and divers die of nostalgia, and bad currents would not bring him back to shore, as had happened with other bodies. But the more they hurried, the more the women thought of ways to waste time. They walked about like startled hens, pecking with the sea charms[6] on their breasts, some interfering on one side to put a scapular[7] of the good wind on the drowned man, some on the other side to put a wrist compass on him, and after a great deal of *get away from there, woman, stay out of the way, look, you almost made me fall on top of the dead man,* the men began to feel mistrust in their livers and started grumbling about why so many main-altar decorations for a stranger, because no matter how many nails and holy-water jars he had on him, the sharks would chew him all the same, but the women kept piling on their junk relics, running back and forth, stumbling, while they released in sighs what they did not in tears, so that the men finally exploded with *since when has there ever been such a fuss over a drifting corpse, a drowned nobody, a piece of cold Wednesday meat.* One of the women, mortified by so much lack of care, then removed the handkerchief from the dead man's face and the men were left breathless too.

He was Esteban. It was not necessary to repeat it for them to recognize him. If they had been told Sir Walter Raleigh, even they might have been impressed with his gringo accent, the macaw[8] on his shoulder, his cannibal-killing blunderbuss,[9] but there could be only one Esteban in the world and there he was, stretched out like a sperm whale, shoeless, wearing the pants of an undersized child, and with those stony nails that had to be cut with a knife. They only had to take the handkerchief off his face to see that he was ashamed, that it was not his fault that he was so big or so heavy or so handsome, and if he had known that this was going to happen, he would have looked for a more discreet place to drown in, seriously, *I even would have tied the anchor off a galleon around my neck and staggered off a cliff like someone who doesn't like things in order not to be upsetting people now with this Wednesday dead body, as you people say, in order not to be bothering anyone with this filthy piece of cold meat that doesn't have anything to do with me.* There was so much truth in his manner that even the most mistrustful men, the ones who felt the bitterness of endless nights at sea fearing that their women would tire of dreaming about them and begin to dream of drowned men, even they and others who were harder still shuddered in the marrow of their bones at Esteban's sincerity.

---

5. **gaffs:** poles used on a boat to support a sail.
6. **sea charms:** magic charms worn to protect from dangers at sea.
7. **scapular** (SKAP yuh luhr): pair of small cloth squares showing images of saints, joined by string and worn under clothing by some Roman Catholics as a symbol of religious devotion.
8. **macaw:** large, brightly colored parrot.
9. **blunderbuss:** now-outdated gun with a short, flaring muzzle.

That was how they came to hold the most splendid funeral they could conceive of for an abandoned drowned man. Some women who had gone to get flowers in the neighboring villages returned with other women who could not believe what they had been told, and those women went back for more flowers when they saw the dead man, and they brought more and more until there were so many flowers and so many people that it was hard to walk about. At the final moment it pained them to return him to the waters as an orphan and they chose a father and mother from among the best people, and aunts and uncles and cousins, so that through him all the inhabitants of the village became kinsmen. Some sailors who heard the weeping from a distance went off course and people heard of one who had himself tied to the mainmast, remembering ancient fables about sirens.[10] While they fought for the privilege of carrying him on their shoulders along the steep escarpment by the cliffs, men and women became aware for the first time of the desolation of their streets, the dryness of their courtyards, the narrowness of their dreams as they faced the splendor and beauty of their drowned man. They let him go without an anchor so that he could come back if he wished and whenever he wished, and they all held their breath for the fraction of centuries the body took to fall into the abyss. They did not need to look at one another to realize that they were no longer all present, that they would never be. But they also knew that everything would be different from then on, that their houses would have wider doors, higher ceilings, and stronger floors so that Esteban's memory could go everywhere without bumping into beams and so that no one in the future would dare whisper the big boob finally died, too bad, the handsome fool has finally died, because they were going to paint their house fronts gay colors to make Esteban's memory eternal and they were going to break their backs digging for springs among the stones and planting flowers on the cliffs so that in future years at dawn the passengers on great liners would awaken, suffocated by the smell of gardens on the high seas, and the captain would have to come down from the bridge in his dress uniform, with his astrolabe,[11] his polestar, and his row of war medals and, pointing to the promontory of roses on the horizon, he would say in fourteen languages, look there, where the wind is so peaceful now that it's gone to sleep beneath the beds, over there, where the sun's so bright that the sunflowers don't know which way to turn, yes, over there, that's Esteban's village.

---

10. **sirens:** In Greek mythology, the sirens are sea maidens whose seductive singing lures men to wreck their boats on coastal rocks. Odysseus, hero of Homer's *Odyssey*, fills his crew's ears with wax so that they can pass the sirens safely. Odysseus, however, has his crew tie him to the ship's mast so that he can listen to the sirens' songs without plunging into the sea.

11. **astrolabe** (AS troh layb): instrument used to find a star's altitude and to help navigators determine their position at sea.

# Luisa Valenzuela
**b. 1938–** (Argentina)

## Meet the Writer

Perhaps one of the most significant facts about **Luisa Valenzuela** (loo EE sah vah lehn soo AY lah) is that she is from Argentina. Before Valenzuela was born, the real power in Argentina had rested with the landed aristocracy—members of the upper class who owned property. The aristocracy viewed democracy as dangerous because it allowed the uneducated masses to have a voice in government. Beginning in 1943, Argentina began to experience one upheaval in government after another, and the leaders of these upheavals, or coups, were all from the military.

Valenzuela, like other writers and artists who lived during these chaotic and dangerous years, worked under the threat of censorship, suppression, even violence. One of her most famous stories, "The Censors," captures the oppressive tone of these times. Valenzuela believed it was her duty to bear witness to the military government's atrocities. She says that she wrote her stories in cafes, "reacting to the generalized paranoia and fear, and thinking that I should write in illegible handwriting so that no one could read over my shoulder." Valenzuela admitted, "Writing about it, unfortunately, does not stop the horror." In 1979, she published a novel and short stories collected in a book called *Strange Things Happen Here*, which exposed the evils of the fascist dictatorship with unflinching honesty. Her novel *The Lizard's Tail,* published in 1983, explored power, politics, and magic.

## Background

Though her work is characterized by the surreal and the absurd, Valenzuela does not accept the label of "magic realism"; she does not want to be limited by labels and styles. Her works explore difficult topics—violence, political oppression, gender discrimination—in a style that is all her own, full of uncanny imagery, ambiguity, and irony.

**Before You Read**  You might have read stories in which a character enters an imaginary world. Alice falls down a rabbit hole and finds herself in a topsy-turvy Wonderland. The children in C. S. Lewis's Narnia stories walk through a wardrobe to find themselves in a world ruled by a wicked witch who has turned everything to winter. A tornado lands a girl named Dorothy in a strange land called Oz. Sometimes the other worlds are examples of wish fulfillment; sometimes the worlds are nightmarish. Usually the people who find themselves in these imaginary worlds learn something valuable, not only about the imaginary world but also about their own worlds—even about themselves. In this story a writer finds a world "up among the eagles." What kind of world does she find there? What does she learn?

# Up Among the Eagles

## Luisa Valenzuela
*translated by* Margaret Sayers Peden

You'll find what I tell you hard to believe, for who knows anything, nowadays, about life in the country? And life here on the mountains, up among the eagles. You get used to it. Oh yes, I can tell you. I who never knew anything but the city, just look at me now, the color of clay, carrying my pails of water from the public fountain. Water for myself and water for others. I've been doing it to eke out a living ever since the day I made the foolish mistake of climbing the path that borders the cliff. I climbed up and, looking down at the green dot of the valley below, I decided to stay here forever. It wasn't that I was afraid; I was just being prudent, as they say: threatening cliffs, beyond imagination—impossible even to consider returning. Everything I owned I traded for food: my shoes, my wristwatch, my key holder with all the keys (I wouldn't be needing them anymore), a ballpoint pen that was almost out of ink.

The only thing of any value I kept is my Polaroid camera; no one wanted it. Up here they don't believe in preserving images, just the opposite: every day they strive to create new images only for the moment. Often they get together to tell each other about the improbable images they've been envisioning. They sit in a circle in the dark on the dirt floor of their communal hut and concentrate on making the vision appear. One day, out of nothing, they materialized a tapestry of nonexistent colors and ineffable design, but they decided that it was just a pale reflection of their mental image, and so they broke the circle to return the tapestry to the nothingness from which it had come.

They are strange creatures; normally they speak a language whose meaning they themselves have forgotten. They communicate by interpreting pauses, intonations, facial expressions, and sighs. I tried to learn this language of silences, but it seems I don't have the right accent. At any rate, they speak our language when they refer to trivial matters, the daily needs that have nothing to do with their images. Even so, some words are missing from their vocabulary. For example, they have no word for yesterday or for tomorrow, before or after, or for one of these days. Here everything is now, and always. An unsatisfactory imitation of eternity like the tapestry I have already mentioned. Have mentioned? Oh yes, I'm the only one to use that verb tense; I may also be the only one who has any notion of conjugation. A vice left over from the world down there, knowledge I can't barter because no one wants it.

Will you trade me some beans for a notion of time, I went around asking the women in the marketplace, but they shook their heads emphatically. (A notion of time? They looked at me with mistrust. A way of moving on a different plane? That has nothing to do with the knowledge they are after.)

Who dares to speak of the passage of time to the inhabitants of this high place where everything endures? Even their bodies endure. Death neither decays nor obliterates them; it merely stops them in their path. Then the others, with exquisite delicacy—a delicacy I've seen them employ in connection with newly dropped kids or with certain mushrooms—carry the corpse beyond the rushing stream with the precise symmetry arrange it in the exact place it occupied in life. With infinite patience they have succeeded in creating, on the other side, a second town that obliterates time, an unmoving reflection of themselves that gives them a feeling of security because it is mummified, unmodifiable.

They only allow themselves changes in respect to the images. They grow, yes, they grow up and reach adulthood with only a suspicion of old age, remaining more or less the same until they die. In contrast, I discover with horror that I have a sprinkling of gray hairs, and wrinkles are lining my face; premature, of course, but who could keep her youth in this dry air, beneath such intense skies? What will become of me when they discover that time passes in my life, and is leaving its marks?

They are absorbed in other concerns, in trying to retain visions of what appear to be jeweled palaces and splendors unknown on this earth. They roam around latitudes of awe while all I can do—and very infrequently and with extreme stealth at that—is take a photo of myself. I am down to earth despite living in this elevated land floating among clouds. And they say the altitude deranges those of us who come from sea level. But it is my belief, my fear, that they are the ones who are deranged; it's something ancestral, inexplicable, especially when they are squatting on their haunches, as they almost always are, looking inward in contemplation. I'm always looking outward, I search every road, almost nonchalantly nourishing my fear. They watch me go by carrying water, the pole across my shoulders and the two pails dangling from it, and I would like to think they do not suspect my fear. This fear has two faces, not at all like the one that kept me from returning after I had climbed the mountain. No, this is not a simple fear; it reflects others, and becomes voracious.

On the other hand, I am here, now. That now grows and changes and expands with time and, if I am lucky, will continue to evolve. I do not want them to be aware of this evolving, as I have already said, and even less do I want to be like them, exempt from time. For what would become of me if I kept this face forever, as if surprised between two ages? I think about the mummies in the mirror city, oh yes, absolutely, only mummies are unchanged by time. Time does not pass for the dead, I told myself one day, and on a different day (because I, if not they, am very careful to relate question to calendar) I added: nor does it pass for those who have no concept of death. Death is a milestone.

The inhabitants here, with their language of silence, could teach me the secrets of the immobility that so closely resembles immortality, but I am not eager to learn them. Life is a movement toward death; to remain static is to be already dead.

*Sit here, little lady, nice and quiet here with us* is

*The India of Tehuantepec,* by Alfredo Ramos Martinez

one of the few things they consent to say to me in my own language, and I shake my head energetically (one more way of insuring movement), and as soon as I am out of their sight, I begin to run like crazy along the neglected paths. More often than not I run up, not down, but either way, I don't want to get too far from the town, I don't want to stumble into the still city and find myself face-to-face with the mummies.

The secret city. I don't know its exact location but I know everything about it—or maybe I only suspect. I know it has to be identical to this humble little clump of huts where we live, a faithful replica with the exact same number of bodies, for when one of them dies the oldest mummy is thrown into the void. It's noisy in the secret city. The noise announces its proximity, but it also serves a more basic purpose: scraps of tin, of every size and shape, hang from the rafters of the huts to scare away the buzzards. They are all that moves in the secret city, those scraps of tin to scare away the vultures, the only thing that moves or makes a sound. On certain limpid nights the wind carries the sound to where the living dwell, and on those nights they gather in the plaza, and dance.

They dance, but oh so slowly, almost without moving their feet, more as if they were undulating, submerged in the dense waters of sound. This happens only rarely, and when it does I feel an almost uncontrollable urge to join in the dance—the need to dance soaks into my bones, sways me—but I resist with all my strength. I am afraid that nothing could be more paralyzing than to yield to this music that comes from death. So that I won't be paralyzed I don't dance. I don't dance and I don't share the visions.

I have not witnessed a birth since I have been here. I know they couple, but they don't reproduce. They do nothing to avoid it, simply the stillness of the air prevents it. As for me, at this point I don't even go near men. It must be admitted that men don't come near me either, and there must be a reason, considering how often and how closely they approach almost anything else. Something in my expression must drive them away, but I've no way of knowing what it is. There are no mirrors here. No reflections. Water is either glaucous[1] or torrential white. I despair. And every so often in the privacy of my cave, sparingly and with extreme caution, I take a new photo of myself.

I do this when I can't stand things any longer, when I have an overwhelming need to know about myself, and then no fear, no caution, can hold me back. One problem is that I am running out of film. In addition, I know perfectly well that if they find my photographs, if they place them in chronological order, two things can happen: they will either abominate or adore me. And neither possibility is to be desired. There are no alternatives. If they put the photos in order and draw the conclusions; if they see that when I arrived, my face was smoother, my hair brighter, my bearing more alert; if they discover the marks of time they will know that I have not controlled time even for a moment. And so if they find I am growing older, they won't want me among them, and they will stone me out of town, and I will have to face the terrifying cliffs.

I don't even want to think about the other possibility: that they will adore me because I have so efficiently, and so concretely, materialized these images of myself. Then I would be like stone to them, like a statue forever captive and contained.

Either of these two lapidary[2] prospects should provide sufficient reason to restrain my suicidal impulse to take yet another photograph, but it doesn't. Each time, I succumb, hoping against hope that they will not be alerted by the glare of the flash. Sometimes I choose stormy nights; perhaps I conjure up the lightning with my pale simulacrum.[3] At other times I seek the protective radiance of dawn, which at this altitude can be incendiary.

I make elaborate preparations for each of my secret snapshots, preparations charged with hope and danger, that is, with life. The resulting picture does not always please me but the emotion of seeing myself—no matter how horrible or haggard I appear—is immeasurable. This is I, changing in a static world that imitates death. And I feel safe. Then I am able to stop and speak of simple things with the women in the market and even understand their silences, and answer them. I can live a little longer without love, without anyone's touch.

Until another relapse, a new photo. And this will be the last. On a day with the sound of death,

---

1. **glaucous** (GLAW kuhs): bluish- or yellowish-green.

2. **lapidary** (LAP uh dehr ee).: having to do with stones.
3. **simulacrum** (sihm yoo LAY kruhm): likeness of something.

when the minimal activities of the town have come to a halt and they have all congregated to dance in the marketplace. That deliberate dancing that is like praying with their feet, a quiet prayer. They will never admit it, but I suspect that they count to themselves, that their dance is an intricate web of steps like knitting, one up, two backward, one to the right. All to the tinkling of the far-off tin scraps: the wind in the house of the dead. A day like any other; a very special day for them because of the sound that they would call music, were they interested in making such distinctions. But all that interests them is the dance, or believing they are dancing, or thinking of the dance, which is the same thing. To the pulse of the sound that floods over us, whose origins I cannot locate though I know it comes from the city of the dead.

They do not call to me; they don't even see me. It's as if I didn't exist. Maybe they're right, maybe I don't exist, maybe I am my own invention, or a peculiar materialization of an image they have evoked. That sound is joyful, and yet the most mournful ever heard. I seem to be alive, and yet . . .

I hide in my cave trying not to think, trying not to hear the tinkling; I don't know where it comes from, but I fear where it may lead me. With the hope of setting these fears to rest, I begin my preparations for the last photo: a desperate attempt to recover my being. To return to myself, which is all I have.

Anxiously, I wait for the perfect moment, while outside, darkness is weaving its blackest threads. Suddenly, an unexpected radiance causes me to trip the shutter before I am ready. No photograph emerges, only a dark rectangle that gradually reveals the blurred image of a stone wall. And that's all. I have no more film so I may as well throw away the camera. A cause for weeping were it not for the fact the radiance is not fading. A cause for uneasiness, then, because when I peer out I see that the blazing light is originating from the very place I wanted not to know about, from the very heart of the sound, from a peak just below us. And the radiance comes from millions of glittering scraps of tin in the moonlight. The city of the dead.

Spontaneously, I set forth with all my stupid photos, responding to an impulse that responds, perhaps, to a summons from the sonorous[4] radiance. They are calling me from down there, over to the left, and I answer, and at first I run along the treacherous path and when the path ends I continue on. I stumble, I climb and descend, I trip and hurt myself; to avoid hurtling into the ravine I try to imitate the goats, leaping across the rocks; I lose my footing, I slip and slide, I try to check my fall, thorns rake my skin and at the same time hold me back. Rashly I pull ahead and it is imperative I must reach the city of the dead and leave my face to the mummies. I will place my successive faces on the mummies and then at last I'll be free to go down without fearing stone for I'll take my last photo with me and I am myself in that photo and I am stone.

---

4. **sonorous** (suh NAWR uhs): full, deep, and rich, said of sound.

# Isabel Allende
## b. 1942– (Chile/United States)

## Meet the Writer

**Isabel Allende** (EE sah behl ah YEHN day) may be the best-known woman writer from Latin America. Her first novel, published in 1982, *The House of the Spirits* (*La casa de los espíritus*), became a bestseller, was widely translated, and was filmed in English in 1993.

Allende, the daughter of a Chilean diplomat, was born in Lima, Peru. She is related to Salvador Allende, who became president of Chile in 1970. He was assassinated in 1973, and the new military government brought about widespread political change. Isabel Allende was dismissed from her job, and increasing repression and fear led to her exile in 1975.

Allende's fame rests chiefly on *The House of the Spirits*, a story of several generations of a family set against the political conflicts of an unnamed Latin American country. The book began when Allende, in exile, was writing a letter to her grandfather, who had remained in Chile. She wanted to prove to him that she had forgotten nothing. In Chile the book was censored at first, and copies had to be smuggled into the country.

Allende has written other novels and short stories, as well as plays and stories for children. She now lives in California, where she teaches and continues to write.

## Background

What sets Allende apart from many writers of Latin American fiction is her feminine perspective. Allende does not accept the stereotype of women as submissive; she sends a message of "female empowerment." In 1989, Allende published *The Stories of Eva Luna* (*Cuentos de Eva Luna*), which is about a twentieth-century Scheherazade who tells stories in order to survive. The stories combine elements of fantasy, satire, and magic realism. Among the stories that deal with strong women is "Two Words" ("Dos palabras"). In this story, a girl survives by selling words. Through the power of language, she is able to enchant a man and transform him.

**Before You Read**  *The power of words is one of the oldest motifs, or recurring thematic elements, in the literature of virtually all world cultures. Many myths and folk tales deal with the "power of the word"; the underlying idea of such tales is that "to name a thing is to have power over that thing." In many cultures, "naming" is associated with magical powers; a baby's name may be chosen in order to protect it from jealous gods or bad luck.*

*Allende, herself a master storyteller, writes about characters who are skillful at using words. Note how this story develops the theme that language has the power to change people. Which characters exhibit changes that were brought about by words—and what are those changes? What does Allende leave unanswered at the end of this story?*

# Two Words

## Isabel Allende
*translated by* Margaret Sayers Peden

She went by the name of Belisa Crepusculario, not because she had been baptized with that name or given it by her mother, but because she herself had searched until she found the poetry of "beauty" and "twilight" and cloaked herself in it. She made her living selling words. She journeyed through the country from the high cold mountains to the burning coasts, stopping at fairs and in markets where she set up four poles covered by a canvas awning under which she took refuge from the sun and rain to minister to her customers. She did not have to peddle her merchandise because from having wandered far and near, everyone knew who she was. Some people waited for her from one year to the next, and when she appeared in the village with her bundle beneath her arm, they would form a line in front of her stall. Her prices were fair. For five *centavos* she delivered verses from memory; for seven she improved the quality of dreams; for nine she wrote love letters; for twelve she invented insults for irreconcilable enemies. She also sold stories, not fantasies but long, true stories she recited at one telling, never skipping a word. This is how she carried the news from one town to another. People paid her to add a line or two: our son was born; so and so died; our children got married; the crops burned in the field. Wherever she went a small crowd gathered around to listen as she began to speak, and that was how they learned about each other's doings, about distant relatives, about what was going on in the civil war. To anyone who paid her fifty centavos in trade, she gave the gift of a secret word to drive away melancholy. It was not the same word for everyone, naturally, because that would have been collective deceit. Each person received his or her own word, with the assurance that no one else would use it that way in this universe or the beyond.

Belisa Crepusculario had been born into a family so poor they did not even have names to give their children. She came into the world and grew up in an inhospitable land where some years the rains became avalanches of water that bore everything away before them and others when not a drop fell from the sky and the sun swelled to fill the horizon and the world became a desert. Until she was twelve, Belisa had no occupation or virtue other than having withstood hunger and the exhaustion of centuries. During one interminable drought, it fell to her to bury four younger brothers and sisters; when she realized that her turn was next, she decided to set out across the plains in the direction of the sea, in hopes that she might trick death along the way. The land was eroded, split with deep cracks, strewn with rocks, fossils of trees and thorny bushes, and skeletons of animals bleached by the sun. From time to time she ran into families who, like her, were heading south, following the mirage of water. Some had begun the march carrying their belongings on their back or in small carts, but they could barely move their own bones, and after a while they had to abandon their possessions. They dragged themselves along painfully, their skin turned to lizard hide and their eyes burned by the reverberating glare. Belisa greeted them with a wave as she passed, but she did not stop, because she had no strength to waste in acts of compassion. Many people fell by the wayside, but she was so stubborn that she survived to cross through that hell and at long last reach the first trickles of water, fine, almost invisible threads that fed spindly vegetation and farther down widened into small streams and marshes.

Belisa Crepusculario saved her life and in the process accidentally discovered writing. In a village near the coast, the wind blew a page of newspaper at her feet. She picked up the brittle yellow paper and stood a long while looking at it, unable to determine its purpose, until curiosity overcame her shyness. She walked over to a man who was washing his horse in the muddy pool where she had quenched her thirst.

"What is this?" she asked.

"The sports page of the newspaper," the man replied, concealing his surprise at her ignorance.

The answer astounded the girl, but she did not want to seem rude so she merely inquired about the significance of the fly tracks scattered across the page.

"Those are words, child. Here it says that Fulgencio Barba knocked out El Negro Tiznao in the third round."

That was the day Belisa Crepusculario found out that words make their way in the world without a master, and that anyone with a little cleverness can appropriate them and do business with them. She made a quick assessment of her situation and concluded that aside from becoming a prostitute or working as a servant in the kitchens of the rich there were few occupations she was qualified for. It seemed to her that selling words would be an honorable alternative. From that moment on, she worked at that profession, and was never tempted by any other. At the beginning, she offered her merchandise unaware that words could be written outside of newspapers. When she learned otherwise, she calculated the infinite possibilities of her trade and with her savings paid a priest twenty pesos to teach her to read and write; with her three remaining coins she bought a dictionary. She pored over it from A to Z and then threw it into the sea, because it was not her intention to defraud her customers with packaged words.

One August morning several years later, Belisa Crepusculario was sitting in her tent in the middle of a plaza, surrounded by the uproar of market day, selling legal arguments to an old man who had been trying for sixteen years to get his pension. Suddenly she heard yelling and thudding hoofbeats. She looked up from her writing and saw, first, a cloud of dust, and then a band of horsemen come galloping into the plaza. They were the Colonel's men, sent under orders of El Mulato, a giant known throughout the land for the speed of his knife and his loyalty to his chief. Both the Colonel and El Mulato had spent their lives fighting in the civil war, and their names were ineradicably linked to devastation and calamity. The rebels swept into town like a stampeding herd, wrapped in noise, bathed in sweat, and leaving a hurricane of fear in their trail. Chickens took wing, dogs ran for their lives, women and children scurried out of sight, until the only living soul left in the market was Belisa Crepusculario. She had never seen El Mulato and was surprised to see him walking toward her.

"I'm looking for you," he shouted, pointing his coiled whip at her; even before the words were out, two men rushed her—knocking over her canopy and shattering her inkwell—bound her hand and foot, and threw her like a duffel bag across the rump of El Mulato's mount. Then they thundered off toward the hills.

Hours later, just as Belisa Crepusculario was near death, her heart ground to sand by the pounding of the horse, they stopped, and four strong hands set her down. She tried to stand on her feet and hold her head high, but her strength failed her and she slumped to the ground, sinking into a confused dream. She awakened several hours later to the murmur of night in the camp, but before she had time to sort out the sounds, she opened her eyes and found herself staring into the impatient glare of El Mulato, kneeling beside her.

"Well, woman, at last you've come to," he said. To speed her to her senses, he tipped his canteen and offered her a sip of liquor laced with gunpowder.

She demanded to know the reason for such rough treatment, and El Mulato explained that the Colonel needed her services. He allowed her to splash water on her face, and then led her to the far end of the camp where the most feared man in all the land was lazing in a hammock strung between two trees. She could not see his face, because he lay in the deceptive shadow of the leaves and the indelible shadow of all his years as a bandit, but she imagined from the way his gigantic aide addressed him with such humility that he must have a very menacing expression. She was surprised by the Colonel's voice, as soft and well modulated as a professor's.

"Are you the woman who sells words?" he asked.

"At your service," she stammered, peering into the dark and trying to see him better.

The Colonel stood up, and turned straight toward her. She saw dark skin and the eyes of a ferocious puma, and she knew immediately that she was standing before the loneliest man in the world.

"I want to be President," he announced.

The Colonel was weary of riding across that Godforsaken land, waging useless wars and suffering defeats that no subterfuge could transform into victories. For years he had been sleeping in the open air, bitten by mosquitoes, eating iguanas and snake soup, but those minor inconveniences were not why he wanted to change his destiny. What truly troubled him was the terror he saw in people's eyes. He longed to ride into a town beneath a triumphal arch with bright flags and flowers everywhere; he wanted to be cheered, and be given newly laid eggs and freshly baked bread. Men fled at the sight of him, children trembled, and women miscarried from fright; he had had enough, and so he had decided to become President. El Mulato had suggested that they ride to the capital, gallop up to the Palace and take over the government, the way they had taken so many other things without anyone's permission. The Colonel, however, did not want to be just another tyrant; there had been enough of those before him and, besides, if he did that, he would never win people's hearts. It was his aspiration to win the popular vote in the December elections.

"To do that, I have to talk like a candidate. Can you sell me the words for a speech?" the Colonel asked Belisa Crepusculario.

She had accepted many assignments, but none like this. She did not dare refuse, fearing that El

*La Gitana,* 1920
Louis Kronberg
Oil on canvas
80 × 63.5 inches

Mulato would shoot her between the eyes, or worse still, that the Colonel would burst into tears. There was more to it than that, however; she felt the urge to help him because she felt . . . a powerful desire . . . to clasp him in her arms.

All night and a good part of the following day, Belisa Crepusculario searched her repertory for words adequate for a presidential speech, closely watched by El Mulato. . . . She discarded harsh, cold words, words that were too flowery, words worn from abuse, words that offered improbable promises, untruthful and confusing words, until all she had left were words sure to touch the minds of men and women's intuition. Calling upon the knowledge she had purchased from the priest for twenty pesos, she wrote the speech on a sheet of paper and then signalled El Mulato to untie the rope that bound her ankles to a tree. He led her once more to the Colonel, and again she felt the throbbing anxiety that had seized her when she first saw him. She handed him the paper and waited while he looked at it, holding it gingerly between thumbs and fingertips.

"What . . . does this say?" he asked finally.

"Don't you know how to read?"

"War's what I know," he replied.

She read the speech aloud. She read it three times, so her client could engrave it on his memory. When she finished, she saw the emotion in the faces of the soldiers who had gathered round to listen, and saw that the Colonel's eyes glittered with enthusiasm, convinced that with those words the presidential chair would be his.

"If after they've heard it three times, the boys are still standing there with their mouths hanging open, it must mean the thing's damn good, Colonel," was El Mulato's approval.

"All right, woman. How much do I owe you?" the leader asked.

"One *peso*, Colonel."

"That's not much," he said, opening the purse he wore at his belt, heavy with proceeds from the last foray.

"The *peso* entitles you to a bonus. I'm going to give you two secret words," said Belisa Crepusculario.

"What for?"

She explained that for every fifty *centavos* a client paid, she gave him the gift of a word for his exclusive use. The Colonel shrugged. He had no interest at all in her offer, but he did not want to be impolite to someone who had served him so well. She walked slowly to the leather stool where he was sitting, and bent down to give him her gift. The man . . . heard the terrible whisper of her hair, and a breath of sweet mint murmured into his ear the two secret words that were his alone.

"They are yours, Colonel," she said as she stepped back. "You may use them as much as you please."

El Mulato accompanied Belisa to the roadside, his eyes as entreating as a stray dog's, but when he reached out to touch her, he was stopped by an avalanche of words he had never heard before; believing them to be an irrevocable curse, the flame of his desire was extinguished.

During the months of September, October and November, the Colonel delivered his speech so many times that had it not been crafted from glowing and durable words, it would have turned to ash as he spoke. He travelled up and down and across the country, riding into cities with a triumphal air, stopping in even the most forgotten villages where only the dump heap betrayed a human presence, to convince his fellow citizens to vote for him. While he spoke from a platform erected in the middle of the plaza, El Mulato and his men handed out sweets and painted his name on all the walls in gold frost. No one paid the least attention to those advertising ploys; they were dazzled by the clarity of the Colonel's proposals and the poetic lucidity of his arguments, infected by his powerful wish to right the wrongs of history, happy for the first time in their lives. When the Candidate had finished his speech, his soldiers would fire their pistols into the air and set off firecrackers, and when finally they rode off, they left behind a wake of hope that lingered for days on the air, like the splendid memory of a comet's tail. Soon the Colonel was the favorite. No one had ever witnessed such a phenomenon: a man who surfaced from the civil war, covered with scars and speaking like a professor, a man whose fame spread to every corner of the land and captured the nation's heart. The press focused their attention on him. Newspapermen came from far away to interview him and repeat his phrases, and the number of his followers and enemies continued to grow.

"We're doing great, Colonel," said El Mulato, after twelve successful weeks of campaigning.

But the Candidate did not hear. He was repeating his secret words, as he did more and more obsessively. He said them when he was mellow with nostalgia; he murmured them in his sleep; he carried them with him on horseback; he thought them before delivering his famous speech; and he caught himself savoring them in his leisure time. And every time he thought of those two words, he thought of Belisa Crepusculario, and his senses were inflamed with the memory of . . . the whisper of her hair and her sweet mint breath in his ear, until he began to go around like a sleepwalker, and his men realized that he might die before he ever sat in the presidential chair.

"What's got hold of you, Colonel," El Mulato asked so often that finally one day his chief broke down and told him the source of his befuddlement: those two words that were buried like two daggers in his gut.

"Tell me what they are and maybe they'll lose their magic," his faithful aide suggested.

"I can't tell them, they're for me alone," the Colonel replied.

Saddened by watching his chief decline like a man with a death sentence on his head, El Mulato slung his rifle over his shoulder and set out to find Belisa Crepusculario. He followed her trail through all that vast country, until he found her in a village in the far south, sitting under her tent reciting her rosary of news. He planted himself, straddle-legged, before her, weapon in hand.

"You! You're coming with me," he ordered.

She had been waiting. She picked up her inkwell, folded the canvas of her small stall, arranged her shawl around her shoulders, and without a word took her place behind El Mulato's saddle. They did not exchange so much as a word in all the trip; El Mulato's desire for her had turned into rage, and only his fear of her tongue prevented his cutting her to shreds with his whip. Nor was he inclined to tell her that the Colonel was in a fog, and that a spell whispered into his ear had done what years of battle had not been able to do. Three days later they arrived at the encampment, and immediately, in view of all the troops, El Mulato led his prisoner before the Candidate.

"I brought this witch here so you can give her back her words, Colonel," El Mulato said, pointing the barrel of his rifle at the woman's head. "And then she can give you back your manhood."

The Colonel and Belisa Crepusculario stared at each other, measuring one another from a distance. The men knew then that their leader would never undo the witchcraft of those two accursed words, because the whole world could see the voracious-puma eyes soften as the woman walked to him and took his hand in hers.

# María Elena Llano

b. 1936–   (Cuba)

## Meet the Writer

**María Elena Llano** (mah REE ah  ay LAY nah  YAH noh) was born in Cuba. She has worked as a journalist for the cultural section of Havana's news agency, Latin Press. In addition to her newspaper work, Llano has written for radio and television; she is also a published poet. A volume of her short stories, *La Reja* (*The Plow*), was published in 1966. The story that follows was read aloud on Chicago Public Radio as part of a group from the series *Stories on Stage* called "It Ain't Necessarily So."

## Background

Llano's story "In the Family" is an example of magic realism, a style of writing that is often associated with the modern literature of Latin America. The magic realists combine the fantastic with the realistic, and they relate their stories in a matter-of-fact tone that suggests that this is all perfectly normal. Today, magic realism is probably most strongly associated with the great Colombian writer and Nobel Prize winner Gabriel García Márquez. In one of his most famous, disturbing, and surprisingly humorous stories, "A Very Old Man with Enormous Wings," a tattered old angel falls from the sky one day into a couple's backyard. They keep the angel in their chicken coop and charge the townspeople admission to see him. By the time the old angel flutters his wings and flies away, like some aged vulture, he has miraculously changed the lives of people in the village. Such transformations are common in magic realist stories, which suggests that, in the meeting of two worlds—the ordinary world and the usually unseen world of the fantastic—there is untold power for marvelous changes.

In Llano's story that follows, the narrator tells us in a most matter-of-fact way that the ancestors of her family all live in a mirror in her house. What happens next is unpredictable; it is also comical and very, very strange.

**Before You Read** "Mirror, mirror, on the wall..." Even though the evil queen in "Snow White" expects that her magic mirror—"which can only tell the truth"—will tell her that her own face is the "fairest one of all," the mirror tells her that Snow White is more beautiful. Although what appears in a mirror is "only" a reflection, mirrors are traditionally seen as symbols of truth, since they reflect with clarity the actual person or object before them. Mirrors also suggest another kind of self-reflection: We may judge the rightness of our actions by asking ourselves if we could look into a mirror after doing something that is questionable or could be wrong.

Here is a story about a mirror that contains an entire world of its own. Like mirrors in certain fantasy stories, which often serve as portals to another world, this mirror brings together two worlds: that of the living and of the dead. As you might expect, the mirror in this story changes the lives of the living family members. What truths does this mirror reveal?

# In the Family

## María Elena Llano
*translated by* Beatriz Teleki

When my mother found out that the large mirror in the living-room was inhabited, we all gradually went from disbelief to astonishment, and from this to a state of contemplation, ending up by accepting it as an everyday thing.

The fact that the old, spotted mirror reflected the dear departed in the family was not enough to upset our life style. Following the old saying of "Let the house burn as long as no one sees the smoke," we kept the secret to ourselves since, after all, it was nobody else's business.

At any rate, some time went by before each one of us would feel absolutely comfortable about sitting down in our favourite chair and learning that, in the mirror, that same chair was occupied by somebody else. For example, it could be Aurelia, my grandmother's sister (1939), and even if cousin Natalie would be on my side of the room, across from her would be the almost forgotten Uncle Nicholas (1927). As could have been expected, our departed reflected in the mirror presented the image of a family gathering almost identical to our own, since nothing, absolutely nothing in the living-room—the furniture and its arrangement, the light, etc.—was changed in the mirror. The only difference was that on the other side it was them instead of us.

I don't know about the others, but I sometimes felt that, more than a vision in the mirror, I was watching an old worn-out movie, already clouded. The deceaseds' efforts to copy our gestures were slower, restrained, as if the mirror were not truly showing a direct image but the reflection of some other reflection.

From the very beginning I knew that everything would get more complicated as soon as my cousin Clara got back from vacation. Because of her boldness and determination, Clara had long given me the impression that she had blundered

*Ladies' Tailor* by Remedios Varo
©2006 Artists Rights Society (ARS), New York/VEGAP, Madrid

into our family by mistake. This suspicion had been somewhat bolstered by her being one of the first women dentists in the country. However, the idea that she might have been with us by mistake went away as soon as my cousin hung up her diploma and started to embroider sheets beside my grandmother, aunts and other cousins, waiting for a suitor who actually did show up but was found lacking in one respect or another—nobody ever really found out why.

Once she graduated, Clara became the family oracle,[1] even though she never practised her profession. She would prescribe painkillers and was the arbiter[2] of fashion; she would choose the theatre shows and rule on whether the punch had the right amount of liquor at each social gathering. In view of all this, it was fitting that she take one month off every year to go to the beach.

That summer when Clara returned from her vacation and learned about my mother's discovery, she remained pensive for a while, as if weighing the symptoms before issuing a diagnosis. Afterwards, without batting an eye, she leaned over the mirror, saw for herself that it was true, and then tossed her head, seemingly accepting the situation. She immediately sat by the book-

---

1. **oracle** (AWR uh kuhl): person of great knowledge and wisdom, often one who can predict the future.

2. **arbiter** (AHR buht uhr): person who settles disputes or makes judgments.

case and craned her neck to see who was sitting in the chair on the other side. "Gosh, look at Gus," was all she said. There in the very same chair the mirror showed us Gus, some sort of godson of Dad, who after a flood in his home town came to live with us and had remained there in the somewhat ambiguous character of adoptive poor relation. Clara greeted him amiably with a wave of the hand, but he seemed busy, for the moment, with something like a radio tube and did not pay attention to her. Undoubtedly, the mirror people weren't going out of their way to be sociable. This must have wounded Clara's self-esteem, although she did not let on.

Naturally, the idea of moving the mirror to the dining-room was hers. And so was its sequel: to bring the mirror near the big table, so we could all sit together for meals.

In spite of my mother's fears that the mirror people would run away or get annoyed because of the fuss, everything went fine. I must admit it was comforting to sit every day at the table and see so many familiar faces, although some of those from the other side were distant relatives, and others, due to their lengthy—although unintentional—absence, were almost strangers. There were about twenty of us sitting at the table every day, and even if their gestures and movements seemed more remote than ours and their meals a little washed-out, we generally gave the impression of being a large family that got along well.

At the boundary between the real table and the other one, on this side, sat Clara and her brother Julius. On the other side was Eulalia (1949), the second wife of Uncle Daniel, aloof and indolent in life, and now the most distant of anyone on the other side. Across from her sat my godfather Sylvester (1952), who even though he was not a blood relative was always a soul relation. I was sad to see that Sylvester had lost his ruddiness, for he now looked like a faded mannequin, although his full face seemed to suggest perfect health. This pallor did not suit the robust Asturian,[3] who undoubtedly felt a bit ridiculous in these circumstances.

For a while we ate all together, without further incidents or problems. We mustn't forget Clara, however, whom we had allowed to sit at the frontier between the two tables, the equator separating what was from what was not. Although we paid no attention to the situation, we should have. Compounding our regrettable oversight was the fact that lethargic Eulalia sat across from her so that one night, with the same cordiality with which she had addressed Gus, Clara asked Eulalia to pass the salad. Eulalia affected the haughty disdain of offended royalty as she passed the spectral salad bowl, filled with dull lettuce and greyish semi-transparent tomatoes which Clara gobbled up, smiling mischievously at the novelty of it all. She watched us with the same defiance in her eyes that she had on the day she enrolled in a man's subject. There was no time to act. We just watched her grow pale, then her smile faded away until finally Clara collapsed against the mirror.

Once the funeral business was over and we sat back down at the table again, we saw that Clara had taken a place on the other side. She was between cousin Baltazar (1940) and a great-uncle whom we simply called "Ito."

This *faux pas*[4] dampened our conviviality somewhat. In a way, we felt betrayed; we felt that they had grievously abused our hospitality. However, we ended up divided over the question of who was really whose guest. It was also plain that our carelessness and Clara's irrepressible inquisi-

---

3. **Asturian** (as TOOR ee uhn): person from a region of northwestern Spain on the Bay of Biscay.
4. *faux pas* (foh PAH): French for "false step"; a social blunder.

tiveness had contributed to the mishap. In fact, a short time later we realized that there wasn't a great deal of difference between what Clara did before and what she was doing now, and so we decided to overlook the incident and get on with things. Nevertheless, each day we became less and less sure about which side was life and which its reflection, and as one bad step leads to another, I ended up taking Clara's empty place.

I am now much closer to them. I can almost hear the distant rustle of the folding and unfolding of napkins, the slight clinking of glasses and cutlery, the movement of chairs. The fact is that I can't tell if these sounds come from them or from us. I'm obviously not worried about clearing that up. What really troubles me, though, is that Clara doesn't seem to behave properly, with either the solemnity or with the opacity owed to her new position; I don't know how to put it. Even worse, the problem is that I—more than anybody else in the family—may become the target of Clara's machinations,[5] since we were always joined by a very special affection, perhaps because we were the same age and had shared the same children's games and the first anxieties of adolescence . . .

As it happens, she is doing her best to get my attention, and ever since last Monday she has been waiting for me to slip up so she can pass me a pineapple this big, admittedly a little bleached-out, but just right for making juice and also a bit sour, just as she knows I like it.

---

5. **machinations** (mak uh NAY shuhnz): plots or schemes.

# Part 3

# Panorama: Latino Writing in the United States

The current state of Latino literature in the United States is vibrant, diverse, and energetic—a constantly evolving scene. Latino literature includes the work of many contemporary writers who claim a dual heritage. Whether they were born in the United States or emigrated from Mexico, Argentina, Cuba, Guatemala, or other Latin American nations, they have lived in the U.S. for a significant period of time—long enough for their artistic consciousness to have been affected by their experiences here. Although the writers have cultural and linguistic ties to their Latin American heritage, they also have roots and identity in the United States.

Among these current writers there is great diversity. Some write solely in Spanish; some write in both Spanish and English; and some write exclusively in English. The works of all, however, reflect a sense of linguistic consciousness of both languages. Some writers remember the pain and embarrassment of being forced to abandon their native language as they learned English, facing reprimands from well-meaning but insensitive teachers if they fell into old habits. Others learned both languages simultaneously, slipping easily from one language to the other, often in the same sentence. The ultimate result, however, is a richness formed by the blend of two languages and two heritages.

## Themes and Subject Matter

Despite its great diversity, certain themes tend to recur in Latino literature. The theme of identity—or rather, dual identity—is perhaps most central to Latino writers, who often find themselves caught between the cultural expectations of two worlds. Closely related to the theme of identity is the theme of "*sin fronteras*," or "without borders"—the idea that the Latino in the United States is a cross-cultural person who blends, or attempts to blend, disparate influences into a new synthesis. Another recurring theme is the importance of family and tradition, which includes ties to the language and customs of parents and grandparents. Conflict is also an important theme: conflict between races and cultures; between the cultures of older generations and new ones; between traditional versus contemporary gender roles; between lower and upper socioeconomic classes; between the government and the individual; between the "native" and the immigrant; and even between the choice to speak Spanish or English. The core conflict for many writers is one that can be traced back to the arrival of the earliest Spanish explorers and colonists: the conflict between the European "conquerors" and the oppressed native populations (the "conquered").

## Latino, Hispanic, or —?

In addition to the diversity among the writers, there is diversity in terminology. The word *Latino* is only one of several words used in discussions of Latino writing and culture. In the 1960s, to emphasize their Mexican roots, some politically active Latinos adopted the name *Chicano*. The choice of this word scandalized their parents and grandparents, who used it as a disparaging term for lower-class Mexicans who moved into rural areas of the U.S. after emigrating from Mexico. By identifying themselves as Chicanos, however, the members of the younger generation were acknowledging and accepting with pride the *mestizo*, or mixed Spanish and Indian side of their heritage, not just the European side.

The term *Chicano* came to be equated with political militancy in urban areas and on high-school and college campuses in the Southwest and, particularly, California, where numerous Chicano political groups and student organizations formed in the mid-1960s. The leaders of these groups actively opposed economic exploitation and other types of discrimination and succeeded in getting candidates elected to local and regional political offices. They also successfully petitioned for the creation of Chicano Studies programs in universities, programs that emphasized a non-Anglo version of Mexican and Mexican American history, literature, and culture. Perhaps the greatest Chicano leader was César Chávez (1927–1993), who, in the mid-1960s, organized Mexican, Mexican American, and Filipino farmworkers in California and led a successful national boycott of California-grown grapes in order to call attention to the plight of migrant farmworkers and institute reforms.

There are yet other terms used to refer to particular Latino groups. Some Latinos from Puerto Rico refer to themselves as *Boricuas*, from *Boriquén*, the pre-Columbian native peoples' name for Puerto Rico.

*Boricuas* is also a name that Puerto Ricans call each other as an endearment. A frequently used term for Puerto Ricans who have an affiliation with New York is *Nuyorican*.

Writers who claim a Cuban heritage usually designate themselves as either "Cuban American" or "Cuban exile," the latter term emphasizing not only their heritage but also the reason they left their country.

The term *Hispanic* is often used interchangeably with *Latino*, although each term has specific history and connotations. *Hispanic* is a term created by the U.S. Department of Education and the Census Bureau in the 1970s to refer to people of Spanish descent. Since the term *Hispanic* has both political and geographic connotations that many find inaccurate, it is often rejected in favor of *Latino*. *Latino*, from the Spanish word *latinoamericano*, refers to the fact that both the Spanish and Portuguese languages are in the family of languages that stem from ancient Latin. (Spanish and Portuguese are also referred to as "Romance"—from Rome—languages, another term for the Latin family of languages.) *Latino* is a broader term than *Hispanic*, as it encompasses the wider area of Mexico, the Caribbean, Central America, and South America. (Because of the masculine and feminine forms inherent in the Spanish language, the term *Latina* is correctly used to speak of an individual female. In this book, the term *Latino* is used to refer to the larger group, though increasingly in the popular media the combined term *Latino/a* is used.)

## Mexican American Literature

In the second half of the nineteenth century, Mexican American literature began to emerge as a vital form. Most of the early writing was primarily in Spanish, for newspaper publication. A great deal of the literature remained oral. The *corrido*, a form of ballad, flourished as antagonisms increased between Mexican Americans and Anglos. After 1920, when the Mexican Revolution intensified immigration to the United States, contributions to Mexican American literature grew. The state of New Mexico became a center of Hispanicism, a type of regional writing that celebrated Spanish heritage by bringing to life the speech, dress, customs, and scenery of a specific locale. One of the leading figures of this type of writing is Fray Angélico Chávez, whose short story "Hunchback Madonna" is reproduced in this anthology.

The first work of fiction by a Mexican American to find a large audience among Anglos was *Mexican Village* (1945) by Josephine Niggli. This novel portrays village life in the mountains of northern Mexico. In her depiction of main character Bob Webster's mixed heritage as both Mexican and American, Niggli creates an archetypal figure whose identity is bicultural. Niggli makes use of folklore, introducing each section of the book with a *dicho*, a proverb or saying. She uses Spanish idioms and syntax to give the flavor of Spanish in English. Niggli, who came to the United States from Mexico in 1913 during the Mexican Revolution, wrote two plays about the revolution: *Soldadera*, a tale of women soldiers, and *The Ring of General Macías*, reprinted here.

## From Spanish to English

In the first half of the twentieth century, many Latino writers continued to write in Spanish; but by the late 1940s, many of them began to write in English. Having fought in Europe and Japan in World War II in defense of their country's values and traditions, many thousands of Mexican Americans and other Latinos returned home ready to participate fully in American society. Unfortunately, they returned home to discrimination and hostility. A new awareness of their rights gripped Latinos, who resolved to become integrated into American society so they could take advantage of all that life in the United States had to offer. Many parents insisted that their children speak only English, the language of the American Dream. Others took an "English at school, Spanish at home" approach.

In the early 1960s, Mexican Americans in particular began to reevaluate the attitudes and practices that had prevailed within their culture since the late 1940s. A new consciousness emerged, especially among younger Mexican Americans, who felt a resurgence of cultural pride. Questioning their parents' drive to try to become like the Anglos, this generation placed value on speaking Spanish and studying the history of their people. Mexican American authors continued to explore sources of discrimination, such as that against farmworkers, and they developed new forms of poetry, as well.

In the 1960s the Teatro Campesino was established. Dramatic forms were used to present farmworker issues. This union of theater with César Chávez's program of political activism stimulated a period of literary activity. A writer who emerged during this period was Tomás Rivera, whose major work . . . *y no se lo tragó la tierra* (*And the Earth Did Not Devour Him*) is a series of stories about migrant farmworkers. Another Rivera account of the migrant farmworker experience, "The Harvest," is reprinted here.

Contemporary Mexican American poets like Gary Soto base their work on ordinary experiences. Soto writes in English about growing up in Fresno, California. Many of his works, including those in this book, show how he has been influenced by popular American culture.

## Puerto Rican American Literature

Puerto Ricans make up the largest Latino group in the northeastern United States. In 1948, the United States and Puerto Rico reached an agreement that became known as Operation Bootstrap. This agreement led to migration from Puerto Rico to the mainland in order to provide labor for American industries. Puerto Ricans arrived in great numbers in the 1950s.

Jesús Colón was among the first writers to describe the immigrant experience of Puerto Ricans in the United States in his collection of newspaper sketches *A Puerto Rican in New York* (1961). Nicholasa Mohr wrote about adolescents growing up in the *barrio* in *Nilda* (1974). Her short story "Mr. Mendelsohn," a selection from *El Bronx Remembered* (1975), is reprinted here. Another writer who describes the experiences of Puerto Ricans in the United States is Judith Ortiz Cofer. She writes about the challenge of living in two cultures. The first half of her novel *The Line of the Sun* (1989) takes place in a village in Puerto Rico; the second part follows her characters to Paterson, New Jersey, where the heroine tries to reconcile the two aspects of her identity. Selections from Ortiz Cofer's fiction and novels in verse are included here. The theme of bicultural identity is also addressed by Esmeralda Santiago in her memoir *When I Was Puerto Rican* (1994). In the excerpt included here, Santiago recalls an experience in junior high school that gave her an opportunity for a better life.

Poetry also began to flourish in the 1960s and 1970s when the Nuyorican Poets' Café was established in New York City. The term *Nuyorican*, which dates from at least 1975, blends the phrases "New York" and "Puerto Rican" and is sometimes used to refer to the Spanish spoken by Puerto Ricans.

A younger generation of Puerto Rican writers includes Ernesto Quiñonez, who has a dual Hispanic heritage—both Puerto Rican and Ecuadorian. His novel *Bodega Dreams* (2000) is set in New York City's Spanish Harlem. He has been admired for his gift for dialect and depiction of the vibrant culture of East Harlem.

## Cuban American Literature

Contemporary Cuba has been ruled by dictators since 1952. These dictatorships led to the emigration and exile of a number of Cuba's citizens, many to Florida. Unlike other Latino groups from the Carribean, the first group of Cuban American exiles came from the middle and professional classes. The next wave of Cubans, the *Marielitos*, 120,000 people who fled from the Cuban port of Mariel, arrived in 1980. They were poor and experienced greater discrimination than earlier arrivals. There are now several generations of exiles living in the United States.

Authors from the first group of exiles continue to write in Spanish, focusing on the life and culture in the country they left behind, expressing nostalgia for Cuba, and hoping to return. Their stories contain distinctive political and ideological recollections. In addition to the literature of exile, these authors write about the search for identity, culture shock and confusion in their new land, conflict between themselves and the Americans, and exploitation of Cuban workers, a subject formerly avoided.

Second-generation texts, by the children of these writers, explore the familiar theme of finding one's cultural identity in a new country. In addition to examining their own experiences, these younger writers absorb and combine information from their parents and grandparents. The result of these identity searches is a more multifaceted literature that goes beyond simple examinations of cultural assimilation. Like other Latino writers, Cuban American authors examine the dynamics and eccentricities of family relationships. (Cuban writer María Elena Llano's short story "In the Family," in Part 2 of this anthology, describes a family whose dead relatives continue to share meals in the family dining room.) Margarita Engle writes about a Cuban American poet who returns to Cuba to visit relatives to assure them that the exiles have not forgotten them. In her short story "Niña," reprinted here, a visit to Cuba reveals the cultural and political conflicts of the Castro era.

## Toward the Future

In recent years, Latino writing has found a huge audience. Many Hispanic presses and *revistas*, or magazines, have helped introduce Latino writers to the public. Readings and book fairs are held regularly. The growing body of Latino literature has undergone significant changes in the last forty years, which some view as a literary renaissance. More and more writers seem to be emphasizing formal literary aspects to a greater degree than before. Their works also tend to be more introspective than those published in the 1960s and 1970s. Latino literature now receives worldwide attention among scholars, and literary conferences are held to discuss the Latino writers of the United States. According to Dr. Roberta Fernández, whose novel *Intaglio: A Novel in Six Stories* was selected as Best Fiction for 1991 by Multicultural Publishers Exchange: "As more writers move into the mainstream and yet hold on to a cultural integrity, their literature promises to become the most exciting and innovative literature of the twenty-first century in the United States."

# Jesús Colón
**1901–1974** (Puerto Rican American)

## Meet the Writer

When **Jesús Colón** (hay SOOS koh LOHN) stowed away on the S.S. *Carolina* in 1918 and landed in Brooklyn, New York, he brought with him more than a few built-in obstacles to success. A Puerto Rican of African descent, he would face discrimination based on both his skin color and his country of origin. Furthermore, he could not speak English, and his socialist political views would ultimately make him unpopular, if not persecuted, especially during the McCarthy era of the early 1950s.

In spite of these obstacles, Colón became a successful writer and a respected journalist, both in his homeland and in the United States. At first he supported himself with various menial jobs and contributed articles to Puerto Rican newspapers and other periodicals. By the 1940s, English-language socialist journals such as *The Daily Worker* and *Mainstream* had published some of his pieces. He also founded a small publishing house, Editorial Hispanica, which published political pamphlets, books on history, and literature by Spanish and Hispanic writers.

Colón was a social activist in addition to being a writer. He was involved in the Puerto Rican independence movement and the labor movement, and he once ran for political office.

## Background

Although his work was not well publicized, Jesús Colón was influential both in affecting perceptions of Puerto Ricans in the United States and in starting a movement in Puerto Rican–American literature. His works exposed the exploitation of working class Puerto Ricans in New York, addressed racism, and brought to light the realities of the immigrant experience. *A Puerto Rican in New York*, Colón's only published volume of essays, was one of the first Latino works of literature to depict the lives of immigrants. The book inspired other Puerto Rican writers living in New York, and Colón eventually became known as the "Father of the Nuyorican Movement."

**Before You Read** *If you've ever hunted for a job, you may be familiar with the Help Wanted section of your local newspaper. Perhaps you've noticed some ads that promise great things but give no information about the job.*

*In this essay, the narrator is intrigued by an ad that reads simply "Easy job. Good wages. No experience necessary." Predict what you think he will find when he gets to the address given in the paper. As you read, consider the predicament of the unskilled worker looking for employment. What does the narrator learn from his experience? What is ironic about the story's title?*

# Easy Job, Good Wages
## from A Puerto Rican in New York
## Jesús Colón

This happened early in 1919. We were both out of work, my brother and I. He got up earlier to look for a job. When I woke up, he was already gone. So I dressed, went out and bought a copy of the *New York World* and turned its pages until I got to the "Help Wanted Unskilled" section of the paper. After much reading and re-reading the same columns, my attention was held by a small advertisement. It read: "Easy job. Good wages. No experience necessary." This was followed by a number and street on the west side of lower Manhattan. It sounded like the job I was looking for. Easy job. Good wages. Those four words revolved in my brain as I was travelling toward the address indicated in the advertisement. Easy job. Good wages. Easy job. Good wages. Easy . . .

The place consisted of a small front office and a large loft on the floor of which I noticed a series of large galvanized tubs half filled with water out of which I noticed protruding the necks of many bottles of various sizes and shapes. Around these tubs there were a number of workers, male and female, sitting on small wooden benches. All had their hands in the water of the tub, the left hand holding a bottle and with the thumb nail of the right hand scratching the labels.

The foreman found a vacant stool for me around one of the tubs of water. I asked why a penknife or a small safety razor could not be used instead of the thumb nail to take off the old labels from the bottles. I was expertly informed that knives or razors would scratch the glass thus depreciating the value of the bottles when they were to be sold.

I sat down and started to use my thumb nail on one bottle. The water had somewhat softened the transparent mucilage used to attach the label to the bottle. But the softening did not work out uniformly somehow. There were always pieces of label that for some obscure reason remained affixed to the bottles. It was on those pieces of labels tenaciously fastened to the bottles that my right hand thumb nail had to work overtime. As the minutes passed I noticed that the coldness of the water started to pass from my hand to my body giving me intermittent body shivers that I tried to conceal with the greatest of effort from those sitting beside me. My hands became deadly clean and tiny little wrinkles started to show especially at the tip of my fingers. Sometimes I stopped a few seconds from scratching the bottles, to open and close my fists in rapid movements in order to bring blood to my hands. But almost as soon as I placed them in the water they became deathly pale again.

But these were minor details compared with what was happening to the thumb of my right hand. From a delicate, boyish thumb, it was growing by the minute into a full blown tomato colored finger. It was the only part of my right hand remaining blood red. I started to look at the workers' thumbs. I noticed that these particular fingers on their right hands were unusually developed with a thick layer of corn-like surface at the top of their right thumb. The nails on their thumbs looked coarser and smaller than on the other fingers—thumb and nail having become one and the same thing—a primitive unnatural human instrument especially developed to detach hard pieces of labels from wet bottles immersed in galvanized tubs.

After a couple of hours I had a feeling that my thumb nail was going to leave my finger and jump into the cold water in the tub. A numb pain imperceptibly began to be felt coming from my right thumb. Then I began to feel such pain as if coming from a finger bigger than all of my body.

After three hours of this I decided to quit fast. I told the foreman so, showing him my swollen finger. He figured I had earned 69 cents at 23 cents an hour.

Early in the evening I met my brother in our furnished room. We started to exchange experiences of our job hunting for the day. "You know what?" my brother started, "early in the morning I went to work where they take labels off old bottles—with your right hand thumb nail . . . Somewhere on the West Side of Lower Manhattan. I only stayed a couple of hours. 'Easy job . . . Good wages' . . . they said. The person who wrote that ad must have had a great sense of humor." And we both had a hearty laugh that evening: when I told my brother that I also went to work at that same place later in the day.

Now when I see ads reading, "Easy job. Good wages," I just smile an ancient, tired, knowing smile.

# Fray Angélico Chávez
1910–1996 (Mexican American)

## Meet the Writer

It was fitting that when Manuel E. Chávez joined the Franciscan Order of Catholic priests he took the name of Fray (Brother) Angélico, after the fifteenth century painter Fra Angélico da Fiesole. The artistic **Fray Angélico Chávez** (ahn HEH lee koh CHAH behs), like his namesake, painted religious murals and frescoes, some of them enormous, often using local people as models. He also lovingly and painstakingly created literary portraits of his people in New Mexico, both Indian and Hispanic, with his pen.

Born in the isolated town of Wagon Mound in northern New Mexico, Chávez grew up in the midst of a Spanish-speaking community rich in traditions and fiercely protective of its heritage. When he was quite young, he went with his parents on a trip to California, and while there he visited the Mission San Diego de Alcala, the first mission established by Father Junipero Serra. Certain that he had a religious calling, Chávez left New Mexico to study for the priesthood when he was only fourteen years old.

Chávez's first assignment took him back to New Mexico, where he spent several years restoring the original Spanish religious art in rural village churches. He served for over three decades as a missionary in New Mexico, ministering to Indian pueblos. When he retired in 1972, he became an archivist and one of the great historians of New Mexico history.

## Background

For many years, critics dismissed Fray Chávez's works as folkloric, "local color" writings. More recently, he has been acknowledged as one of the great contributors to contemporary Mexican American literature. As a historian, he was able to write about New Mexico's history with such insight that he seemed to be recording contemporary events. In all his writings, Chavez captured the unique texture of rural life in northern New Mexico, where the Spanish language, customs, and values of his ancestors have continued to thrive for five centuries.

**Before You Read**  *According to the narrator, the appeal of the tiny, isolated village of El Tordo lies not in its quaint setting but in the village's most prized possession: a curiously "stoop-shouldered" image of the Madonna that hangs in the "old and crumbling" mission. The legend that lies behind this painting is the focus of Fray Angélico Chávez's tale. Like El Tordo's many pilgrims and sightseers, you too may be moved by the story of Mana Seda,[1] or "Sister Silk," the humble old woman who inspired the painting of the Madonna. How might Mana Seda's life stand as an inspiration to others?*

# Hunchback Madonna
## Fray Angélico Chávez

Old and crumbling, the squat-built adobe[2] mission of El Tordo[3] sits in a hollow high up near the snow-capped Truchas.[4] A few clay houses huddle close to it like tawny chicks about a ruffled old hen. On one of the steep slopes, which has the peaks for a background, sleeps the ancient graveyard with all its inhabitants, or what little is left of them. The town itself is quite as lifeless during the winter months, when the few folks that live there move down to warmer levels by the Rio Grande; but when the snows have gone, except for the white crusts on the peaks, they return to herd their sheep and goats, and with them comes a stream of pious pilgrims and curious sightseers which lasts throughout the spring and summer weather.

They come to see and pray before the stoop-shouldered Virgin, people from as far south as Belén[5] who from some accident or some spinal or heart affliction are shoulder-bent and want to walk straight again. Others, whose faith is not so simple or who have no faith at all, have come from many parts of the country and asked the way to El Tordo, not only to see the curiously painted Madonna in which the natives put so much faith, but to visit a single grave in a corner of the *campo santo*[6] which, they have heard, is covered in spring with a profusion of wild flowers, whereas the other sunken ones are bare altogether, or at the most sprinkled only with sagebrush and tumbleweed. And, of course, they want to hear from the lips of some old inhabitant the history of the town and the church, the painting and the grave, and particularly of Mana Seda.

No one knows, or cares to know, when the village was born. It is more thrilling to say, with the natives, that the first settlers came up from the Santa Clara Valley long before the railroad came to New Mexico, when the Indians of Nambé and Taos still used bows and arrows and obsidian clubs; when it took a week to go to Santa Fe, which looked no different from the other northern towns at the time, only somewhat bigger.

---

1. **Mana Seda** (ma NAH SAY dah).
2. **adobe** (ah DOH bay): made of mud brick that has been baked in the sun.
3. **El Tordo** (ehl TOHR doh).
4. **Truchas** (TROO chahs): mountains in New Mexico, northeast of Santa Fe.
5. **Belén** (beh LEHN): a village in central New Mexico, on the Rio Grande.
6. ***campo santo*** (KAHM poh SAHN toh): cemetery.

After the men had allotted the scant farming land among themselves, and each family raised its adobe hut of one or two rooms to begin with, they set to making adobes for a church that would shoulder above their homes as a guardian parent. On a high, untillable slope they marked out as their God's acre a plot which was to be surrounded by an adobe wall. It was not long before large pines from the forest nearby had been carved into beams and corbels and hoisted into their places on the thick walls. The women themselves mud-plastered the tall walls outside with their bare hands; within they made them a soft white with a lime mixture applied with the woolly side of sheepskins.

The padre, whose name the people do not remember, was so pleased with the building, and with the crudely wrought reredos[7] behind the altar, that he promised to get at his own expense a large hand-painted *Nuestra Señora de Guadalupe*[8] to hang in the middle of the *retablo*.[9] But this had to wait until the next traders' ox-drawn caravan left Santa Fe for Chihuahua[10] in Old Mexico and came back again. It would take years, perhaps, if there was no such painting ready and it must be made to order.

With these first settlers of El Tordo had come an old woman who had no relatives in the place they had left. For no apparent reason she had chosen to cast her lot with the emigrants, and they had willingly brought her along in one of their wooden-wheeled *carretas*,[11] had even built her a room in the protective shadow of the new church. For that had been her work before, sweeping the house of God, ringing the Angelus[12] morning, noon and night, adorning the altar with lace cloths and flowers, when there were flowers. She even persuaded the padre, when the first of May came around, to start an ancient custom prevalent in her place of origin: that of having little girls dressed as queens and their maids-in-waiting present bunches of flowers to the Virgin Mary every evening in May. She could not wait for the day when the Guadalupe picture would arrive.

They called her *Mana Seda*, "Sister Silk." Nobody knew why; they had known her by no other name. The women thought she had got it long ago for being always so neat, or maybe because she embroidered so many altar cloths. But the men said it was because she looked so much like a silk-spinning spider; for she was very much humpbacked—so bent forward that she could look up only sideways and with effort. She always wore black, a black shiny dress and black shawl with long leglike fringes and, despite her age and deformity, she walked about quite swiftly and noiselessly. "Yes," they said, "like the black widow spider."

Being the cause of the May devotions at El Tordo, she took it upon herself to provide the happy girls with flowers for the purpose. The geraniums which she grew in her window were used up the first day, as also those that other women had tended in their own homes. So she scoured the slopes around the village for wild daisies and Indian paint brush, usually returning in the late afternoon with a shawlful to spill at the eager children's feet. Toward the end of May she had to push deeper into the forest, whence she came back with her tireless, short-stepped

---

7. *reredos* (RIHR dahs): ornamental screen or partition behind an altar.
8. *Nuestra Señora de Guadalupe* (NWES trah seh NYOHR ah deh gwah dah LOO peh): Our Lady of Guadalupe (the Virgin Mary), the patron saint of Mexico.
9. *retablo* (reh TAH bloh): a shelf or ledge for holding altar ornaments.
10. *Chihuahua* (chee WAH wah): a state in northern Mexico.
11. *carretas* (kahr REH tahs): long, narrow carts.

---

12. *Angelus* (AHN heh loos): a bell rung to call people to prayer.

spider-run, her arms and shawl laden with wild iris and cosmos, verbenas and mariposa lilies from the pine shadows.

This she did year after year, even after the little "queens" of former Mays got married and new tots grew up to wear their veils. Mana Seda's one regret was that the image of the Virgin of Guadalupe had not come, had been lost on the way when the Comanches or Apaches attacked and destroyed the Chihuahua–Santa Fe ox-train.

One year in May (it was two days before the close of the month), when the people were already whispering among themselves that Mana Seda was so old she must die soon, or else last forever, she was seen hurrying into the forest early in the morning, to avail herself of all the daylight possible, for she had to go far into the wooded canyons this time. At the closing services of May there was to be not one queen but a number of them with their attendants. Many more flowers were needed for this, and the year had been a bad one for flowers, since little snow had fallen the winter before.

Fray Angélico Chávez

Mana Seda found few blooms in her old haunts, here and there an aster with half of its petals missing or drought-toasted, or a faded columbine fast wilting in the cool but moistureless shade. But she must find enough flowers; otherwise the good heavenly Mother would have a sad and colorless farewell this May. On and on she shuttled in between the trunks of spruce and fir, which grew thicker and taller and closer-set as the canyon grew narrower. Farther up she heard the sound of trickling water; surely the purple iris and freckled lily flames would be riot- ing there, fresh and without number. She was not disappointed, and without pausing to recover her breath, began lustily to snap off the long, luscious stems and lay them on her shawl, spread out on the little meadow. Her haste was prompted by the darkness closing in through the evergreens, now turning blacker and blacker, not with approaching dusk, but with the smoky pall of thunderheads that had swallowed up the patches of blue among the tops of the forest giants.

Far away arose rumblings that grew swiftly louder and nearer. The great trees, which always whispered to her even on quiet, sunny days, began to hiss and whine angrily at the unseen wind that swayed them and swung their arms like maidens unwilling to be kissed or danced with. And then a deafening sound exploded nearby with a blinding bluish light. Others followed, now on the right or on the left, now before or behind, as Mana Seda, who had thrown her flower-weighted mantle on her arched back, started to run—in which direction she knew not, for the rain was slashing down in sheets that blurred the dark boles and boulders all around her.

At last she fell, whimpering prayers to the Holy Virgin with a water-filled mouth that choked her. Of a sudden, sunlight began to fall instead between the towering trees, now quiet and dripping with emeralds and sapphires. The storm had passed by, the way spring rains in the Truchas Mountains do, as suddenly as it had come. In a clearing not far ahead, Mana Seda saw a little adobe hut. On its one chimney stood a wisp of smoke, like a white feather. Still clutching her heavy, rain-soaked shawl, she ran to it and knocked at the door, which was opened by an astonished young man with a short, sharp knife in his hand.

"I thought the mountain's bowels where the springs come from had burst," she was telling the youth, who meanwhile stirred a pot of brown beans that hung with a pail of coffee over the flames in the corner fireplace. "But our most Holy Lady saved me when I prayed to her, *gracias a Dios*.[13] The lightning and the water stopped, and I saw her flying above me. She had a piece of sky for a veil, and her skirt was like the beautiful red roses at her feet. She showed me your house."

Her host tried to hide his amusement by taking up his work again, a head he had been carving on the end of a small log. She saw that he was no different from the grown boys of El Tordo, dark and somewhat lean-bodied in his plain homespun. All about, against the wall and in niches, could be seen several other images, wooden and gaily colored *bultos*,[14] and more *santos*[15] painted on pieces of wood or hide. Mana Seda guessed that this must be the young stranger's trade, and grew more confident because of it. As she spread out her shawl to dry before the open fire, her load of flowers rolled out soggily on the bare earth floor. Catching his questioning stare, she told him what they were for, and about the church and the people of El Tordo.

"But that makes me think of the apparition of Our Lady of Guadalupe," he said. "Remember how the Indian Juan Diego filled his blanket with roses, as Mary most holy told him to do? And how, when he let down his *tilma*[16] before the bishop, out fell the roses, and on it was the miraculous picture of the Mother of God?"

Yes, she knew the story well; and she told him about the painting of the Guadalupe which the priest of El Tordo had ordered brought from Mexico and which was lost on the way. Perhaps, if the padre knew of this young man's ability, he would pay him for making one. Did he ever do work for churches? And what was his name?

"My name is Esquipula," he replied. "*Sí*,[17] I have done work for the Church. I made the *retablo* of 'San Francisco' for his church in Ranchos de Taos, and also the 'Cristo' for Santa Cruz. The 'Guadalupe' at San Juan, I painted it. I will gladly paint another for your chapel." He stopped all of a sudden, shut his eyes tight, and then quickly leaned toward the bent old figure who was helping herself to some coffee. "Why do you not let me paint one right now—on your shawl!"

She could not answer at first. Such a thing was unheard of. Besides, she had no other *tápalo*[18] to wear. And what would the people back home say when she returned wearing the Virgin on her back? What would She say?

---

13. ***gracias a Dios*** (GRAH syahs ah dyohs): thanks be to God.
14. ***bultos*** (BOOL tohs): busts.
15. ***santos*** (SAHN tohs): images of saints.
16. ***tilma*** (TEEL mah): a blanket used as a cloak.
17. ***Sí*** (see): yes.
18. ***tápalo*** (TAH pah loh): a woman's shawl.

"You can wear the picture turned inside where nobody can see it. Look! You will always have Holy Mary with you, hovering over you, hugging your shoulders and your breast! Come," he continued, seeing her ready to yield, "it is too late for you to go back to El Tordo. I will paint it now, and tomorrow I and Mariquita will take you home."

"And who is Mariquita?" she wanted to know.

"Mariquita is my little donkey," was the reply.

Mana Seda's black shawl was duly hung and spread tight against a bare stretch of wall, and Esquipula lost no time in tracing with white chalk the outlines of the small wood-print which he held in his left hand as a model. The actual laying of the colors, however, went much slower because of the shawl's rough and unsized texture. Darkness came, and Esquipula lit an oil lamp, which he held in one hand as he applied the pigments with the other. He even declined joining his aged guest at her evening meal of beans and stale *tortillas*,[19] because he was not hungry, he explained, and the picture must be done.

Once in a while the painter would turn from his work to look at Mana Seda, who had become quite talkative, something the people back at El Tordo would have marveled at greatly. She was recounting experiences of her girlhood which, she explained, were more vivid than many things that had happened recently.

Only once did he interrupt her, and that without thinking first. He said, almost too bluntly: "How did you become hunchbacked?"

Mana Seda hesitated, but did not seem to take the question amiss. Patting her shoulder as far as she could reach to her bulging back, she answered, "The woman who was nursing me dropped me on the hard dirt floor when I was a baby, and I grew up like a ball. But I do not remember, of course. My being bent out of shape did not hurt me until the time when other little girls of my age were chosen to be flowermaids in May. When I was older, and other big girls rejoiced at being chosen May queens, I was filled with bitter envy. God forgive me, I even cursed. I at last made up my mind never to go to the May devotions, nor to mass either. In the place of my birth, the shores of the Rio Grande are made up of wet sand which sucks in every living creature that goes in; I would go there and return no more. But something inside told me the Lord would be most pleased if I helped the other lucky girls with their flowers. That would make me a flower-bearer every day. Esquipula, my son, I have been doing this for seventy-four Mays."

Mana Seda stopped and reflected in deep silence. The youth, who had been painting absent-mindedly and looking at her, now noticed for the first time that he had made the Virgin's shoulders rather stooped, like Mana Seda's, though not quite so much. His first impulse was to run the yellow sun-rays into them and cover up the mistake, but for no reason he decided to let things stand as they were. By and by he put the last touches to his *oeuvre de caprice*,[20] offered the old lady his narrow cot in a corner, and went out to pass the night in Mariquita's humble shed.

The following morning saw a young man leading a gray burro through the forest, and on the patient animal's back swayed a round black shape, grasping her mantle with one hand while the other held tight to the small wooden saddle. Behind her, their bright heads bobbing from its wide mouth, rode a sack full of iris and tiger lilies from the meadow where the storm had caught Mana Seda the day before. Every once in a while, Esquipula had to stop the beast and go after some new flower which the rider had spied from her perch; sometimes she made him climb up a steep rock for a crannied blossom he would have passed unnoticed.

---

**19.** *tortillas* (tohr TEE yahs): thin bread made of unleavened cornmeal.

**20.** *oeuvre de caprice* (EUH vreh deh kah PREES): French for "work of impulse."

The sun was going down when they at last trudged into El Tordo and halted before the church, where the priest stood surrounded by a bevy of inquiring, disappointed girls. He rushed forth immediately to help Mana Seda off the donkey, while the children pounced upon the flowers with shouts of glee. Asking questions and not waiting for answers, he led the stranger and his still stranger charge into his house, meanwhile giving orders that the burro be taken to his barn and fed.

Mana Seda dared not sit with the padre at table and hied herself to the kitchen for her supper. Young Esquipula, however, felt very much at ease, answering all his host's questions intelligently, at which the pastor was agreeably surprised, but not quite so astonished as when he heard for the first time of Mana Seda's childhood disappointments.

"Young man," he said, hurriedly finishing his meal, "there is little time to lose. Tonight is closing of May—and it will be done, although we are unworthy." Dragging his chair closer to the youth, he plotted out his plan in excited whispers which fired Esquipula with an equal enthusiasm.

The last bell was calling the folk of El Tordo in the cool of the evening. Six queens with their many white-veiled maids stood in a nervous, noisy line at the church door, a garden of flowers in their arms. The priest and the stranger stood on guard facing them, begging them to be quiet, looking anxiously at the people who streamed past them into the edifice. Mana Seda finally appeared and tried to slide quietly by, but the padre barred her way and pressed a big basket filled with flowers and lighted candles into her brown, dry hands. At the same time Esquipula took off her black shawl and dropped over her gray head and hunched form a precious veil of Spanish lace.

In her amazement she could not protest, could not even move a step, until the padre urged her on, whispering into her ear that it was the Holy Virgin's express wish. And so Mana Seda led all the queens that evening, slowly and smoothly, not like a black widow now, folks observed, but like one of those little white moths moving over alfalfa fields in the moonlight. It was the happiest moment of her long life. She felt that she must die from pure joy, and many others observing her thought so too.

She did not die then; for some years afterward, she wore the new black *tápalo* the padre gave her in exchange for the old one, which Esquipula installed in the *retablo* above the altar. But toward the last she could not gather any more flowers on the slopes, much less in the forest. They buried her in a corner of the *campo santo*, and the following May disks of daisies and bunches of verbenas came up on her grave. It is said they have been doing it ever since, for curious travelers to ask about, while pious pilgrims come to pray before the hunchback Madonna.

# Josephina Niggli
**1910–1983** (Mexican American)

## Meet the Writer

Born in Hidalgo, Mexico, to a family with a culturally rich background—her father's ethnicity was Swiss and Alsatian; her mother's, Irish, French, and German—**Josephina Niggli** (hoh seh FEE nah NEEG glee) developed a deep understanding of Mexican American culture.

As a child Niggli lived in both Mexico and the United States. As the daughter of the Anglo cement plant manager who employed many people in her village, Niggli felt separate from the rest of her community in Mexico. Yet, while in the United States because of the political turmoil of the Mexican Revolution, she felt homesick for Mexico.

Niggli, a dramatist, poet, and prose writer, displayed a gift for writing at an early age. Her mother taught her daughter at home until Niggli entered a Catholic high school in San Antonio, Texas. The combination of her bicultural upbringing and an unconventional education gave her a keen imagination and an unusual perspective. Niggli wrote prolifically as a teenager, publishing short stories and poems. At eighteen, she published her first poetry collection, *Mexican Silhouettes*.

When she entered the University of North Carolina to study playwriting, Niggli's work as a dramatist began in earnest; many of the plays she wrote during this time were produced.

After spending time in Hollywood writing film scripts, Niggli moved to North Carolina. She taught at Western Carolina University until she retired in 1975.

## Background

The Mexican Revolution of 1910 was a response to the dictatorship of Porfirio Díaz. In 1910, Francisco I. Madero decided to run for office against Díaz. Díaz ensured his own victory by having Madero put in prison until after the election. Once released, Madero fled to Texas and encouraged revolutionary armies to attack federal troops, ruin railroads, and damage estates. Díaz was forced to resign from office, and Madero was later elected president. The Mexican Revolution continued many years, but eventually Mexico's government was transformed from a dictatorship to a constitutional republic.

**Before You Read**  While reading the play, keep in mind the details of the Mexican Revolution you read in the Background feature: Federalists want to keep Porfirio Díaz, a leader who has many wealthy supporters, in power. The revolutionaries are fighting to oust Díaz and want a reformed government that will improve the standing of Mexican citizens, many of whom are poor and uneducated.

Differences in the characters' class standing are a main factor in this play, informing the characters' beliefs about who "real soldiers" are and why they are fighting. Take careful note of how class distinctions affect the characters' views: What reasons do they give for fighting, and what do they hold dear? As you read, keep in mind the quotation from Joaquin Peralta at the beginning of the play.

# The Ring of General Macías
## A Drama of the Mexican Revolution
### Josephina Niggli

"The Federal troops were fighting for a way of living; the Revolutionists were fighting for life itself. The outcome of such a struggle could never be in doubt."

> Joaquin Peralta,
> *Essay on The Great Revolution.*

### CHARACTERS
**Marica,** the sister of General Macías
**Raquel,** the wife of General Macías
**Andrés de la O,** a captain in the Revolutionary Army
**Cleto,** a private in the Revolutionary Army
**Basilio Flores,** a captain in the Federal Army

**Place:** Just outside Mexico City.
**Time:** A night in April, 1912.

[*The living room of General Macías's home is luxuriously furnished in the gold and ornate style of Louis XVI. In the Right wall are French windows leading into the patio. Flanking these windows are low bookcases. In the Back wall is, Right, a closet door; and, Center, a table holding a wine decanter and glasses. The Left wall has a door Upstage, and Downstage a writing desk with a straight chair in front of it. Near the desk is an armchair. Down Right is a small sofa with a table holding a lamp at the Upstage end of it. There are pictures on the walls. The room looks rather stuffy and unlived in.*

*When the curtains part, the stage is in darkness save for the moonlight that comes through the French windows. Then the house door opens and a young girl in negligee enters stealthily. She is carrying a lighted candle. She stands at the door a moment listening for possible pursuit, then moves quickly across to the bookcase Down Right. She puts the candle on top of the bookcase and begins searching behind the books. She finally finds what she wants: a small bottle. While she is searching, the house door opens silently and a woman, also in negligee, enters. (These negligees are in the latest Parisian style.) She moves silently across the room to the table by the sofa, and as the girl turns with the bottle, the woman switches on the light. The girl gives a half-scream and draws back, frightened. The light reveals her to be quite young—no more than twenty—a timid, dovelike creature. The woman has a queenly air, and whether she is actually beautiful or not, people think she is. She is about thirty-two.*]

**The Ring of General Macías**     **175**

**Marica.** [*Trying to hide the bottle behind her.*] Raquel! What are you doing here?
**Raquel.** What did you have hidden behind the books, Marica?
**Marica.** [*Attempting a forced laugh.*] I? Nothing. Why do you think I have anything?
**Raquel.** [*Taking a step toward her.*] Give it to me.
**Marica.** [*Backing away from her.*] No. No, I won't.
**Raquel.** [*Stretching out her hand.*] I demand that you give it to me.
**Marica.** You have no right to order me about. I'm a married woman I . . . I . . . [*She begins to sob and flings herself down on the sofa.*]
**Raquel.** [*Much gentler.*] You shouldn't be up. The doctor told you to stay in bed. [*She bends over Marica and gently takes the bottle out of the girl's hand.*] It was poison. I thought so.
**Marica.** [*Frightened.*] You won't tell the priest, will you?
**Raquel.** Suicide is a sin, Marica. A sin against God.
**Marica.** I know. I . . . [*She catches Raquel's hand.*] Oh, Raquel, why do we have to have wars? Why do men have to go to war and be killed?
**Raquel.** Men must fight for what they believe is right. It is an honorable thing to die for your country as a soldier.
**Marica.** How can you say that with Domingo out there fighting, too? And fighting what? Men who aren't even men. Peasants. Ranch slaves. Men who shouldn't be allowed to fight.
**Raquel.** Peasants are men, Marica. Not animals.
**Marica.** Men. It's always men. But how about the women? What becomes of us?
**Raquel.** We can pray.
**Marica.** [*Bitterly.*] Yes, we can pray. And then comes the terrible news, and it's no use praying any more. All the reason for our praying is dead. Why should I go on living with Tomás dead?
**Raquel.** Living is a duty.
**Marica.** How can you be so cold, so hard? You are a cold and hard woman, Raquel. My brother worships you. He has never even looked at another woman since the first day he saw you. Does he know how cold and hard you are?
**Raquel.** Domingo is my — honored husband.
**Marica.** You've been married for ten years. And I've been married for three months. If Domingo is killed, it won't be the same for you. You've had ten years. [*She is crying wildly.*] I haven't anything . . . anything at all.
**Raquel.** You've had three months — three months of laughter. And now you have tears. How lucky you are. You have tears. Perhaps five months of tears. Not more. You're only twenty. And in five months Tomás will become just a lovely memory.
**Marica.** I'll remember Tomás all my life.
**Raquel.** Of course. But he'll be distant and far away. But you're young . . . and the young need laughter. The young can't live on tears. And one day in Paris, or Rome, or even Mexico City, you'll meet another man. You'll marry again. There will be children in your house. How lucky you are.
**Marica.** I'll never marry again.
**Raquel.** You're only twenty. You'll think differently when you're twenty-eight, or nine, or thirty.
**Marica.** What will you do if Domingo is killed?
**Raquel.** I shall be very proud that he died in all his courage . . . in all the greatness of a hero.
**Marica.** But you'd not weep, would you? Not you! I don't think there are any tears in you.
**Raquel.** No, I'd not weep. I'd sit here in this empty house and wait.
**Marica.** Wait for what?
**Raquel.** For the jingle of his spurs as he walks across the tiled hall. For the sound of his laughter in the patio. For the echo of his voice as he shouts to the groom to put away his horse. For the feel of his hand . . .
**Marica.** [*Screams.*] Stop it!
**Raquel.** I'm sorry.

**Marica.** You do love him, don't you?
**Raquel.** I don't think even he knows how much.
**Marica.** I thought that after ten years people slid away from love. But you and Domingo—why, you're all he thinks about. When he's away from you he talks about you all the time. I heard him say once that when you were out of his sight he was like a man without eyes or ears or hands.
**Raquel.** I know. I, too, know that feeling.
**Marica.** Then how could you let him go to war? Perhaps to be killed? How could you?
**Raquel.** [*Sharply.*] Marica, you are of the family Macías. Your family is a family of great warriors. A Macías man was with Ferdinand when the Moors were driven out of Spain. A Macías man was with Cortés when the Aztecans surrendered. Your grandfather fought in the War of Independence. Your own father was executed not twenty miles from this house by the French. Shall his son be any less brave because he loves a woman?
**Marica.** But Domingo loved you enough to forget that. If you had asked him, he wouldn't have gone to war. He would have stayed here with you.
**Raquel.** No, he would not have stayed. Your brother is a man of honor, not a whining, creeping coward.
**Marica.** [*Beginning to cry again.*] I begged Tomás not to go. I begged him.
**Raquel.** Would you have loved him if he had stayed?
**Marica.** I don't know. I don't know.
**Raquel.** There is your answer. You'd have despised him. Loved and despised him. Now come, Marica, it's time for you to go to bed.
**Marica.** You won't tell the priest—about the poison, I mean?
**Raquel.** No. I won't tell him.
**Marica.** Thank you, Raquel. How good you are. How kind and good.
**Raquel.** A moment ago I was hard and cruel. What a baby you are. Now, off to bed with you.
**Marica.** Aren't you coming upstairs, too?
**Raquel.** No . . . I haven't been sleeping very well lately. I think I'll read for a little while.
**Marica.** Good night, Raquel. And thank you.
**Raquel.** Good night, little one.

[*Marica goes out through the house door Left, taking her candle with her. Raquel stares down at the bottle of poison in her hand, then puts it away in one of the small drawers of the desk. She next selects a book from the Downstage case and sits on the sofa to read it, but feeling chilly, she rises and goes to the closet, Back Right, and takes out an afghan. Coming back to the sofa, she makes herself comfortable, with the afghan across her knees. Suddenly she hears a noise in the patio. She listens, then convinced it is nothing, returns to her reading. But she hears the noise again. She goes to the patio door and peers out.*]

**Raquel.** [*Calling softly.*] Who's there? Who's out there? Oh! [*She gasps and backs into the room. Two men—or rather a man and a young boy—dressed in the white pajama suits of the Mexican peasants, with their sombreros tipped low over their faces, come into the room. Raquel draws herself up regally. Her voice is cold and commanding.*] Who are you, and what do you want here?
**Andrés.** We are hunting for the wife of General Macías.
**Raquel.** I am Raquel Rivera de Macías.
**Andrés.** Cleto, stand guard in the patio. If you hear any suspicious noise, warn me at once.
**Cleto.** Yes, my captain. [*The boy returns to the patio.*]

[*The man, hooking his thumbs in his belt, strolls around the room, looking it over. When he reaches the table at the back he sees the wine. With a small bow to Raquel he pours himself a glass of wine and drains it. He wipes his mouth with the back of his hand.*]

**Raquel.** How very interesting.
**Andrés.** [*Startled.*] What?
**Raquel.** To be able to drink wine with that hat on.
**Andrés.** The hat? Oh, forgive me, señora. [*He flicks the brim with his fingers so that it drops off his head and dangles down his back from the neck cord.*] In a military camp one forgets one's polite manners. Would you care to join me in another glass?
**Raquel.** [*Sitting on the sofa.*] Why not? It's my wine.
**Andrés.** And very excellent wine. [*He pours two glasses and gives her one while he is talking.*] I would say Amontillado of the vintage of '87.
**Raquel.** Did you learn that in a military camp?
**Andrés.** I used to sell wines . . . among other things.
**Raquel.** [*Ostentatiously hiding a yawn.*] I am devastated.
**Andrés.** [*Pulls over the armchair and makes himself comfortable in it.*] You don't mind, do you?
**Raquel.** Would it make any difference if I did?
**Andrés.** No. The Federals are searching the streets for us, and we have to stay somewhere. But women of your class seem to expect that senseless sort of question.
**Raquel.** Of course I suppose I could scream.
**Andrés.** Naturally.
**Raquel.** My sister-in-law is upstairs asleep. And there are several servants in the back of the house. Mostly men servants. Very big men.
**Andrés.** Very interesting. [*He is drinking the wine in small sips with much enjoyment.*]
**Raquel.** What would you do if I screamed?
**Andrés.** [*Considering the request as though it were another glass of wine.*] Nothing.
**Raquel.** I am afraid you are lying to me.
**Andrés.** Women of your class seem to expect polite little lies.
**Raquel.** Stop calling me "woman of your class."
**Andrés.** Forgive me.
**Raquel.** You are one of the fighting peasants, aren't you?
**Andrés.** I am a captain in the Revolutionary Army.
**Raquel.** This house is completely loyal to the Federal government.
**Andrés.** I know. That's why I'm here.
**Raquel.** And now that you are here, just what do you expect me to do?
**Andrés.** I expect you to offer sanctuary[1] to myself and to Cleto.
**Raquel.** Cleto? [*She looks toward the patio and adds sarcastically.*] Oh, your army.
**Cleto.** [*Appearing in the doorway.*] I'm sorry, my captain. I just heard a noise. [*Raquel stands. Andrés moves quickly to her and puts his hands on her arms from the back. Cleto has turned and is peering into the patio. Then the boy relaxes.*] We are still safe, my captain. It was only a rabbit. [*He goes back into the patio. Raquel pulls away from Andrés and goes to the desk.*]
**Raquel.** What a magnificent army you have. So clever. I'm sure you must win many victories.
**Andrés.** We do. And we will win the greatest victory, remember that.
**Raquel.** This farce[2] has gone on long enough. Will you please take your army and climb over the patio wall with it?
**Andrés.** I told you that we came here so that you could give us sanctuary.
**Raquel.** My dear captain—captain without a name . . .
**Andrés.** Andrés de la O, your servant. [*He makes a bow.*]
**Raquel.** [*Startled.*] Andrés de la O!
**Andrés.** I am flattered. You have heard of me.
**Raquel.** Naturally. Everyone in the city has heard of you. You have a reputation for politeness—especially to women.

---

1. **sanctuary** (SANGK choo er ee): here, protection or refuge.
2. **farce:** absurd situation.

**Andrés.** I see that the tales about me have lost nothing in the telling.
**Raquel.** I can't say. I'm not interested in gossip about your type of soldier.
**Andrés.** Then let me give you something to heighten your interest. [*He suddenly takes her in his arms and kisses her. She stiffens for a moment, then remains perfectly still. He steps away from her.*]
**Raquel.** [*Rage forcing her to whisper.*] Get out of here—at once!
**Andrés.** [*Staring at her in admiration.*] I can understand why Macías loves you. I couldn't before, but now I can understand it.
**Raquel.** Get out of my house.
**Andrés.** [*Sits on the sofa and pulls a small leather pouch out of his shirt. He pours its contents into his hand.*] So cruel, señora, and I with a present for you? Here is a holy medal. My mother gave me this medal. She died when I was ten. She was a street beggar. She died of starvation. But I wasn't there. I was in jail. I had been sentenced to five years in prison for stealing five oranges. The judge thought it a great joke. One year for each orange. He laughed. He had a very loud laugh. [*Pause.*] I killed him two months ago. I hanged him to the telephone pole in front of his house. And I laughed. [*Pause.*] I also have a very loud laugh. [*Raquel abruptly turns her back on him.*] I told that story to a girl the other night and she thought it very funny. But of course she was a peasant girl—a girl who could neither read nor write. She hadn't been born in a great house in Tabasco. She didn't have an English governess. She didn't go to school to the nuns in Paris. She didn't marry one of the richest young men in the Republic. But she thought my story very funny. Of course she could understand it. Her brother had been whipped to death because he had run away from the plantation that owned him. [*He pauses and looks at her. She does not move.*] Are you still angry with me? Even though I have brought you a present? [*He holds out his hand.*] A very nice present—from your husband.
**Raquel.** [*Turns and stares at him in amazement.*] A present! From Domingo?
**Andrés.** I don't know him that well. I call him the General Macías.
**Raquel.** [*Excitedly.*] Is he well? How does he look? [*With horrified comprehension.*] He's a prisoner . . . your prisoner!
**Andrés.** Naturally. That's why I know so much about you. He talks about you constantly.
**Raquel.** You know nothing about him. You're lying to me.

[*Cleto comes to the window.*]

**Andrés.** I assure you, señora . . .
**Cleto.** [*Interrupting.*] My captain . . .
**Andrés.** What is it, Cleto? Another rabbit?
**Cleto.** No, my captain. There are soldiers at the end of the street. They are searching all the houses. They will be here soon.
**Andrés.** Don't worry. We are quite safe here. Stay in the patio until I call you.
**Cleto.** Yes, my captain. [*He returns to the patio.*]
**Raquel.** You are not safe here. When those soldiers come I shall turn you over to them.
**Andrés.** I think not.
**Raquel.** You can't escape from them. And they are not kind to you peasant prisoners. They have good reason not to be.
**Andrés.** Look at this ring. [*He holds his hand out, with the ring on his palm.*]
**Raquel.** Why, it's—a wedding ring.
**Andrés.** Read the inscription inside of it. [*As she hesitates, he adds sharply.*] Read it!
**Raquel.** [*Slowly takes the ring. While she is reading her voice fades to a whisper.*] "D. M.—R. R.—June 2, 1902." Where did you get this?
**Andrés.** General Macías gave it to me.
**Raquel.** [*Firmly and clearly.*] Not this ring. He'd never give you this ring. [*With dawning horror.*]

He's dead. You stole it from his dead finger. He's dead.
**Andrés.** Not yet. But he will be dead if I don't return to camp safely by sunset tomorrow.
**Raquel.** I don't believe you. I don't believe you. You're lying to me.
**Andrés.** This house is famous for its loyalty to the Federal government. You will hide me until those soldiers get out of this district. When it is safe enough Cleto and I will leave. But if you betray me to them, your husband will be shot tomorrow evening at sunset. Do you understand? [*He shakes her arm. Raquel looks dazedly at him. Cleto comes to the window.*]
**Cleto.** The soldiers are coming closer, my captain. They are at the next house.
**Andrés.** [*To Raquel.*] Where shall we hide? [*Raquel is still dazed. He gives her another little shake.*] Think, woman! If you love your husband at all—think!
**Raquel.** I don't know. Marica upstairs—the servants in the rest of the house—I don't know.
**Andrés.** The General has bragged to us about you. He says you are braver than most men. He says you are very clever. This is a time to be both brave and clever.
**Cleto.** [*Pointing to the closet.*] What door is that?
**Raquel.** It's a closet . . . a storage closet.
**Andrés.** We'll hide in there.
**Raquel.** It's very small. It's not big enough for both of you.
**Andrés.** Cleto, hide yourself in there.
**Cleto.** But, my captain . . .
**Andrés.** That's an order! Hide yourself.
**Cleto.** Yes, Sir. [*He steps inside the closet.*]
**Andrés.** And now, señora, where are you going to hide me?
**Raquel.** How did you persuade my husband to give you his ring?
**Andrés.** That's a very long story, señora, for which we have no time just now. [*He puts the ring and medal back in the pouch and thrusts it inside his shirt.*] Later I will be glad to give you all the details. But at present it is only necessary for you to remember that his life depends upon mine.
**Raquel.** Yes—yes, of course. [*She loses her dazed expression and seems to grow more queenly as she takes command of the situation.*] Give me your hat. [*Andrés shrugs and passes it over to her. She takes it to the closet and hands it to Cleto.*] There is a smoking jacket hanging up in there. Hand it to me. [*Cleto hands her a man's velvet smoking jacket. She brings it to Andrés.*] Put this on.
**Andrés.** [*Puts it on and looks down at himself.*] Such a pity my shoes are not comfortable slippers.
**Raquel.** Sit in that chair. [*She points to the armchair.*]
**Andrés.** My dear lady . . .
**Raquel.** If I must save your life, allow me to do it in my own way. Sit down. [*Andrés sits. She picks up the afghan from the couch and throws it over his feet and legs, carefully tucking it in so that his body is covered to the waist.*] If anyone speaks to you, don't answer. Don't turn your head. As far as you are concerned, there is no one in this room—not even me. Just look straight ahead of you and . . .
**Andrés.** [*As she pauses.*] And what?
**Raquel.** I started to say "and pray," but since you're a member of the Revolutionary Army I don't suppose you believe in God and prayer.
**Andrés.** My mother left me a holy medal.
**Raquel.** Oh, yes, I remember. A very amusing story. [*There is the sound of men's voices in the patio.*] The Federal soldiers are here. If you can pray, ask God to keep Marica upstairs. She is very young and very stupid. She'll betray you before I can shut her mouth.
**Andrés.** I'll . . .
**Raquel.** Silence! Stare straight ahead of you and pray. [*She goes to the French window and speaks loudly to the soldiers.*] Really! What is the meaning of this uproar?

**Flores.** [*Off.*] Do not alarm yourself, señora. [*He comes into the room. He wears the uniform of a Federal officer.*] I am Captain Basilio Flores, at your service, señora.
**Raquel.** What do you mean, invading my house and making so much noise at this hour of the night?
**Flores.** We are hunting for two spies. One of them is the notorious Andrés de la O. You may have heard of him, señora.
**Raquel.** [*Looking at Andrés.*] Considering what he did to my cousin—yes, I've heard of him.
**Flores.** Your cousin, señora?
**Raquel.** [*Comes to Andrés and puts her hand on his shoulder. He stares woodenly in front of him.*] Felipe was his prisoner before the poor boy managed to escape.
**Flores.** Is it possible? [*He crosses to Andrés.*] Captain Basilio Flores, at your service. [*He salutes.*]
**Raquel.** Felipe doesn't hear you. He doesn't even know you are in the room.
**Flores.** Eh, it is a sad thing.
**Raquel.** Must your men make so much noise?
**Flores.** The hunt must be thorough, señora. And now if some of my men can go through here to the rest of the house . . .
**Raquel.** Why?
**Flores.** But I told you, señora. We are hunting for two spies . . .
**Raquel.** [*Speaking quickly from controlled nervousness.*] And do you think I have them hidden someplace, and I the wife of General Macías?
**Flores.** General Macías! But I didn't know . . .
**Raquel.** Now that you do know, I suggest you remove your men and their noise at once.
**Flores.** But, señora, I regret—I still have to search this house.
**Raquel.** I can assure you, captain, that I have been sitting here all evening, and no peasant spy has passed me and gone into the rest of the house.
**Flores.** Several rooms open off the patio, señora. They needn't have come through here.
**Raquel.** So . . . you do think I conceal spies in this house. Then search it by all means. Look under the sofa . . . under the table. In the drawers of the desk. And don't miss that closet, captain. Inside that closet is hidden a very fierce and wicked spy.
**Flores.** Please, señora . . .
**Raquel.** [*Goes to the closet door.*] Or do you prefer me to open it for you?
**Flores.** I am only doing my duty, señora. You are making it very difficult.
**Raquel.** [*Relaxing against the door.*] I'm sorry. My sister-in-law is upstairs. She has just received word that her husband has been killed. They were married three months ago. She's only twenty. I didn't want . . .
**Marica.** [*Calling off.*] Raquel, what is all that noise downstairs?
**Raquel.** [*Goes to the house door and calls.*] It is nothing. Go back to bed.
**Marica.** But I can hear men's voices in the patio.
**Raquel.** It is only some Federal soldiers hunting for two peasant spies. [*She turns and speaks rapidly to Flores.*] If she comes down here, she must not see my cousin. Felipe escaped, but her husband was killed. The doctor thinks the sight of my poor cousin might affect her mind. You understand?
**Flores.** Certainly, señora. What a sad thing.
**Marica.** [*Still off.*] Raquel, I'm afraid! [*She tries to push past Raquel into the room. Raquel and Flores stand between her and Andrés.*] Spies! In this house. Oh, Raquel!
**Raquel.** The doctor will be very angry if you don't return to bed at once.
**Marica.** But those terrible men will kill us. What is the matter with you two? Why are you standing there like that? [*She tries to see past them, but they both move so that she can't see Andrés.*]
**Flores.** It is better that you go back to your room, señora.
**Marica.** But why? Upstairs I am alone. Those terrible men will kill me. I know they will.

**Flores.** Don't be afraid, señora. There are no spies in this house.

**Marica.** Are you sure?

**Raquel.** Captain Flores means that no spy would dare to take refuge in the house of General Macías. Isn't that right, captain?

**Flores.** [*Laughing.*] Of course. All the world knows of the brave General Macías.

**Raquel.** Now go back to bed, Marica. Please, for my sake.

**Marica.** You are both acting very strangely. I think you have something hidden in this room you don't want me to see.

**Raquel.** [*Sharply.*] You are quite right. Captain Flores has captured one of the spies. He is sitting in the chair behind me. He is dead. Now will you please go upstairs!

**Marica.** [*Gives a stifled sob.*] Oh! That such a terrible thing could happen in this house. [*She runs out of the room, still sobbing.*]

**Flores.** [*Worried.*] Was it wise to tell her such a story, señora?

**Raquel.** [*Tense with repressed relief.*] Better that than the truth. Good night, captain, and thank you.

**Flores.** Good night, señora. And don't worry. Those spies won't bother you. If they were anywhere in this district, my men would have found them.

**Raquel.** I'm sure of it.

[*The Captain salutes her, looks toward Andrés and salutes him, then goes into the patio. He can be heard calling his men. Neither Andrés nor Raquel moves until the voices outside die away. Then Raquel staggers and nearly falls, but Andrés catches her in time.*]

**Andrés.** [*Calling softly.*] They've gone, Cleto. [*Andrés carries Raquel to the sofa as Cleto comes out of the closet.*] Bring a glass of wine. Quickly.

**Cleto.** [*As he gets the wine.*] What happened?

**Andrés.** It's nothing. Just a faint. [*He holds the wine to her lips.*]

**Cleto.** She's a great lady, that one. When she wanted to open the closet door my knees were trembling, I can tell you.

**Andrés.** My own bones were playing a pretty tune.

**Cleto.** Why do you think she married Macías?

**Andrés.** Love is a peculiar thing, Cleto.

**Cleto.** I don't understand it.

**Raquel.** [*Moans and sits up.*] Are they—are they gone?

**Andrés.** Yes, they're gone. [*He kisses her hand.*] I've never known a braver lady.

**Raquel.** [*Pulling her hand away.*] Will you go now, please?

**Andrés.** We'll have to wait until the district is free of them—but if you'd like to write a letter to your husband while we're waiting . . .

**Raquel.** [*Surprised at his kindness.*] You'd take it to him? You'd really give it to him?

**Andrés.** Of course.

**Raquel.** Thank you. [*She goes to the writing desk and sits down.*]

**Andrés.** [*To Cleto, who has been staring steadily at Raquel all the while.*] You stay here with the señora. I'm going to find out how much of the district has been cleared.

**Cleto.** [*Still staring at Raquel.*] Yes, my captain.

[*Andrés leaves by the French windows. Cleto keeps on staring at Raquel as she starts to write. After a moment she turns to him.*]

**Raquel.** [*Irritated.*] Why do you keep staring at me?

**Cleto.** Why did you marry a man like that one, señora?

**Raquel.** You're very impertinent.

**Cleto.** [*Shyly.*] I'm sorry, señora.

**Raquel.** [*After a brief pause.*] What do you mean: "a man like that one"?

**Cleto.** Well, you're very brave, señora.
**Raquel.** [*Lightly.*] And don't you think the general is very brave?
**Cleto.** No, señora. Not very.
**Raquel.** [*Staring at him with bewilderment.*] What are you trying to tell me?
**Cleto.** Nothing, señora. It is none of my affair.
**Raquel.** Come here. [*He comes slowly up to her.*] Tell me what is in your mind.
**Cleto.** I don't know, señora. I don't understand it. The captain says love is a peculiar thing, but I don't understand it.
**Raquel.** Cleto, did the general willingly give that ring to your captain?
**Cleto.** Yes, señora.
**Raquel.** Why?
**Cleto.** The general wanted to save his own life. He said he loved you and he wanted to save his life.
**Raquel.** How would giving that ring to your captain save the general's life?
**Cleto.** The general's supposed to be shot tomorrow afternoon. But he's talked about you a lot, and when my captain knew we had to come into the city, he thought perhaps we might take refuge here if the Federals got on our trail. So he went to the general and said that if he fixed it so we'd be safe here, my captain would save him from the firing squad.
**Raquel.** Was your trip to the city very important—to your cause, I mean?
**Cleto.** Indeed yes, señora. The captain got a lot of fine information. It means we'll win the next big battle. My captain is a very clever man, señora.
**Raquel.** Did the general know about this information when he gave his ring to your captain?
**Cleto.** I don't see how he could help knowing it, señora. He heard us talking about it enough.
**Raquel.** Who knows about that bargain to save the general's life beside you and your captain?
**Cleto.** No one, señora. The captain isn't one to talk, and I didn't have time to.

**Raquel.** [*While the boy has been talking, the life seems to have drained completely out of her.*] How old are you, Cleto?
**Cleto.** I don't know, señora. I think I'm twenty, but I don't know.
**Raquel.** [*Speaking more to herself than to him.*] Tomás was twenty.
**Cleto.** Who is Tomás?
**Raquel.** He was married to my sister-in-law. Cleto, you think my husband is a coward, don't you?
**Cleto.** [*With embarrassment.*] Yes, señora.
**Raquel.** You don't think any woman is worth it, do you? Worth the price of a great battle, I mean?
**Cleto.** No, señora. But as the captain says, love is a very peculiar thing.
**Raquel.** If your captain loved a woman as much as the general loves me, would he have given an enemy his ring?
**Cleto.** Ah, but the captain is a great man, señora.
**Raquel.** And so is my husband a great man. He is of the family Macías. All of that family have been great men. All of them—brave and honorable men. They have always held their honor to be greater than their lives. That is a tradition of their family.
**Cleto.** Perhaps none of them loved a woman like you, señora.
**Raquel.** How strange you are. I saved you from the Federals because I want to save my husband's life. You call me brave, and yet you call him a coward. There is no difference in what we have done.
**Cleto.** But you are a woman, señora.
**Raquel.** Has a woman less honor than a man, then?
**Cleto.** No, señora. Please, I don't know how to say it. The general is a soldier. He has a duty to his own cause. You are a woman. You have a duty to your husband. It is right that you should try to save him. It is not right that he should try to save himself.

**Raquel.** [*Dully.*] Yes, of course. It is right that I should save him. [*Becoming practical again.*] Your captain has been gone some time, Cleto. You'd better find out if he is still safe.

**Cleto.** Yes, señora. [*As he reaches the French windows she stops him.*]

**Raquel.** Wait, Cleto. Have you a mother—or a wife, perhaps?

**Cleto.** Oh, no, señora. I haven't anyone but the captain.

**Raquel.** But the captain is a soldier. What would you do if he should be killed?

**Cleto.** It is very simple, señora. I should be killed, too.

**Raquel.** You speak about death so calmly. Aren't you afraid of it, Cleto?

**Cleto.** No, señora. It's like the captain says . . . dying for what you believe in—that's the finest death of all.

**Raquel.** And you believe in the Revolutionary cause?

**Cleto.** Yes, señora. I am a poor peasant, that's true. But still I have a right to live like a man, with my own ground, and my own family, and my own future. [*He stops speaking abruptly.*] I'm sorry, señora. You are a fine lady. You don't understand these things. I must go and find my captain. [*He goes out.*]

**Raquel.** [*Rests her face against her hand.*] He's so young. But Tomás was no older. And he's not afraid. He said so. Oh, Domingo—Domingo! [*She straightens abruptly, takes the bottle of poison from the desk drawer and stares at it. Then she crosses to the decanter and laces the wine with the poison. She hurries back to the desk and is busy writing when Andrés and Cleto return.*]

**Andrés.** You'll have to hurry that letter. The district is clear now.

**Raquel.** I'll be through in just a moment. You might as well finish the wine while you're waiting.

**Andrés.** Thank you. A most excellent idea. [*He pours himself a glass of wine. As he lifts it to his lips she speaks.*]

**Raquel.** Why don't you give some to—Cleto?

**Andrés.** This is too fine a wine to waste on that boy.

**Raquel.** He'll probably never have another chance to taste such wine.

**Andrés.** Very well. Pour yourself a glass, Cleto.

**Cleto.** Thank you. [*He pours it.*] Your health, my captain.

**Raquel.** [*Quickly.*] Drink it outside, Cleto. I want to speak to your captain. [*The boy looks at Andrés, who jerks his head toward the patio. Cleto nods and goes out.*] I want you to give my husband a message for me. I can't write it. You'll have to remember it. But first, give me a glass of wine, too.

**Andrés.** [*Pouring the wine.*] It might be easier for him if you wrote it.

**Raquel.** I think not. [*She takes the glass.*] I want you to tell him that I never knew how much I loved him until tonight.

**Andrés.** Is that all?

**Raquel.** Yes. Tell me, captain, do you think it possible to love a person too much?

**Andrés.** Yes, señora. I do.

**Raquel.** So do I. Let us drink a toast, captain—to honor. To bright and shining honor.

**Andrés.** [*Raises his glass.*] To honor. [*He drains his glass. She lifts hers almost to her lips and then puts it down. From the patio comes a faint cry.*]

**Cleto.** [*Calling faintly in a cry that fades into silence.*] Captain. Captain.

[*Andrés sways, his hand trying to brush across his face as though trying to brush sense into his head. When he hears Cleto he tries to stagger toward the window but stumbles and can't quite make it. Hanging on to the table by the sofa he looks accusingly at her. She shrinks back against her chair.*]

**Andrés.** [*His voice weak from the poison.*] Why?

**Raquel.** Because I love him. Can you understand that?
**Andrés.** We'll win. The Revolution will win. You can't stop that.
**Raquel.** Yes, you'll win. I know that now.
**Andrés.** That girl—she thought my story was funny—about the hanging. But you didn't . . .
**Raquel.** I'm glad you hanged him. I'm glad.

[*Andrés looks at her and tries to smile. He manages to pull the pouch from his shirt and extend it to her. But it drops from his hand.*]

**Raquel.** [*Runs to French window and calls.*] Cleto. Cleto! [*She buries her face in her hands for a moment, then comes back to Andrés. She kneels beside him and picks up the leather pouch. She opens it and, taking the ring, puts it on her finger. Then she sees the medal. She rises and, pulling out the chain from her own throat, she slides the medal on to the chain. Then she walks to the sofa and sinks down on it.*]
**Marica.** [*Calling off.*] Raquel! Raquel! [*Raquel snaps off the lamp, leaving the room in darkness.* MARICA *opens the house door. She is carrying a candle which she shades with her hand. The light is too dim to reveal the dead Andrés.*] What are you doing down here in the dark? Why don't you come to bed?
**Raquel.** [*Making an effort to speak.*] I'll come in just a moment.
**Marica.** But what are you doing, Raquel?
**Raquel.** Nothing. Just listening . . . listening to an empty house.

QUICK CURTAIN

# Américo Paredes

**1915–1999** (Mexican American)

## Meet the Writer

A man of diverse talents and interests, **Américo Paredes** (ah MAY ree coh pah RAY dees) might be referred to as "the Renaissance man of Mexican American studies." Whether he was teaching folklore or writing poetry, studying music or writing scholarly essays, Paredes played a major role in developing the foundations of modern Mexican American scholarship.

Born and raised in Brownsville, Texas, near the Mexican border, Paredes grew up amidst border tensions and anti-Mexican sentiment. He would spend summer evenings listening to border "Mexicanos" recount ballads and folk tales around the campfire. In high school, Paredes encountered various forms of discrimination. His counselor assumed Paredes would not go on to college because of his ethnicity. He proved the counselor wrong, however, when he graduated *summa cum laude* from the University of Texas at Austin and later earned an M.A. and a doctorate.

Paredes immediately gained widespread recognition for his doctoral dissertation, *With His Pistol in His Hand: A Border Ballad and Its Hero,* about the famous *corrido* "The Ballad of Gregorio Cortez." During a thirty-year teaching career at the University of Texas, he published profusely, became a giant in the English and anthropology departments, fought for the creation of a center for Mexican American studies (and won), and founded the Center for Intercultural Studies of Folklore and Ethnomusicology. For his substantial contributions, Américo Paredes came to be considered one of the preeminent Latino scholars of the twentieth century.

## Background

"The Hammon and the Beans" appears in Paredes' short story collection *The Hammon and the Beans and Other Stories,* published in 1994. It is one of several stories in the collection that are set in the fictional Texas town of Jonesville-on-the-Grande. The town—including Fort Jones with its tall wire fence—is probably based on Paredes' childhood home of Brownsville and Fort Brown. Fort Brown was established in 1846 to house troops during the Mexican-American War. It was later used to defend the border.

**Before You Read** *This story depicts a town that consists of two different groups of people—the people of Mexican heritage who have historically lived there and the Anglo soldiers living at the fort. As you read, consider the differences between the two groups. What might be the reasons the two tend to clash or at the very least remain distinctly separate from one another? Be on the lookout for symbols that will help you understand the impact upon the townspeople of having the fort and the soldiers in their midst.*

# The Hammon and the Beans
## Américo Paredes

Once we lived in one of my grandfather's houses near Fort Jones. It was just a block from the parade grounds, a big frame house painted a dirty yellow. My mother hated it, especially because of the pigeons that cooed all day about the eaves. They had fleas, she said. But it was a quiet neighborhood at least, too far from the center of town for automobiles and too near for musical, night-roaming drunks.

At this time Jonesville-on-the-Grande was not the thriving little city that it is today. We told off our days by the routine on the post. At six sharp the flag was raised on the parade grounds to the cackling of the bugles, and a field piece thundered out a salute. The sound of the shot bounced away through the morning mist until its echoes worked their way into every corner of town. Jonesville-on-the-Grande woke to the cannon's roar, as if to battle, and the day began.

At eight the whistle from the post laundry sent us children off to school. The whole town stopped for lunch with the noon whistle, and after lunch everybody went back to work when the post laundry said that it was one o'clock, except for those who could afford to be old-fashioned and took the siesta. The post was the town's clock, you might have said, or like some insistent elder person who was always there to tell you it was time.

At six the flag came down, and we went to watch through the high wire fence that divided the post from the town. Sometimes we joined in the ceremony, standing at salute until the sound of the cannon made us jump. That must have been when we had just studied about George Washington in school, or recited "The Song of Marion's Men" about Marion the Fox and the British cavalry that chased him up and down the broad Santee. But at other times we stuck out our tongues and jeered at the soldiers. Perhaps the night before we had hung at the edges of a group of old men and listened to tales about Aniceto Pizaña and the "border troubles," as the local paper still called them when it referred to them gingerly in passing.

It was because of the border troubles, ten years or so before, that the soldiers had come back to old Fort Jones. But we did not hate them for that; we admired them even, at least sometimes. But when we were thinking about the border troubles instead of Marion the Fox, we hooted them and the flag they were lowering, which for the moment was theirs alone, just as we would have jeered an opposing ball team, in a friendly sort of way. On these occasions even Chonita would join in the mockery, though she usually ran home at the stroke of six. But whether we taunted or saluted, the distant men in khaki uniforms went about their motions without noticing us at all.

The last word from the post came in the night when a distant bugle blew. At nine it was all right because all the lights were on. But sometimes I heard it at eleven when everything was dark and still, and it made me feel that I was all alone in the world. I would even doubt that I was me, and that put me in such a fright that I felt like yelling out just to make sure I was really there. But next morning the sun shone and life began all over again, with its whistles and cannon shots and bugles blowing. And so we lived, we and the post, side by side with the wire fence in between.

The wandering soldiers whom the bugle called home at night did not wander in our neighborhood, and none of us ever went into Fort Jones. None except Chonita. Every evening when the flag came down she would leave off playing and go down towards what was known as the "lower" gate of the post, the one that opened not on main street but against the poorest part of town. She went into the grounds and to the mess halls and pressed her nose against the screens and watched the soldiers eat. They sat at long tables calling to each other through food-stuffed mouths.

"Hey bud, pass the coffee!"

"Give me the ham!"

"Yeah, give me the beans!"

After the soldiers were through, the cooks came out and scolded Chonita, and then they gave her packages with things to eat.

Chonita's mother did our washing, in gratefulness—as my mother put it—for the use of a vacant lot of my grandfather's which was a couple of blocks down the street. On the lot was an old one-room shack which had been a shed long ago, and this Chonita's father had patched up with flattened-out pieces of tin. He was a laborer. Ever since the end of the border troubles there had been a development boom in the Valley, and Chonita's father was getting his share of the good times. Clearing brush and building irrigation ditches, he sometimes pulled down as much as six dollars a week. He drank a good deal of it up, it was true. But corn was just a few cents a bushel in those days. He was the breadwinner, you might say, while Chonita furnished the luxuries.

Chonita was a poet too. I had just moved into the neighborhood when a boy came up to me and said, "Come on! Let's go hear Chonita make a speech."

She was already on top of the alley fence when we got there, a scrawny little girl of about nine, her bare dirty feet clinging to the fence almost like hands. A dozen other kids were there below her, waiting. Some were boys I knew at school; five or six were her younger brothers and sisters.

"Speech! Speech!" they all cried. "Let Chonita make a speech! Talk in English, Chonita!"

They were grinning and nudging each other except for her brothers and sisters, who looked up at her with proud serious faces. She gazed out beyond us all with a grand, distant air and then she spoke.

"Give me the hammon and the beans!" she yelled. "Give me the hammon and the beans!"

She leaped off the fence and everybody cheered and told her how good it was and how she could talk English better than the teachers at the grammar school.

I thought it was a pretty poor joke. Every evening almost, they would make her get up on the fence and yell, "Give me the hammon and the beans!" And everybody would cheer and make her think she was talking English. As for me, I would wait there until she got it over with so we could play at something else. I wondered how long it would be before they got tired of it all. I never did find out because just about that time I got the chills and fever, and when I got up and around, Chonita wasn't there anymore.

In later years I thought of her a lot, especially during the thirties when I was growing up. Those years would have been just made for her. Many's the time I have seen her in my mind's eye, in the picket lines demanding not bread, not cake, but the hammon and the beans. But it didn't work out that way.

One night Doctor Zapata came into our kitchen through the back door. He set his bag on the table and said to my father, who had opened the door for him, "Well, she is dead."

My father flinched. "What was it?" he asked.

The doctor had gone to the window and he stood with his back to us, looking out toward the lights of Fort Jones. "Pneumonia, flu, malnutrition, worms, the evil eye," he said without turning around. "What the hell difference does it make?"

"I wish I had known how sick she was," my father said in a very mild tone. "Not that it's really my affair, but I wish I had."

The doctor snorted and shook his head.

My mother came in and I asked her who was dead. She told me. It made me feel strange but I did not cry. My mother put her arm around my shoulders. "She is in Heaven now," she said. "She is happy."

I shrugged her arm away and sat down in one of the kitchen chairs.

"They're like animals," the doctor was saying. He turned round suddenly and his eyes glistened in the light. "Do you know what that brute of a father was doing when I left? He was laughing! Drinking and laughing with his friends."

"There's no telling what the poor man feels," my mother said.

My father made a deprecatory gesture. "It wasn't his daughter, anyway."

"No?" the doctor said. He sounded interested.

"This is the woman's second husband," my father explained. "First one died before the girl was born, shot and hanged from a mesquite limb. He

*Girl Sitting (Niña Sentada)*, 1959
Jesus Guerrer Galvan (b. 1912)

was working too close to the tracks the day the Olmito train was derailed."

"You know what?" the doctor said. "In classical times they did things better. Take Troy, for instance. After they stormed the city they grabbed the babies by the heels and dashed them against the wall. That was more humane."

My father smiled. "You sound very radical. You sound just like your relative down there in Morelos."

"No relative of mine," the doctor said. "I'm a conservative, the son of a conservative, and you know that I wouldn't be here except for that little detail."

**The Hammon and the Beans** 189

"Habit," my father said. "Pure habit, pure tradition. You're a radical at heart."

"It depends on how you define radicalism," the doctor answered. "People tend to use words too loosely. A dentist could be called a radical, I suppose. He pulls up things by the roots."

My father chuckled.

"Any bandit in Mexico nowadays can give himself a political label," the doctor went on, "and that makes him respectable. He's a leader of the people."

"Take Villa, now . . ." my father began.

"Villa was a different type of man," the doctor broke in.

"I don't see any difference."

The doctor came over to the table and sat down. "Now look at it this way," he began, his finger in front of my father's face. My father threw back his head and laughed.

"You'd better go to bed and rest," my mother told me. "You're not completely well, you know."

So I went to bed, but I didn't go to sleep, not right away. I lay there for a long time while behind my darkened eyelids Emiliano Zapata's cavalry charged down to the broad Santee, where there were grave men with hoary hairs. I was still awake at eleven when the cold voice of the bugle went gliding in and out of the dark like something that couldn't find its way back to wherever it had been. I thought of Chonita in Heaven, and I saw her in her torn and dirty dress, with a pair of bright wings attached, flying round and round like a butterfly shouting, "Give me the hammon and the beans!"

Then I cried. And whether it was the bugle, or whether it was Chonita or what, to this day I do not know. But cry I did, and I felt much better after that.

# Sabine Ulibarrí

1919–1988 (Mexican American)

## Meet the Writer

Born in Santa Fe, New Mexico, **Sabine Ulibarrí** (sah BEE neh  oo lee bahr REE) grew up in the northern New Mexican town of Tierra Amarilla and attended the University of New Mexico, teaching for a time before joining the United States Air Force as a gunner during World War II.

Ulibarrí earned his master's degree and his doctorate before returning to teach at the University of New Mexico. There, his many students remember "Uli" as an agreeable man whose recitations of Spanish poetry still echo through the halls.

Ulibarrí is perhaps best known for his essays, which established him as a leading voice in contemporary Mexican American literature. Yet it is in his creative writing that he made his strongest attempts to preserve his Hispanic heritage. Ulibarrí long urged Mexican Americans not to abandon their native Spanish; he felt that losing their language would lead to losing their heritage.

In 1966, Ulibarrí published two books of poetry: *Al cielo se sube a pie* (*You Get to Heaven on Foot*) and *Amor y Ecuador* (*Love and Ecuador*). His collections of short stories, *Tierra Amarilla* (1964) and *Mi abuela fumaba puros* (*My Grandma Smoked Cigars*) (1977), reflect the traditional values, customs, and sentiments of northern New Mexico.

## Background

In many of his stories, Ulibarrí wistfully recounts incidents of his childhood in Tierra Amarilla with awe, humor, and excitement. In "My Wonder Horse," the author takes the legend of a fabulous white horse that roamed the countryside and transforms it into a living symbol of beauty, strength, and freedom. In this story and others, the young narrator (perhaps representing Ulibarrí himself) gains key insights about himself and about life, insights that mark significant steps in the passage from youth to maturity.

**Before You Read** *The transition from childhood to adulthood is often marked by "rites of passage"—challenging tests of skill, strength, endurance, and character that a young person must face. In the following story, the narrator describes his physical and emotional experiences as he seeks the object of his waking and sleeping dreams—a magnificent white horse. The narrator's challenges, victory, and ultimate loss during his quest change him in a way neither he nor readers anticipate.*

*As you read, notice how Ulibarrí uses vivid figures of speech to heighten the drama and the sense of intense, personal experience. What key insights does the narrator gain about himself and life in this experience, which marks the passage from youth to maturity?*

# My Wonder Horse
## Sabine Ulibarrí

He was white. White as memories lost. He was free. Free as happiness is. He was fantasy, liberty, and excitement. He filled and dominated the mountain valleys and surrounding plains. He was a white horse that flooded my youth with dreams and poetry.

Around the campfires of the country and in the sunny patios of the town, the ranch hands talked about him with enthusiasm and admiration. But gradually their eyes would become hazy and blurred with dreaming. The lively talk would die down. All thoughts fixed on the vision evoked by the horse. Myth of the animal kingdom. Poem of the world of men.

White and mysterious, he paraded his harem through the summer forests with lordly rejoicing. Winter sent him to the plains and sheltered hillsides for the protection of his females. He spent the summer like an oriental potentate in his woodland gardens. The winter he passed like an illustrious warrior celebrating a well-earned victory.

He was a legend. The stories told of the Wonder Horse were endless. Some true, others fabricated. So many traps, so many snares, so many searching parties, and all in vain. The horse always escaped, always mocked his pursuers, always rose above the control of man. Many a valiant cowboy swore to put his halter and his brand on the animal. But always he had to confess later that the mystic horse was more of a man than he.

I was fifteen years old. Although I had never seen the Wonder Horse, he filled my imagination and fired my ambition. I used to listen open-mouthed as my father and the ranch hands talked about the phantom horse who turned into mist and air and nothingness when he was trapped. I joined in the universal obsession—like the hope of winning the lottery—of putting my lasso on him some day, of capturing him and showing him off on Sunday afternoons when the girls of the town strolled through the streets.

It was high summer. The forests were fresh, green, and gay. The cattle moved slowly, fat and sleek in the August sun and shadow. Listless and drowsy in the lethargy of late afternoon, I was dozing on my horse. It was time to round up the herd and go back to the good bread of the cowboy camp. Already my comrades would be sitting around the campfire, playing the guitar, telling stories of past or present, or surrendering to the languor of the late afternoon. The sun was setting behind me in a riot of streaks and colors. Deep, harmonious silence.

I sit drowsily still, forgetting the cattle in the glade. Suddenly the forest falls silent, a deafening quiet. The afternoon comes to a standstill. The breeze stops blowing, but it vibrates. The sun flares hotly. The planet, life, and time itself have stopped in an inexplicable way. For a moment, I don't understand what is happening.

Then my eyes focus. There he is! The Wonder Horse! At the end of the glade, on high ground surrounded by summer green. He is a statue. He is an engraving. Line and form and white stain on a green background. Pride, prestige, and art incarnate in animal flesh. A picture of burning beauty and virile freedom. An ideal, pure and invincible, rising from the eternal dreams of humanity. Even today my being thrills when I remember him.

A sharp neigh. A far-reaching challenge that soars on high, ripping the virginal fabric of the rosy clouds. Ears at the point. Eyes flashing. Tail waving active defiance. Hoofs glossy and destructive. Arrogant ruler of the countryside.

The moment is never ending, a momentary eternity. It no longer exists, but it will always live. . . . There must have been mares. I did not see them. The cattle went on their indifferent way. My horse followed them, and I came slowly back from the land of dreams to the world of toil. But life could no longer be what it was before.

That night under the stars I didn't sleep. I dreamed. How much I dreamed awake and how much I dreamed asleep, I do not know. I only know that a white horse occupied my dreams and filled them with vibrant sound, and light, and turmoil.

Summer passed and winter came. Green grass gave place to white snow. The herds descended from the mountains to the valleys and the hollows. And in the town they kept saying that the Wonder Horse was roaming through this or that secluded area. I inquired everywhere for his whereabouts. Every day he became for me more of an ideal, more of an idol, more of a mystery.

It was Sunday. The sun had barely risen above the snowy mountains. My breath was a white cloud. My horse was trembling with cold and fear like me. I left without going to mass. Without any breakfast. Without the usual bread and sardines in my saddle bags. I had slept badly, but had kept the vigil well. I was going in search of the white light that galloped through my dreams.

On leaving the town for the open country, the roads disappear. There are no tracks, human or animal. Only a silence, deep, white, and sparkling. My horse breaks trail with his chest and leaves an unending wake, an open rift, in the white sea. My trained, concentrated gaze covers the landscape from horizon to horizon, searching for the noble silhouette of the talismanic horse.

It must have been midday. I don't know. Time had lost its meaning. I found him! On a slope stained with sunlight. We saw one another at the same time. Together, we turned to stone. Motionless, absorbed, and panting, I gazed at his beauty, his pride, his nobility. As still as sculptured marble, he allowed himself to be admired.

A sudden, violent scream breaks the silence. A glove hurled into my face. A challenge and a mandate. Then something surprising happens. The horse that in summer takes his stand between any threat and his herd, swinging back and forth from left to right, now plunges into the snow. Stronger than they, he is breaking trail for his mares. They follow him. His flight is slow in order to conserve his strength.

I follow. Slowly. Quivering. Thinking about his intelligence. Admiring his courage. Understanding his courtesy. The afternoon advances. My horse is taking it easy.

One by one the mares become weary. One by one, they drop out of the trail. Alone! He and I. My inner ferment bubbles to my lips. I speak to him. He listens and is quiet.

He still opens the way, and I follow in the path he leaves me. Behind us a long, deep trench crosses the white plain. My horse, which has eaten grain and good hay, is still strong. Undernourished as the Wonder Horse is, his strength is waning. But he keeps on because that is the way he is. He does not know how to surrender.

I now see black stains over his body. Sweat and the wet snow have revealed the black skin beneath the white hair. Snorting breath, turned to steam, tears the air. White spume above white snow. Sweat, spume, and steam. Uneasiness.

I felt like an executioner. But there was no turning back. The distance between us was growing relentlessly shorter. God and Nature watched indifferently.

I feel sure of myself at last. I untie the rope. I open the lasso and pull the reins tight. Every nerve, every muscle is tense. My heart is in my mouth. Spurs pressed against trembling flanks. The horse leaps. I whirl the rope and throw the obedient lasso.

A frenzy of fury and rage. Whirlpools of light and fans of transparent snow. A rope that whistles and burns the saddle tree. Smoking, fighting gloves. Eyes burning in their sockets. Mouth parched. Fevered forehead. The whole earth shakes and shudders. The long, white trench ends in a wide, white pool.

Deep, gasping quiet. The Wonder Horse is mine! Both still trembling, we look at one another squarely for a long time. Intelligent and realistic, he stops struggling and even takes a hesitant step toward me. I speak to him. As I talk, I approach him. At first, he flinches and recoils. Then he waits for me. The two horses greet one another in their own way. Finally, I succeed in stroking his mane. I tell him many things, and he seems to understand.

Ahead of me, along the trail already made, I drove him toward the town. Triumphant. Exultant. Childish laughter gathered in my throat. With my newfound manliness, I controlled it. I wanted to sing, but I fought down the desire. I wanted to shout, but I kept quiet. It was the ultimate in happiness. It was the pride of the male adolescent. I felt myself a conqueror.

Occasionally the Wonder Horse made a try for his liberty, snatching me abruptly from my thoughts. For a few moments, the struggle was renewed. Then we went on.

It was necessary to go through the town. There was no other way. The sun was setting. Icy streets and people on the porches. The Wonder Horse full of terror and panic for the first time. He ran and my well-shod horse stopped him. He slipped and fell on his side. I suffered for him. The indignity. The humiliation. Majesty degraded. I begged him not to struggle, to let himself be led. How it hurt me that other people should see him like that!

Finally we reached home.

"What shall I do with you, Mago? If I put you into the stable or the corral, you are sure to hurt yourself. Besides, it would be an insult. You aren't a slave. You aren't a servant. You aren't even an animal."

I decided to turn him loose in the fenced pasture. There, little by little, Mago would become accustomed to my friendship and my company. No animal had ever escaped from that pasture.

My father saw me coming and waited for me without a word. A smile played over his face, and a spark danced in his eyes. He watched me take the rope from Mago, and the two of us thoughtfully observed him move away. My father clasped my hand a little more firmly than usual and said, "That was a man's job." That was all. Nothing more was needed. We understood one another very well. I was playing the role of a real man, but the childish laughter and shouting that bubbled up inside me almost destroyed the impression I wanted to create.

That night I slept little, and when I slept, I did not know that I was asleep. For dreaming is the same when one really dreams, asleep or awake. I was up at dawn. I had to go to see my Wonder Horse. As soon as it was light, I went out into the cold to look for him.

The pasture was large. It contained a grove of trees and a small gully. The Wonder Horse was not visible anywhere, but I was not worried. I walked slowly, my head full of the events of yesterday and my plans for the future. Suddenly I realized that I had walked a long way. I quicken my steps. I look apprehensively around me. I begin to be afraid. Without knowing it, I begin to run. Faster and faster.

He is not there. The Wonder Horse has escaped. I search every corner where he could be hidden. I follow his tracks. I see that during the night he walked incessantly, sniffing, searching for a way out. He did not find one. He made one for himself.

I followed the track that led straight to the fence. And I saw that the trail did not stop but continued on the other side. It was a barbed-wire fence. There was white hair on the wire. There was blood on the barbs. There were red stains on the snow and little red drops in the hoofprints on the other side of the fence.

I stopped there. I did not go any farther. The rays of the morning sun on my face. Eyes clouded and yet filled with light. Childish tears on the cheeks of a man. A cry stifled in my throat. Slow, silent sobs.

Standing there, I forgot myself and the world and time. I cannot explain it, but my sorrow was mixed with pleasure. I was weeping with happiness. No matter how much it hurt me, I was rejoicing over the flight and the freedom of the Wonder Horse, the dimensions of his indomitable spirit. Now he would always be fantasy, freedom, and excitement. The Wonder Horse was transcendent. He had enriched my life forever.

My father found me there. He came close without a word and laid his arm across my shoulders. We stood looking at the white trench with its flecks of red that led into the rising sun.

# Rolando Hinojosa-Smith

b. 1929–   (Mexican American)

## Meet the Writer

In his writing as well as in person, **Rolando Hinojosa-Smith** (roh LAHN doh ee noh HOH sah smith) is eloquent yet plain-spoken, good-humored yet deeply serious. One of the most well-respected Latino writers in the United States, he won the 1973 Quinto Sol Prize for his first novel, *Estampas del valle y otras obras* (*Sketches of the Valley and Other Works*).

Born in Mercedes, Texas, in the Rio Grande Valley, Hinojosa-Smith's life and works reflect the cultural synthesis of the border area. His mother was Anglo; his father was a Mexican American whose Spanish ancestors first settled in the Valley in 1749. His early immersion in Hispanic culture (he did not speak to any Anglo children until he was eleven or twelve years old) had a profound influence on his sense of identity.

Hinojosa-Smith began his education in a private school run by Mexican exiles, which reinforced his ties to Mexican culture. His love of words and reading was obvious at an early age. Often sick as a child, he spent many days at home, where he read constantly. His first attempts at writing began in high school, and the school's library still makes these early attempts available to those who visit.

Regarding himself as a Mexican American with strong ties to that culture, Hinojosa-Smith is equally fluent in Spanish and English and feels at home writing in both languages. He has enjoyed a long and illustrious academic career at the University of Texas at Austin.

## Background

Hinojosa-Smith believes that his role as a writer is to present the "eternal verities" (truths) of human nature and experience—to address the lives and concerns not only of Mexican Americans but of human beings in general. Much of his writing exhibits a sharp irony that is wise and knowing rather than bitter or cynical. Hinojosa-Smith's best-known works are his novels, which reflect the characters' memories of their pasts and their reflections on their present lives.

**Before You Read**  Hinojosa-Smith's memories in this essay are richly detailed and lovingly narrated. The author's appreciation for his dual-language heritage and the subtle and painless methods his parents used to enhance his obvious fascination with language create a warm reflection of a pleasant childhood. What memories do you have of something precious to you? How do those memories affect your life?

# Words and Palabras
## Rolando Hinojosa-Smith

There are certain words I remember hearing for the first time, learning what they meant, and I can usually remember who said them and where. At the instant of hearing those early words, sometimes they invoke people, images and memories; a whiff of nostalgia, almost. Considerable talent and distance aside, a produced sensation much like Proust's madeleine.[1]

At age twelve, for example, although I must have *read* the word *infamy* somewhere, I'd not heard it until Roosevelt's speech before Congress those many years ago. A high-sounding phrase it was, that day which was to live in infamy, and millions who heard it then are now dead and perhaps forgotten, I dare say. For me, I keep that late president and his words alive through my memory of him.

Out of the mouth of a man named Antonio García, a grocery store owner in my hometown, Mercedes, Texas, Mexican-born and American-naturalized, came the phrase *la serie mundial* which one of my brothers translated for me as the World Series. (This was in the days of radio and the Yankees versus the Giants in the thirties; the days of Hubbell, Bill Terry, Gehrig and Bill Dickey).

The listening to the games was an annual rite; I worked at the store as a sackboy, and there they were, in front of the García store, a group of some fifty to sixty middle-aged Texas Mexican men sitting on long benches, while a man named Carlos Leal, standing before them, did the play-by-play in Spanish. Leal, a man of scant formal education in English, was, as my father put it, *un autodidacta.*

Leal was a reader. The word doesn't need an adjective, I don't think. In brief, his pronunciation was Northern Mexican, but his knowledge of history and politics, particularly Lower Rio Grande Valley history and politics, was encyclopaedic. He was also a great storyteller, an impenitent digressor, and a man who, at age forty-two, took and passed his army physical during World War II.

I come from a rural background, and I learned the Spanish words for mace, nutmeg, thyme, rosemary, clove, and so on, from him. And so, it was a constant crisscrossing of English and Spanish vocabulary-building under his informal tutelage. Later, when my father sent me to Luis Salinas' office to learn the use of the typewriter in preparation for high school, it was from Salinas I learned the Spanish names for one's fingers: *el meñique,* the little finger; *el anular,* the ring fin-

---

1. Proust's madeleine [usually spelled *madeleine*]: allusion to an incident in *Remembrance of Things Past* by Marcel Proust in which a character bites into a madeleine (cookie), thus releasing a flood of childhood memories.

ger; *el cordial,* the middle finger; *el índice* for the index; and *el pulgar* (*pulgada* = inch) for the thumb. As for some of the other body parts, I think I knew them by then, although I can't recall in which language I first learned them. My father too had little formal education; but he'd garnered enough to read and write in both English and Spanish; since he too was a reader (at times he would read to my mother and vice versa), my vocabulary in both languages grew painlessly, unconsciously even. But even now, whenever I hear certain words that he used, I see his face clearly: a full head of brownish hair turning gray, blue eyes, as blue as my mother's, a reddish face, and even teeth; too even I thought as a child, because I thought them false; I was wrong.

My mother, Carrie Effie Smith, spoke the same regional Spanish as the people just mentioned. Her father, Abraham Neumann Smith and her mother, Mary Phillips, had been enticed to the Valley by Lawyer Jim Wells. My mother was but six weeks old when the Smiths came down from Rockport, Texas, via a series of small South Texas towns and settlements. The year was 1887.

Her childhood friends in the villages of Relámpago and Progreso, where my grandfather served as postmaster, were both Texas Anglo and Texas Mexican. Among them were the Jeffords brothers, Harold and Julius. Harold was called Jarito (close to Harry in sound with the Spanish J pronounced as the English H); Julius was called Julio. As children, they, along with my mother spoke both languages, again crisscrossing them as fluent speakers can and do, whenever it suits them.

Jarito (this is the story my mother told me) must've been sixteen years old and ready to be sent to Brownsville to attend high school, when he learned that he, Jarito Jeffords, was an Anglo, of all things. My uncle Jack was the one who told him; needless to say, my uncle Jack also spoke Spanish like a native. From him, I learned *nejayote, nixtamal,* and *machiguas.* The first (*nejayotl*, in Nahuatl) is the yellowish water left over when lye is used to soften the corn for making *nixtamal;* the *nixtamal* is then ground into dough (*masa*) for making tortillas, tamales, and so on. The third word, *machiguas,* is the clean water used to keep the hands moist as the tortillas are slapped and shaped by hand. (A word to the purists: Mexican women, in the home, have been using cast-iron tortilla presses for over thirty years; the reason? They are fast, practical, and cheap).

I first attended a Spanish-language school from ages four to five; a school, incidentally, run by a Mexican exile biding his time in the Valley while one stage or another of the Mexican Revolution played itself out. He would read sections from *La Prensa* to us on Fridays. *La Prensa* was the Spanish-language daily published in San Antonio by the Ignacio Lozano family; it ran from 1912 until 1962, and was mailed or sent by train to its subscribers all over Texas and northern Mexico. The school and the newspaper filled the voids in politics, social notes, sports, and so on.

Later, in high school, the two teachers I remember most clearly were Merle Blankenship and Amy Cornish. The two English teachers also served as the school's toughest hurdles; it wasn't that English presented a problem for Texas Mexicans alone since our fellow students, the Texas Anglos, had a time of it just as we did.

One incident stands out: In an oral book report, in my junior year, I used the term *nary;* God alone knows where *that* came from. The point is one of the students objected to its use, and as usual in those cases, we turned to Miss Cornish for *adjudication* (this last word I learned from my brother-in-law, an attorney). To go on, Miss Cornish overruled my usage and went on to talk about *diction.* She then defined enunciation and pronunciation as well.

One of the words Miss Blankenship dropped on us in Freshman English was *colloquialisms.* I have used this term to my students on occasion; many claim never to have heard it before. I believe them.

The Army and college, later on, introduced me to regionalisms. Too many for me to go into here, although some do stand out. *Tonic* is one such word, as used by some New Englanders, for what we called soda water or pop or, as a Louisiana friend of mine called it, "a cold drank." The other word refers to a sandwich that went by many names: gyro, pronounced and written at times as hero; there was also hoagy or hoagie, poor boy, and my favorite, grinder; this was a New England word, as I recall. I may be wrong in this, but one of the pleasures of being a teacher is that I'm always open to "any corrections and or additions" (a little phrase picked up in junior high homeroom during the reading of something called "the minutes").

Obviously, mathematics and the various sciences brought new words, but there was always Carlos Leal or my father to give me the Spanish *sodio cloruro* for sodium chloride, for one example; I'd gone for an easy guess, for what I thought was a cognate: *clorido.* The word doesn't exist.

As a youngster, however, my parents, naturally enough, introduced me to most of the new words. It wasn't a class nor did they make it a point of being teachers and I their student. Come to that, the words would flow in conversations among themselves, their friends, and our relatives. Too, both sensed, knew perhaps, that I was a ready-made market for new words.

I chose the list that follows, because they are not ordinary words; ordinary in the sense that they're not much heard in everyday speech anymore, it doesn't seem to me.

The first one, but in no particular order, was *generalísimo;* I heard it (and of this I am sure) on a Sunday morning while my mother shaved my father; this she did only on Sundays after Mass since he shaved himself on the other days of the week. And Sundays were special since *La Prensa,* the Spanish-language daily I mentioned, came in at a hefty four pounds. There was reading there for the family for the whole day. It rankled my father that Francisco Franco had assumed that high-sounding title; my father didn't much like the term *caudillo,* also assumed by Franco; as a former military man, *generalísimo* was too much for him.

At home, my father referred to Franco as *El usurpador,* The Usurper. When Chiang Kai-Shek, used the same title he too was unacceptable; the man was, in a word, *corrompido,* corrupt. This was a word my father also reserved for Stalin. He didn't have kind words for Hitler, either.

It's not often nowadays one hears, or reads, *usurper* to describe the military men in charge of state governments. In passing, it's only natural that I learned *junta* from him; I suppose it was in high school or through English-language newspapers that I learned the same word existed as a borrowing in English, but with the usual English pronunciation where the J is pronounced much like the G in *page.*

The Spanish Civil war also introduced me to *la quinta columna, the fifth column.* The emigration of Spaniards to Mexico did not necessarily revive, although it did reinforce, the use of the pejorative[2] *gachupín,* a word used principally in Mexico to describe the Spaniards. The word *refugiados* (refugee) must have been added to my vocabulary around this time, much like the term Displaced Persons (*la gente desplazada*), at the end of World War II.

That war brought more words; my father would read to us from *La Prensa* and from *El Heraldo de Brownsville;* for my part, I read from

---

2. **pejorative** (pih JAWR uh tihv): word or term that is disparaging or derogatory.

*The Brownsville Herald*, which I delivered in the Texas Anglo part of town. As an aside, it seems to me that newspapers were better written in those days; it's an impression, and only that.

I also heard the words *Eje* (the Axis Powers) and *quisling*[3] from my parents; to them, I also owe the terms for the various army units from squad to platoon to company, battalion, regiment, and so on; and almost immediately, they would be filled in with their Spanish equivalents. These words took their place alongside destroyer, cruiser, battleship, and a fairly new one at the time, *portaviones* for aircraft carriers. The rest of that wartime vocabulary I must have picked up on my own, and since the seven of us ate as a group, the dinner table, always an exciting time.

The few months' respite between the end of the Spanish Civil War and the beginning of World War II, provided two social notes for me: *compromiso* and *noviazgo*. I learned that my oldest sister, Clarissa Effie, was engaged at the time: *estaba comprometida*, and was thus in her courtship stage, *el noviazgo*. I liked the sound of the words, but I don't think I found a reason or an excuse to use them with anyone at the time.

Finally, the word *scapegoat;* I heard it in Spanish first, and then in English on another Sunday morning. My father was referring to General Jonathan Wainwright. MacArthur was now stationed in Australia, and Skinny Wainwright had been left to face General Homma's terms of surrender when the Philippines fell.

The Sunday *La Prensa* was spread out around the house, and I was reading the American comics in Spanish (Mickey Mouse or *El ratón Miguelito*; Donald Duck aka *El Pato Pascual*); of marginal interest: the widespread use of English since 1945 has now caused Donald to be referred to as such in most Spanish-speaking countries.

---

3. **quisling** (KWIHZ lihng): a traitor.

My father's voice, even and tempered usually, rose a bit; that was the signal for an opinion. Something was said, but I couldn't make it out. Walking into their room, I heard him say something on the order of:

*Eso es lo que es, ni más ni menos, ¿eh?* " 'Cause that's what he is; no more no less, right?"

I'd missed what the word was, and so I asked.

*"El general Wainwright es nada menos que un chivo expiatorio."*

My mother turned to me and said, *scapegoat*.

Well! I'd no idea what either one was talking about; so, it was to some room or other to find myself a dictionary.

The meaning in the Merriam-Webster's was clear enough, but my father's editorializing and use of examples brought the word to life to me. A lesson I've banked on in my career.

Years later, after war's end, the city of Brownsville invited General Wainwright to a local celebration; the General had served there, in Fort Brown, as a young cavalry officer.

The war spirit was still on despite the peace treaties signed aboard the USS Missouri a few months back, and the citizenry turned out to see that frail old man who'd survived captivity along with Manuel Chacón from Mercedes and Valentín Gavito from Brownsville, both of whom had also been captured in the Philippines.

My father who was grateful that my oldest brothers had survived their wars in the Pacific, cried that day; he mourned another Mercedes youngster, Clemente García, who numbered among the fallen in the Philippines, the fortress of Corregidor, another Spanish word.

Some innocent orator was extolling Wainwright, as he should have, I guess, but the speech was rather windy; nothing new, then. And, the speaker must have gone on to repeat himself, as often happens on those occasions.

On the drive home, my mother said the General looked embarrassed, and the poor man probably was. He was certainly uncomfortable, and then there was that *speech*.

My father had one word for the speech: *pedantería*. I don't think this needs translating, and I had fun with it on the way home. I asked since the orator used *pedantería*, what did that make him?

*Ese loco es un pedante, hijo.* That was clear enough.

No mention was ever made as to my career, if indeed I was to have one. One thing was clear enough, however: words were meant to be used not abused, *usadas pero no abusadas.* Words to live by.

When he died, my father left us no money, no land, and no property of any kind. He left us words, *good* words, and a sense of respect for them; he also meant us to use them, as he said:

*Con frugalidad, por favor.*

# Nicholasa Mohr

b. 1938–    (Puerto Rican American)

## Meet the Writer

When it comes to young adult literature, **Nicholasa Mohr** (nee coh LAHS ah mohr) is one of the most critically acclaimed Latino writers working today. Her portraits of the lives of Puerto Rican families in New York City's barrios have been hailed as "realistic and uncompromising." Mohr does not see herself, however, as trying to capture the quintessential immigrant experience. "I just write about what I know and care deeply about," she says. "I think the more specific you are in your work, the more universal you become. . . . I write about Puerto Ricans because that is what I am."

Mohr's success is all the more remarkable when one considers that writing is her second career. Visual art was her first love. She studied it in high school and continued her training at the Art Students League in New York. Her large, bold paintings filled with words attracted interest, and her career as an artist took off. When a collector of her art, who also happened to be the head of a publishing company, contacted her and suggested she try writing, the eventual result was a first novel titled *Nilda*. Portraying a Puerto Rican girl's transition from childhood to adolescence, the award-winning novel explores poverty and discrimination in the United States. Mohr's later short story collections and novels also draw on her own coming-of-age memories and on her firsthand experience of life in the barrio.

## Background

Mohr is primarily interested in people's lives. In her collection *El Bronx Remembered: A Novella and Stories,* Mohr documents the experiences of everyday people and the development of the Puerto Rican community in the Bronx from the early stages of immigration through the middle 1950s. As the stories progress, the largely homogeneous community is increasingly exposed to interaction with other ethnic minorities, leading to friction and eventually to a stratification, or separation of the different ethnic groups within the community.

**Before You Read**  *This story, about an elderly Jewish man and his Puerto Rican neighbors, illuminates the ways in which ethnic heritage influences family life. As the contrast between Mr. Mendelsohn's lifestyle and that of the Suárezes is made clear, the reader can meditate upon what constitutes "family" and why there are so many different types of "family."*

*As you read the story, think about why Mr. Mendelsohn gravitates toward the Suárezes even though they are so different from him. How is it that he is so comfortable participating in their family life? Why does he not share the same kind of time with his own family?*

# Mr. Mendelsohn
## Nicholasa Mohr

"Psst . . . psst, Mr. Mendelsohn, wake up. Come on now!" Mrs. Suárez said in a low quiet voice. Mr. Mendelsohn had fallen asleep again, on the large armchair in the living room. He grasped the brown shiny wooden cane and leaned forward, his chin on his chest. The small black skullcap that was usually placed neatly on the back of his head had tilted to one side, covering his right ear. "Come on now. It's late, and time to go home." She tapped him on the shoulder and waited for him to wake up. Slowly, he lifted his head, opened his eyes, and blinked.

"What time is it?" he asked.

"It's almost midnight. Caramba! I didn't even know you was still here. When I came to shut off the lights, I saw you was sleeping."

"Oh . . . I'm sorry. O.K., I'm leaving." With short, slow steps he followed Mrs. Suárez over to the front door.

"Go on now," she said, opening the door. "We'll see you tomorrow."

He walked out into the hallway, stepped about three feet to the left, and stood before the door of his apartment. Mrs. Suárez waited, holding her door ajar, while he carefully searched for the right key to each lock. He had to open seven locks in all.

A small fluffy dog standing next to Mrs. Suárez began to whine and bark.

"Shh—sh, Sporty! Stop it!" she said. "You had your walk. Shh."

"O.K.," said Mr. Mendelsohn, finally opening his door. "Good night." Mrs. Suárez smiled and nodded.

"Good night," she whispered, as they both shut their doors simultaneously.

Mr. Mendelsohn knocked on the door and waited; then tried the doorknob. Turning and pushing, he realized the door was locked, and knocked again, this time more forcefully. He heard Sporty barking and footsteps coming toward the door.

"Who's there?" a child's voice asked.

"It's me—Mr. Mendelsohn! Open up, Yvonne." The door opened, and a young girl, age nine, smiled at him.

"Mami! It's el Señor Mr. Mendelsohn again."

"Tell him to come on in, muchacha!" Mrs. Suárez answered.

"My mother says come on in."

He followed Yvonne and the dog, who leaped up, barking and wagging his tail. Mr. Mendelsohn stood at the kitchen entrance and greeted everyone.

"Good morning to you all!" He had just shaved and trimmed his large black mustache. As he smiled broadly, one could see that most of his teeth were missing. His large bald head was partially covered by his small black skullcap. Thick dark grey hair grew in abundance at the lower back of his head, coming around the front above his ears into short sideburns. He wore a clean white shirt, frayed at the cuffs. His worn-out pinstripe trousers were held up by a pair of dark suspenders. Mr. Mendelsohn leaned on his brown shiny cane and carried a small brown paper bag.

"Mr. Mendelsohn, come into the kitchen," said Mrs. Suárez, "and have some coffee with us." She stood by the stove. A boy of eleven, a young man of about seventeen, and a young pregnant woman were seated at the table.

"Sit here," said the boy, vacating a chair. "I'm finished eating." He stood by the entrance with his sister Yvonne, and they both looked at Mr. Mendelsohn and his paper bag with interest.

"Thank you, Georgie," Mr. Mendelsohn said. He sat down and placed the bag on his lap.

The smell of freshly perked coffee and boiled milk permeated the kitchen.

Winking at everyone, the young man asked, "Hey, what you got in that bag you holding onto, huh, Mr. Mendelsohn?" They all looked at each other and at the old man, amused. "Something special, I bet!"

"Well," the old man replied, "I thought your mama would be so kind as to permit me to make myself a little breakfast here today . . . so." He opened the bag, and began to take out its contents. "I got two slices of rye bread, two tea bags. I brought one extra, just in case anybody would care to join me for tea. And a jar of herring in sour cream."

"Sounds delicious!" said the young man, sticking out his tongue and making a face. Yvonne and Georgie burst out laughing.

"Shh . . . sh." Mrs. Suárez shook her head and looked at her children disapprovingly. "Never mind, Julio!" she said to the young man. Turning to Mr. Mendelsohn, she said, "You got the same like you brought last Saturday, eh? You can eat with us anytime. How about some fresh coffee? I just made it. Yes?" Mr. Mendelsohn looked at her, shrugging his shoulders. "Come on, have some," she coaxed.

"O.K.," he replied. "If it's not too much bother."

"No bother," she said, setting out a place for the old man. "You gonna have some nice fresh bread with a little butter—it will go good with your herring." Mrs. Suárez cut a generous slice of freshly baked bread with a golden crust and buttered it. "Go on, eat. There's a plate and everything for your food. Go on, eat. . . ."

"Would anyone care for some?" Mr. Mendelsohn asked. "Perhaps a tea bag for a cup of tea?"

"No . . . no thank you, Mr. Mendelsohn," Mrs. Suárez answered. "Everybody here already ate. You go ahead and eat. You look too skinny; you better eat. Go on, eat your bread."

The old man began to eat vigorously.

"Can I ask you a question?" Julio asked the old man. "Man, I don't get you. You got a whole apartment next door all to yourself—six rooms! And you gotta come here to eat in this crowded kitchen. Why?"

"First of all, today is Saturday, and I thought I could bring in my food and your mama could turn on the stove for me. You know, in my religion you can't light a fire on Saturday."

"You come here anytime. I turn on the stove for you, don't worry," Mrs. Suárez said.

"Man, what about other days? We been living here for about six months, right?" Julio persisted. "And you do more cooking here than in your own place."

"It doesn't pay to turn on the gas for such a little bit of cooking. So I told the gas company to turn it off . . . for good! I got no more gas now, only an electric hot plate," the old man said.

Julio shook his head and sighed, "I don't know—"

"Julio, chico!" snapped Mrs. Suárez, interrupting him, "Basta—it doesn't bother nobody."

She looked severely at her son and shook her head. "You gotta go with your sister to the clinic today, so you better get ready now. You too, Marta."

"O.K., Mama," she answered, "but I wanted to see if I got mail from Ralphy today."

"You don't got time. I'll save you the mail; you read it when you get back. You and Julio better get ready; go on." Reluctantly, Marta stood up and yawned, stretching and arching her back.

"Marta," Mr. Mendelsohn said, "you taking care? . . . You know, this is a very delicate time for you."

"I am, Mr. Mendelsohn. Thank you."

"I raised six sisters," the old man said. "I ought to know. Six . . . and married them off to fine husbands. Believe me, I've done my share in life." Yvonne and Georgie giggled and poked each other.

"He's gonna make one of his speeches," they whispered.

". . . I never had children. No time to get married. My father died when I was eleven. I went to work supporting my mother and six younger sisters. I took care of them, and today they are all married, with families. They always call and want me to visit them. I'm too busy and I have no time. . . ."

"Too busy eating in our kitchen," whispered Julio. Marta, Georgie and Yvonne tried not to laugh out loud. Mrs. Suárez reached over and with a wooden ladle managed a light but firm blow on Julio's head.

". . . Only on the holidays, I make some time to see them. But otherwise, I cannot be bothered with all that visiting." Mr. Mendelsohn stopped speaking and began to eat again.

"Go on, Marta and Julio, you will be late for the clinic," Mrs. Suárez said. "And you two? What are you doing there smiling like two monkeys? Go find something to do!"

Quickly, Georgie and Yvonne ran down the hallway, and Julio and Marta left the kitchen.

Mrs. Suárez sat down beside the old man.

"Another piece of bread?" she asked.

"No, thank you very much. . . . I'm full. But it was delicious."

"You too skinny—you don't eat right, I bet." Mrs. Suárez shook her head. "Come tomorrow and have Sunday supper with us."

"I really couldn't."

"Sure, you could. I always make a big supper and there is plenty. All right? Mr. Suárez and I will be happy to have you."

"Are you sure it will be no bother?"

"What are you talking for the bother all the time? One more person is no bother. You come tomorrow. Yes?"

The old man smiled broadly and nodded. This was the first time he had been invited to Sunday supper with the family.

Mrs. Suárez stood and began clearing away the dishes. "O.K., you go inside; listen to the radio or talk to the kids or something. I got work to do."

Mr. Mendelsohn closed his jar of herring and put it back into the bag. "Can I leave this here till I go?"

"Leave it; I put it in the refrigerator for you."

Leaning on his cane, Mr. Mendelsohn stood up and walked out of the kitchen and down the long hallway into the living room. It was empty. He went over to a large armchair by the window. The sun shone through the window, covering the entire armchair and Mr. Mendelsohn. A canary cage was also by the window, and two tiny yellow birds chirped and hopped back and forth energetically. Mr. Mendelsohn felt drowsy; he shut his eyes. So many aches and pains, he thought. It was hard to sleep at night, but here, well . . . the birds began to chirp in unison and the old man opened one eye, glancing at them, and smiled. Then he shut his eyes once more and fell fast asleep.

When Mr. Mendelsohn opened his eyes, Georgie and Yvonne were in the living room. Yvonne held a deck of playing cards and Georgie read a comic book. She looked at the old man and, holding up the deck of cards, asked, "Do you wanna play a game of War? Huh, Mr. Mendelsohn?"

"I don't know how to play that," he answered.

"It's real easy. I'll show you. Come on . . . please!"

"Well," he shrugged, "sure, why not? Maybe I'll learn something."

Yvonne took a small maple end table and a wooden chair, and set them next to Mr. Mendelsohn. "Now . . ." she began, "I'll shuffle the cards and you cut, and then I throw down a card and you throw down a card and the one with the highest card wins. O.K.? And then, the one with the most cards of all wins the game. O.K.?"

"That's all?" he asked.

"That's all. Ready?" she asked, and sat down. They began to play cards.

"You know, my sister Jennie used to be a great card player," said Mr. Mendelsohn.

"Does she still play?" asked Yvonne.

"Oh . . ." Mr. Mendelsohn laughed. "I don't know anymore. She's already married and has kids. She was the youngest in my family—like you."

"Did she go to P.S. 39? On Longwood Avenue?"

"I'm sure she did. All my sisters went to school around here."

"Wow! You must be living here a long time, Mr. Mendelsohn."

"Forty-five years!" said the old man.

"Wowee!" Yvonne whistled. "Georgie, did you hear? Mr. Mendelsohn been living here for forty-five whole years!"

Georgie put down his comic book and looked up.

"Really?" he asked, impressed.

"Yes, forty-five years this summer we moved here. But in those days things were different, not like today. No sir! The Bronx has changed. Then, it was the country. That's right! Why, look out the window. You see the elevated trains on Westchester Avenue? Well, there were no trains then. That was once a dirt road. They used to bring cows through there."

"Oh, man!" Georgie and Yvonne both gasped.

"Sure. These buildings were among the first apartment houses to go up. Four stories high, and that used to be a big accomplishment in them days. All that was here was mostly little houses, like you still see here and there. Small farms, woodlands . . . like that."

"Did you see any Indians?" asked Georgie.

"What do you mean, Indians?" laughed the old man. "I'm not that old, and this here was not the Wild West." Mr. Mendelsohn saw that the children were disappointed. He added quickly, "But we did have carriages with horses. No cars and lots of horses."

"That's what Mami says they have in Puerto Rico—not like here in El Bronx," said Yvonne.

"Yeah," Georgie agreed. "Papi says he rode a horse when he was a little kid in Puerto Rico. They had goats and pigs and all them things. Man, was he lucky."

"Lucky?" Mr. Mendelsohn shook his head. "You—you are the lucky one today! You got school and a good home and clothes. You don't have to go out to work and support a family like your papa and I had to do, and miss an education. You can learn and be somebody someday."

"Someday," said Yvonne, "we are gonna get a house with a yard and all. Mami says that when Ralphy gets discharged from the Army, he'll get a loan from the government and we can pay to buy a house. You know, instead of rent."

Mrs. Suárez walked into the living room with her coat on, carrying a shopping bag.

"Yvonne, take the dog out for a walk, and Georgie, come on! We have to go shopping. Get your jacket."

Mr. Mendelsohn started to rise. "No," she said, "stay . . . sit down. It's O.K. You can stay and rest if you want."

"All right, Mrs. Suárez," Mr. Mendelsohn said.

"Now don't forget tomorrow for Sunday supper, and take a nap if you like."

Mr. Mendelsohn heard the front door slam shut, and the apartment was silent. The warmth of the bright sun made him drowsy once more. It was so nice here, he thought, a house full of people and kids—like it used to be. He recalled his sisters and his parents . . . the holidays . . . the arguments . . . the laughing. It was so empty next door. He would have to look for a smaller apartment, near Jennie, someday. But not now. Now, it was just nice to sleep and rest right here. He heard the tiny birds chirping and quietly drifted into a deep sleep.

Mr. Mendelsohn rang the bell, then opened the door. He could smell the familiar cooking odors of Sunday supper. For two years he had spent every Sunday at his neighbors'. Sporty greeted him, jumping affectionately and barking.

"Shh—sh . . . down. Good boy," he said, and walked along the hallway toward the kitchen. The room was crowded with people and the stove was loaded with large pots of food, steaming and puffing. Mrs. Suárez was busy basting a large roast. Looking up, she saw Mr. Mendelsohn.

"Come in," she said, "and sit down." Motioning to Julio, who was seated, she continued, "Julio, you are finished, get up and give Mr. Mendelsohn a seat." Julio stood up.

"Here's the sponge cake," Mr. Mendelsohn said, and handed the cake box he carried to Julio, who put it in the refrigerator.

"That's nice. . . . Thank you," said Mrs. Suárez, and placed a cup of freshly made coffee before the old man.

"Would anyone like some coffee?" Mr. Mendelsohn asked. Yvonne and Georgie giggled, looked at one another, and shook their heads.

"You always say that!" said Yvonne.

"One of these days," said Ralphy, "I'm gonna say, 'Yes, give me your coffee,' and you won't have none to drink." The children laughed loudly.

"Don't tease him," Mrs. Suárez said, half smiling. "Let him have his coffee."

"He is just being polite, children," Mr. Suárez said, and shifting his chair closer to Mr. Mendelsohn, he asked, "So . . . Mr. Mendelsohn, how you been? What's new? You O.K.?"

"So-so, Mr. Suárez. You know, aches and pains when you get old. But there's nothing you can do, so you gotta make the best of it."

Mr. Suárez nodded sympathetically, and they continued to talk.

Mr. Mendelsohn saw the family every day, except for Mr. Suárez and Ralphy, who both worked a night shift.

Marta appeared in the entrance, holding a small child by the hand.

"There he is, Tato," she said to the child, and pointed to Mr. Mendelsohn.

"Oh, my big boy! He knows, he knows he's my best friend," Mr. Mendelsohn said, and held the brown shiny cane out toward Tato. The small boy grabbed the cane and, shrieking with delight, walked toward Mr. Mendelsohn.

"Look at that, will you?" said Ralphy. "He knows Mr. Mendelsohn better than me, his own father."

"That's because they are always together," smiled Marta. "Tato is learning to walk with his cane!"

Everyone laughed as they watched Tato climbing the old man's knee. Bending over, Mr. Mendelsohn pulled Tato onto his lap.

"Oh . . . he's getting heavy," said Mrs. Suárez. "Be careful."

"Never mind," Mr. Mendelsohn responded, hugging Tato. "That's my best boy. And look how swell he walks, and he's not even nineteen months."

"What a team," Julio said. "Tato already walks

*Portrait of Johann Harms,* 1916  Egon Schiele
Oil with wax on canvas  54½ × 42½ inches
Solomon R. Guggenheim Museum, New York. Partial gift, Dr. and Mrs. Otto Kallir, 1969. 69.1884

like Mr. Mendelsohn and pretty soon he's gonna complain like him, too. . . ." Julio continued to tease the old man, who responded good-naturedly, as everyone laughed.

After coffee, Mr. Mendelsohn sat on the large armchair in the living room, waiting for supper to be ready. He watched with delight as Tato walked back and forth with the cane. Mr. Mendelsohn held Tato's blanket, stuffed bear, and picture book.

"Tato," he called out, "come here. Let me read you a book—come on. I'm going to read you a nice story."

Tato climbed onto the chair and into Mr. Mendelsohn's lap. He sucked his thumb and waited. Mr. Mendelsohn opened the picture book.

"O.K. Now . . ." He pointed to the picture. "A is for Alligators. See that? Look at that big mouth and all them teeth. . . ." Tato yawned, nestled back, and closed his eyes. The old man read a few more pages and shut the book.

The soft breathing and sucking sound that Tato made assured Mr. Mendelsohn that the child was asleep. Such a smart kid. What a great boy, he said to himself. Mr. Mendelsohn was vaguely aware of a radio program, voices, and the small dog barking now and then, just before he too fell into a deep sleep.

This Sunday was very much like all the others; coffee first, then he and Tato would play a bit before napping in the large armchair. It had become a way of life for the old man. Only the

High Holy Days and an occasional invitation to a family event, such as a marriage or funeral and so on, would prevent the old man from spending Sunday next door.

It had all been so effortless. No one ever asked him to leave, except late at night when he napped too long. On Saturdays, he tried to observe the Sabbath and brought in his meal. They lit the stove for him.

Mrs. Suárez was always feeding him, just like Mama. She also worried about me not eating, the old man had said to himself, pleased. At first, he had been cautious and had wondered about the food and the people that he was becoming so involved with. That first Sunday, the old man had looked suspiciously at the food they served him.

"What is it?" he had asked. Yvonne and Georgie had started giggling, and had looked at one another. Mrs. Suárez had responded quickly and with anger, cautioning her children; speaking to them in Spanish.

"Eat your food, Mr. Mendelsohn. You too skinny," she had told him.

"What kind of meat is it?" Mr. Mendelsohn insisted.

"It's good for you, that's what it is," Mrs. Suárez answered.

"But I—" Mr. Mendelsohn started.

"Never mind—it's good for you. I prepare everything fresh. Go ahead and eat it," Mrs. Suárez had interrupted. There was a silence as Mr. Mendelsohn sat still, not eating.

"You know, I'm not allowed to eat certain things. In my religion we have dietary laws. This is not—pork or something like it, is it?"

"It's just . . . chicken. Chicken! That's what it is. It's delicious . . . and good for you," she had said with conviction.

"It doesn't look like chicken to me."

"That's because you never ate no chicken like this before. This here is—is called Puerto Rican chicken. I prepare it special. So you gonna eat it. You too skinny."

Mr. Mendelsohn had tried to protest, but Mrs. Suárez insisted. "Never mind. Now I prepare everything clean and nice. You eat the chicken; you gonna like it. Go on!"

And that was all.

Mr. Mendelsohn ate his Sunday supper from then on without doubt or hesitation, accepting the affection and concern that Mrs. Suárez provided with each plateful.

That night in his own apartment, Mr. Mendelsohn felt uneasy. He remembered that during supper, Ralphy had mentioned that his G.I. loan had come through. They would be looking for a house soon, everyone agreed. Not in the Bronx; farther out, near Yonkers. It was more like the country there.

The old man tossed and turned in his bed. That's still a long way off. First, they have to find the house and everything. You don't move just like that! he said to himself. It's gonna take a while, he reasoned, putting such thoughts out of his mind.

Mr. Mendelsohn looked at his new quarters.

"I told you, didn't I? See how nice this is?" his sister Jennie said. She put down the large sack of groceries on the small table.

It was a fair-sized room with a single bed, a bureau, a wooden wardrobe closet, a table, and two chairs. A hot plate was set on a small white refrigerator, and a white metal kitchen cabinet was placed alongside.

"We'll bring you whatever else you need, Louis," Jennie went on. "You'll love it here, I'm sure. There are people your own age, interested in the same things. Here—let's get started. We'll put your things away and you can get nicely settled."

Mr. Mendelsohn walked over to the window and looked out. He saw a wide avenue with cars, taxis and buses speeding by. "It's gonna take me two buses, at least, to get back to the old neighborhood," he said.

"Why do you have to go back there?" Jennie asked quickly. "There is nobody there any more, Louis. Everybody moved!"

"There's shul. . . ."

"There's shul right here. Next door you have a large temple. Twice you were robbed over there. It's a miracle you weren't hurt! Louis, there is no reason for you to go back. There is nothing over there, nothing," Jennie said.

"The trouble all started with that rooming house next door. Those people took in all kinds. . . ." He shook his head. "When the Suárez family lived there we had no problems. But nobody would talk to the landlord about those new people—only me. Nobody cared."

"That's all finished," Jennie said, looking at her watch. "Now look how nice it is here. Come on, let's get started." She began to put the groceries away in the refrigerator and cabinet.

"Leave it, Jennie," he interrupted. "Go on . . . I'll take care of it. You go on home. You are in a hurry."

"I'm only trying to help," Jennie responded.

"I know, I know. But I lived in one place for almost fifty years. So don't hurry me." He looked around the room. "And I ain't going nowhere now."

Shaking her head, Jennie said, "Look—this weekend we have a wedding, but next weekend Sara and I will come to see you. I'll call the hotel on the phone first, and they'll let you know. All right?"

"Sure." He nodded.

"That'll be good, Louis. This way you will get a chance to get settled and get acquainted with some of the other residents." Jennie kissed Mr. Mendelsohn affectionately. The old man nodded and turned away. In a moment, he heard the door open and shut.

Slowly, he walked to the sack of groceries and finished putting them away. Then, with much effort, he lifted a large suitcase onto the bed. He took out several photographs. Then he set the photographs upright, arranging them carefully on the bureau. He had pictures of his parents' wedding and of his sisters and their families. There was a photograph of his mother taken just before she died, and another one of Tato.

That picture was taken when he was about two years old, the old man said to himself. Yes, that's right, on his birthday. . . . There was a party. And Tato was already talking. Such a smart kid, he thought, smiling. Last? Last when? he wondered. Time was going fast for him. He shrugged. He could hardly remember what year it was lately. Just before they moved! He remembered. That's right, they gave him the photograph of Tato. They had a nice house around Gunhill Road someplace, and they had taken him there once. He recalled how exhausted he had been after the long trip. No one had a car, and they had had to take a train and buses. Anyway, he was glad he remembered. Now he could let them know he had moved, and tell them all about what happened to the old neighborhood. That's right, they had a telephone now. Yes, he said to himself, let me finish here, then I'll go call them. He continued to put the rest of his belongings away.

Mr. Mendelsohn sat in the lobby, holding on to his cane and a cake box. He had told the nurse at the desk that his friends were coming to pick him up this Sunday. He looked eagerly toward the revolving doors. After a short while, he saw Ralphy, Julio, and Georgie walk through into the lobby.

"Deliveries are made in the rear of the building," he heard the nurse at the desk say as they walked toward him.

"These are my friends, Mrs. Read," Mr. Mendelsohn said, standing. "They are here to take me out."

"Oh, well," said the nurse. "All right; I didn't realize. Here he is then. He's been talking about nothing else but this visit." Mrs. Read smiled.

Ralphy nodded, then spoke to Georgie. "Get Mr. Mendelsohn's overcoat."

Quickly, Mr. Mendelsohn put on his coat, and all four left the lobby.

"Take good care of him now . . ." they heard Mrs. Read calling. "You be a good boy now, Mr. Mendelsohn."

Outside, Mr. Mendelsohn looked at the young men and smiled.

"How's everyone?" he asked.

"Good," Julio said. "Look, that's my pickup truck from work. They let me use it sometimes when I'm off."

"That's a beautiful truck. How's everyone? Tato? How is my best friend? And Yvonne? Does she like school? And your Mama and Papa? . . . Marta? . . ."

"Fine, fine. Everybody is doing great. Wait till you see them. We'll be there in a little while," said Julio. "With this truck, we'll get there in no time."

Mr. Mendelsohn sat in the kitchen and watched as Mrs. Suárez packed food into a shopping bag. Today had been a good day for the old man; he had napped in the old armchair and spent time with the children. Yvonne was so grown up, he almost had not recognized her. When Tato remembered him, Mr. Mendelsohn had been especially pleased. Shyly, he had shaken hands with the old man. Then he had taken him into his room to show Mr. Mendelsohn all his toys.

"Now I packed a whole lotta stuff in this shopping bag for you. You gotta eat it. Eat some of my Puerto Rican chicken—it's good for you. You too skinny. You got enough for tomorrow and for another day. You put it in the refrigerator. Also I put some rice and other things."

He smiled as she spoke, enjoying the attention he received.

"Julio is gonna drive you back before it gets too late," she said. "And we gonna pick you up again and bring you back to eat with us. I bet you don't eat right." She shook her head. "O.K.?"

"You shouldn't go through so much bother," he protested mildly.

"Again with the bother? You stop that! We gonna see you soon. You take care of yourself and eat. Eat! You must nourish yourself, especially in such cold weather."

Mr. Mendelsohn and Mrs. Suárez walked out into the living room. The family exchanged good-byes with the old man. Tato, feeling less shy, kissed Mr. Mendelsohn on the cheek.

Just before leaving, Mr. Mendelsohn embraced Mrs. Suárez for a long time, as everybody watched silently.

"Thank you," he whispered.

"Thank you? For what?" Mrs. Suárez said. "You come back soon and have Sunday supper with us. Yes?" Mr. Mendelsohn nodded and smiled.

It was dark and cold out. He walked with effort. Julio carried the shopping bag. Slowly, he got into the pickup truck. The ride back was bumpy and uncomfortable for Mr. Mendelsohn. The cold wind cut right through into the truck, and the old man was aware of the long winter ahead.

His eyelids were so heavy he could hardly open them. Nurses scurried about busily. Mr. Mendelsohn heard voices.

"Let's give him another injection. It will help his breathing. Nurse! Nurse! The patient needs . . ."

The voices faded. He remembered he had gone to sleep after supper last—last when? How many days have I been here . . . here in the hospital? Yes, he thought, now I know where I am. A heart attack, the doctor had said, and then he had felt even worse. Didn't matter; I'm too tired. He heard voices once more, and again he barely opened his eyes. A tall thin man dressed in white spoke to him.

"Mr. Mendelsohn, can you hear me? How do you feel now? More comfortable? We called your family. I spoke to your sister, Mrs. Wiletsky. They should be here very soon. You feeling sleepy? Good. . . . Take a little nap—go on. We'll wake you when they get here, don't worry. Go on now. . . ."

He closed his eyes, thinking of Jennie. She'll be here soon with Esther and Rosalie and Sara. All of them. He smiled. He was so tired. His bed was by the window and a bright warm sash of sunshine covered him almost completely. Nice and warm, he thought, and felt comfortable. The pain had lessened, practically disappeared. Mr. Mendelsohn heard the birds chirping and Sporty barking. That's all right, Mrs. Suárez would let him sleep. She wouldn't wake him up, he knew that. It looked like a good warm day; he planned to take Tato out for a walk later. That's some smart kid, he thought. Right now he was going to rest.

"This will be the last of it, Sara."

"Just a few more things, Jennie, and we'll be out of here." The two women spoke as they packed away all the items in the room. They opened drawers and cabinets, putting things away in boxes and suitcases.

"What about these pictures on the bureau?" asked Sara.

Jennie walked over and they both looked at the photographs.

"There's Mama and Papa's wedding picture. Look, there's you, Sara, when Jonathan was born. And Esther and . . . look, he's got all the pictures of the entire family." Jennie burst into tears.

"Come on, Jennie. It's all over, honey. He was sick and very old." The older woman comforted the younger one.

Wiping her eyes, Jennie said, "Well, we did the best we could for him, anyway."

"Who is this?" asked Sara, holding up Tato's photo.

"Let me see," said Jennie. "Hummm . . . that must be one of the people in that family that lived next door in the old apartment on Prospect Avenue. You know—remember that Spanish family? He used to visit with them. Their name was . . . Díaz or something like that, I think. I can't remember."

"Oh yes," said Sara. "Louis mentioned them once in a while, yes. They were nice to him. What shall we do with it? Return it?"

"Oh," said Jennie, "that might be rude. What do you think?"

"Well, I don't want it, do you?"

"No." Jennie hesitated. ". . . But let's just put it away. Maybe we ought to tell them what happened. About Louis." Sara shrugged her shoulders. "Maybe I'll write to them," Jennie went on, "if I can find out where they live. They moved. What do you say?"

"I don't care, really." Sara sighed. "I have a lot to do yet. I have to meet Esther at the lawyer's to settle things. And I still have to make supper. So let's get going."

Both women continued to pack, working efficiently and with swiftness. After a while, everything was cleared and put away in boxes and suitcases.

"All done!" said Sara.

"What about this?" asked Jennie, holding up Tato's photograph.

"Do what you want," said Sara. "I'm tired. Let's go."

Looking at the photograph, Jennie slipped it into one of the boxes. "I might just write and let them know."

The two women left the room, closing the door behind them.

# Tomás Rivera
**1935–1984** (Mexican American)

## Meet the Writer

**Tomás Rivera** (toh MAHS ree VAY rah) has had a powerful influence on Chicano literature, not only through his writing but also in the model he provided for aspiring young writers whose backgrounds were similar to his own.

Rivera was born in Crystal City, Texas, to Mexican parents who had migrated to Texas in search of seasonal farm work. From the time he was a little boy, Rivera worked in the fields alongside his parents. Like the children of other migrant workers, young Rivera attended school whenever and wherever he could. Even as a young child, he read what he could find—discarded books that he fished out of trash dumps, old magazines that his father collected. In high school he became interested in American writers such as Ernest Hemingway, John Steinbeck, and Walt Whitman. Rivera wrote his first story when he was only twelve years old—a story he later pronounced as "crummy"—but it was the start of what would become a lifelong love of writing.

Rivera, overcoming tremendous obstacles, graduated from Southwest Texas State University, but he was unable to find a teaching position because he was Mexican American. Rejection made him more determined: He went on to earn a master's degree in English and administration and a doctorate in Spanish literature. By the time of his premature death, he was chancellor of the University of California, Riverside.

## Background

Rivera's great work is a novel published in 1971 called . . . *y no se lo tragó la tierra* (*And the Earth Did Not Devour Him*). Based on Rivera's own experiences, the novel traces the experiences of a year in the life of a child of migrant farmworkers. The novel is set squarely in the Mexican Americans' struggle for social and political justice. Rivera said that he wanted to capture "the suffering and the strength and the beauty" of the people he grew up among. The title of this, his only novel, . . . *y no se lo tragó la tierra*, suggests their triumph in the face of great hardships.

**Before You Read** *The lives of migrant workers are filled with grueling, monotonous work, and children are pulled into the fields to help as soon as they are physically able. Despite their backbreaking work in the fields, the workers have an appreciation of the land and the bounty it yields. Why do you think Don Trine digs holes in the field? What do you think he gains through this unusual behavior?*

# The Harvest
## Tomás Rivera

The end of September and the beginning of October. That was the best time of the year. First, because it was a sign that the work was coming to an end and that the return to Texas would start. Also, because there was something in the air that the folks created, an aura of peace and death. The earth also shared that feeling. The cold came more frequently, the frosts that killed by night, in the morning covered the earth in whiteness. It seemed that all was coming to an end. The folks felt that all was coming to rest. Everyone took to thinking more. And they talked more about the trip back to Texas, about the harvests, if it had gone well or bad for them, if they would return or not to the same place next year. Some began to take long walks around the grove. It seemed like in these last days of work there was a wake[1] over the earth. It made you think.

That's why it wasn't very surprising to see Don Trine take a walk by himself through the grove and to walk along the fields every afternoon. This was at the beginning, but when some youngsters asked him if they could tag along, he even got angry. He told them he didn't want anybody sticking behind him.

"Why would he want to be all by hisself, anyway?"
"To heck with him; it's his business."
"But, you notice, it never fails. Every time, why, sometimes I don't even think he eats supper, he takes his walk. Don't you think that's a bit strange?"
"Well, I reckon. But you saw how he got real mad when we told him we'd go along with him. It wasn't anything to make a fuss over. This ain't his land. We can go wherever we take a liking to. He can't tell us what to do."
"That's why I wonder, why'd he want to walk by hisself?"

And that's how all the rumors about Don Trine's walks got started. The folks couldn't figure out why or what he got out of taking off by himself every afternoon. When he would leave, and somebody would spy on him, somehow or other he would catch on, then take a little walk, turn around and head right back to his chicken coop. The fact of the matter is that everybody began to say he was hiding the money he had earned that year or that he had found some buried treasure and every day, little by little, he was bringing it back to his coop. Then they began to say that when he was young he had run around with a gang in Mexico and that he always

---

1. **wake** (wayk): watch kept over the body of a dead person before burial.

carried around a lot of money with him. They said, too, that even if it was real hot, he carried a belt full of money beneath his undershirt. Practically all the speculation centered on the idea that he had money.

"Let's see, who's he got to take care of? He's an old bachelor. He ain't never married or had a family. So, with him working so many years . . . Don't you think he's bound to have money? And then, what's that man spend his money on? The only thing he buys is his bit of food every Saturday. Once in a while, a beer, but that's all."
"Yeah, he's gotta have a pile of money, for sure. But, you think he's going to bury it around here?"
"Who said he's burying anything? Look, he always goes for his food on Saturday. Let's check close where he goes this week, and on Saturday, when he's on his errand, we'll see what he's hiding. Whadda you say?" "Good 'nuff. Let's hope he doesn't catch on to us."

That week the youngsters closely watched Don Trine's walks. They noticed that he would disappear into the grove, then come out on the north side, cross the road then cross the field until he got to the irrigation ditch. There he dropped from sight for a while, then he reappeared in the west field. It was there where he would disappear and linger the most. They noticed also that, so as to throw people off his track, he would take a different route, but he always spent more time around the ditch that crossed the west field. They decided to investigate the ditch and that field the following Saturday.

When that day arrived, the boys were filled with anticipation. The truck had scarcely left and they were on their way to the west field. The truck had not yet disappeared and they had already crossed the grove. What they found they almost expected. There was nothing in the ditch, but in the field that had been harrowed[2] after pulling the potatoes they found a number of holes.

"You notice all the holes here? The harrow didn't make these. Look, here's some foot prints, and notice that the holes are at least a foot deep. You can stick your arm in them up to your elbow. No animal makes these kind of holes. Whadda you think?"
"Well, it's bound to be Don Trine. But, what's he hiding? Why's he making so many holes? You think the landowner knows what he's up to?"
"Naw, man. Why, look, you can't see them from the road. You gotta come in a ways to notice they're here. What's he making them for? What's he using them for? And, look, they're all about the same width. Whadda you think?"
"Well, you got me. Maybe we'll know if we hide in the ditch and see what he does when he comes here."
"Look, here's a coffee can. I bet you this is what he digs with."
"I think you're right."

The boys had to wait until late the following Monday to discover the reason for the holes. But the word had spread around so that everybody already knew that Don Trine had a bunch of holes in that field. They tried not to let on but the allusions they made to the holes while they were out in the fields during the day were very obvious. Everybody thought there had to be a big explanation. So, the youngsters spied more carefully and astutely.

---

2. **harrowed** (HAR ohd): broken up and leveled by a harrow, a frame with spikes or disks pulled over plowed ground.

The Harvest    215

That afternoon they managed to fool Don Trine and saw what he was doing. They saw, and as they had suspected, Don Trine used the coffee can to dig a hole. Every so often, he would measure with his arm the depth of the hole. When it went up to his elbow, he stuck in his left arm, then filled dirt in around it with his right hand, all the way up to the elbow. Then he stayed like that for some time. He seemed very satisfied and even tried to light a cigarette with one hand. Not being able to, he just let it hang from his lips. Then he dug another hole and repeated the process. The boys could not understand why he did this. That was what puzzled them the most. They had believed that, with finding out what it was he did, they would understand everything. But it didn't turn out that way at all. The boys brought the news to the rest of the folks in the grove and nobody there understood either. In reality, when they found out that the holes didn't have anything to do with money, they thought Don Trine was crazy and even lost interest in the whole matter. But not everybody.

The next day one of the boys who discovered what Don Trine had been up to went by himself to a field. There he went through the same procedure that he had witnessed the day before. What he experienced and what he never forgot was feeling the earth move, feeling the earth grasp his fingers and even caressing them. He also felt the warmth of the earth. He sensed he was inside someone. Then he understood what Don Trine was doing. He was not crazy, he simply liked to feel the earth when it was sleeping.

That's why the boy kept going to the field every afternoon, until one night a hard freeze came on so that he could no longer dig any holes in the ground. The earth was fast asleep. Then he thought of next year, in October at harvest time, when once again he could repeat what Don Trine did. It was like when someone died. You always blamed yourself for not loving him more before he died.

# Rudolfo Anaya
b. 1937–    (Mexican American)

## Meet the Writer

**Rudolfo Anaya** (ruh DOHL foh  ah NAH yah) has a woman in black to thank for helping him develop a style that would be his own. Born in the small town of Pastura, New Mexico, to a poor family, Anaya moved to Albuquerque when he was fifteen. There he encountered a cultural and ethnic diversity that was unsettling. Entry into the University of New Mexico sent him into an identity crisis—the classes and writers seemed irrelevant to his culture.

Anaya eventually started writing. One night he had a strange, otherworldly experience that changed his life: He was visited by an old woman dressed in black. That vision inspired his first novel, *Bless Me, Ultima*. The woman in his vision became Ultima, a healer who helps the story's main character find his way to adulthood.

Anaya struggled to get his book published; all mainstream publishers rejected it because it was too Latino in style and language. Finally, a small publisher in California, Quinto Sol Publications, accepted his manuscript. That was the beginning of a distinguished literary and professional career. Anaya went on to teach at the University of New Mexico, where years before he had encountered prejudice and isolation. He retired from teaching in 1993 and still lives in Albuquerque.

## Background

In 1531 the Spanish conquistador Francisco Pizarro invaded the empire of the Incas in Peru. Pizarro and his soldiers were greatly outnumbered by the well-equipped Incan army, but Pizarro used trickery to subdue the Incas. By the 1560s the Spanish had gained control of the huge Incan empire.

The center of Incan power was the beautiful city of Cuzco (COOZ coh). Seventy-five miles away was the Incas' fortress of Machu Picchu, which soars over the deep canyon of the Urubamba River. The city was abandoned, but no one knows why or when. Its ruins were discovered in 1911. The fortress is thought to have been a sanctuary or temple inhabited by "Virgins of the Sun," women chosen to tend the temples and offer tributes.

**Meet the Writer**

**Before You Read** *What if people and events from the past still existed in the present in some way that we couldn't understand? What, for example, might a tourist at Valley Forge witness if he could see the freezing soldiers still sleeping in those little wood huts that dot the valley? What ghosts might be seen at Machu Picchu today, hundreds of years after the last Inca passed from this earth?*

# Message from the Inca
## Rudolfo Anaya

He prayed and drank the coca tea,[1] preparing himself for the run. He concentrated only on the task ahead of him, blocking out the sound of the fire sticks that sounded outside in the streets. The city of Cuzco, the capital city of the Inca, was under siege. The barbarians, speaking a strange tongue, had come, casting fire and death from their pointed sticks.

Even now the runner could hear the cries and screams of the people, and the terrifying curses of the barbarians. These bearded sorcerers were too powerful to stop; they rode huge beasts that trampled the people in their path. The runner had caught a glimpse of the carnage before the priest pulled him into the secret rooms beneath the Inca's temple. But even these sacred rooms would soon be discovered, and the barbarians' wrath would destroy everything.

Through the small window cut into the stone wall, he could see the glare of the holy city as it burned. The sight saddened the runner. All the Inca's warriors were powerless to stop the calamity. If Cuzco fell, the empire of the Inca would be lost.

Outside the cell, the runner heard the footsteps of the priest as he approached. The priest opened the door and looked at the young man, who had been taken from his parents when he was a child and trained to be a runner in the service of the Inca. He had run up and down the Mountains of the Gods, even to the sea coast. Now he was the only runner left in Cuzco. The others had been sent in all directions, carrying messages to the people, and none had returned. One, as he tried to escape from the city, had been attacked by the dogs of the barbarians. He had died in the arms of the priests, crying that there was no way out.

The message this runner would carry to Machu Picchu would be the last communication to leave Cuzco before it fell. The salvation of the people of Vilcampa depended on the runner.

"Are you ready, my son?" the priest asked.

"Yes," the runner replied.

"Cuzco cannot be saved," the priest said. There was no fear in his voice, only finality. "Come," he said, and the runner stood and followed the priest down a dark corridor.

The runner could hear the faint reports of the fire sticks outside, and the cries of women. For a moment he thought of the woman he had known as a mother, then he shook the thought away.

He shivered. A horrifying time had come to the land of the Inca. The priests had warned the people that the bearded barbarians would destroy everything in their search for gold, but it

---

1. **coca tea:** tea made from the leaf of the coca plant, used to numb pain.

was worse than they could have imagined. Time itself was ending.

The young man and the priest entered the room of the Inca, the room of gold. Here the torches reflected the glitter of the precious metal, this metal used to create the art of the Inca. This gift from the Sun God, used as decorations to please those one loved, was the obsession of the barbarians.

The runner bowed, low to the ground, not daring to look into the face of the Inca. Even so, he had caught a glimpse of the noble family, huddling in the shadows of the room. Only the Inca remained unperturbed. He sat on his throne like the god he was.

"My house is about to fall," the great king spoke to those gathered. The runner shivered. He had never before heard words from the Inca.

"My time is ending," the Inca continued. "I accept my destiny, but we must keep the Sun God crossing the heavens and giving warmth to the earth. Otherwise the earth will die. Send the runner to Vilcampa. Send him to the mountain of Machu Picchu, there where the virgins tie the Sun God to the post on the mountain. Let him warn them of the barbarians; let them guard our secrets."

The runner felt the eyes of the Inca upon him and heard the words entrusting him with the last message from the Inca.

"Leave no trail, cut the bridges behind you. Here we accept death at the hands of the barbarians, but we must save Vilcampa. We have been told, even time dies, but a new time must be born. Our knowledge is also for the time that is being born" were the Inca's last words.

The priest pulled the runner away from the presence of the Inca. In the corridor he handed him an intricately knotted cord, the quipu,[2] which contained the message from the ruler.

---

2. **quipu** (KEE poo): an arrangement of cords variously colored and knotted, used by the ancient Incas to keep accounts, record events, and so on. The Incas did not have a written language.

"This is the message for the virgins of Vilcampa," the priest said. "It tells the chief priestess how long they must remain hidden from the world if they are to escape the wrath of the barbarians. The city of the virgins must be sealed; no one must pass through the portals of Machu Picchu. The city clothed in mountain mists will now be clothed in secrecy for all time. There the virgins will guard the knowledge of the Inca. Perhaps in a future time someone will read the message in the quipu and shed tears for the Inca."

Outside the thunder of the fire sticks grew louder, the murderous shouts of the barbarians closer.

"Go now." The priest hurried the runner down the corridor and to the secret door. "Take the message to the priestess of Vilcampa. Do not fail us."

The priest opened the door, the screams and thunder grew louder. In the air floated a strange, acrid smoke. He pressed a pouch of dried coca leaves into the runner's hands. The runner would chew the leaves, and they would deaden the pain during the long run to Vilcampa. Many of the tambos, the rest houses along the trails in the Mountains of the Gods, had been destroyed. Now there were no runners to help relay the message; this runner would run a full day and a full night.

Without incident, he climbed out of the mountain bowl which was the Valley of Cuzco. The Inca had thrown all of his warriors into one last stand against the barbarians, a distraction to allow the runner to slip out of the palace. Now as the runner stood on the edge of the cliff looking down on the burning city, a great sadness filled him.

The people of the Inca were being destroyed, there was no family left. Frightening sounds filled the air, sounds that echoed across the centuries of time. Cuzco was dying; now there was only the hope of Vilcampa in Machu Picchu.

Panting from the climb, the runner opened the pouch and took out the coca leaves. Now he would run continually, stopping only to cut the bridges that spanned the mountain ravines. These bridges, constructed of lianas,[3] the vines from the Amazon, were the most valued possession of the Inca. The runner's instructions were to cut all the bridges on the trail to Vilcampa. He would not take time to rest.

He touched the quipu. There at the end, the priest had tied a piece of metal, perhaps a piece taken from one of the breastplates the barbarians wore. This hard and cold object was the symbol of the new age. The virgins of Vilcampa would shiver when they touched the metal.

Into the evening he ran, climbing higher and higher, following the hidden foot trail above the river valley. Behind him plumes of smoke rose into the orange sky, the fires of Cuzco burning. In the sky the runner saw a strange omen, a silver bird flying over the mountain. Below him he saw a giant snake made of metal twisting its way along the Urubamba Valley. He shivered. These were the strange omens of the new time the Inca predicted.

He entered the dusk, knowing his world had come to an end. Who would read the quipu when the children of the Inca were dead? Who would know the glory of Vilcampa and the virgins who tethered the Sun God at the Post of the Sun? Who would keep the calendars of the Inca, and the memory of the people?

He ran along the plain of the Urubamba, and all around him the terraced fields of the people were deserted. The people had fled into the mountains. He had tied the quipu to his belt, and as he ran, the corded string bounced on his thigh. The piece of metal at the end of the cord beat against his leg, bruising and then cutting open his flesh.

He ascended the mountains, pausing only to cut the footbridges, sealing off the road to Vilcampa. He did not rest. The tambos on the trail were deserted, the ashes in the fireplaces cold. All runners and warriors had been called to defend the Inca. He was the only runner on the trail to Vilcampa.

He ran to the rhythm taught to the runners of the Inca, and still his lungs began to burn. He chewed the coca leaves, swallowing the bitter juice. The rhythm he kept and the deadening effect of the coca produced a new rhythm, a new awareness. He sang the songs of the Inca as he ran; his heart grew happy, and he knew he could run forever.

He could fly, yes, this is what the runners of the Inca could do. They had been taught by the shamans to fly. The runners are birds circling the Mountains of the Gods, the priests of the Inca had said, the runners are the sons of the Inca, sons of the Sun.

Below him the mighty waters of the Urubamba raged and rumbled as they surged down the mountain. The runner heard the rush of the river, and he heard another sound. It was the hiss of the iron serpent winding its way along the valley. A dark plume of smoke trailed the roaring viper.

Very well, the runner thought, I will run faster than the serpent of the barbarians. Let the new time come to the land of the Inca; I will deliver my message.

All night he ran, and visions came to him. He moved out of the time of the Inca into a new time. The old priests had taught him to run, and they had taught him that visions would come as he ran. He spoke to his father as if he were running by his side, remembering the stories his father had taught him. He moved back into the navel of time and spoke to runners of the past, runners who had run from the ocean to Cuzco, bearing fresh fish for the Inca's dinner. He moved so far back in time that he saw the first people arriving to settle the mountains, the first Incas in their thrones of gold. He saw the first stones laid to construct Vilcampa, the city guarded by Machu Picchu. Then the ultimate vi-

---

3. **lianas** (lee AH nuhs): climbing, woody, tropical vines.

sion came, and he saw the virgins of Vilcampa tie the Sun God to its post. With perfect clarity he saw the golden disc tethered for a moment on the solstice day of rest, and peace filled him.

For a moment he saw the harmony, the earth and sun as one, the prayers of the virgins answered. Then visions of the future came, and he saw the devastation of his people. The people were enslaved; the old calendars of the sun were broken. The runner felt fatigue spreading in his muscles, and the visions became a clutter of people swarming around him, people from another time and place.

The light of dawn glowed around him, and still he had not stopped to rest. Into the new day he ran until there before him was the gate of Vilcampa. He had broken the stream of time to arrive with the message. He did not feel the exhaustion, even though the muscles of his legs quivered. He thanked the sun for his swiftness and safety; he had brought the message to Vilcampa.

He slowed to a walk as he passed through the stone gate. Just below, an alert sentry waved him forward. He paused to look at the city of the votaries[4] of the sun, the virgins who cared for Vilcampa. The Urubamba River cut a wide curve around the promontory on which stood the city; the city was a fortress of the sun, protected by the mountains Machu and Picchu. The barbarians could follow the river, but from below they could not see the city. And he had cut the bridges and obliterated the signs on the trail. Now Vilcampa could be sealed off and exist in its own time.

Just below the sentry hut was the entry door. There in the middle of the city was the meadow where the dances were held. To the left stood the houses of the virgins, and nearby, the temple. And there was the sundial! Here was the center of the universe, the ombligo[5] of time. He gazed upon the sundial and felt he was returning home, as others would come in future times. Vilcampa would stand for all time and belong to all people. That is what the Inca meant, that the message was also for the time being born.

Here, it was known, the virgins could tie the Sun God to the Post of the Sun. Only for a moment, only to renew its energy. Here the sun gazed on the altar of sacrifice, the smooth monolith where prayers and penance were done. . . . This was the navel of the world where time converged.

The runner stood transfixed, feeling the luminous moment. The quality of light was so pure it was like the light of the first dawn on earth. The air was clear and scintillating. The green mountains of the Urubamba rose around him, clouds drifted across the peaks, dappling Vilcampa with bright sun, then shadow. An immense peace filled the runner's heart. Below him he could see the stone masons working at the quarry, and on the terraces, those who tended the maíz and potatoes. It was a serene image, and he wished he could sit and rest, but he had to deliver the message from the Inca.

He descended and was met at the sentry hut by a young woman. She greeted him. They had been expecting him.

"You are hurt," she said and looked at his thigh where the piece of metal on the metal tip of the quipu had drawn blood.

"It is nothing," he answered. "I bring a message from the Inca."

"Follow me," she said. At the gate she called to the others, and many stepped forward to help push the large stone into place. The city was now sealed.

"Our chief priestess had a vision," the young woman said as they walked toward the temple.

---

4. **votaries** (VOHT uh rees): persons bound by vows, especially religious vows; worshippers.

5. **ombligo** (awm BLEE goh): Spanish for "navel."

"Strangers have come to burn Cuzco. We hear strange sounds in the valley."

She paused and looked at him.

"Behind me, everything is destroyed," he said sadly. "The time of the Inca is no more."

"And Vilcampa?" she asked.

He saw the fright in her eyes, and he wished he could say that Vilcampa was forever. But nothing was forever, only the path of the sun and the knowledge of the virgins. A weariness filled his body.

"For now, Vilcampa is safe. I will live here," he said.

He wanted to tell her that while he ran he'd had a vision of others trudging up the slopes of the mountain to the secret city, new generations who came seeking the knowledge of the Incas.

"The quipu carries the message," he said. "It will be passed on."

She led him through the narrow streets of the city, turning left toward the altar. There she invited him to sit. She left him for a moment and returned with water. She cleansed his wound, washing the blood away, and she washed his body. He closed his eyes while she washed him, enjoying the softness of her hands. Around him gathered other women, the virgins who kept Vilcampa, eager to know what message he had brought.

"Now you may deliver your message," the young woman said and led him toward the temple. They passed the sundial, the Post of the Sun, which was carved from one piece of stone.

She led him to the temple where the chief priestess waited. She was surrounded by other women, priestesses of the sun and workers from the fields and the quarry.

"Welcome, runner of the Inca," the priestess spoke and stepped forward. "Welcome to our home. We have been waiting for you."

The runner undid the quipu from the leather thong at his waist and handed it to her. She received it tremulously.

She read the message in a loud voice, and the wind of the mountain carried her sad words down the canyon of the Urubamba. She read the date the barbarians had come to destroy Cuzco, and of the many warriors of the Inca who had been killed. In the words of the Inca, time had come to an end; now a new time had to be born. Vilcampa was to keep the calendars of the sun and the knowledge of the Inca.

A deep silence filled the air. Only the moan of the wind could be heard. Then she showed them the piece of metal tied to the tip of the quipu, and she told them this was the cause of all the destruction.

"Did you cut the bridges on the mountain passes?" she asked the runner.

"Yes," he answered.

"The Inca has commanded," she said to all gathered, "no one is to leave Vilcampa. No one can enter. Our fate is sealed. We are the last city of the Inca; we will praise and renew the sun as always."

All nodded in assent. The time of the Inca had died, and now Vilcampa was a capsule anchored to the mountains of Machu Picchu. How long they would survive was not for them to say, for time on earth was short and the visions of the priests forever. They knew the secret of Vilcampa, and in the future others would come to know it. Of that they were sure.

The priestess returned the quipu to the runner. "It is yours," she said. "A message to be passed down through the centuries. Many people will come here seeking the knowledge of the Inca. They will want to know how we were attentive to the Sun God. They will seek knowledge of the harmony of our world. We will share that message," she said.

The runner nodded. The message of catastrophe and chaos had been received with courage. These women, these votaries of the sun, were all women of courage. They accepted the end of time because they knew a new time would be born. In their wombs they carried the rays of the sun, the penetrating light of the Giver of Life.

"Take the runner to the eating area," the priestess said to the young woman. "See that he is fed. See that he has a place to rest. He is one of us now. This is his home."

The young woman bowed and took the runner's hand. She led him through the open meadow, past a flock of alpacas and the houses of the workers.

"There," she said, "is the place to eat. The women will serve you. I will return for you."

He turned to look at the terrace where people were eating. They were clothed in garments he had never seen; they spoke a strange language. For a moment he was afraid. Was he, too, slipping away from the time of the Inca? Was there no spot of earth that was fixed forever? Had he died in Cuzco or in the mountain ravines? Was this his ghost moving across time to come to sit with the strangers?

"Do not be afraid," he heard the voice of the young woman. "You are one of us."

The runner's hand tightened on the quipu, as if holding tight to the cord, he could hold onto reality. His body ached with fatigue; the effect of the coca had worn away. He felt hunger. He walked to the eating area. There was an empty chair, and the man next to it motioned the runner.

"Sit here," the man said. He spoke the language of the barbarians, but his smile was kind. "I have come a long way to listen to the memories of Vilcampa," he said. He had been writing on the notebook that lay on the table.

A woman served the runner food and drink. The drink was cold and bitter. It was served in a marvelous glass bottle. The food was cold and tasteless; he couldn't eat. A swarm of people moved around him. Who are these strangers? he wondered. What has happened to the Vilcampa I knew? He looked for the young woman, and spotted her near workers who stood by the large metal huts. Smoke poured from these cabins even as people stepped out of them.

"Too many tourists, too many buses," the man sitting by the runner whispered. He pointed to the long line of people disembarking. "We come looking for the magic, and we find only each other." He smiled.

It was a kind smile, the runner thought. This stranger from another country had dark curly hair and a dark face, but he was not a child of the Inca. The children of the Inca were the workers who spoke Quechua as they ate their lunches by the side of the road.

The runner looked at the quipu. He understood now what had happened during his run, and that it was time to pass on the message. This man, too, was a messenger; he wrote his stories in the notebook. The runner pushed the quipu across the table to the man, and the man took it. Their eyes met for a moment, and in that instant each knew the message from the Inca would never die. It would be passed on, generation to generation.

The runner nodded and rose. He bowed, and the man responded. Then the runner walked away from the eating place to join the workers. These were his people, men of strong backs and honest brown faces. They talked and joked in a language he could understand. They were cleaning the road that led down to the valley, but they had paused to eat their noonday meal. They accepted the runner easily into their company.

The young woman he had met when he entered the gate of Vilcampa handed him Quechua food, and he ate. Here he felt at ease. These men had been in the Mountains of the Sun a long time. They were the new workers in the city of Vilcampa. They ate and talked in the shadow of Machu Picchu. They will be here forever, the runner thought.

He relaxed, looked at the young woman, and smiled. He had delivered the message from the Inca; now it was in the hands of the man who sat at the table. That man would read the secret of the quipu, record it in his language, and pass it on. Each new time had its runners, those whose work carried them into new visions of reality.

**Before You Read**   *Anaya's nonfiction is as rich in imagery and a sense of place as his fictional prose. In this personal essay, Anaya shares childhood memories of Christmas activities that are full of his family's traditions. The combination of Spanish, native Indian, Christian, and Anglo elements created simple, but meaningful, holiday joy. Unlike Christmases today, so often driven by commercialism, Anaya's childhood Christmases emphasized sharing the holiday with family, friends, and even strangers, not the amount or size of the presents he received. Have you experienced special holiday celebrations? What memories do you treasure most?*

# A New Mexico Christmas
## Rudolfo Anaya

Christmas in New Mexico is unique. It is a time of celebration and a time of memories.

When I was a child, my mother's preparations for Christmas meant a week's work in the kitchen. Pots of posole[1] would bubble on the stove, the plump tamales[2] wrapped in their corn husks steamed in the pressure cooker. The aroma of these foods made from corn, the sacred food of the New World, pervaded the kitchen.

There were also desserts. Plates of empanadas[3] made with fruit and sweetmeats were piled high. The anise and nutmeg fragrance of the biscochitos,[4] the traditional sugar cookies, filled the house. These were just some of the Christmas foods prepared to celebrate Christ's birth.

It was my father's job to scour the countryside for a piñon tree. It was a treasure trip for me as I accompanied him in search of the green tree that would grace our simple home. It would be decorated with an old and frayed string of lights, bright streamers of cloth my mother sewed. My sisters would add the store-bought icicles and the angel hair.

On Christmas Eve we hung our stockings on the stout branches of the tree. In the morning the stockings would be stuffed with hard candy, nuts, and fruit. There were always plenty of apples and dried fruit, the bounty of the harvest from the farms of my uncles in Puerto de Luna. Oranges were a favorite, but they were expensive, available only if my father was working.

Christmas Eve meant bundling up at eleven o'clock at night to make the long trek into town to celebrate la Misa del Gallo, midnight Mass. The long walk into town was also a time for contemplation. Under the starry sky of the New Mexico llano[5] it was the family unit that made its way to church. My mother led, we followed close behind, my father came after us.

---

1. ***posole*** (puh ZOH lay): a hominy stew.
2. ***tamale*** (*tamal*) (tah MAH lay): thick masa harina (corn dough) wrapped around a spicy meat filling, enclosed in corn husks, and steamed.
3. ***empanadas*** (ehm puh NAH duhs): meat or fruit turnovers.
4. ***biscochitos*** (bihs koh CHEE tohs): Christmas cookies.
5. ***llano*** (YAH noh): a wide plain or prairie.

That walk rekindles memories of my childhood. The night was cold. Over us sparkled the mystery of the universe, the stars of the Milky Way. Once, long ago, one star lighted the way to Bethlehem. I learned then that to celebrate the religious spirit one had to be attentive. Each person could renew the spirit within, but each had to make an offering. My mother's offering was her belief in the birth of Christ, el Cristo. My father offered the green tree, the symbol of life everlasting, the tree of life itself. And we offered the long, cold walk to join the community of the Mass.

It is that individual and communal offering that cannot be packaged in the modern department store.

After Mass we hurried home. At two in the morning the cold of the llano had set in. Plumes of our breath filled the blue night. We hurried home, where my mother prepared hot chocolate and biscochitos. Then it was off to blissful sleep under warm covers.

In the morning we would awaken to search in the stockings and to open gifts, gifts we usually made ourselves for each other, because there was little money for store-bought gifts. If lucky I might receive a pair of gloves—that is, if the fingers were showing in the old pair. My sisters received clothing, curlers, and prized nylons—as bobby socks gave way to young womanhood.

Then I would run out to join my friends to visit the houses of our neighbors. Our shout was, "¡Mis Crismes![6] ¡Mis Crismes!" We asked for and received the traditional gifts of Christmas, much as the trick-or-treaters do today on Halloween. Our flour sacks bulged with candy, nuts, and fruits when we returned home.

Later in the morning the family would start arriving, brothers from afar, aunts and uncles, and the entire potpourri of padrinos and madrinas, compadres and comadres, cousins, friends, the extended family.

For a child lost in the wonder of the celebration everyone was a welcome sight. They all brought gifts. If the piñon season had been good that fall, someone would arrive with a gunnysack full of piñones, those sweet, little nuts we would crack and eat in front of the stove as we listened to the stories. Another might bring carne seca, jerky to be cooked with red chile from the ristra hanging in the pantry.

Perhaps someone had been working in Texas, and his truck would be loaded with oranges and ruby red grapefruits, gifts from el Valle de Tejas where some went to make a living.

Then we would compare gifts, and my cousins would ask, "What did Santo Clos bring you?"

Our Santo Clos was the Santa Claus we knew at school, where we also decorated the classroom tree and acted in the annual Christmas play. Santo Clos, the stockings, and the Perry Como Christmas songs on the radio were the influence of the Anglo culture filtering into our way of life. The cultures were interacting, exchanging customs, and yet each group still retained its own ways, borrowing from each other and forming the mosaic of celebration that Christmas has come to be in New Mexico.

At the center of the celebration was the tree. For my father it was important to have it ready on December 21, the day of the winter solstice. This was indeed the tree of life, and its importance and the importance of the day were fixed in the religious nature of the Indians of New Mexico, as it has been fixed since time immemorial in most of the cultures of the world. The shortest day of the year reminds us all that the sun has reached the end of its winter journey. It will return northward to renew the earth, but for one day it hangs in precarious balance.

Long ago on this day in ancient Mexico, and throughout the Americas, sacrifices were made in honor of the sun, the life giver. Incense was

---

6. *"¡Mis Crismes!"* (mees KREES mays): "Where's my Christmas gift!"

burned and sprigs of green were gathered. Ancient man understood his relation to the cosmos. For him the race of the sun was a mystery to be celebrated. One had to be attentive to the workings of the planets and stars, as one had to attend to the working of the spirit within.

I wonder how much of that awe we have lost today.

Our child's Christmas in New Mexico did not involve expensive toys. There were no malls beckoning with sales to distract the spirit and exhaust the mind. We gathered together to celebrate two ways of life, the Christian and the indigenous religious spirit that came to us through the traditions founded in ancient Mexico. Our Christmas Day was not intent on football games, but on listening to the history of the families who came to visit.

They brought many stories. The kitchen was warm and filled with good food, and after we ate we listened to the stories.

My child's Christmas was a celebration because it was a sharing. Out of that past I have evolved the rituals that are important for me to celebrate. I decorate with lights the piñon tree near the entrance to my home. I make sure it is lighted on the night of December 21. It also serves me well for Christmas.

There are other celebrations to share in as the year draws to a close. When it is possible I go to Jemez Pueblo on December 12, el Día de Nuestra Señora de Guadalupe. The Matachines dances at Jemez are among the most exquisite I have ever witnessed. The color of the earth is red, the hills are dotted with junipers and pines, and above the pueblo loom the dark Jemez Mountains. As one approaches, the pueblo appears serene and quiet, then one hears the violin of the fiddler. It is time to hurry to the plaza, where two brightly colored lines of dancers move to the music.

Each dancer wears an ornate, colorful corona, the headdress. The rattle of hollow gourds fills the air as the dancers move back and forth to the lively, repetitive strains of the fiddle. The drama is a mixture of a pueblo step and a polka, more Spanish than Indian. The Malinche, the little girl in white, symbolizing innocence, dances with the old Abuelo, the grandfather. Near her lurks the dancer dressed as El Toro. The presence of the bull frightens the children, for El Toro symbolizes evil.

This dance, brought by the Spaniards to the New World, is now danced both in the Hispano villages and in the Indian pueblos of New Mexico. It is a unique and enthralling way to start the season of renewal. An hour or two spent visiting with friends at Jemez and sitting in the winter sun while the dance drama unfolds can remind the most depressed of spirits that this community is still attentive to its spiritual needs.

All of the homes are open, strangers are fed. The tables are heaped high with posole, meat, chile dishes, tortillas and Indian bread from the hornos, pies, and biscochitos. Imagine what a better life this would be if all the homes in the cities and suburbs enacted this noble sense of community.

Another experience not to be missed is to be at the Taos Pueblo on Christmas Day, but it could be any one of the other pueblos, because they are all celebrating. It is the end of a season, a time of dancing and singing. But in Taos at dusk on Christmas Eve the Mass is celebrated. After Mass the people come pouring out of the church in a winding line.

I was there one Christmas Eve when my friend Cruz pulled me into the procession to weave around the luminarias,[7] stacks of crisscrossed piñon wood which are bonfires lighting the way of the celebrants. And what are these luminarias but a symbol of everlasting light. The bonfires roaring into the night sky are a reflection on earth of the stars that light the way, the star that guided the shepherds to Bethlehem. The fires symbolize the renewal of the sun, and renewal of the light within.

Those roaring fires at the pueblo rekindle the memory of the stars I contemplated as a child. The sweet perfume of the burning piñon rises into the dark, cold sky. So it is with the votive candles in the church. The smoke rises with its message for harmony and peace.

On Christmas Day the deer dance is performed, a dance both for the Taoseños and for their guests. One has to be attentive to brave the sharp cold of the winter morning. Then from the direction of the blue Taos Mountain the cry of the deer is heard, and the frozen spectators stamp their feet and wait eagerly. The cold is numbing, but worth the effort. The deer dancers unite the elements of earth, sky, and community, symbolizing the deep, religious nature of the pueblo.

In Albuquerque, my home, there are other old and lasting rituals to be enacted. Even in the city the barrios preserve their traditions. *Los Pastores,* an old miracle play that originated in Spain, is a favorite. Many of the barrios and villages have their version of this nativity play. Each of the shepherds in the play represents a vice, and when Bartolo, the laziest of the group, is finally converted, the audience rejoices.

*Las Posadas* is another favorite miracle play. It is one of the oldest plays of the Western world continually reenacted in the New World. The story tells how Joseph and Mary sought an inn, a posada. Those who play the parts of Joseph and

---

7. **luminarias** (loo muh NAH ree uhs): bonfires usually lit at the church on Christmas Eve.

Mary go from home to home, seeking shelter for the night. They knock at the first door and are refused. The procession moves to another home, singing carols, until finally they are admitted at a designated home and all the guests are fed. There is singing and great rejoicing.

There is something beneath the ritual that must be the real message. Even when *Las Posadas* is not enacted as a play, the idea of welcoming the stranger to the feast persists. That is why so many people met in my mother's kitchen in those Christmases of long ago.

Time changes the customs in small ways; it does not dim the memory. Now the farolitos[8] are not the stacks of piñon wood to be lighted, they are votive candles placed in paper sacks with sand at the bottom. When we were children the brown paper bags from the grocery store were saved not only for sack lunches but so we would have enough sacks to use for the farolitos of Christmas.

The farolitos are a traditional New Mexico custom. Hundreds adorn homes, walkways, and street curbs. On a cold Christmas night even the most humble home is transformed as the candles flicker and glow in the dark.

In a city like Albuquerque, caravans of tourists fill the streets in the evenings to view the symphony of light that glows to announce that in this home there is posada. Neighborhoods become united as they gather in community effort to decorate their homes and streets. Candles and paper sacks are shared, even if today they are bought at the store. The children vie to light the candles, for the lighting of the farolitos keeps the child's sense of Christmas. More than one enterprising company is now making electric farolitos. Perhaps the important thing is that the lights continue to be lit.

In our memory we know that it is important to light the fire at the end of this season, whether the fire be the yule log or the luminarias of New Mexico. A fire shall light the way, just as the evergreen will remind us that life will renew itself.

Deep within the celebration of these customs there lies the flicker of hope. Christmas celebrates the birth of Christ, and it is also the celebration of the ending of the year, the cycle of the sun. Now the sun will return north and the days will grow longer, and those who were attentive to this mysterious spirit of renewal will be fulfilled.

---

8. *farolitos* (far uh LEE tohs): lights created by placing a candle in a bag, also called *luminarias*.

# Luis Omar Salinas
b. 1937–   (Mexican American)

## Meet the Writer

**Luis Omar Salinas** (loo EES OH mahr suh LEE nuhs) has described his task in writing as "somehow to come to terms with the tragic and through the tragic gain a vision which transcends this world in some way." Salinas, who was born in Robstown, Texas, faced tragedy at an early age. When he was only four years old, his mother died of tuberculosis.

During college, Salinas endured another dark period, this time caused by his own bout with mental illness. Reflecting on his life struggles, Salinas has said, "At age four I was sort of predestined to a tragic vision of life. . . . Yet poetry became like a kind of saving grace."

Salinas's "saving grace" took root at Fresno State University, where he worked as the editor of a literary magazine and became part of the Chicano movement. In his creative writing courses, Salinas began writing many of the poems that later appeared in the first collection of his work, *Crazy Gypsy* (1971).

The 1970s were prolific years for Salinas. In much of his poetry from that time, Salinas dwells on the feelings of alienation, exploitation, and loss of identity that many Mexicans have experienced after immigrating to the United States.

In the 1980s, Salinas began to create works with more conventional content and structure, using metaphors and images that were less shocking than those found in his earlier poems. Today, Salinas lives in Sanger, California, and works as a poet, editor, interpreter, and translator.

## Background

Perhaps the most distinguishing feature of Salinas's work is his abstract, metaphysical style, influenced by surrealist poets such as Pablo Neruda, César Vallejo, and Miguel Hernández. Salinas uses striking and unsettling metaphors that are meant to startle his readers from the comfort of their customary perceptions of life. He feels that only through such a powerful change of perspective can readers be free from their fixed views of social order and see the injustices taking place around them.

**Before You Read**   *In this touching poem about the death of his mother, Salinas reveals the memories of his childhood that he associates with her and the deep sense of emptiness that he still feels at her loss. What specific details and abstract images does he use in this poem to express the confusion he felt when he was a child and the grief he continues to feel?*

# Olivia
## Luis Omar Salinas

I walk on the edge
of my mother's grave
sadly touching her rain
as if it were her dress
5   disguised as silk, I
wander on, a shadow
speaks as softly
as my hands
and we must leave off
10   where it began
the coughing
and my four year old
arms ready to please
mother you have
15   made the cold into fire
and your beauty the talk
of the town
I know death like I know
you mother
20   leavened bread in the oven
a dog,
my sister Irma,
and the neighbors
wailing like our kitchen
25   I didn't come to this world
to be frightened
yet your death sticks
in my stomach
and I must clean the kitchen
30   with my hands
and I must wander on
into the night of leavened bread
and pursue truth
like a tube needing air.

**Before You Read** *The speaker in this poem says that he has "difficult thoughts" that sometimes cause him to doubt whether he will ever be able to figure them out. He also has powerful memories he finds difficult to "translate." Reflect on the thoughts and feelings you have "deep inside" you. How successful are you at gaining an understanding of them?*

# This Is What I Said
## Luis Omar Salinas

"I'm a very metaphysical cat,
someday I'll be slicing apples
in heaven," I tell my companion
the Estonian. The night
5   is just right for this, and
he laughs, and we both laugh.
Deep inside me, I think
difficult thoughts and wonder
whether my intellect is sharp
10  enough for this, or if I can
translate the feeling that
overcame me when my grandfather died,
or the time I had a high fever
and saw ghosts in the garden
15  and my mother consoled me.
There was a time when I chased
butterflies in Mexico, and the
mad nearby grinned with huge
faces which seemed to be made
20  of my mother's apron.
I realize I'm nothing;
yet if something kind were
to come from nowhere,
I'd start believing all over
25  again, and smile at a girl's
fancifulness, gather myself,
and make a life.

**Before You Read**  *While walking outdoors, thinking private thoughts, you may have sensed strong yet elusive connections between the natural world around you and the inner world of your ideas and feelings. As you read this poem, look for such connections between the speaker's inner and outer worlds. How does the natural world reflect or influence the speaker's thoughts?*

# Coming Back from It
## Luis Omar Salinas

I've been thinking about falling
in love, but the weather has been harsh,
a hair shirt° of sorts, some ashes,
and I've noticed
5   a blind leaf fall on my black boots.
I catch my breath, lift
my white handkerchief up to my face
and look at my palm, where ambition crosses
and recrosses like the traffic at 5:00.
10   The cat from up the street
breaks toward a bird
and the sunlight catches
at my pulse
like a leaf puzzled in the air.

°**hair shirt:** In early Christian and medieval times, a shirt made of some rough, scratchy material like goat's or camel's hair, worn to show repentence for sins or remind the wearer of the limitations of earthly flesh.

# José Antonio Burciaga
1940–1996 (Mexican American)

## Meet the Writer

Perhaps his involvement as a founding member of the comedy group Culture Clash gave **José Antonio Burciaga** (hoh SAY ahn TOH nee oh boor see AH gah) an opportunity to polish the humor that often is found in his writing. Burciaga was born in El Paso, Texas. His mother, who had been a schoolteacher in Mexico, instilled in him a love of storytelling and reading. After completing service in the United States Air Force, he earned a degree in fine arts from the University of Texas at El Paso and began work as an illustrator and graphic artist. He moved to California and started writing for the syndicated news column "Hispanic Link" while he continued working as an artist. He also became a Resident Fellow at Stanford University, where he painted murals, including his well-known *Last Supper of Chicano Heroes*.

Burciaga has written fiction, poetry, and essays of social criticism, often laced with satiric humor. His books include *Restless Serpents* (1976); *Weedee Peepo: A Collection of Essays* (1988); *Undocumented Love* (1992), which won the Before Columbus Foundation American Book Award; and *Drink Cultura: Chicanismo* (1993), which includes "The Great Taco War," an ironic essay on the success of fast-food taco restaurants serving inferior food in Latino neighborhoods.

In the journal *Aztlan*, Carlos G. Velez-Ibañez says of Burciaga: "He offers a moral center that provides everyone with an insight into their potential selves and gives hope and optimism."

## Background

"La Puerta" (Spanish for "the door") is set in a Mexican village where the inhabitants often buy lottery tickets, hoping to win one hundred million pesos. The Mexican National Lottery has been in existence since 1771, when Mexico was a colony of Spain. Lottery profits are used to support health and welfare programs. The holder of a winning ticket must present it to lottery officials before a deadline. As long as the ticket's numbers are readable—even if the ticket is torn, in pieces, or soggy—the ticket is redeemable.

**Before You Read** There is a saying that "necessity is the mother of invention"—in other words, if you need something badly enough, you will figure out a way to get it. Have you ever come close to reaching a goal only to meet with an unexpected difficulty that you had to overcome? What did you do?

# La Puerta[1]

## José Antonio Burciaga

It had rained in thundering sheets every afternoon that summer. A dog-tired Sinesio returned home from his job in a mattress sweat shop. With a weary step from the *autobús,* Sinesio gathered the last of his strength and darted across the busy *avenida* into the ramshackle *colonia* where children played in the meandering pathways that would soon turn into a noisy *arroyo* of rushing water. The rain drops striking the *barrio*'s[2] tin, wooden and cardboard roofs would soon become a sheet of water from heaven.

Every afternoon Sinesio's muffled knock on their two-room shack was answered by Faustina, his wife. She would unlatch the door and return to iron more shirts and dresses of people who could afford the luxury. When thunder clapped, a frightened Faustina would quickly pull the electric cord, believing it would attract lightning. Then she would occupy herself with preparing dinner. Their three children would not arrive home for another hour.

On this day Sinesio laid down his tattered lunch bag, a lottery ticket and his week's wages on the oily tablecloth. Faustina threw a glance at the lottery ticket.

Sinesio's silent arrival always angered Faustina so she glared back at the lottery ticket, "Throwing money away! Buying paper dreams! We can't afford dreams, and you buy them!"

Sinesio ignored her anger. From the table, he picked up a letter, smelled it, studied the U.S. stamp, and with the emphatic opening of the envelope sat down at the table and slowly read aloud the letter from his brother Aurelio as the rain beat against the half tin, half wooden rooftop.

*Dear Sinesio,*

*I write to you from this country of abundance, the first letter I write from los Estados Unidos.[3] After two weeks of nerves and frustration I finally have a job at a canning factory. It took me that long only because I did not have the necessary social security number. It's amazing how much money one can make, but just as amazing how fast it goes. I had to pay for the social security number, two weeks of rent, food, and a pair of shoes. The good pair you gave me wore out on our journey across the border. From the border we crossed two mountains, and the desert in between.*

*I will get ahead because I'm a better worker than the rest of my countrymen. I can see that already and so does the "boss." Coming here will be hard for you, leaving Faustina and the children. It was hard enough for me and I'm single without a worry*

---

1. **la puerta** (lah PWEHR tuh): the door.
2. **barrio's** (BAHR ee ohz): A barrio is a neighborhood or district in a large town or city.

3. **los Estados Unidos** (lohs ehs TAH dohs oo NEE dohs): the United States.

*in life. But at least you will have me here if you come and I'm sure I can get you a job. All you've heard about the crossing is true. Even the lies are true. "Saludos" from your "compadres" Silvio and Ramiro. They are doing fine. They're already bothering me for the bet you made against the Dodgers.*

*Next time we get together I will relate my adventures and those of my "compañeros" . . . things to laugh and cry about.*

Aurelio signed the letter *Saludos y abrazo*. Sinesio looked off into space and imagined himself there already. But this dreaming was interrupted by the pelting rain and Faustina's knife dicing *nopal*,[4] cactus, on the wooden board.

*¿Qué crees?*—"What do you think?" Faustina asked Sinesio.

*¡No sé!*—"I don't know," Sinesio responded with annoyance.

"But you do know, Sinesio. How could you not know? There's no choice. We have turned this over and around a thousand times. That miserable mattress factory will never pay you enough to eat with. We can't even afford the mattresses you make!"

Sinesio's heart sank as if he was being pushed out or had already left his home. She would join her *comadres*[5] as another undocumented widow. Already he missed his three children, Celso, Jenaro, and Natasia his eldest, a joy every time he saw her. "An absence in the heart is an empty pain," he thought.

Faustina reminded Sinesio of the inevitable trip with subtle statements and proverbs that went straight to the heart of the matter. "Necessity knows no frontiers," she would say. The dicing of the *nopal* and onions took on the fast clip of the rain. Faustina looked up to momentarily study a trickle of water that had begun to run on the inside of a heavily patched glass on the door. It bothered her, but unable to fix it at the moment she went back to her cooking.

Sinesio accepted the answer to a question he wished he had never asked. The decision was made. There was no turning back. "I will leave for *el norte* in two weeks," he said gruffly and with authority.

Faustina's heart sank as she continued to make dinner. After the rain, Sinesio went out to help his *compadre* widen a ditch to keep the water from flooding in front of his door. The children came home, and it became Faustina's job to inform them that *Papá* would have to leave for a while. None of them said anything. Jenaro refused to eat. They had expected and accepted the news. From their friends, they knew exactly what it meant. Many of their friends' fathers had already left and many more would follow.

Throughout the following days, Sinesio continued the same drudgery at work but as his departure date approached he began to miss even that. He secured his family and home, made all the essential home repairs he had put off and asked his creditors for patience and trust. He asked his sisters, cousins and neighbors to check on his family. Another *compadre* lent him money for the trip and the coyote.[6] Sinesio did not know when he would return but told everyone, "One year, no more. Save enough money, buy things to sell here and open up a *negocio*, a small business the family can help with."

The last trip home from work was no different except for the going-away gift, a bottle of *mezcal*,[7] and the promise of his job when he returned. As usual, the *autobús* was packed. And as

---

4. ***nopal*** (noh PAHL): a kind of cactus found chiefly in Mexico.
5. ***comadres*** (koh MAH drehs): intimate women friends; gossips.

---

6. ***coyote*** (koh YOH tay): slang for a smuggler.
7. ***mezcal*** (mehs KAHL): a liquor made from the agave plant.

usual, the only ones to talk were two loud young men, *sinvergüenzas*—without shame.

The two young men talked about the *Lotería Nacional* and a lottery prize that had gone unclaimed for a week. "*¡Cien millones de pesos!*—One hundred million pesos! *¡Caray!*" one of them kept repeating as he slapped the folded newspaper on his knees again and again. "Maybe the fool that bought it doesn't even know!"

"Or can't read!" answered the other. And they laughed with open mouths.

This caught Sinesio's attention. Two weeks earlier he had bought a lottery ticket. "Could . . . ? No!" he thought. But he felt a slight flush of blood rush to his face. Maybe this was his lucky day. The one day out of the thousands that he had lived in poverty.

The two jumped off the bus, and Sinesio reached for the newspaper they had left behind. There on the front page was the winning number. At the end of the article was the deadline to claim the prize: 8 that night.

Sinesio did not have the faintest idea if his ticket matched the winning number. So he swung from the highest of hopes and dreams to resigned despair as he wondered if he had won one hundred million pesos.

Jumping off the bus, he ran home, at times slowing to a walk to catch his breath. The times he jogged, his heart pounded, the newspaper clutched in his hand, the heavy grey clouds ready to pour down.

Faustina heard his desperate knock and swung the door open.

"*¿Donde está?*" Sinesio pleaded. "Where is the lottery ticket I bought?" He said it slowly and clearly so he wouldn't have to repeat himself.

Faustina was confused, "What lottery ticket?"

Sinesio searched the table, under the green,

oily cloth, on top of the dresser and through his papers, all the while with the jabbing question, "What did you do with the *boleto de lotería*?"

Thunder clapped. Faustina quit searching and unplugged the iron. Sinesio sounded off about no one respecting his papers and how no one could find anything in that house. *¿Dónde está el boleto de lotería?*—Where is the lottery ticket?

They both stopped to think. The rain splashed into a downpour against the door. Faustina looked at the door to see if she had fixed the hole in the glass.

*¡La puerta!*—"The door!" blurted Faustina, "I put it on the door to keep the rain from coming in!"

Sinesio turned to see the ticket glued on the broken window pane. It was light blue with red numbers and the letters "*Lotería Nacional.*" Sinesio brought the newspaper up to the glued lottery ticket and with his wife compared the numbers off one by one—*Seis—tres—cuatro—uno—ocho—nueve—uno—¡SIETÉ-DOS!*—Sinesio yelled.

"¡No!" trembled a disbelieving and frightened Sinesio, "One hundred million pesos!" His heart pounded, afraid this was all a mistake, a bad joke. They checked it again and again only to confirm the matching numbers.

Sinesio then tried to peel the ticket off. His fingernail slid off the cold, glued lottery ticket. Faustina looked at Sinesio's stubby fingernails and moved in. But Faustina's thinner fingernails also slid off the lottery ticket. Sinesio walked around the kitchen table looking, thinking, trying to remain calm.

Then he grew frustrated and angry. "What time is it?"

"A quarter to seven," Faustina said looking at the alarm clock above the dresser. They tried hot water and a razor blade with no success. Sinesio then lashed out at Faustina in anger, "You! I never answered your mockery! Your lack of faith in me! I played the lottery because I knew this day would come! *¡Por Dios Santo!*" and he swore and kissed his crossed thumb and forefinger. "And now? Look what you have done to me, to us, to your children!"

"We can get something at the *farmacia*! The doctor would surely have something to unglue the ticket."

"*¡Sí! ¡O sí!*" mocked Sinesio. "Sure! We have time to go there."

Time runs faster when there is a deadline. The last bus downtown was due in a few minutes. They tried to take the broken glass pane off the door but he was afraid the ticket would tear more. Sinesio's fear and anger mounted with each glance at the clock.

In frustration, he pushed the door out into the downpour and swung it back into the house, cracking the molding and the inside hinges. One more swing, pulling, twisting, splintering, and Sinesio broke the door completely off.

Faustina stood back with hands over her mouth as she recited a litany to all the *santos* and virgins in heaven as the rain blew into their home and splashed her face wet.

Sinesio's face was also drenched. But Faustina could not tell if it was from the rain or tears of anger, as he put the door over his head and ran down the streaming pathway to catch the *autobús*.

# Gloria Anzaldúa

**1942–2004** (Mexican American)

## Meet the Writer

**Gloria Anzaldúa** (GLOH ree ah ahn sahl DOO ah) is best known for *Borderlands/La Frontera: The New Mestiza* (1987), a work that defies easy classification. It mixes several genres—fiction, history, biography, and poetry—and switches between English and Spanish. It has been called a "creative autobiography." The subtitle calls attention to the word *mestiza*—a female who is half white and half Indian—which to Anzaldúa refers to a woman living between different cultures and different countries.

Anzaldúa was born in South Texas, where her father worked on a ranch. After her father's death, her family labored in the fields for a time in Arkansas. During this period, Anzaldúa came to understand the life of migrant Chicanos. She has written of her desire when she was young to escape from the Chicano culture of the Valley and from family traditions she considered oppressive. In college, she was often at odds with academic advisors because of her interest in feminist studies. The idea for *Borderlands* came to her while she was teaching creative writing and feminist studies in Vermont. It grew out of her sense of alienation, of feeling like a foreigner because there were so few people of color.

## Background

*Borderlands/La Frontera* is divided into two sections. The first part consists of seven essays; the second part is a collection of poems. The book focuses on the experiences of the people who occupy the border between Mexico and the United States. In the last essay, "La conciencia de la mestiza: Towards a New Consciousness," Anzaldúa presents her idea of a *mestiza* consciousness. She believes it results in a synthesis of different cultures, races, and languages. From her perspective, cultural boundaries are broken down in the borderlands. She ends her poem about the borderlands with the paradoxical statement that to survive there, one must live *without* borders and "be a crossroads."

**Before You Read**  *The title of this poem is repeated with slight variations in most stanzas of the poem and provides a framework for the poet's ideas. Note that the poet integrates Spanish words and expressions into her text. How does this technique emphasize the poet's identity as a* mestiza?

# To live in the Borderlands means you
## Gloria Anzaldúa

        To live in the Borderlands means you

   are neither *hispana india negra española*
   *ni gabacha, eres mestiza, mulata,*[1] half-breed
   caught in the crossfire between camps
5   while carrying all five races on your back
   not knowing which side to turn to, run from;

To live in the Borderlands means knowing
   that the *india in you*, betrayed for 500 years,
   is no longer speaking to you,
10   that *mexicanas* call you *rajetas*,[2]
   that denying the Anglo inside you
   is as bad as having denied the Indian or Black;

*Cuando vives en la frontera*[3]
   people walk through you, the wind steals your voice,
15   you're a *burra, buey,*[4] scapegoat,
   forerunner of a new race,
   half and half—both woman and man, neither—
   a new gender;

---

1. *hispana india . . . mestiza, mulata:* Hispanic Indian black Spanish nor white woman, you are mestiza (Indian/white), mulata (black/white).
2. *rajetas:* literally, "split," that is, having betrayed your word.
3. *cuando vives en la frontera:* when you live on the border.
4. *burra, buey:* female donkey, ox.

To live in the Borderlands means to
20    put *chile* in the borscht,
      eat whole wheat *tortillas*,
      speak Tex-Mex with a Brooklyn accent;
      be stopped by *la migra*[5] at the border checkpoints;

Living in the Borderlands means you fight hard to
25    resist the gold elixir beckoning from the bottle,
      the pull of the gun barrel,
      the rope crushing the hollow of your throat;

In the Borderlands
      you are the battleground
30    where enemies are kin to each other;
      you are at home, a stranger,
      the border disputes have been settled
      the volley of shots have shattered the truce
      you are wounded, lost in action
35    dead, fighting back;

To live in the Borderlands means
      the mill with the razor white teeth wants to shred off
      your olive-red skin, crush out the kernel, your heart
      pound you pinch you roll you out
40    smelling like white bread but dead;

To survive the Borderlands
      you must live *sin fronteras*[6]
      be a crossroads.

---
5. *la migra:* the U.S. Immigration Service.
6. *sin fronteras:* without borders.

# Pat Mora

b. 1942– (Mexican American)

## Meet the Writer

**Pat Mora** says that she learned the power of storytelling from her aunt Ignacia (Nacha) Delgado, whom the Mora children called *Tía Lobo*, "Aunt Wolf." Nacha would tell the children tales in Spanish and English and read to them. Something else Pat Mora learned from her aunt was "loving well." In her work, Mora acknowledges the importance of her family's influence. She and the other children were taught both English and Spanish so that they "could derive pleasure from both cultures."

Mora has dedicated much of her professional life to the preservation of her culture. Believing that a person's sense of identity is firmly rooted in his or her culture, she has worked to raise awareness among Mexican Americans of the rich history and traditions that make up their heritage. Her artistic goals are similar: to write about the Mexican American experience not only as a contemporary phenomenon but also as the culmination of centuries-old values, languages, and customs.

Mora, who now lives in Santa Fe, New Mexico, was born and raised in El Paso, Texas. She completed her undergraduate degree at Texas Western College and her graduate degrees in English and speech at the University of Texas at El Paso. Although she showed an early interest in books and language, she did not consider a career as a writer until she had worked as a teacher and university administrator. As she started writing, Mora became interested in discovering her own heritage and sharing it with others. Her first book, a collection of poetry called *Chants*, was published in 1984. *Borders* appeared in 1986. Both were awarded the Southwest Book Award from the Border Regional Library. Mora also received the Creative Writing Award from the National Association for Chicano Studies in 1983 and the Women Artists and Writers of the Southwest poetry award in 1984.

## Background

Mora's poetry often springs from her geographical surroundings: the high desert that extends from Mexico in the south to the Rocky Mountains in the north, creating a common bond between two countries and two diverse cultures. In *Borders,* she "posits the metaphor that unifies most of her work." One writer has noted that "while recognizing that Mexican Americans live a type of border existence no matter where they live, [Mora] sees the border as a powerful image of healing, a place to bridge divisions and to foster mutual understanding."

Mora has written many books for children. In 1997, she and her illustrator received the third annual Tomás Rivera Mexican American Children's Book Award for their book *Tomás and the Library Lady.* Mora also became an advocate for the establishment of a national day to celebrate language and bilingual literacy. *El día de los niños/El día de los libros* (*Children's Day/Book Day*) is now celebrated on April 30.

Mora has also published a collection of autobiographical essays, *Nepantla: Essays from the Land in the Middle* (1993) and a memoir, *House of Houses* (1997). *My Own True Name: New and Selected Poems for Young Adults* is a collection of sixty poems divided into three sections: blooms, thorns, and roots. Her most recent collection of poetry, *Adobe Odes,* was inspired, she says, by Pablo Neruda's odes.

**Before You Read** Do you, as the speaker of this poem does, feel drawn to a particular kind of terrain—a place that offers you comfort and seems to reflect your inner thoughts? Consider why the speaker characterizes the desert as a *madre*, or mother.

# Mi Madre[1]

## Pat Mora

I say feed me.
She serves red prickly pear on a spiked cactus.

I say tease me.
She sprinkles raindrops in my face on a sunny day.

5   I say frighten me.
She shouts thunder, flashes lightning.

I say comfort me.
She invites me to lay on her firm body.

I say heal me.
10   She gives me *manzanilla, orégano, dormilón*[2]

I say caress me.
She strokes my skin with her warm breath.

I say make me beautiful.
She offers turquoise for my fingers, a pink blossom for my hair.

15   I say sing to me.
She chants lonely women's songs of femaleness.

I say teach me.
She endures: glaring heat
          numbing cold
20             frightening dryness.

She: the desert
She: strong mother.

---

1. *Mi Madre* (mee MAH dray): my mother.

2. *manzanilla, orégano, dormilón* (mahn sah NEE yah oh REH gah noh dawr mee LOHN): three spices commonly used as herbal medicines.

**Before You Read** *What is the speaker's attitude toward the child, the tourists at the spring, and herself? What do the contrasts in the poem imply about how the tourists view the Peruvians—and how the Peruvians view the tourists?*

# Peruvian Child
## Pat Mora

Still in the middle of my path is the child
with no smile who stared at us. Her eyes
even then the eyes of women who sell chickens
and onions in outdoor markets. The women
5  who stare at us as if we are guards.

She whispered to the doll with no face,
smoothed the red and blue scraps
of cloth on the path, ironed them with her hand,
wrapped and re-wrapped the doll, hair
10  mud-tangled as the child's, and the dog's,
and the llama's that followed the child's
small bare feet after she bundled the doll
in the striped *manta°* on her back.

The matted group stood by the edge of the spring
15  watching us drink clear, holy water of the Inca,
a fountain of youth, our guide said.
We wanted, as usual, to hold a picture
of the child in a white border, not to hold her
mud-crusted hands or feet or face,
20  not to hold her, the child in our arms.

---

° ***manta*** (MAHN tah): mantle.

**Before You Read** *During her many years as housekeeper to his family, the woman in this poem has become like a mother to the boy whose graduation she now attends. Having cared for him throughout his childhood, she feels intense emotions as she witnesses the event that marks his becoming an adult. What images and details express the strong mutual affection between the woman and the boy?*

# Graduation Morning
## Pat Mora

*for Anthony*

She called him *Lucero*,[1] morning star,
snared him with sweet coffee, pennies,
Mexican milk candy, brown bony hugs.

Through the years she'd cross the Rio
5   Grande to clean his mother's home. "*Lucero,
mi[2] lucero,*" she'd cry, when she'd see him
running toward her in the morning,
when she pulled stubborn cactus thorns
from his small hands, when she found him
10  hiding in the creosote.[3]

Though she's small and thin,
black sweater, black scarf,
the boy in the white graduation robe
easily finds her at the back of the cathedral,
15  finds her amid the swirl of sparkling clothes,
finds her eyes.

Tears slide down her wrinkled cheeks.
Her eyes, *luceros,* stroke his face.

---

1. ***Lucero*** (loo SEH roh).
2. ***mi*** (mee): my.
3. **creosote:** an evergreen shrub with a pungent odor; it grows in the southwestern United States and northern Mexico.

**Before You Read** *In this poem the speaker pays homage to the various folk arts ("arte popular") of Mexico: the colorful, fanciful creations made by Mexican villagers and admired throughout the world. How does the imagery in this poem bring the museum's objects to life?*

# Arte Popular
## Pat Mora

    A hot breath among the pale crystal,
    and polite watercolors of this tidy museum,
    a breathing
    in these new rooms,
5   and faint drums, whistles, chants.

    Judas figures° puffed with sins rise
    to the ceiling ready to explode into
    pure white smoke,
    dragons' eyes bulge, and green claws reach
10  to pull your hair
    as masks sneer down
    at skeletons dressed as bride and groom.

    In Mexican villages
    wrinkled hands lure and trap
15  dark spirits,
    snakes
    slide into woven reeds
    dogs
    growl softly in wood
20  frogs
    blow their wet song into clay flutes
    jaguars
    pant in papier-mâché

    a breathing those spirits poised
25  to inhale deeply, fly out museum windows,
    leap down steps three at a time, slither
    on cool white marble into the night, into the full moon.

---

°**Judas figures:** large papier-maché figures that are exploded; they represent the disciple who betrayed Jesus.

# Alma Luz Villanueva

b. 1944–    (Mexican American)

## Meet the Writer

Now a recognized poet and novelist, **Alma Luz Villanueva** (AHL mah LOOS vee yah NWAY vah) had a rough start in life. Born in Lompoc, California, she never knew her father. For her first eleven years, she was raised by her grandmother, a Yaqui Indian from Sonora, Mexico; when her grandmother died, her mother and aunt took care of her. By the tenth grade, Villanueva had dropped out of high school. By the time she was seventeen years old, she had two children, was trapped in a violent marriage, and was living on welfare in a brutal public housing project in San Francisco. When she ended that marriage and moved to a beautiful farm in Sebastopol on the edge of the Santa Rosa plain in Sonoma County, "the poetry, all the words, all the crying, all the laughter, just erupted."

Villanueva graduated from City College of San Francisco and Norwich University and earned a master of fine arts degree from Vermont College. She now teaches at Antioch University in Los Angeles.

Her novel *Ultraviolet Sky* won the 1989 American Book Award from the Before Columbus Foundation. *Planet*, a collection of poems published in a volume with the previously published *Mother May I?*, was awarded the 1994 Latino Literature Prize. Villanueva teaches workshops in creative writing and does readings throughout the United States. In one poetry workshop, she asked her students to think about these words from the Buddha: "These things matter most: How well do you love? How fully did you live? How deeply did you learn to let go?"

## Background

Many of Villanueva's stories take place in California, where she has spent most of her life. Vida, the name of the mother in this story, means "life" in Spanish. A woman named Vida is also the focus of a book of Villanueva's poems (titled *Vida*). Those poems about Vida express some of Villanueva's common themes, which are also found in the following story: a celebration of womanhood, love, relationships, and children.

**Before You Read**  *Coming-of-age is a theme in literature that can be found in stories as early as those told by the ancient Greeks. In most coming-of-age stories, a young person endures an initiation period, usually one that involves some kind of physical or psychological hardship. The self-knowledge that the boy or girl gains from this experience helps in the quest for independence—for eventual separation from parental control. The young people learn how to take charge of their own lives, while maintaining the connection with the family that is so important for a sense of continuity. What actions and events could mark the coming-of-age of a boy or girl today? What problems might the young people encounter before the coming-of-age is successfully completed?*

# Golden Glass
## Alma Luz Villanueva

It was his fourteenth summer. He was thinning out, becoming angular and clumsy, but the cautiousness, the old-man seriousness he'd had as a baby, kept him contained, ageless and safe. His humor, always dry and to the bone since a small child, let you know he was watching everything.

He seemed always to be at the center of his own universe, so it was no surprise to his mother to hear Ted say: "I'm building a fort and sleeping out in it all summer, and I won't come in for anything, not even food. Okay?"

This had been their silent communion, the steady presence of love that flowed regularly, daily—food. The presence of his mother preparing it, his great appetite and obvious enjoyment of it—his nose smelling everything, seeing his mother more vividly than with his eyes.

He watched her now for signs of offense, alarm, and only saw interest. "Where will you put the fort?" Vida asked.

She trusted him to build well and not ruin things, but of course she had to know where. She looked at his dark, contained face and her eyes turned in and saw him when he was small, with curly golden hair, when he wrapped his arms around her neck. Their quiet times—undemanding—he could be let down, and a small toy could delight him for hours. She thought of the year he began kissing her elbow in passing, the way he preferred. Vida would touch his hair, his forehead, his shoulders—the body breathing out at the touch, his stillness. Then the explosion out the door told her he needed her touch, still.

"I'll build it by the redwoods, in the cypress trees. Okay?"

"Make sure you keep your nails together and don't dig into the trees. I'll be checking. If the trees get damaged, it'll have to come down."

"Jason already said he'd bring my food and stuff."

"Where do you plan to shower and go to the bathroom?" Vida wondered.

"With the hose when it's hot and I'll dig holes behind the barn," Ted said so quietly as to seem unspoken. He knew how to slither under her, smoothly, like silk.

"Sounds interesting, but it better stay clean—this place isn't that big. Also, on your dinner night, you can cook outdoors."

His eyes flashed, but he said, "Okay."

He began to gather wood from various stacks, drying it patiently from the long rains. He kept in his room one of the hammers and a supply of nails that he'd bought. It was early June and the seasonal creek was still running. It was pretty dark out there and he wondered if he'd meant what he'd said.

Ted hadn't seen his father in nearly four years, and he didn't miss him like you should a regular father, he thought. His father's image blurred with the memory of a football hitting him too hard, pointed (a bullet), right in the stomach, and the punishment for the penny candies—a test his father had set up for him to fail. His stomach hardened at the thought of his father, and he found he didn't miss him at all.

He began to look at the shapes of the trees, where the limbs were solid, where a space was provided (he knew his mother really would make him tear down the fort if he hurt the trees). The cypress was right next to the redwoods, making it seem very remote. Redwoods do that—they suck up sound and time and smell like another place. So he counted the footsteps, when no one was looking, from the fort to the house. He couldn't believe it was so close; it seemed so separate, alone—especially in the dark, when the only safe way of travel seemed flight (invisible at best).

Ted had seen his mother walk out to the bridge at night with a glass of wine, looking into the water, listening to it. He knew she loved to see the moon's reflection in the water. She'd pointed it out to him once by a river where they camped, her face full of longing—too naked somehow, he thought. Then, she swam out into the water, at night, as though trying to touch the moon. He wouldn't look at her. He sat and glared at the fire and roasted another marshmallow the way he liked it: bubbly, soft and brown (maybe six if he could get away with it). Then she'd be back, chilled and bright, and he was glad she went. Maybe I like the moon too, he thought, involuntarily, as though the thought weren't his own—but it was.

He built the ground floor directly on the earth, with a cover of old plywood, then scattered remnant rugs that he'd asked Vida to get for him. He concocted a latch and a door, with his hand ax over it, just in case. He brought his sleeping bag, some pillows, a transistor radio, some clothes, and moved in for the summer. The first week he slept with his buck knife open in his hand and his pellet gun loaded on the same side, his right. The second week Ted sheathed the knife and put it under his head, but kept the pellet gun loaded at all times. He missed no one in the house but the dog, so he brought him into the cramped little space, enduring dog breath and farts because he missed *someone*.

Ted thought of when his father left, when they lived in the city, with forty kids on one side of the block and forty on the other. He remembered that one little kid with the funny sores on his body who chose an apple over candy every time. He worried they would starve or something worse. That time he woke up screaming in his room (he forgot why), and his sister began crying at the same time, "Someone's in here," as though they were having the same terrible dream. Vida ran in with a chair in one hand and a kitchen knife in the other, which frightened them even more. But when their mother realized it was only their hysteria, she became angry and left. Later they all laughed about this till they cried, including Vida, and things felt safer.

He began to build the top floor now but he had to prune some limbs out of the way. Well, that was okay as long as he was careful. So he stacked them to one side for kindling and began to brace things in place. It felt weird going up into the tree, not as safe as his small, contained place on the ground. He began to build it, thinking of light. He could bring his comic books, new ones, sit up straight, and eat snacks in the daytime. He would put in a side window facing the house to watch them, if he wanted, and a tunnel from the bottom floor to the top. Also, a ladder he'd found and repaired—he could pull it up and place it on hooks, out of reach. A hatch at the top of the ceiling for leaving or entering, tied down inside with a rope. He began to sleep up here, without the dog, with the tunnel closed off.

Vida noticed Ted had become cheerful and would stand next to her, to her left side, talking sometimes. But she realized she mustn't face him or he'd become silent and wander away. So she stood listening, in the same even breath and heartbeat she kept when she spotted the wild pheasants with their long, lush tails trailing the grape arbor, picking delicately and greedily at the unpicked grapes in the early autumn light. So sharp, so perfect, so rare to see a wild thing at peace.

She knew he ate well—his brother brought out a half gallon of milk that never came back, waiting to be asked to join him, but never daring to ask. His sister made him an extra piece of ham for his four eggs; most always he ate cold cereal and fruit or got a hot chocolate on the way to summer school. They treated Ted somewhat like a stranger, because he was.

Ted was taking a makeup course and one in stained glass. There, he talked and acted relaxed, like a boy; no one expected any more or less. The colors of the stained glass were deep and beautiful, and special—you couldn't waste this glass. The sides were sharp, the cuts were slow and meticulous with a steady pressure. The design's plan had to be absolutely followed or the beautiful glass would go to waste, and he'd curse himself.

It was late August and Ted hadn't gone inside the house once. He liked waking up, hearing nothing but birds—not his mother's voice or his sister's or his brother's. He could tell the various

bird calls and liked the soft brown quail call the best. He imagined their taste and wondered if their flesh was as soft as their song. Quail would've been okay to kill, as long as he ate it, his mother said. Instead, he killed jays because they irritated him so much with their shrill cries. Besides, a neighbor paid Ted per bird because he didn't want them in his garden. But that was last summer and he didn't do that anymore, and the quail were proud and plump and swift, and Ted was glad.

The stained glass was finished and he decided to place it in his fort facing the back fields. In fact, it looked like the back fields—trees and the sun in a dark sky. During the day the glass sun shimmered a beautiful yellow, the blue a much better color than the sky outside: deeper, like night.

He was so used to sleeping outside now he didn't wake up during the night, just like in the house. One night, toward the end when he'd have to move back with everyone (school was starting, frost was coming and the rains), Ted woke up to see the stained glass full of light. The little sun was a golden moon and the inside glass sky and the outside sky matched.

In a few days he'd be inside, and he wouldn't mind at all.

# Lucha Corpi

b. 1945–    (Mexican American)

## Meet the Writer

Describing her reasons for becoming a writer, **Lucha Corpi** (LOO chah KOHR pee) recalls her grandmother saying that there is no justice in the world. Corpi adds, "I think that's why I write—to bring justice into the world." Her work often focuses on social issues, especially the struggles of women, immigrants, and the powerless people in society.

Born in a small village in Veracruz, Mexico, Corpi immigrated to the United States with her husband when she was nineteen years old. At the University of California at Berkeley, she became involved in the free speech and Chicano rights movements. She went on to earn a master's degree from San Francisco State University and has taught in Oakland public schools for many years.

Corpi's first book of poetry, *Palabras de mediodia/Noon Words*, was published in 1980. Written in Spanish and translated into English, these poems are highly expressive with striking and original imagery. This volume includes her best-known work, "The Marina Poems," a series of four poems about the historical figure Doña Marina, who gave birth to the son of Hernán Cortés, the conqueror of Mexico. Although Doña Marina was condemned by her people as a traitor, Corpi portrays her sympathetically as a wise woman caught between two worlds.

Corpi has written a second volume of poetry, an autobiographical book for children, and several novels. Even Corpi's detective novels continue to explore themes related to social issues.

## Background

Like many Mexican Americans, Corpi has felt torn between two conflicting sets of values: those of her native Mexican culture and those of modern American society. Her divorce from her husband intensified these conflicts, leading her to question her identity as a Mexican woman in her adopted American culture. Corpi's poem "Mexico" reflects the deep influence of Mexican culture on her identity. The poem "Emily Dickinson" shows Corpi's feelings of solidarity with one of America's most famous poets.

**Before You Read** *A prominent theme in Corpi's poetry is her dual identity as a Mexican American. What images can you find that show a sense of division and opposition between two cultures?*

# México
## Lucha Corpi

Partí
como nota dividida
buscándose a sí misma.

Busqué
5  en colores de noche
sombras de día.

Perseguí
luces de ríos
en sueños viejos.

10  Esencia doble tan cercana
Cuerda floja de mi orden natural.

México.

A veces pienso en ti
en tardes así
15  Me acaece viejo mal.

Buscar senderos de tierra
a vera de profundidades.

En bancales tibios
garzas de plumaje azul
20  perlas rojas cultivaron.

No hay tiempo de llorar
si has de vivir en mí.

Recuerdos nunca fueron
medida líquida de amar.

# Mexico

I parted
like a note divided
in search of itself.

I looked
5  in the colors of night
for day's shadows.

I hunted
river lights
in old dreams.

10  Double essence so closely bound
tightrope of my natural order.

Mexico.

Sometimes I think of you
on afternoons like this
15  An old distress comes over me.

Search for paths of earth
at the edge of the depth.

On warm banks
blue-feathered herons
20  cultivate red pearls.

There is no time for weeping
if you are to live in me.

Memories were never
the liquid measure of love.

**Before You Read**  You have probably read at least one poem by the nineteenth-century poet Emily Dickinson. A quiet, solitary person, Dickinson created powerful works that reveal an intense inner life. She was a startlingly "modern" poet whose unique poetry was ahead of its time. As you read Corpi's poem, consider why Corpi might feel that she is like Dickinson. What do these two poets have in common?

# Emily Dickinson
## Lucha Corpi

Como tú, soy de ayer,
de las bahías en donde
se ancla el día a
esperar su propia hora.

5  Como yo, eres de hoy,
del andar de esa hora
en la que apenas palpita
lo que aún no ha nacido.

Somos cultivadoras de
10  indecibles, tejedoras
de singulares, campesinas
migratorias en busca de
chinampas aún sin
siembra y sin cosecha.

# Emily Dickinson

Like you, I belong to yesterday,
to the bays where
day is anchored to
wait for its hour.

5  Like me, you belong to today,
the progression of that hour
when what is unborn
begins to throb.

We are cultivators of
10  the unsayable, weavers
of singulars, migrant
workers in search of
floating gardens as yet
unsown, as yet unharvested.

# Esmeralda Santiago
b. 1948–  (Puerto Rican American)

## Meet the Writer

**Esmeralda Santiago** (ehs mah RAHL dah sahn tee AH goh) was born in Santurce, Puerto Rico, a suburb of San Juan. She was the eldest of eleven children. During her childhood, her family moved frequently between Santurce and Macún, a barrio without running water or electricity. In 1961, Santiago moved to New York City with her mother and siblings. She attended junior high school in Brooklyn, where she overcame problems of language and cultural differences to become an outstanding student. After she graduated from Performing Arts High School in Manhattan, she attended community colleges and eventually transferred to Harvard on a scholarship. She is married to Frank Cantor, a filmmaker, and has two children.

## Background

Santiago has been asked why she used the past tense in the title of her memoir, *When I Was Puerto Rican*. She responded, "The 'was' in the title refers to the strong sense of self I had as a rural Puerto Rican." When she returned to Puerto Rico after graduating from college, she found that she was no longer considered Puerto Rican because she had lived in the United States for too long: "My Spanish was rusty, my gaze too direct, my personality too assertive for a Puerto Rican woman. . . ." Until she arrived in Brooklyn, she had never heard the words *Hispanic* and *Latina* used to identify her. She felt that these words, which ignored her place of birth, took away an aspect of her identity. "In writing the book I wanted to get back to that feeling of Puertoricanness I had before I came here. Its title reflects who I was then, and asks, who am I today?"

**Before You Read**  This excerpt, taken from the final pages of Santiago's memoir, When I Was Puerto Rican, tells the story of the author's audition for the Performing Arts High School, a public school for students wishing to follow careers in theater, music, and dance. As you read, try to put yourself in Santiago's shoes. Think about times when you have had to audition for something you really wanted or had to prove to others that you had a particular talent, knowledge, or skill. How was your experience similar to or different from Santiago's?

# A Shot at It
*from* When I Was Puerto Rican
## Esmeralda Santiago

*Te conozco bacalao, aunque vengas disfrazao.*

*I recognize you salted codfish, even if you're in disguise.*

While Francisco[1] was still alive, we had moved to Ellery Street. That meant I had to change schools, so Mami walked me to P.S. 33, where I would attend ninth grade. The first week I was there I was given a series of tests that showed that even though I couldn't speak English very well, I read and wrote it at the tenth-grade level. So they put me in 9-3, with the smart kids.

One morning, Mr. Barone, a guidance counsellor, called me to his office. He was short, with a big head and large hazel eyes under shapely eyebrows. His nose was long and round at the tip. He dressed in browns and yellows and often perched his tortoiseshell glasses on his forehead, as if he had another set of eyes up there.

"So," he pushed his glasses up, "what do you want to be when you grow up?"

"I don't know."

He shuffled through some papers. "Let's see here . . . you're fourteen, is that right?"

"Yes, sir."

"And you've never thought about what you want to be?"

When I was very young, I wanted to be a *jíbara*.[2] When I was older, I wanted to be a cartographer, then a topographer. But since we'd come to Brooklyn, I'd not thought about the future much.

"No, sir."

He pulled his glasses down to where they belonged and shuffled through the papers again.

"Do you have any hobbies?" I didn't know what he meant. "Hobbies, hobbies," he flailed his hands, as if he were juggling, "things you like to do after school."

"Ah, yes." I tried to imagine what I did at home that might qualify as a hobby. "I like to read."

He seemed disappointed. "Yes, we know that about you." He pulled out a paper and stared at it. "One of the tests we gave you was an aptitude

---

1. **Francisco:** her mother's suitor.
2. ***jíbara*** (HEE bah rah): someone from the mountains of Puerto Rico; a peasant, but in this context it carries with it a certain romanticism [Author's note].

test. It tells us what kinds of things you might be good at. The tests show that you would be good at helping people. Do you like to help people?"

I was afraid to contradict the tests. "Yes, sir."

"There's a high school we can send you where you can study biology and chemistry which will prepare you for a career in nursing."

I screwed up my face. He consulted the papers again.

"You would also do well in communications. Teaching maybe."

I remembered Miss Brown standing in front of a classroom full of rowdy teenagers, some of them taller than she was.

"I don't like to teach."

Mr. Barone pushed his glasses up again and leaned over the stack of papers on his desk. "Why don't you think about it and get back to me," he said, closing the folder with my name across the top. He put his hand flat on it, as if squeezing something out. "You're a smart girl, Esmeralda. Let's try to get you into an academic school so that you have a shot at college."

On the way home, I walked with another new ninth grader, Yolanda. She had been in New York for three years but knew as little English as I did. We spoke in Spanglish, a combination of English and Spanish in which we hopped from one language to the other depending on which word came first.

"*Te preguntó el* Mr. Barone, you know, *lo que querías hacer*[3] when you grow up?" I asked.

"*Sí, pero*, I didn't know. *¿Y tú?*"[4]

"*Yo tampoco.*[5] He said, *que* I like to help people. *Pero*, you know, *a mí no me gusta la gente.*"[6] When she heard me say I didn't like people much, Yolanda looked at me from the corner of her eye, waiting to become the exception.

---

3. *Te preguntó . . . hacer:* He asked you . . . what you wanted to be.
4. *Sí, pero, . . . ¿Y tú?:* Yes, but, . . . And you?
5. *Yo tampoco:* me neither.
6. *a mí . . . gente:* I don't much like people.

**256** Latino Literature

By the time I said it, she had dashed up the stairs of her building. She didn't wave as she ducked in, and the next day she wasn't friendly. I walked around the rest of the day in embarrassed isolation, knowing that somehow I had given myself away to the only friend I'd made at Junior High School 33. I had to either take back my words or live with the consequences of stating what was becoming the truth. I'd never said that to anyone, not even to myself. It was an added weight, but I wasn't about to trade it for companionship.

A few days later, Mr. Barone called me back to his office.

"Well?" Tiny green flecks burned around the black pupils of his hazel eyes.

The night before, Mami had called us into the living room. On the television "fifty of America's most beautiful girls" paraded in ruffled tulle dresses before a tinsel waterfall.

"Aren't they lovely?" Mami murmured, as the girls, escorted by boys in uniform, floated by the camera, twirled, and disappeared behind a screen to the strains of a waltz and an announcer's dramatic voice calling their names, ages, and states. Mami sat mesmerized through the whole pageant.

"I'd like to be a model," I said to Mr. Barone.

He stared at me, pulled his glasses down from his forehead, looked at the papers inside the folder with my name on it, and glared. "A model?" His voice was gruff, as if he were more comfortable yelling at people than talking to them.

"I want to be on television."

"Oh, then you want to be an actress," in a tone that said this was only a slight improvement over my first career choice. We stared at one another for a few seconds. He pushed his glasses up to his forehead again and reached for a book on the shelf in back of him. "I only know of one school that trains actresses, but we've never sent them a student from here."

Performing Arts, the write-up said, was an academic, as opposed to a vocational, public school that trained students wishing to pursue a career in theater, music, and dance.

"It says here that you have to audition." He stood up and held the book closer to the faint gray light coming through the narrow window high on his wall. "Have you ever performed in front of an audience?"

"I was announcer in my school show in Puerto Rico," I said. "And I recite poetry. There, not here."

He closed the book and held it against his chest. His right index finger thumped a rhythm on his lower lip. "Let me call them and find out exactly what you need to do. Then we can talk some more."

I left his office strangely happy, confident that something good had just happened, not knowing exactly what.

"I'm not afraid . . . I'm not afraid . . . I'm not afraid." Every day I walked home from school repeating those words. The broad streets and sidewalks that had impressed me so on the first day we had arrived had become as familiar as the dirt road from Macún to the highway. Only my curiosity about the people who lived behind these walls ended where the façades of the buildings opened into dark hallways or locked doors. Nothing good, I imagined, could be happening inside if so many locks had to be breached to go in or step out.

It was on these tense walks home from school that I decided I had to get out of Brooklyn. Mami had chosen this as our home, and just like every other time we'd moved, I'd had to go along with her because I was a child who had no choice. But I wasn't willing to go along with her on this one.

"How can people live like this?" I shrieked once, desperate to run across a field, to feel grass under my feet instead of pavement.

"Like what?" Mami asked, looking around our apartment, the kitchen and living room crisscrossed with sagging lines of drying diapers and bedclothes.

"Everyone on top of each other. No room to do anything. No air."

"Do you want to go back to Macún, to live like savages, with no electricity, no toilets . . ."

"At least you could step outside every day without somebody trying to kill you."

"Ay, Negi,[7] stop exaggerating!"

"I hate my life!" I yelled.

"Then do something about it," she yelled back.

Until Mr. Barone showed me the listing for Performing Arts High School, I hadn't known what to do.

"The auditions are in less than a month. You have to learn a monologue, which you will perform in front of a panel. If you do well, and your grades here are good, you might get into the school."

Mr. Barone took charge of preparing me for my audition to Performing Arts. He selected a speech from *The Silver Cord*, a play by Sidney Howard, first performed in 1926, but whose action took place in a New York drawing room circa 1905.

"Mr. Gatti, the English teacher," he said, "will coach you. . . . And Mrs. Johnson will talk to you about what to wear and things like that."

I was to play Christina, a young married woman confronting her mother-in-law. I learned the monologue phonetically from Mr. Gatti. It opened with "You belong to a type that's very common in this country, Mrs. Phelps—a type of self-centered, self-pitying, son-devouring tigress, with unmentionable proclivities[8] suppressed on the side."

"We don't have time to study the meaning of

---

7. **Negi:** Esmeralda's nickname.
8. **proclivities:** tendencies.

every word," Mr. Gatti said. "Just make sure you pronounce every word correctly."

Mrs. Johnson, who taught Home Economics, called me to her office.

"Is that how you enter a room?" she asked the minute I came in. "Try again, only this time, don't barge in. Step in slowly, head up, back straight, a nice smile on your face. That's it." I took a deep breath and waited. "Now sit. No, not like that. Don't just plop down. Float down to the chair with your knees together." She demonstrated, and I copied her. "That's better. What do you do with your hands? No, don't hold your chin like that; it's not ladylike. Put your hands on your lap, and leave them there. Don't use them so much when you talk."

I sat stiff as a cutout while Mrs. Johnson and Mr. Barone asked me questions they thought the panel at Performing Arts would ask.

"Where are you from?"

"Puerto Rico."

"No," Mrs. Johnson said, "Porto Rico. Keep your *r*'s soft. Try again."

"Do you have any hobbies?" Mr. Barone asked. Now I knew what to answer.

"I enjoy dancing and the movies."

"Why do you want to come to this school?"

Mrs. Johnson and Mr. Barone had worked on my answer if this question should come up.

"I would like to study at Performing Arts because of its academic program and so that I may be trained as an actress."

"Very good, very good!" Mr. Barone rubbed his hands together, twinkled his eyes at Mrs. Johnson. "I think we have a shot at this."

"Remember," Mrs. Johnson said, "when you shop for your audition dress, look for something very simple in dark colors."

Mami bought me a red plaid wool jumper with a crisp white shirt, my first pair of stockings, and penny loafers. The night before, she rolled

up my hair in pink curlers that cut into my scalp and made it hard to sleep. For the occasion, I was allowed to wear eye makeup and a little lipstick.

"You look so grown up!" Mami said, her voice sad but happy, as I twirled in front of her and Tata.

"*Toda una senorita,*"9 Tata said, her eyes misty.

We set out for the audition on an overcast January morning heavy with the threat of snow.

"Why couldn't you choose a school close to home?" Mami grumbled as we got on the train to Manhattan. I worried that even if I were accepted, she wouldn't let me go because it was so far from home, one hour each way by subway. But in spite of her complaints, she was proud that I was good enough to be considered for such a famous school. And she actually seemed excited that I would be leaving the neighborhood.

---

9. ***Toda una señorita:*** All a young lady should be [Author's note]; Tata: Esmeralda's grandmother.

"You'll be exposed to a different class of people," she assured me, and I felt the force of her ambition without knowing exactly what she meant.

Three women sat behind a long table in a classroom where the desks and chairs had been pushed against a wall. As I entered I held my head up and smiled, and then I floated down to the chair in front of them, clasped my hands on my lap, and smiled some more.

"Good morning," said the tall one with hair the color of sand. She was big boned and solid, with intense blue eyes, a generous mouth, and soothing hands with short fingernails. She was dressed in shades of beige from head to toe and wore no makeup and no jewelry except for the gold chain that held her glasses just above her full bosom. Her voice was rich, modulated, each word pronounced as if she were inventing it.

Next to her sat a very small woman with very high heels. Her cropped hair was pouffed around her face, with bangs brushing the tips of her long false lashes, her huge dark brown eyes were thickly lined in black all around, and her small mouth was carefully drawn in and painted cerise. Her suntanned face turned toward me with the innocent curiosity of a lively baby. She was dressed in black, with many gold chains around her neck, big earrings, several bracelets, and large stone rings on the fingers of both hands.

The third woman was tall, small boned, thin, but shapely. Her dark hair was pulled flat against her skull into a knot in back of her head. Her face was all angles and light, with fawnlike dark brown eyes, a straight nose, full lips painted just a shade pinker than their natural color. Silky forest green cuffs peeked out from the sleeves of her burgundy suit. Diamond studs winked from perfect earlobes.

I had dreamed of this moment for several weeks. More than anything, I wanted to impress the panel with my talent, so that I would be accepted into Performing Arts and leave Brooklyn every day. And, I hoped, one day I would never go back.

But the moment I faced these three impeccably groomed women, I forgot my English and Mrs. Johnson's lessons on how to behave like a lady. In the agony of trying to answer their barely comprehensible questions, I jabbed my hands here and there, forming words with my fingers because the words refused to leave my mouth.

"Why don't you let us hear your monologue now?" the woman with the dangling glasses asked softly.

I stood up abruptly, and my chair clattered onto its side two feet from where I stood. I picked it up, wishing with all my strength that a thunderbolt would strike me dead to ashes on the spot.

"It's all right," she said. "Take a breath. We know you're nervous."

I closed my eyes and breathed deeply, walked to the middle of the room, and began my monologue.

"Ju bee lonh 2 a type dats berry cómo in dis kuntree, Meessees Felps. A type off selfcent red self pee tee in sun de boring tie gress wid on men shon ah ball pro klee bee tees on de side."

In spite of Mr. Gatti's reminders that I should speak slowly and enunciate every word, even if I didn't understand it, I recited my three-minute monologue in one minute flat.

The small woman's long lashes seemed to have grown with amazement. The elegant woman's serene face twitched with controlled laughter. The tall one dressed in beige smiled sweetly.

"Thank you, dear," she said. "Could you wait outside for a few moments?"

I resisted the urge to curtsy. The long hallway had narrow wainscoting halfway up to the high ceiling. Single bulb lamps hung from long cords, creating yellow puddles of light on the polished brown linoleum tile. A couple of girls my age sat on straight chairs next to their mothers, waiting their turn. They looked up as I came out and the door shut behind me. Mami stood up from her chair at the end of the hall. She looked as scared as I felt.

"What happened?"

"Nothing," I mumbled, afraid that if I began telling her about it, I would break into tears in front of the other people, whose eyes followed me and Mami as we walked to the EXIT sign. "I have to wait here a minute."

"Did they say anything?"

"No. I'm just supposed to wait."

We leaned against the wall. Across from us there was a bulletin board with newspaper clippings about former students. On the ragged edge, a neat person had printed in blue ink, "P.A." and the year the actor, dancer, or musician had graduated. I closed my eyes and tried to picture myself on that bulletin board, with "P.A. '66" across the top.

The door at the end of the hall opened, and the woman in beige poked her head out.

"Esmeralda?"

"*Sí*, I mean, here." I raised my hand.

She led me into the room. There was another girl in there, whom she introduced as Bonnie, a junior at the school.

"Do you know what a pantomime is?" the woman asked. I nodded. "You and Bonnie are sisters decorating a Christmas tree."

Bonnie looked a lot like Juanita Marín, whom I had last seen in Macún four years earlier. We decided where the invisible Christmas tree would be, and we sat on the floor and pretended we were taking decorations out of boxes and hanging them on the branches.

My family had never had a Christmas tree, but I remembered how once I had helped Papi wind colored lights around the eggplant bush that divided our land from Doña Ana's. We started at the bottom and wound the wire with tiny red bulbs around and around until we ran out; then Papi plugged another cord to it and we kept going until the branches hung heavy with light and the bush looked like it was on fire.

Before long I had forgotten where I was, and that the tree didn't exist and Bonnie was not my sister. She pretended to hand me a very delicate ball, and just before I took it, she made like it fell to the ground and shattered. I was petrified that Mami would come in and yell at us for breaking her favorite decoration. Just as I began to pick up the tiny fragments of nonexistent crystal, a voice broke in. "Thank you."

Bonnie got up, smiled, and went out.

The elegant woman stretched her hand out for me to shake. "We will notify your school in a few weeks. It was very nice to meet you."

I shook hands all around then backed out of the room in a fog, silent, as if the pantomime had taken my voice and the urge to speak.

On the way home Mami kept asking what had happened, and I kept mumbling, "Nothing. Nothing happened," ashamed that, after all the hours of practice with Mrs. Johnson, Mr. Barone, and Mr. Gatti, after the expense of new clothes and shoes, after Mami had to take a day off from work to take me into Manhattan, after all that, I had failed the audition and would never, ever, get out of Brooklyn.

## Epilogue: One of These Days

*El mismo jíbaro con diferente caballo.*
*Same jíbaro, different horse.*

A decade after my graduation from Performing Arts, I visited the school. I was by then living in Boston, a scholarship student at Harvard University. The tall, elegant woman of my audition had become my mentor through my three years there. Since my graduation, she had married the school principal.

"I remember your audition," she said, her chiseled face dreamy, her lips toying with a smile that she seemed, still, to have to control.

I had forgotten the skinny brown girl with the curled hair, wool jumper, and lively hands. But she hadn't. She told me that the panel had had to ask me to leave so that they could laugh, because it was so funny to see a fourteen-year-old Puerto Rican girl jabbering out a monologue about a possessive mother-in-law at the turn of the century, the words incomprehensible because they went by so fast.

"We admired," she said, "the courage it took to stand in front of us and do what you did."

"So you mean I didn't get into the school because of my talent, but because I had chutzpah?"[10] We both laughed.

"Are any of your sisters and brothers in college?"

"No, I'm the only one, so far."

"How many of you are there?"

"By the time I graduated from high school there were eleven of us."

"Eleven!" She looked at me for a long time, until I had to look down. "Do you ever think about how far you've come?" she asked.

"No." I answered. "I never stop to think about it. It might jinx the momentum."

"Let me tell you another story, then," she said. "The first day of your first year, you were absent. We called your house. You said you couldn't come to school because you had nothing to wear. I wasn't sure if you were joking. I asked to speak to your mother, and you translated what she said. She needed you to go somewhere with her to interpret. At first you wouldn't tell me where, but then you admitted you were going to the welfare office. You were crying, and I had to assure you that you were not the only student in this school whose family received public assistance. The next day you were here, bright and eager. And now here you are, about to graduate from Harvard."

"I'm glad you made that phone call," I said.

"And I'm glad you came to see me, but right now I have to teach a class." She stood up, as graceful as I remembered. "Take care."

Her warm embrace, fragrant of expensive perfume, took me by surprise. "Thank you," I said as she went around the corner to her classroom.

I walked the halls of the school, looking for the room where my life had changed. It was across from the science lab, a few doors down from the big bulletin board where someone with neat handwriting still wrote the letters "P.A." followed by the graduating year along the edges of newspaper clippings featuring famous alumni.

"P.A. '66," I said to no one in particular. "One of these days."

---

10. **chutzpah:** brazenness; daring boldness (Yiddish slang).

# Mark Smith-Soto

**b. 1948–**   (Costa Rican American)

## Meet the Writer

During an interview, **Mark Smith-Soto** revealed his feelings about writing poetry: "Writing poetry is not putting embroidery on things . . . it is a cry from the heart, a prayer, a song, a human yearning to express the inexpressible." One reviewer has said that Smith-Soto is "brilliant at depicting moments from the past."

Mark Smith-Soto is representative of many Latino writers in the United States who straddle two worlds. He was born in Washington, D.C., his father's hometown, but until he was eleven, he lived in Costa Rica with his mother's family. He grew up speaking Spanish at home and English outside his home. His mother and grandfather recited poetry to him, and he learned many passages of poetry verbatim. He claims to have learned English by memorizing Shakespeare. As a result of his bilingual childhood, Smith-Soto has always been fascinated with the process of translation.

He is now a professor of Romance languages at the University of North Carolina at Greensboro, a specialist in late-nineteenth- and early-twentieth-century Spanish American poetry. In addition, he is director of the Center for Creative Writing in the Arts.

## Background

In his poetry Mark Smith-Soto connects his American and Hispanic cultures. Some of his poems focus on the sensory memories of his childhood in Costa Rica. Others focus on the different dimensions of time, the transitoriness of life, and the interactions between generations of family.

His poems have appeared in many literary magazines. *Green Mango Collage* and *Shafts*, his first two collections of poetry, have earned prestigious awards. His first full-length book of poetry, *Our Lives Are Rivers,* was published in 2003. His latest collection, *Any Second Now*, appeared in 2006. Smith-Soto has also written a series of one-act plays.

**Before You Read** *What do you think the speaker means by "the ancient places in my soul"? What clues to meaning are provided in the poem?*

# What I Mean
## Mark Smith-Soto

—*for Bruce, Lyn, Tom, Vince*

    So many words when what I mean is only
    I have forgotten the ancient places in my soul.
    Will they know me, these places, when I return?
    Will they receive the child climbing broken walls

5    into the garden? A strange boy, something
    of the Jew, the Costa Rican, the Spanish, something
    of the Indian eyes that saw the Irazú volcano[1]
    burst alive, and the river Marañón[2]

    mix the violent cocktail of different bloods.
10   I am a little bit afraid of what I mean.
    What I mean is only I have forgotten
    the ancient places in my soul. Are they still

    there waiting? Must I go there after all?
    Hush, my heart, hear what you are saying:
15   They are there, yes, or you would not fear them;
    and you would not fear them if you did not have to go.

---

1. **Irazú volcano:** in Costa Rica, near the city of Cartago. It has a history of eruptions dating back to the Spanish Colonial period. Its first recorded eruption was in 1723. It is the only place on the continent of North America where one can see both the Atlantic and Pacific Oceans. The name *Irazú* comes from the Indian name *Istarú*, which means "Thunder and Earthquake Mountain."
2. **Marañón:** a tributary of the Amazon River. It rises in the Andes Mountains in Peru and flows north, then bends to join the Ucayali River to form the Amazon.

# Victor Hernández Cruz

**b. 1949–** (Puerto Rican American)

## Meet the Writer

"My family life was full of music, guitars and conga drums, maracas and songs. My mother sang songs. Even when it was five below zero in New York she sang warm tropical ballads." Perhaps as a result of this musical family life, **Victor Hernández Cruz** writes poetry that is full of a particularly personal music.

Born in Aguas Buenas, Puerto Rico, Cruz immigrated to New York City when he was five years old. He starting writing in his mid-teens and even self-published his first book of poetry while he was still in high school. Although Cruz left high school without graduating, his education was not over. He went to Berkeley, California, where he further developed his writing talent by joining a vibrant community of artists and writers and reading the works of authors such as Richard Wright, Pablo Neruda, and Octavio Paz.

An essential part of the Nuyorican movement—a movement of Puerto Rican writers who have spent much of their lives in the United States, especially New York—Cruz records in his poetry a life lived in two languages and in two contrasting worlds: a tropical island and a muticultural concrete city.

In addition to publishing many acclaimed collections of poetry, Cruz has lectured and taught at the University of Michigan and the University of California. His poems have been translated into five languages. In 1989, Cruz returned to Puerto Rico, where he continues to write.

## Background

As a child, Cruz absorbed the music of the spoken language of Puerto Rico as he listened to his grandfather read aloud. In New York City, he grew aware of the music of a large city—street sounds, a mixture of languages, and English spoken with many accents. Cruz blends sensory details to create poetry that sings with rhythm and repetition and that abounds in his personal, energetic music.

**Before You Read** As you read this poem, consider how the campesino°, as quoted by the speaker of the poem, views death and nature. What comment might Cruz be making through his description of this dark and absurd, yet humorous, situation?

# Problems with Hurricanes
## Victor Hernández Cruz

A campesino looked at the air
And told me:
With hurricanes it's not the wind
or the noise or the water.
5   I'll tell you he said:
it's the mangoes, avocados
Green plantains and bananas
flying into town like projectiles.

How would your family
10  feel if they had to tell
The generations that you
got killed by a flying
Banana.

Death by drowning has honor
15  If the wind picked you up
and slammed you
Against a mountain boulder

This would not carry shame
But
20  to suffer a mango smashing
Your skull
or a plantain hitting your
Temple at 70 miles per hour
is the ultimate disgrace.

25  The campesino takes off his hat—
As a sign of respect
towards the fury of the wind
And says:
Don't worry about the noise
30  Don't worry about the water
Don't worry about the wind—
If you are going out
beware of mangoes
And all such beautiful
35  sweet things.

---

°**campesino** (kahm peh SEE noh): farmer or peasant.

# Julia Alvarez
b. 1950–    (Dominican American)

## Meet the Writer

Speaking of her life and work, **Julia Alvarez** (AHL vah rehs) says, "I am a Dominican, hyphen, American. As a fiction writer, I find that the most exciting things happen in the realm of that hyphen—the place where two worlds collide or blend together." It is precisely the meeting of these two worlds—the Dominican Republic and the United States—that leads to one of the main themes in Alvarez's work: the relationship of identity to language and culture.

Alvarez was born in the United States but moved to the Dominican Republic shortly after her birth. When she was ten years old, her family was forced to flee the country because of her father's involvement in a plot to overthrow the dictator Rafael Trujillo Molina.

According to Alvarez, the move to the United States is what caused her to become a writer. Although she had attended an American school in the Dominican Republic, she was completely unprepared for the fast-spoken English she encountered in the United States. As she tried to learn this new language, she became acutely aware of the uses and nuances of words.

In the United States, Alvarez encountered the world of books for the first time. Although she had heard many stories told aloud, her family owned few books. Feeling out of place in American culture, Alvarez began to seek refuge in books. Reading made her dream that she might one day become a writer.

Alvarez's first collection of poems, *Homecoming*, was published in 1984, but her first novel, *How the Garcia Girls Lost Their Accents*, earned her widespread recognition upon its publication in 1991. Like many of Alvarez's works, this novel is autobiographical, exploring the conflict between American customs and her parents' more traditional Dominican views. Her 1997 novel, *¡Yo!*, also centers around the lives of immigrants. The book's title reflects Alvarez's love of wordplay. The word *Yo* is at once the nickname of the book's main character, the Spanish word for "I," and an informal way to get someone's attention in English.

Alvarez has written historical novels in addition to autobiographical fiction. *In the Time of Butterflies* (1994) is a fictionalized account of the lives and deaths of three sisters who were married to political prisoners in the Dominican Republic. *In the Name of Salomé* (2000) is based on the true story of the Dominican political poet Salomé Ureña and her daughter, two women who dedicated themselves to revolutionary causes.

Alvarez's collection of autobiographical essays, *Something to Declare* (1998), includes her ten commandments for writing. Her fourth commandment is a quotation from Saint Thomas: "If you bring forth what is inside you, what you bring forth will save you. If you do not bring forth what is inside you, what is inside you will destroy you." By bringing forth her experiences as a Dominican American, Alvarez sheds light on the significance of her own journey as well as the journeys of others who leave one homeland for another and struggle to embrace them both.

## Background

The relationship of identity to culture and language is a recurring theme not only in Alvarez's novels but also in her nonfiction and poetry. The title *Something to Declare* refers both to the act of declaring belongings as one travels from one country to another and to the act of using language to state something important. The book's first section, "Customs," details Alvarez's family's flight from the Dominican Republic and their adjustment to their new life in the United States. Included here are "El Doctor," a portrait of Alvarez's father, and "My English," a reflection on the importance of the English language in Alvarez's life.

In *Homecoming*, the poems collected under the heading "Housekeeping" reflect on the childhood lessons Alvarez learned about the role of women in traditional Dominican society. "Washing the Windows" and "Woman's Work" show Alvarez's keen observation of her mother's "high art" of housekeeping—an art that Alvarez both admires and rejects. "Audition" continues to explore the domestic roles of women. Despite Alvarez's rejection of the idea that women's lives should focus on housekeeping, the discipline she learned from such attention to detail seems to have transferred to her process of writing poetry. According to Alvarez's sixth commandment of writing, "One must write a poem the way one rules an empire, the way one cooks a small fish."

**Before You Read**  In "El Doctor," Alvarez paints a complex portrait of her father as a man who is both reserved and deeply attached to his family. As you read the essay, consider in what ways his experience as an immigrant affects his attitudes toward life. How does this experience affect his relationship with his daughter Julia?

# El Doctor

## Julia Alvarez

"Lights! At this hour?" my father asks, looking up from his empty dinner plate at the glowing lamp my mother has just turned on above the table. "Are we in Plato's cave, Mami?" He winks at me; as the two readers in the family we show off by making allusions my mother and sisters don't understand. He leans his chair back and picks up the hem of the curtain. A dim gray light falls into the room. "See, Mami. It's still light out there!"

"Ya, ya!" she snaps, and flips the switch off.

"Your mother is a wonder," he announces, then he adds, "El Doctor is ready for bed." Dinner is over; every night my father brings the meal to a close with a third-person goodnight before he leaves the room.

Tonight he lingers, watching her. She says nothing, head bent, intent on her mashed plantains with oil and onions. "Yessir," he elaborates, "El Doctor—" The rest is garbled, for he's balled up his napkin and rubbed his lips violently as if he meant to erase them from his face. Perhaps he shouldn't have spoken up? She is jabbing at the few bites of beefsteak on her plate. Perhaps he should have just let the issue drop like water down his chest or whatever it is the Americans say. He scrapes his chair back.

Her scowl deepens. "Eduardo, please." And then, because he already knows better, she adds only, "The wax finish."

"Por supuesto," he says, his voice full of false concern as he examines her spotless kitchen floor for damages. Then, carefully, he lifts his chair up and tucks it back in its place. "This old man is ready for bed." He leans over and kisses the scowl off her face. "Mami, this country agrees with you. You look more beautiful every day. Doesn't she, girls?" And with a wink of encouragement to each of us, he leaves us in the dark.

I remember my mother at all times of the day: slapping around in her comfortable slippers, polishing her windows into blinding panes of light. But I remember him mostly at night, moving down the dark halls, undressing as he climbed the dark stairs to bed.

I want to say there were as many buttons on his vest as stairs up to the bedroom: it seemed he unbuttoned a button on each step so that by the time he reached the landing, his vest was off. His armor, I thought, secretly pleased with all I believed I understood about him. But his vest couldn't have had more than six buttons, and the stairs were long and narrow. Then again, I couldn't see that well in the dark he insisted on.

"I'm going to take this dollar," he showed me, holding a bill in one hand, a flickering lighter in the other, "and I'm going to set fire to it." He never actually did. He spoke in parables, he complained in metaphors, because he had never learned to say things directly. I already knew what he meant, but I had my part to play.

"Why would you want to do something like that?" I asked.

"Exactly! Why burn up money with all these lights in the house?"

As we grew up, confirmed in our pyromania, he did not bother to teach us to economize, but went through the house, turning off lights in every room, not noticing many times that we were there, reading or writing a letter, and leaving us in the dark, hurt that he had overlooked us.

At the bedroom door he loosened his tie and, craning his neck, undid the top button of his shirt. Then he sat at the edge of the bed and turned on his bedside lamp. Not always; if a little reflected sun dappled the room with shadowy light, if it was late spring or early fall or summertime, he waited until the last moment to turn on the lamp, sometimes reading in the dark until we came in and turned it on for him. "Papi, you're going to ruin your eyes," we scolded.

Once I worked it out for him with the pamphlet the electric company had sent me. Were he to leave his bedside light, say, burning for the rest of his evenings—and I allowed him a generous four decades ("I won't need it for that long," he protested; I insisted)—the cost (side by side we multiplied, added, carried over to the next column) would be far less than if he lost his eyesight, was forced to give up his practice, and had to spend the next four decades—

"Like your friend Milton," he said, pleased with the inspired possibilities of blindness. Now that I was turning out to be the family poet, all the greats were my personal friends. "'When I consider how my light is spent,'" he began. Just like my mother's father, my own father loved to recite, racing me through poems to see who would be the first one to finish.

"'How my light is spent,'" I echoed and took the lead. "'Ere half my days, in this dark world and wide...'"

Just as I was rounding the line break to the last line, he interjected it, "'They also serve who only stand and wait.'"

I scowled. How dare he clap the last line on after I had gone through all the trouble of reciting the poem! "Not every blind man is a Milton," I said, and I gave him the smirk I wore all through adolescence.

"Nutrition," he said mysteriously.

"What about nutrition?"

"Good nutrition. We're starting to see the effects: children grow taller; they have better teeth, better bones, better minds than their elders." And he reached for his book on the bedside table.

Actually, the reading came later. First there is the scene that labels him immigrant and shows why I could never call him, sweetly, playfully, "Daddy." He took from his back pocket a wad of bills so big his hand could not close over it. And he began to count. If at this point we disturbed him, he waved us away. If we called from downstairs, he did not answer. All over the bed he shared with my mother were piles of bills. I do not know the system; no one ever did. Perhaps all the fives were together, all the tens? Perhaps each pile was a specific amount? But this was the one private moment he insisted on. Not even catching him undressing, which I never did, seems as intimate a glimpse of him.

After the counting came the binding and marking: each pile was held together with rubber bands he saved up from the rolled-up *New York Times*, and the top bill was scribbled on. He marked them as a reminder of how much was in each pile, I'm sure, but I can't help thinking it was also his way of owning what he had earned, much as ranchers brand their cattle. The secretary of the treasury had signed this twenty; there was Andrew Jackson's picture; he had to add his hand to it to make it his—to try to convince himself that it was his, for he never totally believed it was. Even after he was a successful doctor in New York with a house in the suburbs and lands at "home," his daughters in boarding schools and summer camps, a second car with enough gadgets to keep him busy in bad traffic, he was turning off lights, frequenting thrift shops for finds in ties, taking the 59th Street bridge even if it was out of his way to avoid paying a toll to cross the river.

He could not afford the good life; he could only pass it on. And he did. Beneath the surface penny-pinching, his extravagance might have led him to bankruptcy several times had my mother not been there to remind him that the weather was apt to change. "Save for a snowy day," she advised him.

"Isn't it 'rainy day'?" he enlisted me. He was always happy to catch his wife in an error since she spoke English so much better than he did. "Save it for a rainy day?"

Eager to be an authority on anything, I considered my role as Arbiter of Clichés a compliment to my literary talent. "Save it for a rainy day," I agreed.

"See, Mami."

She defended herself. "Snow is much worse than rain. For one thing, you need to own more clothes in the winter. You get more colds in the winter."

Out from his pocket came a ten when we needed small change for the subway. Away at college I opened the envelope, empty but for the money order for fifty, a hundred; typed out in the blank beside *memo* was his note: "Get yourself a little something in my name." It was the sixties, and parental money was under heavy suspicion; my friends needed me as a Third World person to be a good example of poverty and oppression by the capitalist, military-industrial complex. I put my little somethings quietly in the bank. By the time I graduated from college, I had a small, corrupt fortune.

But my rich father lived in the dark, saving string, going the long way. I've analyzed it with my economist friends. Perhaps since his fortune came from the same work which in his country had never earned him enough, he could not believe that his being well-to-do wasn't an I.R.S. oversight. My psychologist friends claim that it is significant that he was the youngest of twenty-five children. Coming after so many, he would always fear that the good things would run out. And indeed he had a taste for leftovers, which made his compliments come a day or two after a special meal. Whenever we had chicken, he insisted on the wings and the neck bone because those had been the portions left by the time the platter got to him, the baby. He liked the pale, bitter center of the lettuce. ("The leaves were gone when I got the salad bowl.") And when we had soup, he was surprised to find a bit of meat bobbing at the surface. "Someone missed this one."

Unlike my mother, he saved for a sunny day. Extravaganza! On his birthday, at Christmas, on his saint's day (which was never celebrated for anyone else), his presents multiplied before us. Beside the ones we had bought for him, there were always other glossy packages, ribboned boxes, which dwarfed ours. The cards were forged: "To my dearest Papi from his loving daughter." "Which of you gave me this?" he asked with mock surprise and real delight. Cordelias all, we shook our heads as he unwrapped a silk lounging jacket or a genuine leather passport case. I wish he had allowed us to give him something of value.

Perhaps we did, on those evenings after the money was counted and put away, and he was ready for company. With an instinct for his rituals, we knew when it was time to come into the bedroom. We heard the bathroom door click shut; he was undressing, putting on his pajamas. The hamper lid clapped on its felt lip. We heard steps. The bed creaked. We found him in the darkening room with a book. "Papi, you're ruining your eyes!"

"Oh my God, it's gotten dark already," he would say, almost thanking us.

He wanted company, not conversation. He had us turn on the television so we could learn our English. This after years here, after his money had paid for the private schools that unrolled our *r*s and softened our accents; after American boyfriends had whispered sweet colloquialisms in our ears. As the television cowboys

and beauty queens and ladies with disappointing stains in their wash droned on in their native English, he read the usual: a history book in Spanish. We sat at the edge of the king-size bed and wondered what he wanted from us. He wanted presences: his children, his wife, Walter Cronkite, the great men of the past, Napoleon, Caesar, Maximilian. If one of us, bored with his idea of company, got up to leave, he lowered his book. "Did you know that in the campaign of 1808, Napoleon left his general behind to cut off the enemy from the rear, and the two divisions totally missed each other?" That was the only way he knew to ask us to stay, appealing to history and defeat, to wintry campaigns, bloody frost-bitten feet, a field strewn with war dead.

I taste the mints that he gave us, one each. He kept a stash of them in a drawer next to his bed like a schoolboy and ate exactly one each night and gave away four. That was the other way he kept us there if we got up to go after Napoleon's troops had been annihilated. "Don't you want a mint?" He didn't mean right then and there. It was a promise we had to wait for, perhaps until the chapter ended or the Roman empire fell or he was sure we had given up on the evening and decided to stay, talking in code with each other about school, our friends, our wild (for that room) adventures.

We were not fooled into rash confessions there, for at the merest hint of misadventure, the book came down like a coffin lid on Caesar or Claudius. Oh, we confessed, we were just exaggerating! Of course we didn't raid the dorm kitchen at midnight; our friends did. "Tell me who your friends are," he said in Spanish, "and I'll tell you who you are." No, we hadn't gotten help on our math. "The man who reaches the summit following another's trail will not find his way back to his own valley." If he caught us, hurrying, scurrying, here, there, he stopped us midflight to tell us what Napoleon had said to his valet, "Dress me slowly—I'm in a hurry."

But why look beyond one's own blood for good examples? "You come from good stock," he bragged when I came home from boarding school, my pride wounded. I'd been called names by some great-great-granddaughters of the American Revolution. "You tell them your great-grandfather was the son of a count." He had paid a lot of money on a trip to Barcelona to find that out from a man who claimed he was licensed to do family trees. The elaborate chart, magnificently framed in curlicued wood, hung in the waiting room of his office in Spanish Brooklyn, along with his medical degrees. His patients, I suppose, were meant to be reassured that their ailments would be treated, not only by the valedictorian of the faculty of medicine of La Universidad de Santo Domingo, but also by the descendant of a count. "We were in this hemisphere before they were. In fact, the first Americans—"

"You don't understand, you don't understand," I wailed, hot tears welling in my eyes. And I closed the door of my room, forbidding anyone to enter.

"What's she doing in there, Mami?" I heard him ask her.

"I don't know. Writing poetry or something."

"Are you sure? You think she's all right?"

I had been reading Sylvia Plath, and my talk was spiked with suicide.

"These girls are going to drive me crazy!" my mother said. "That's what I'm sure of. One of them has to have straight hair. Straight hair, at this stage of the show! Another wants to spend the weekend at a boy's school. All the other girls get to! This one wants to die young and miserable!" She glared at my father as if it were all his fault. "I'm going to end up in Bellevue!" she yelled. "And then you'll all be safe and sorry!" I heard her rushed steps down the stairs, the bang of the screen door, finally the patter of water as she hosed down the obedient grass in the growing darkness.

He knocked first. "Hello?" he asked tentatively, the door ajar. "Hello, hello, Edgar Allan Poe," he teased, entering. He sat at the foot of my bed and told me the story of his life.

"The point is," he concluded, "'La vida es sueño y los sueños, sueños son.'" He stood by the window and watched Mami watering her fussy bushes as if she could flush roses out of them. "My father," he turned to me, "used to say that to my mother: 'Life is a dream, Maurán, and dreams are dreams.'"

He came across the shadowy room as if he did not want anyone to overhear. It was getting late. In the darkening garden she would be winding the hose into drooping coils. "Always, always," he said. "I always wanted to be a poet. 'La vida es sueño. They also serve who only stand and wait. To be or not to be.' Can you imagine? To say things that can fill the mind of another human being!" I nodded, too stunned at his flood of words to ask him what he meant. "Everyone gets a little something," he cupped his hands towards me, "and some make a great building." He made a building with a wave of his hand. "Some," he rubbed his thumb and index finger together, "make money. Some make friends, connections, you know. But some, some make something that can change the thinking of mankind!" He smacked his forehead with his palm in amazement. "Think of the Bible. Think of your friend Edgar Allan Poe. But then," he mused, "then you grow older, you discover . . ." He looked down at me. I don't know what he saw in my eyes, perhaps how young I still was, perhaps his eyes duplicated in my face. He stopped himself.

"You discover?" I said.

But he was already halfway across the room. "Papi?" I tried to call him back.

"Your mother," he explained, letting himself out of the room and the revelation. "I think she is calling for me."

**Before You Read**  Alvarez likes to quote the Polish poet Czeslaw Milosz, who said, "Language is the only homeland." As you read "My English," consider why this statement might have particular significance for Alvarez. In what ways does the English language become her "homeland"?

# My English
## Julia Alvarez

Mami and Papi used to speak it when they had a secret they wanted to keep from us children. We lived then in the Dominican Republic, and the family as a whole spoke only Spanish at home, until my sisters and I started attending the Carol Morgan School, and we became a bilingual family. Spanish had its many tongues as well. There was the castellano of Padre Joaquín from Spain, whose lisp we all loved to imitate. Then the educated español my parents' families spoke, aunts and uncles who were always correcting us children, for we spent most of the day with the maids and so had picked up their "bad Spanish." Campesinas, they spoke a lilting, animated campuno, *s*s swallowed, endings chopped off, funny turns of phrases. This campuno was my true mother tongue, not the Spanish of Calderón de la Barca or Cervantes or even Neruda, but of Chucha and Iluminada and Gladys and Ursulina from Juncalito and Licey and Boca de Yuma and San Juan de la Maguana. Those women yakked as they cooked, they storytold, they gossiped, they sang—boleros, merengues, canciones, salves. Theirs were the voices that belonged to the rain and the wind and the teeny, teeny stars even a small child could blot out with her thumb.

Besides all these versions of Spanish, every once in a while another strange tongue emerged from my papi's mouth or my mami's lips. What I first recognized was not a language, but a tone of voice, serious, urgent, something important and top secret being said, some uncle in trouble, someone divorcing, someone dead. *Say it in English so the children won't understand.* I would listen, straining to understand, thinking that this was not a different language but just another and harder version of Spanish. *Say it in English so the children won't understand.* From the beginning, English was the sound of worry and secrets, the sound of being left out.

I could make no sense of this "harder Spanish," and so I tried by other means to find out what was going on. I knew my mother's face by heart. When the little lines on the corners of her eyes crinkled, she was amused. When her nostrils flared and she bit her lips, she was trying hard not to laugh. She held her head down, eyes glancing up, when she thought I was lying. Whenever she spoke that gibberish English, I translated the general content by watching the Spanish expressions on her face.

· · ·

Soon, I began to learn more English, at the Carol Morgan School. That is, when I had stopped gawking. The teacher and some of the American children had the strangest coloration: light hair, light eyes, light skin, as if Ursulina had soaked them in bleach too long, to' deteñío. I did have some blond cousins, but they had deeply tanned skin, and as they grew older, their hair darkened, so their earlier paleness seemed a phase of their acquiring normal color. Just as strange was the little girl in my reader who had a *cat* and a *dog*, that looked just like un gatito y un perrito. Her mami was *Mother* and her papi *Father*. Why have a whole new language for school and for books with a teacher who could speak it teaching you double the amount of words you really needed?

*Butter, butter, butter, butter.* All day, one English word that had particularly struck me would go round and round in my mouth and weave through all the Spanish in my head until by the end of the day, the word did sound like just another Spanish word. And so I would say, "Mami, please pass la mantequilla." She would scowl and say in English, "I'm sorry, I don't understand. But would you be needing some butter on your bread?"

Why my parents didn't first educate us in our native language by enrolling us in a Dominican school, I don't know. Part of it was that Mami's family had a tradition of sending the boys to the States to boarding school and college, and she had been one of the first girls to be allowed to join her brothers. At Abbot Academy, whose school song was our lullaby as babies ("Although Columbus and Cabot never heard of Abbot, it's quite the place for you and me"), she had become quite Americanized. It was very important, she kept saying, that we learn our English. She always used the possessive pronoun: *your* English, an inheritance we had come into and must wisely use. Unfortunately, my English became all mixed up with our Spanish.

Mix-up, or what's now called Spanglish, was the language we spoke for several years. There wasn't a sentence that wasn't colonized by an English word. At school, a Spanish word would suddenly slide into my English like someone butting into line. Teacher, whose face I was learning to read as minutely as my mother's, would scowl but no smile played on her lips. Her pale skin made her strange countenance hard to read, so that I often misjudged how much I could get away with. Whenever I made a mistake, Teacher would shake her head slowly, "In English, YU-LEE-AH, there's no such word as *columpio*. Do you mean a *swing*?"

I would bow my head, humiliated by the smiles and snickers of the American children around me. I grew insecure about Spanish. My native tongue was not quite as good as English, as if words like *columpio* were illegal immigrants trying to cross a border into another language. But Teacher's discerning grammar-and-vocabulary-patrol ears could tell and send them back.

Soon, I was talking up an English storm. "Did you eat English parrot?" my grandfather asked one Sunday. I had just enlisted yet one more patient servant to listen to my rendition of "Peter Piper picked a peck of pickled peppers" at breakneck pace. "Huh?" I asked impolitely in English, putting him in his place. *Cat got your tongue? No big deal! So there! Take that! Holy Toledo!* (Our teacher's favorite "curse word.") *Go jump in the lake! Really dumb. Golly. Gosh.* Slang, clichés, sayings, hotshot language that our teacher called, ponderously, idiomatic expressions. Riddles, jokes, puns, conundrums. *What is yellow and goes click-click? Why did the chicken cross the road? See you later, alligator.* How wonderful to call someone an alligator and not be scolded for being disrespectful. In fact, they were supposed to say back, *In a while, crocodile.*

There was also a neat little trick I wanted to try on an English-speaking adult at home. I had learned it from Elizabeth, my smart-alecky friend in fourth grade, whom I alternately worshiped and resented. I'd ask her a question that required an explanation, and she'd answer, "Because . . ." "Elizabeth, how come you didn't go to Isabel's birthday party?" "Because . . ." "Why didn't you

put your name in your reader?" "Because . . ." I thought that such a cool way to get around having to come up with answers. So, I practiced saying it under my breath, planning for the day I could use it on an unsuspecting English-speaking adult.

One Sunday at our extended family dinner, my grandfather sat down at the children's table to chat with us. He was famous, in fact, for the way he could carry on adult conversations with his grandchildren. He often spoke to us in English so that we could practice speaking it outside the classroom. He was a Cornell man, a United Nations representative from our country. He gave speeches in English. Perfect English, my mother's phrase. That Sunday, he asked me a question. I can't even remember what it was because I wasn't really listening but lying in wait for my chance. "Because . . .," I answered him. Papito waited a second for the rest of my sentence and then gave me a thumbnail grammar lesson, "*Because* has to be followed by a clause."

"Why's that?" I asked, nonplussed.

"Because," he winked, "Just because."

A beginning wordsmith, I had so much left to learn; sometimes it was disheartening. Once Tío Gus, the family intellectual, put a speck of salt on my grandparents' big dining table during Sunday dinner. He said, "Imagine this whole table is the human brain. Then this teensy grain is all we ever use of our intelligence!" He enumerated geniuses who had perhaps used two grains, maybe three: Einstein, Michelangelo, da Vinci, Beethoven. We children believed him. It was the kind of impossible fact we thrived on, proving as it did that the world out there was not drastically different from the one we were making up in our heads.

Later, at home, Mami said that you had to take what her younger brother said "with a grain of salt." I thought she was still referring to Tío Gus's demonstration, and I tried to puzzle out what she was saying. Finally, I asked what she meant. "Taking what someone says with a grain of salt is an idiomatic expression in English," she explained. It was pure voodoo is what it was— what later I learned poetry could also do: a grain of salt could symbolize both the human brain and a condiment for human nonsense. And it could be itself, too: a grain of salt to flavor a bland plate of American food.

**My English**     **275**

When we arrived in New York, I was shocked. A country where everyone spoke English! These people must be smarter, I thought. Maids, waiters, taxi drivers, doormen, bums on the street, all spoke this difficult language. It took some time before I understood that Americans were not necessarily a smarter, superior race. It was as natural for them to learn their mother tongue as it was for a little Dominican baby to learn Spanish. It came with "mother's milk," my mother explained, and for a while I thought a mother tongue was a mother tongue because you got it from your mother's breast, along with proteins and vitamins.

Soon it wasn't so strange that everyone was speaking in English instead of Spanish. I learned not to hear it as English, but as sense. I no longer strained to understand, I understood. I relaxed in this second language. Only when someone with a heavy southern or British accent spoke in a movie, or at church when the priest droned his sermon—only then did I experience that little catch of anxiety. I worried that I would not be able to understand, that I wouldn't be able to "keep up" with the voice speaking in this acquired language. I would be like those people from the Bible we had studied in religion class, whom I imagined standing at the foot of an enormous tower that looked just like the skyscrapers around me. They had been punished for their pride by being made to speak different languages so that they didn't understand what anyone was saying.

But at the foot of those towering New York skyscrapers, I began to understand more and more—not less and less—English. In sixth grade, I had one of the first in a lucky line of great English teachers who began to nurture in me a love of language, a love that had been there since my childhood of listening closely to words. Sister Maria Generosa did not make our class interminably diagram sentences from a workbook or learn a catechism of grammar rules. Instead, she asked us to write little stories imagining we were snowflakes, birds, pianos, a stone in the pavement, a star in the sky. What would it feel like to be a flower with roots in the ground? If the clouds could talk, what would they say? She had an expressive, dreamy look that was accentuated by the wimple that framed her face.

Supposing, just supposing . . . My mind would take off, soaring into possibilities, a flower with roots, a star in the sky, a cloud full of sad, sad tears, a piano crying out each time its back was tapped, music only to our ears.

Sister Maria stood at the chalkboard. Her chalk was always snapping in two because she wrote with such energy, her whole habit shaking with the swing of her arm, her hand tap-tap-tapping on the board. "Here's a simple sentence: 'The snow fell.'" Sister pointed with her chalk, her eyebrows lifted, her wimple poked up. Sometimes I could see wisps of gray hair that strayed from under her headdress. "But watch what happens if we put an adverb at the beginning and a prepositional phrase at the end: 'Gently, the snow fell on the bare hills.'"

I thought about the snow. I saw how it might fall on the hills, tapping lightly on the bare branches of trees. Softly, it would fall on the cold, bare fields. On toys children had left out in the yard, and on cars and on little birds and on people out late walking on the streets. Sister Maria filled the chalkboard with snowy print, on and on, handling and shaping and moving the language, scribbling all over the board until English, those verbal gadgets, those tricks and turns of phrases, those little fixed units and counters, became a charged, fluid mass that carried me in its great fluent waves, rolling and moving onward, to deposit me on the shores of my new homeland. I was no longer a foreigner with no ground to stand on. I had landed in the English language.

**Before You Read** In the following poem, Alvarez describes a childhood experience of helping to wash windows. As you read the poem, consider the child's attitude toward the work she is doing. Is she bored by her work or only by her limited involvement in it? What words and phrases show window washing as a powerful act?

# Washing the Windows
## Julia Alvarez

I helped with the windows,
hosing them down,
while she plunged her sponge
into a soapy bucket
5   clouding them up.

She stretched for the top panes
and squatted on the ladder
level with my shoulder
for the low ones
10   I might have done.

I handed her the towels,
took them crumpled back
and grew bored
emptying her bucket,
15   giving her what she needed

up there on a ladder
too dangerous for a child.
Only when I aimed the hose up
making the glass drum and the suds scatter
20   did I get the feel of the job.

On the tip of her sneakers,
she made the high glasses
glow like mirrors
and lowered the sky back
25   into each window.

**Before You Read**  "Woman's Work" is a villanelle, a nineteen-line poem divided into five tercets (three-line stanzas), each with the rhyme scheme aba, and a final quatrain with the rhyme scheme abaa. In a traditional villanelle, line 1 is repeated entirely to form lines 6, 12, and 18, and line 3 is repeated as lines 9, 15, and 19. As you read the poem, consider the ways in which it both conforms to and differs from a traditional villanelle. How does rejecting the rules of a traditional villanelle suit the theme of the poem?

# Woman's Work
## Julia Alvarez

Who says a woman's work isn't high art?
She challenged as she scrubbed the bathroom tiles.
Keep house as if the address were your heart.

We cleaned the whole upstairs before we started
5   downstairs. I sighed, hearing my friends outside.
Doing her woman's work was a hard art

to practice when the summer sun would bar
the floor I swept till she was satisfied.
She kept me prisoner in her housebound heart.

10  She shined the tines of forks, the wheels of carts,
cut lacy lattices for all her pies.
Her woman's work was nothing less than art.

And I, her masterpiece since I was smart,
was primed, praised, polished, scolded, and advised
15  to keep a house much better than my heart.

I did not want to be her counterpart!
I struck out . . . but became my mother's child:
a woman working at home on her art,
housekeeping paper as if it were her heart.

*for Judy Yarnall*

**Before You Read** In "Audition," the speaker and her mother go to a mountain village to hire a new maid. When they hear a young woman named Gladys singing, the mother is captivated by Gladys's voice and decides to hire her. Consider the reasons that Gladys stops singing. In what way is the title of the poem ironic?

# Audition
## Julia Alvarez

Porfirio drove Mami and me
to Cook's mountain village
to find a new pantry maid.
Cook had given Mami a tip
5   that her home town was girl-heavy,
the men lured away to the cities.
We drove to the interior,
climbing a steep, serpentine,
say-your-last-prayers road.
10  I leaned toward my mother
as if my weight could throw
the car's balance away
from the sheer drop below.
Late morning we entered
15  a dusty village of huts.
Mami rolled down her window
and queried an old woman,
Did she know of any girls
looking for work as maids?
20  Soon we were surrounded
by a dozen señoritas.
Under the thatched cantina
Mami conducted interviews—
a mix of personal questions
25  and Sphinx-like intelligence tests.
*Do you have children, a novio?*
*Would you hit a child who hit you?*
*If I give you a quarter to buy*
*guineos at two for a nickel,*
30  *how many will you bring back?*
As she interviewed I sat by,
looking the girls over;
one of them would soon
be telling me what to do,

35 reporting my misbehaviors.
Most seemed nice enough,
befriending me with smiles,
exclamations on my good hair,
my being such a darling.
40 Those were the ones I favored.
I'd fool them with sweet looks,
improve my bad reputation.
As we interviewed we heard
by the creek that flowed nearby
45 a high, clear voice singing
a plaintive lullaby . . .
as if the sunlight filling
the cups of the allamandas,
the turquoise sky dappled
50 with angel-feather clouds,
the creek trickling down
the emerald green of the mountain
had found a voice in her voice.
We listened. Mami's hard-line,

55 employer-to-be face
softened with quiet sweetness.
The voice came closer, louder—
a slender girl with a basket
of wrung rags on her head
60 passed by the cantina,
oblivious of our presence.
*Who is she?* my mother asked.
*Gladys,* the girls replied.
*Gladys!* my mother called
65 as she would for months to come.
*Gladys, come clear the plates!*
*Gladys, answer the door!*
*Gladys!* the young girl turned—
Abruptly, her singing stopped.

# Dagoberto Gilb

b. 1950–  (Mexican American)

## Meet the Writer

**Dagoberto Gilb** admits to being a wild youth of the 1960s in a bad part of Los Angeles, California. His mother was an immigrant from Mexico, and his father was an ex-marine whose ancestors had come from Germany. Their unhappy marriage ended in divorce.

The 1960s were also a time of the military draft and the Vietnam War. With these grim realities looming in his future, Gilb realized that he needed to change direction. He became very serious about his education. He entered the University of California, Santa Barbara, earned degrees in philosophy and religion, and began writing fiction. He decided to also become a carpenter—the perfect job for a writer.

Getting his work published in mainstream literary magazines, however, was another matter. Most editors weren't interested in stories dealing with Mexican American laborers and carpenters; however, Wendy Lesser, editor of *The Threepenny Review,* published some of Gilb's stories. She says, "I remember thinking this guy was like Chekhov [the famous Russian short story writer] with a working-class Hispanic environment and language. He had this really tough, detailed, interesting world that I hadn't seen much access to in fiction."

Gilb gave up on New York publishers and sent his work to the University of New Mexico Press, which in 1993 published *The Magic of Blood*, his first collection of short stories. The book won several writing awards and eased the way for Gilb to publish more works.

## Background

Gilb's stories often deal with characters trying to live from one paycheck to the next, pay bills, work with mean bosses, or contend with racism. According to Gilb, "Place should be considered as though a major character—or the character's surrounding—is at least defined by it." "Birthday" is a story showing the effects of place, or setting, on character.

**Before You Read**  *The setting for "Birthday" is Los Angeles, complete with congested and roaring freeways, loud radios, and police with helicopters and bullhorns. In this chaos, one island of safety and sanity can be the family. What effect does setting have on the family in this story?*

# Birthday
## Dagoberto Gilb

There was traffic on his birthday. The Hollywood Freeway to the downtown area. His father sighed and got off and got back on going in the other direction and then jumped on again saying he'd catch the 5 Freeway and then they got there but the ramp was closed for repair. His father started grumbling and talking about how he should have thought of this before, that he shouldn't have promised to go to that toy store because it was so far away and saying he couldn't understand how people could live like this all the time, back home nothing was as complicated as here, when he was a kid he didn't have toys like they have now and kids didn't expect as much. His mother said that maybe they should go somewhere else, to the shopping center, that toy store will be open and he can pick out what he wants over there, that'll be all right. His father said he should have called around like a smart man, that he didn't even know really if the store way out here had the toy the boy wanted. The boy, who was six today, let his happy pucker loosen from his lips and his body sag into the backseat as they drove in what seemed to him like a direction of home. But then his father, eyes at him in the rearview mirror, said no, I told him we'd go there, he expects to go and I'm going to take him there and I think I even have an idea. And he drove a little faster, made a turn and another, and got on the Glendale Freeway and then onto the 5 and boomed okay! and we're gonna get there now and it's my son's birthday and it is his day.

It was a long drive and the boy, his arms looped over the front seat now between his parents, worried that this wasn't right either. Was his daddy sure? Was he sure they shouldn't turn around or maybe they weren't going the right way, or maybe they'd gone too far, he'd never seen this freeway before and it didn't look like the one the toy store was next to last time. His mother said look over there, it must be a zoo she teased, because there's a picture of a giraffe on the building. It was the toy store and his baby brother was excited too and pointed ah ah! but his baby sister still slept. The boy controlled his body but not his smile and said oh yeah mommy that must be the zoo so let's go to the zoo and everybody laughed and felt happy and good and they parked and set up a collapsible stroller, the freeway visible and roaring beside them, and, pushing the thick glass doors, they went inside.

It was at least twelve feet high with toys, a trucker's warehouse big, more toys than all the days of childhood, all squeals and squeaks and putts, little kids running and whining and wanting, bouncing and rolling things. The father and the mother and the two boys and the baby sister each were twisting their necks and stopping, look at this, look at this. Get anything you want, the father told his six-year-old, but he didn't say but not for too much, he couldn't talk about money on his son's birthday, didn't want to explain about paying bills, all the other expenses, prob-

lems, how it was in this new place. There's so many things, the boy said, it's so hard. Well, get what you want, what we came here for, that one you saw last time. I just don't know if it's the best one, the boy said, and his father said oh yes it is, it's the best one in the whole place, and his father thought that the price was right too, and he said it's got 145 pieces and a big mountain, and tanks, and landing craft to cross the river, and fighter planes. The boy wanted to know who the good guys were and who were the bad guys and how could you tell? His father said he guessed it was those Germans, yeah these are the Nazi men and they were bad men, they really were bad guys and the Americans really were good guys. And the boy smiled and his father found a new unopened box almost as tall as the boy who glowed with excitement. They were all ready to go home now but the mother wanted to buy some party plates and the younger boy had to get something so he didn't cry so they chose an $.87 package of horses and for the baby girl a soft, pink bracelet-like teething ring for $1.19. They stood in line to pay. There were long lines. The boy waited contentedly, but the other two could not and the mother took them away. The boy just stared at his box, at the pictures, and his father stood there and waited with all the other waiting people. When he got to the stand he asked the young girl is it always crowded like this? and she said always and he shook his head. Life in the big city, she said, and he said life in the big city, and he paid, and the boy pulled the box off the counter, I want to carry it myself, and everyone in the family seemed as happy as him.

The boy had picked out a cake at the supermarket the night before. He didn't want his mother to make it, he knew exactly where the cakes that he wanted were and he guided them through the aisles of the market and squinted at the plastic windows of the cake boxes. His mother and father suggested one but he said no, not that, and found one with a clown and said this one. His father and mother saw the price and said that's a little too expensive and inside it's pink strawberry but the boy had already changed his mind, saying this is it, this one, this one here. It was chocolate devil's food with three white flowers and green leaves and white spiraled frosting in longhand happy birthday. How about this other one? his mother asked. It's the same, except I can write happy birthday on it, and it's less expensive. No, the boy said, this is the one, please, this is the one. Well if you get that, his mother told him, we probably can't get ice cream. His father's silence agreed, and the boy thought about it, then said okay and picked up the chocolate cake anyway. I'll get it, his father said, and he carried it but said we have to get ice cream and the mother helped choose the brand of vanilla.

His mother stabbed six candles into the brown frosting. She arranged them so there were five blue ones at each corner of an imaginary star and one yellow one in the middle. His father posed the boy next to the cake and took a picture, then he found some matches and lit the candles, and then his mother and father sang, only their voices, the father's loud, the mother's soft, the baby girl in her arms drooling, the younger boy, eyes open, learning. It was overcast outside the window near this. The man next door who nagged and screamed at his wife was sweet-talking his dog, and there was a police helicopter swirling around and black-and-whites filling up the street behind them. A radio not so far away played a love song by Yolanda del Río. The father snapped a picture with a flash of the boy blowing out the candles. His mother brought out two more presents, each wrapped in paper that had been around the house, without ribbon or bows. She said, the little one's from your brother and sister, the big one's from your mommy and daddy. The little one was comic books and the boy smiled, so pleased, and grabbed the other and ripped it open. It was called the Sword of Grayskull, which was from his favorite TV show, and now he was happy beyond words. His mother cut up the cake and his father scooped out ice cream and they all sat around quietly eating off the party plates. The radio outside was off and instead they heard a police bullhorn mumbling on the street behind them. His father told the boy to wait a minute, he thought he had a couple of batteries. He loaded them in the black plastic handle of the sword and then handed it to the boy. The six-year-old held it above his head with both hands and lit up the yellow plastic blade. Slicing the darkening air, his whole family admired him as he stood in the center of the room saying I have the power!

# Margarita Engle

b. 1951– (Cuban American)

## Meet the Writer

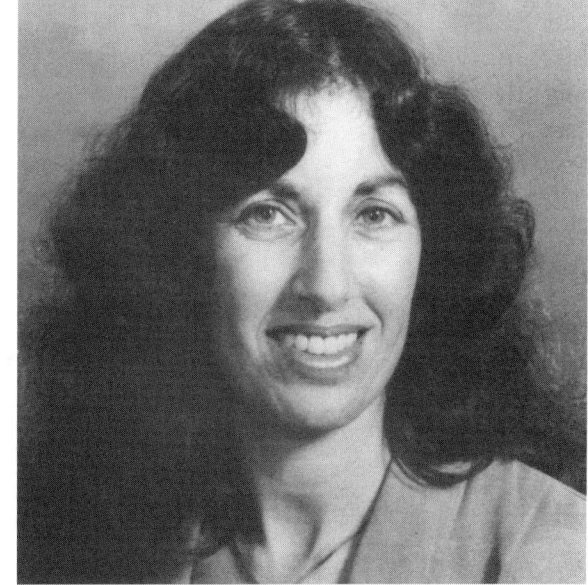

One reviewer has written, "Reading **Margarita Engle's** prose is like stepping from the stale air of an office building into a humid rainforest dense with impossibly tangled vines and birds so brilliantly colored they seem faintly unreal." Engle's prose is sometimes labeled "magic realism." In accepting the label, Engle has remarked that her style "grows out of the strangeness of life, an acceptance of the childlike spirit of wonder, an acceptance of not-knowing."

Engle draws on her own experiences in her writing. A native of California, she visited her relatives in Cuba when she was a child. Two of her novels center on Cuba: *Singing to Cuba* (1993) and *Skywriting* (1995). In *Singing to Cuba*, a woman from California visits her relatives in Cuba and assures them that they have not been forgotten. In *Skywriting*, a woman from California meets her half brother just before he attempts to escape from Cuba on a raft.

Engle began writing when her children were young. Her work has appeared in such publications as *Atlanta Review, California Quarterly,* and *Caribbean Writer*. *Word Wings* (2005) is a collection of poetry for children. Her latest book, *The Poet-Slave of Cuba: A Biography in Poems of Juan Francisco Manzano*, was published in 2006.

## Background

The revolution that forms the background for the following short story was a struggle in which Fulgencio Batista, Cuban dictator, was overthrown by Fidel Castro. As Castro extended his powers, the relationship between Cuba and the United States deteriorated. In 1961, the United States broke off diplomatic relations with Cuba. Trade with Cuba and travel between the two countries were restricted, resulting in economic hardship for the Cuban people and separation of families for long periods.

**Before You Read** *The differences between the two cultures in this story are dramatic. Consider what the family in Cuba may have thought of the behavior of their relatives from the United States. What do you think the children from the United States learned from their visit to Cuba?*

# Niña
## Margarita Engle

My mother was afraid it might be our last chance to visit her family in Cuba. The revolution was almost two years old, and already there was talk of an impending crisis.

At the airport in Miami she gave us three instructions.

"Never tell anyone you are tomboys."

"Why?"

"They wouldn't understand. Also, don't tell the other children about your allowance. You have more money in the bank than their fathers make in a year."

"So?"

"So, they would feel bad."

"Oh."

"And most important, don't bring animals into your grandmother's house."

"But Mom . . ."

"No animals. They don't like having animals in the house. Do you understand?"

At the airport in Havana we released the caterpillars we had hidden in our luggage.

"Just in case there are no butterflies here," my sister and I reassured each other.

We had no idea what to expect, but the island did not disappoint us. Abuelita's house was on the outer fringe of Havana, and there were animals everywhere. We put lizards in beds, and tarantulas and scorpions in the living room. The fisherman who lived across the street gave us a ripe swordfish snout to play with. When it really started to stink, my mother threw it on the roof, where it rotted quickly in the sun.

The fisherman's daughter asked me if I had money for ice cream. "Yes," I said with pride, "I have eighty dollars in the bank, which I saved all by myself."

"Dollars? Really?" I could see she didn't believe a word of it. I squirmed inside, remembering my mother's admonition.

"Well, I have something better," the girl offered. "Crabs. When my father gets home, you can have one to cook for your dinner."

She was right, of course. The crabs were better than my money. Her father came home with a truckload of them, bright orange crabs as big as cats. We put ours on a leash and led it up and down the street until it died.

My sister liked dogs better than crabs. She begged my mother for a can of dog food for my great-grandmother's mangy hound. We had to go all the way downtown, to Woolworth's, just to find dog food in cans. It cost more than a month's supply of real food, corn meal, black beans and rice.

Just to make sure there were no sins left uncommitted, I went across the street and told the fisherman's daughter I was a tomboy.

"Oh no," she said, horrified. "You're not a tomboy, don't worry. You will be fine." She fluffed her petticoats and curled a lock of hair with her fingers.

My collection of revolutionary bullets was growing. They were everywhere—in Abuelita's front yard and in the weeds where we searched for tarantulas, which we caught with wads of gum attached to strings. There were bullets in the open fields beyond the city, and in the passion vines which clung to the walls of houses.

On one of my solitary expeditions I wandered far beyond those walls, beyond the open fields, and into a mud-floored hut with a thatched roof and many inhabitants. The family greeted me as if I had some right to invade their home. The children came outside to introduce me to their mule, their chickens and the sensitive Mimosa plant which closed its leaves at the touch of a child's fingers.

One of the children was called Niña, meaning "girl." I assumed her parents had simply run out of names by the time they got around to her. In Niña's case, her name was no more unusual than her appearance. She was hardly there, just bones and eyes, and a few pale whisps of hair bleached by malnutrition.

"Doesn't she get enough to eat?" I asked my mother when I reached home.

"They say she has a hole in her stomach."

One day I was standing in the sun of the front porch, watching a black storm cloud sweep across the sky, bringing toward me its thunder and lightning, which fell only in one small corner of the sky. A motionless circle of vultures hung from the cloud, listless, with black wings barely trembling in the wind.

"Come in," my mother warned. "Don't forget your uncle who was killed by lightning, right in his own kitchen."

I ignored her. If it could happen in the kitchen, then why bother to go inside? I was just as safe outside.

Niña crept up to the porch, smiling her death's head smile, like the skull and crossbones on a bottle of medicine.

"Here," she said, offering me half of the *anon*[1] fruit she was eating. I took it. Together we ate and stared and smiled at each other, not knowing what to say. We both knew my half of the seedy, juicy fruit was going into my body, making flesh and fat, while hers was going right out the gaping invisible hole in her stomach.

Something like a shiver passed through my shoulders.

"Someone stepped on your grave," Niña giggled.

"What do you mean?"

"They say when you shiver like that it's because someone stepped on the spot where your grave will be."

I stared at Niña's huge eyes, wondering who could have been cruel enough to inform her that she would ever have a grave.

When we trooped down the street to the bingo games at my great-grandmother's house, Niña tagged along. An endless array of uncles and cousins filed in and out, a few boasting revolutionary beards and uniforms, but most outfitted in their farmers' Sunday best, their hands brown and calloused.

Niña was quiet. She poured burnt-milk candy through the hole in her stomach, and watched. The size of her eyes made her watching feel like

---

1. *anon* (ah NOHN): custard apple.

staring, but no one seemed to notice. Children like Niña surprised no one.

On the anniversary of the revolution, the streets filled with truckloads of bearded men on their way to the mountains to celebrate. A man with a loudspeaker walked along our street announcing the treachery of the Yanquis.[2] I was listening inside my grandmother's house. Suddenly his voice changed.

"Let me clarify," he was saying, "that it is not the common people of the United States who we oppose, but the government which has . . ." I stopped listening. Niña was at the open door, smiling her bony smile.

"I told him," she said very quietly, "that you are from *Estados Unidos*. I didn't want him to hurt your feelings."

At the beach, my sister and I went swimming inside shark fences. We imagined the gliding fins beyond the fence. Afterwards, our mother extracted the spines of bristly sea urchins from the soles of our feet.

We visited huge caverns gleaming with stalactites. How wonderfully the Cuban Indians must have lived, I thought, with no home but a cave, nothing to eat but fruit and shellfish, nothing to do but swim and sing. "We were born a thousand years too late," I told my sister.

With a square old-fashioned camera, I took pictures of pigs, dogs, turkeys, horses and mules. Not once did it occur to me to put a friend or relative into one of my photos. I was from Los Angeles. There were more than enough people in my world, and far too few creatures. When my uncle cut sugarcane, it was the stiff, sweet cane itself which caught my eye, and the gnats clinging to his eyes. His strong arms and wizened face were just part of the landscape. When my cousins picked *mamonsillo*[3] fruit, it was the tree I looked at, and not the boys showing off by climbing it. I thrived on the wet smell of green land after a rain, and the treasures I found crawling in red mud or dangling from the leaves of weeds and vines. I trapped lizards, netted butterflies, and once, with the help of my sister, I snared a vulture with an elaborate hand-rigged snare. Our relatives were horrified. What could one do with a vulture? It was just the way I felt about everything which mattered to them. If the goal of the revolution was to uproot happy people from their thatched havens, and deposit them in concrete high-rise apartment buildings, who needed it? Thatched huts, after all, were natural, wild, primitive. They were as good as camping. When my mother explained that the people living in the *bohíos*[4] were tired of it, I grew sulky. Only an adult would be foolish enough to believe that any normal human being could prefer comfort to wildness, roses to weeds, radios to the chants of night-singing frogs.

I knew the hole in Niña's stomach was growing. She was disappearing, vanishing before my eyes. Her parents seemed resigned to her departure. People spoke of her as if she had never really been there. Niña was not solid. She didn't really exist.

On the day of her death, it occurred to me to ask my mother, "Why didn't they just take her to a doctor?"

"They had no money."

I went out to the front porch, abandoning the tarantula I had been about to feed. As I gazed across the open fields toward Niña's *bohío,* the reality of her death permeated the humid summer air. In my mind, I sifted through a stack of foals and ducks, caterpillars and vultures. Somewhere in that stack, I realized, there should have been an image of Niña.

---

2. **Yanquis:** Yankees.
3. ***mamonsillo*** (mah mohn SEE yoh): tropical fruit also known as canip or Spanish lime.

---

4. ***bohíos*** (boh EE ohs): thatched huts.

# Carmen Tafolla

b. 1951–   (Mexican American)

## Meet the Writer

**Carmen Tafolla** has said that her work is inspired by her ancestors "whispering over her shoulders." She believes that she has such a clear and proud awareness of her Chicano identity and history partly because of an awareness of her ancestry.

In fact, Tafolla's vigorous poetry does celebrate the Chicana experience in the United States, but at the same time the author mingles both Spanish and English to create poetry that celebrates the power of both languages.

Tafolla was born in the Mexican American barrios on the west side of San Antonio, Texas. Even when she was a child, she was aware of the way society discriminated against her and other people in the barrios. Her junior high school principal told her that she had the potential to "make it all the way to high school." Despite limited assessments of her abilities, Tafolla received a doctorate in bilingual education from the University of Texas at Austin in 1981.

Tafolla has published five books of poetry, seven television screenplays, a nonfiction book, children's stories, short stories, and numerous academic articles. She is perhaps best known for her collection of poetry *Sonnets to Human Beings,* which won the University of California at Irvine's 1989 National Chicano Literature Contest. She currently lives in San Antonio.

## Background

The poem "marked" is written in free verse, which means that the poet has decided not to restrict her expression to the traditional rules of meter and rhyme. Although free verse is free of a strict meter and of a strict rhyme scheme, it is not free of other poetic devices. Notice how the repetition of certain lines, sentence patterns, and words creates a rhythm.

Free verse is written to imitate the rise and fall of the human voice. When you read this poem aloud, be aware of which words the speaker would stress and where she might pause to emphasize a point.

**Before You Read** *Tafolla has been criticized for her support of bilingualism, but she stands firm in taking pride in her Spanish heritage and will not let anyone erase it from her. Her forcefulness on that issue can be seen in the poem that follows. Notice the title of this poem. How many meanings of "marked" can you think of?*

# marked
## Carmen Tafolla

Never write with pencil,
m'ija.°
It is for those
who would
5    erase.
Make your mark proud
    and open,
Brave,
        beauty folded into
10    its imperfection,
Like a piece of turquoise
    marked.

Never write
with pencil,
15    m'ija.
Write with ink
    or mud,
or berries grown in
gardens never owned,
20    or, sometimes,
        if necessary,
           blood.

---

°*m'ija* (MEE hah): abbreviation for the Spanish words *mi hija*, my daughter, in Spanish.

# Jimmy Santiago Baca

**b. 1952–**   (Mexican American/ Native American)

## Meet the Writer

Faced with almost every imaginable disadvantage in his early years, **Jimmy Santiago Baca** eventually found a way to transform his life from one of despair and incarceration to one of creativity and productivity. The way he found was poetry. As a young man serving time in prison, he taught himself to read and to write poetry. In an interview for the *Los Angeles Times*, Baca explained the transformative power of language this way: "I was tired of being treated like an animal. I wanted to learn how to read and to write and to understand. . . . I wanted to know how to function in this world. . . . The only way of transcending was through language and understanding. Had I not found the language, I would have been a guerrilla in the mountains."

Baca's mother was Chicana, and his father was Apache. When Baca was just two years old, his parents abandoned him. He lived with his grandmother for a few years but ended up in a New Mexico orphanage at the age of five. By this time, his father had died of alcoholism. Later, his mother was murdered by her second husband. Although he officially lived at St. Anthony's Home for Boys in Albuquerque until the age of eleven, Baca fled the orphanage frequently. He would stay with relatives or survive on the streets of Albuquerque's urban barrios.

At age twenty-one, Baca was convicted on drug charges and sentenced to several years at one of the toughest maximum-security prisons in Arizona. He spent more than six years there, enduring solitary confinements, electroshock therapy, and beatings by prison guards. Feeling himself "disintegrate," Baca began a process of trying to find himself through literacy and education. He earned his GED (General Equivalency Diploma) and immersed himself in reading. Soon Baca began writing poetry, and with the encouragement of a fellow inmate, he sent some of his poems to *Mother Jones* magazine. The poetry editor for *Mother Jones* at the time was poet and professor Denise Levertov. Impressed with Baca's raw talent, Levertov had his poems printed in the magazine, began corresponding with him, and eventually found a publisher for his first book.

Baca's first poetry collection, *Immigrants in Our Own Land*, which appeared in 1979, was greeted with great critical acclaim. It was followed by a ten-poem collection in 1982 and then by the publication in 1987 of *Martin and Meditations on the South Valley*, a semiautobiographical work that some call "a novel in verse." *Martin* tells the story of an orphaned Apache boy who travels the country looking for stability and meaning in his life. With this book, Baca gained international attention. Requests for poetry readings and teaching services came pouring in. In 1989, Baca published *Black Mesa Poems*, which, according to critic A. Gabriel Meléndez, "represents the culmination of a long process of recovery and vindication through language and poetry."

For a time Baca settled in Albuquerque's South Valley with his wife and young son. Many of his works speak to the significance of reconnecting with his roots and with the Chicano community there. The family later moved into a hundred-year-old adobe home on Black Mesa, an ancient volcanic tableland south of Albuquerque, and a second son was born. Baca continued to write: a play, several screenplays, a memoir of his childhood and young adulthood, a short story collection, and several more poetry collections. In addition, he works with disadvantaged people in the inner city and is founder of Black Mesa Enterprises, a grassroots cooperative for inner-city youth.

## Background

Jimmy Santiago Baca found a way to tell his own story through poetry. In his works readers can hear the emotional pain of his troubled childhood, the anger and rage of his time in prison, and the healing and salvation of his post-prison years. With each collection published, a leg of Baca's journey into selfhood seems to be revealed. Therefore, to read his works in order of publication would be almost like reading an autobiography in verse.

"It Started" appears in Baca's first book, *Immigrants in Our Own Land*, a work that gives voice to Baca's struggles to gain a sense of self within the prison environment, which so effectively strips its inhabitants of dignity and self-worth. "Tomás Lucero" and "Accountability" were published later, in *Black Mesa Poems*. This collection focuses on Baca's identification with the Chicano community. In addition, it tells how Baca and his family acquired their home on Black Mesa and describes in vivid detail the people and the landscapes that surround the home. Baca conveys in beautiful language the mythic significance of his Indian, Spanish, and Mexican ancestors and their abiding presence in the lands and customs of New Mexico. Baca's ties to both the urban Chicano community and the traditions of the Southwest became important elements in his journey toward self-actualization.

**Before You Read** *The autobiographical nature of Baca's poetry is particularly evident in "It Started." As you read, consider what you know about Baca's life, especially his time in prison. Who do you think might be the "you" in this poem? Why is the relationship Baca has established with this person so important to him?*

# It Started
## Jimmy Santiago Baca

A little state-funded barrack
in the desert, in a prison. A poetry workshop,
an epicenter of originality, companionship,
pain and openness,
5                  For some,
the first time in their life writing,
for others the first time saying openly what they felt,
the first time finding something in themselves,
worthwhile, ugly and beautiful.

10          I think of you and me. Last night I was
thinking of you. I am your friend. I don't want you
to think otherwise.

         I was thinking, when we first wrote to each other.
         I remember instances, of tremendous joy
15          when receiving your letters,
         what cells I was in,
         what emotional state, under
         what circumstances.
         Your letters always fell like meteorites
20          into my lap.
         You were my first friendship
         engendered in this state, perhaps,
         all my past life.
I showed you my first poem ever written,
25 "They Only Came to See the Zoo"

        But you didn't treat me like a wild ape,
        or an elephant. You treated me like Jimmy.
        And who was Jimmy?
A mass of molten fury in this furnace of steel,
and yet, my thoughts became ladles, sifting carefully
through my life, the pain and endurance,
to the essence of my being.
        I gently, into the long night, unmolding
        my shielded heart, the fierce figures
        of war and loss, I remolding them,
        my despair and anger into a cry and song.
I took the path alone, nuded myself to my own caged animals,
and learned their tongues and their spirits,
and roamed the desert, went to my place of birth. . . .
        Now tonight, I am a burning bush,
        my bones a grill of fire,
        I burn these words in praise,
        of our meeting, our friendship.

**Before You Read**  This poem tells the story of a man who has been taken to prison on a train. Notice that the story is not told in chronological order. First, the speaker describes the man being escorted to the train. Then, as the poem continues, the speaker reveals what crime the man committed and why.

As you read, notice how emotionally close the speaker is to the people in the poem and to the tragic events they have experienced. The speaker even addresses the poem to the imprisoned man. What is the significance of Baca's speaker taking such a personal tone? That is, how does the speaker's tone affect the meaning of the poem?

# Tomás Lucero
## Jimmy Santiago Baca

I wept when the police escorted you to the train.
For years, when the train darkly whipped across the *llano*
at midnight, shuddering my cot, the trembling ground
was your voice still mourning your brother
5   killed in your yard by the police.
I wept when your small son was engulfed in a blast of steam,
as the Santa Fe train chugged off he stood there,
choking, breast heaving with tears, a dark small shadow
in ghostly smoke.

10   You have given me hope, Tomás.
I knew you were not a strong man. When you knelt
clutching your bloody brother in your front yard,
across from my house, I saw
how you wept, begging the blood back, the bullet holes healed,
15   the terrible nightmare erased. The dark cloudy features
of your face were an omen—
           you looked up at the policeman,
               took your brother's gun and shot him—
because of that one tragic moment
20   you had to become who you were not.
Sniff air, a hunted coyote,
try to charm the moon—
now hunted, you held alien weight of your brother's gun
in your hands

25     instead of your son's little body,
       now earth became your bed, *arroyos* your paths,
       instead of your wife's arms,
       now you rest on canyon rockrim that overlooks
       Estancia, Tajíque, and Willard.
30     You must have wept for a return, to just sit on your porch,
       watch your children playing in the yard
       as you scold your oldest son for trampling chile plants
       in the garden.

       We sent you food, and every day
35     I have walked to your house to see how your family is doing.
       When the police came to ask of you,
       our silence asked them to leave our yard.

       When you were finally caught,
       I looked into your son's face
40     watching you embark the train for prison.
       I saw the most beautiful, inexpressible love and adoration
       burst over and effuse his sorrowful face.
       And then months after, a mysterious nobility
       filled his eyes, two dark wounds bleeding your image
45     on everything they looked on—
       Never have I seen anything as beautiful, Tomás,
       as your son who is becoming a man.

**Before You Read**   In this poem, Baca compares "Who we are and what we do" to a bill collector who presents an official paper that we have to sign. His comparison goes a long way in presenting questions about what identity really is. Do you think the "man dressed in a long black coat" would present *you with a paper you would want to sign? What feeling are you left with as you read the last few lines?*

# Accountability
## Jimmy Santiago Baca

    Who we are and what we do
    appears to us
    like a man dressed in a long black coat,
    a bill collector
5   who offers a paper to sign
    and says we have no choice
    but to sign it.
    In it,
    we read who we are—
10  we should change this paragraph,
    or the color of the hair,
    or the time we took a trip,
    or the woman we met in a coffeeshop,
    it's not true,
15  or it didn't turn out quite that way.
    "Sign it,"
    he says,
    "I have many others to see today."

# Judith Ortiz Cofer

**b. 1952–** (Puerto Rican American)

## Meet the Writer

**Judith Ortiz Cofer** was born in Hormigueros, Puerto Rico. When she was a small child, her father joined the United States Navy and moved the family to New Jersey. Because her mother spoke only Spanish, Cofer soon learned English in order to help her run the household. The family moved back and forth from their homeland to the United States several times. While growing up, Cofer found that her experiences of American culture often came into conflict with her parents' traditional values. Her struggles to reconcile those different values are reflected in her writing.

After graduating from Augusta College in Georgia, Cofer earned a master's degree and did graduate work at Oxford University. During her years as a graduate student and as a teacher of English, Cofer began writing poetry. Her works soon appeared in magazines, chapbooks, and collections published by small presses. Later she wrote novels, short stories, and even a play.

Cofer has received numerous awards for her writing, including a Pulitzer Prize nomination in 1989 for her novel *The Line of the Sun*. Her collection of autobiographical essays and poems, *Silent Dancing: A Partial Remembrance of a Puerto Rican Childhood*, won awards from PEN (International Association of Poets, Playwrights, Editors, Essayists, and Novelists) and from the New York Public Library. *Silent Dancing* focuses on Cofer's relationships with her parents and grandmother and explores the cultural split she faced as she was growing up.

## Background

"An Hour with Abuelo" is one of twelve stories in Cofer's collection titled *An Island Like You: Stories from the Barrio*. The main characters in these stories are Puerto Rican teenagers living in a barrio in Paterson, New Jersey. Like all teenagers, these young people are struggling to find their place in the world and to establish their own identities. Because they straddle two cultures, their individuation process must somehow integrate their Puerto Rican heritage with the cultural influences of American society. In "An Hour with Abuelo," as in many of the other stories in the collection, the young narrator's look at the older generation becomes an important means of discovering his individual identity.

Cofer explores similar themes through her poetry. Both "Picture of Whoopee" and "Confessions of a Non-Native Speaker," for example, reveal in all their painful glory the tensions associated with being a young person from an ethnic minority. In the former, the subject of the poem, Whoopee, struggles to fit in to American society while trying to retain her unique ethnic identity and courageous personality. In the latter, Cofer's tightly worded description of the experience of learning English brings to light one of the major challenges facing most immigrants to the United States.

Although Cofer has also been prolific as a novelist, essayist, and short story writer, she says she "will never stop writing poetry." According to Cofer, writing poetry helps make her more disciplined. "Poetry contains the essence of language. Every word weighs a ton. . . . Poetry taught me about economizing in language and about the power of language." Cofer has published a number of collections of poetry, including *Peregrina* and *Terms of Survival*. Her poems also appear along with some of her prose works in *The Latin Deli: Prose and Poetry* and *The Year of Our Revolution: New and Selected Stories and Poems*.

**Before You Read**   For the young narrator of this story, an hour with his grandfather at the nursing home is not an appealing prospect. He sees it as waste of valuable time. He would rather be reading and getting ready to advance at school. What might this driven young man have to gain from a visit with his grandfather?

As you read, look for ironic twists in the story. How does Arturo's time with his grandfather turn out differently than you would expect? Also, consider how Arturo's interaction with his grandfather offers him insight into his own goals and priorities.

# An Hour with Abuelo
## Judith Ortiz Cofer

"Just one hour, *una hora,* is all I'm asking of you, son." My grandfather is in a nursing home in Brooklyn, and my mother wants me to spend some time with him, since the doctors say that he doesn't have too long to go now. *I* don't have much time left of my summer vacation, and there's a stack of books next to my bed I've got to read if I'm going to get into the AP English class I want. I'm going stupid in some of my classes, and Mr. Williams, the principal at Central, said that if I passed some reading tests, he'd let me move up.

Besides, I hate the place, the old people's home, especially the way it smells like industrial-strength ammonia and other stuff I won't mention, since it turns my stomach. And really the abuelo always has a lot of relatives visiting him, so I've gotten out of going out there except at Christmas, when a whole vanload of grandchildren are herded over there to give him gifts and a hug. We all make it quick and spend the rest of the time in the recreation area, where they play checkers and stuff with some of the old people's games, and I catch up on back issues of *Modern Maturity.* I'm not picky, I'll read almost anything.

Anyway, after my mother nags me for about a week, I let her drive me to Golden Years. She drops me off in front. She wants me to go in alone and have a "good time" talking to Abuelo. I tell her to be back in one hour or I'll take the bus back to Paterson. She squeezes my hand and says, "*Gracias, hijo,*" in a choked-up voice like I'm doing her a big favor.

I get depressed the minute I walk into the place. They line up the old people in wheelchairs in the hallway as if they were about to be raced to the finish line by orderlies who don't even look at them when they push them here and there. I walk fast to room 10, Abuelo's "suite." He is sitting up in his bed writing with a pencil in one of those old-fashioned black hardback notebooks. It has the outline of the island of Puerto Rico on it. I slide into the hard vinyl chair by his bed. He sort of smiles and the lines on his face get deeper, but he doesn't say anything. Since I'm supposed to talk to him, I say, "What are you doing, Abuelo, writing the story of your life?"

It's supposed to be a joke, but he answers, "Sí, how did you know, Arturo?"

His name is Arturo too. I was named after him. I don't really know my grandfather. His children, including my mother, came to New York and New Jersey (where I was born) and he stayed on the Island until my grandmother died. Then he got sick, and since nobody could leave

their jobs to go take care of him, they brought him to this nursing home in Brooklyn. I see him a couple of times a year, but he's always surrounded by his sons and daughters. My mother tells me that Don Arturo had once been a teacher back in Puerto Rico, but had lost his job after the war. Then he became a farmer. She's always saying in a sad voice, "Ay, bendito! What a waste of a fine mind." Then she usually shrugs her shoulders and says, "*Así es la vida.*" That's the way life is. It sometimes makes me mad that the adults I know just accept whatever crap is thrown at them because "that's the way things are." Not for me. I go after what I want.

Anyway, Abuelo is looking at me like he was trying to see into my head, but he doesn't say anything. Since I like stories, I decide I may as well ask him if he'll read me what he wrote.

I look at my watch: I've already used up twenty minutes of the hour I promised my mother.

Abuelo starts talking in his slow way. He speaks what my mother calls book English. He taught himself from a dictionary, and his words sound stiff, like he's sounding them out in his head before he says them. With his children he speaks Spanish, and that funny book English with us grandchildren. I'm surprised that he's still so sharp, because his body is shrinking like a crumpled-up brown paper sack with some bones in it. But I can see from looking into his eyes that the light is still on in there.

"It is a short story, Arturo. The story of my life. It will not take very much time to read it."

"I have time, Abuelo." I'm a little embarrassed that he saw me looking at my watch.

"Yes, hijo. You have spoken the truth. La verdad. You have much time."

Abuelo reads: "'I loved words from the beginning of my life. In the *campo* where I was born one of seven sons, there were few books. My mother read them to us over and over: the Bible, the stories of Spanish conquistadors and of pirates that she had read as a child and brought with her from the city of Mayagüez; that was before she married my father, a coffee bean farmer; and she taught us words from the newspaper that a boy on a horse brought every week to her. She taught each of us how to write on a slate with chalks that she ordered by mail every year. We used those chalks until they were so small that you lost them between your fingers.

"'I always wanted to be a writer and a teacher. With my heart and my soul I knew that I wanted to be around books all of my life. And so against the wishes of my father, who wanted all his sons to help him on the land, she sent me to high school in Mayagüez. For four years I boarded with a couple she knew. I paid my rent in labor, and I ate vegetables I grew myself. I wore my clothes until they were thin as parchment. But I graduated at the top of my class! My whole family came to see me that day. My mother brought me a beautiful *guayabera,* a white shirt made of the finest cotton and embroidered by her own hands. I was a happy young man.

"'In those days you could teach in a country school with a high school diploma. So I went back to my mountain village and got a job teaching all grades in a little classroom built by the parents of my students.

"'I had books sent to me by the government. I felt like a rich man although the pay was very small. I had books. All the books I wanted! I taught my students how to read poetry and plays, and how to write them. We made up songs and put on shows for the parents. It was a beautiful time for me.

"'Then the war came, and the American President said that all Puerto Rican men would be drafted. I wrote to our governor and explained that I was the only teacher in the mountain village. I told him that the children would go back to the fields and grow up ignorant if I could not teach them their letters. I said that I thought I was a better teacher than a soldier. The governor did not answer my letter. I went into the U.S. Army.

"'I told my sergeant that I could be a teacher in the army. I could teach all the farm boys their letters so that they could read the instructions on the ammunition boxes and not blow themselves up. The sergeant said I was too smart for my own good, and gave me a job cleaning latrines. He said to me there is reading material for you there, scholar. Read the writing on the walls. I spent the war mopping floors and cleaning toilets.

"'When I came back to the Island, things had changed. You had to have a college degree to teach school, even the lower grades. My parents were sick, two of my brothers had been killed in the war, the others had stayed in Nueva York. I was the only one left to help the old people. I became a farmer. I married a good woman who gave me many good children. I taught them all how to read and write before they started school.'"

Abuelo then puts the notebook down on his lap and closes his eyes.

"*Así es la vida* is the title of my book," he says in a whisper, almost to himself. Maybe he's forgotten that I'm there.

For a long time he doesn't say anything else. I think that he's sleeping, but then I see that he's watching me through half-closed lids, maybe waiting for my opinion of his writing. I'm trying to think of something nice to say. I liked it and all, but not the title. And I think that he could've been a teacher if he had wanted to bad enough. Nobody is going to stop me from doing what I want with my life. I'm not going to let la vida get in my way. I want to discuss this with him, but the words are not coming into my head in Spanish just yet. I'm about to ask him why he didn't keep fighting to make his dream come true, when an old lady in hot-pink running shoes sort of appears at the door.

She is wearing a pink jogging outfit too. The world's oldest marathoner, I say to myself. She calls out to my grandfather in a flirty voice, "Yoo-hoo, Arturo, remember what day this is? It's poetry-reading day in the rec room! You promised us you'd read your new one today."

I see my abuelo perking up almost immediately. He points to his wheelchair, which is hanging like a huge metal bat in the open closet. He makes it obvious that he wants me to get it. I put it together, and with Mrs. Pink Running Shoes's help, we get him in it. Then he says in a strong deep voice I hardly recognize, "Arturo, get that notebook from the table, please."

I hand him another map-of-the-Island notebook—this one is red. On it in big letters it says, *POEMAS DE ARTURO.*

I start to push him toward the rec room, but he shakes his finger at me.

"Arturo, look at your watch now. I believe your time is over." He gives me a wicked smile.

Then with her pushing the wheelchair—maybe a little too fast—they roll down the hall. He is already reading from his notebook, and she's making bird noises. I look at my watch and the hour *is* up, to the minute. I can't help but think that my abuelo has been timing *me*. It cracks me up. I walk slowly down the hall toward the exit sign. I want my mother to have to wait a little. I don't want her to think that I'm in a hurry or anything.

**Before You Read** *"Picture of Whoopee" is a portrait in words of an extraordinary little girl. Is she a childhood friend whom the speaker admires as a hero, or a figment of the speaker's imagination—or something else? As you read the poem, notice imagery that appeals to the senses of sight and hearing. How does the sensory imagery help you see and hear Whoopee in your imagination? As you get to know her, think about the contrast between the persona Whoopee projects to the rest of the world and the way she feels inside. Why do you think she "does not know her own beauty"?*

# Picture of Whoopee
## Judith Ortiz Cofer

*Hair* wild as hurricane winds over the Caribbean.
*Skin*, a bright new penny.
*Eyes*, black, ebony, three A.M. on a clear night black;
deepest part of the ocean black, almond-shaped
5    black mirror. "Look into my eyes, María," Whoopee talks me
out of my black moods and my dark days. "Follow me,
María." She pretends to be Whoopee the Magnificent,
Sorceress and Mistress of the Universe. I pretend I am
being propelled out of my sadness
10   like a sleepwalker, controlled by eyes
like two black laser beams. I follow Whoopee
into the sunlight
where she opens that *mouth*,
painted Puerto Rican red, and lets out
15   a glass-shattering Tarzan howl, or maybe
it is a sort of yodel from the Swiss Alps.
                               It is a song too,
a wordless scatting song half jazz, half salsa,
intended to wake me out of my apathy,
20   and everyone on the block out of our boring lives.
Sometimes her call is high pitched, other times
soft and mournful like a dove. Whoopee
is a one-woman band, mainly horns, trombones,
sometimes a flute. Other people whistle or hum,
25   Whoopee belts out musical notes. The sadder

*Portrait of Clara* by Rosa Ibarra

Whoopee is, the angrier Whoopee is,
the louder she yodels. Whoopee
sometimes sings so long and so hard
that her voice sounds like a rusty hinge on a door.
30  She moves like a cat,
she is built low to the ground. She stalks
and pounces on life, takes steps two at a time.
I have seen Whoopee
leaping from rooftop to rooftop
35  in my dreams. I have seen her stop bullets
from a drive-by shooting with her bare hands,
Whoopee the Magnificent! I have seen her

stop the woman who just moved in our building, the one
with the wild look in her sunken eyes, from hitting
40    her little girl. Whoopee,
The Puerto Rican Superhero,
I have heard her send her powerful voice
up from the street and into the crying child's room.
I have heard her call out a warning
45    to the wild-eyed woman, "You will spew toads
and worms if you say ugly things to your child,
and you will turn into a warty frog yourself
if you hit your little daughter
ever again."
50    Whoopee, my best friend and my hero
fears nothing and no one. My friend Whoopee
fears nothing in the world except mirrors in her path.
She turns away from her own reflection. Whoopee
fears herself. She is afraid
55    that if she does not make us laugh
we will laugh at her.
She does not see her own beauty.
She performs for us. She gives us herself
as a clown. This is her gift and her secret
60    sadness. Whoopee does not know
her beauty. She thinks we will not love her
unless she is louder, faster, and stronger
than anyone else. Whoopee
does not know
65    her own beauty.

If Whoopee could go back in time
and walk by Frida Kahlo° on a street
in Mexico, in a place where her brown skin,
wild black hair, and small solid body
70    were like those of goddesses and queens
sculpted into the sides of temples,
she would be immortalized in a painting called
*Girl with the Black Pearl Eyes.*
*Niña de los ojos*
75    *como perlas negras.*

---

°**Frida Kahlo:** One of Mexico's most famous artists. She lived from 1907–1956 and was known for her unusual physical appearance and shocking, often autobiographical paintings.

**Before You Read**  This poem is an extended metaphor in which the speaker compares herself to a thief and the English language to a priceless treasure. Notice that the speaker's voice in the first stanza does sound much like that of a criminal confessing to a crime. How does the voice change as the poem continues? What does that change tell you about how the speaker feels about her "crime"?

# Confessions of a Non-Native Speaker
## Judith Ortiz Cofer

*A poem by María Alegre*

    I confess,
    I had to steal English
    because what I had
    was never enough.
5  The sly taking
    started as a word here,
    a word there.
    It was easy.
    I slipped words
10  into my pockets,
    my crime unnoticed
    as the precious *palabras*°
    spilled out
    of unguarded mouths,
15  and when they were left behind
    like empty glasses and china
    after a banquet,
    or like familiar jewelry,
    the everyday gold
20  tossed anywhere
    at bedtime.

---

°***palabras*** (pah LAH brahs): words.

I took what I needed
and a little more
from places I slipped easily into
25 wearing my heavy accent,
my cloak of invisibility.
I slipped in
while the ones who had more
than they could ever use, dreamed
30 their long, luxurious dreams,
spoiled children
unaware of the real value,
their inherited wealth,
language.

35 It is different now.
What I had to steal then
is legally mine
since no one has ever claimed
a word, taken back a sentence.
40 My treasure room is full.
My second language
is a silver cup
from which I intend to drink
the best wine.
45 Each word I make mine
is a pearl, a diamond,
a ruby, I will someday string
into a necklace
and wear everywhere,
50 as if I had been born
rich in English.

# Alberto Ríos

b. 1952–    (Mexican American)

## Meet the Writer

**Alberto Ríos** (ahl BEHR toh REE ohs) was born in Nogales, Arizona, where he could literally stand with "one foot in Mexico and one foot in the United States at the same time." Since his father was born in Mexico and his mother was born in England, he grew up speaking both Spanish and English. However, when Ríos started elementary school, his teachers forced him to abandon Spanish and speak only English. In fact, students were physically punished for speaking Spanish.

In high school and college, Ríos relearned the language that had once been so familiar—a process that gave him a fresh sense of the worth and dignity of his cultural roots. He says, "In having to pay double and triple attention to language—first to forget, and then to relearn—I began to see earnestly how everything, every object, every idea, had at *least* two names." He recalls that when he began taking creative writing courses at Arizona State University, "The more I wrote, the more I realized I had been writing almost all my life—I simply had had no name for it." He received his undergraduate and graduate degrees from the University of Arizona and currently teaches as Regents' Professor of English at Arizona State University.

In both his poetry and fiction, Ríos explores aspects of his Chicano heritage in a writing style that one critic sums up in this way: "Ríos's poetry is a kind of magical storytelling, and his stories are a kind of magical poetry." Ríos attributes much of his imaginative power to his mother, saying that she ". . . gave me a sense of what I might call the science of the imagination. . . . The whole time I was growing up she would talk about kings and queens, castles, snow, great gardens and countrysides—things that did not appear in the Sonoran Desert I was surrounded by. And she described them in such detail that they were undeniable." Ríos would eventually draw on his own experiences and memories or on those of family and relatives as inspiration for his stories and poems.

The characters in *The Iguana Killer* (1984), his first collection of short stories, often see the world through childhood innocence. The title story depicts a precocious, resourceful boy in southern Mexico who receives a baseball bat from his grandmother in the United States. Since neither the boy nor his family have ever heard of baseball, he concludes that she has sent him the perfect object for killing iguanas to eat. The boy becomes famous for his bat and his ability to provide food for his family.

The stories in *Pig Cookies* (1995) are set in Nogales, Mexico, during the first half of the twentieth century. In them, the village is portrayed as a communal character that shapes its inhabitants. In *The Curtain of Trees* (1999), Ríos continues to probe the Chicano experience in small villages along the border. In these stories, the author examines the complicated bonds of family.

In his fiction, Ríos has moved from an autobiographical to a more objective style. However, his poetry has usually remained intensely personal and subjective, from *Whispering to Fool the Wind* (1982), which recounts his coming-of-age experiences, to *The Smallest Muscle in the Human Body* (2002), in which he returns to early memories to illuminate universal truths. His writing has won numerous awards, and *The Smallest Muscle in the Human Body* was a National Book Award nominee in the 2002 poetry category.

## Background

"Breaking Piñatas" comes from *Capirotada: A Nogales Memoir* (1999), Ríos's often humorous account of growing up in Nogales. A piñata is a papier-mâché figure filled with candy and toys that is suspended and then broken by a blindfolded child with a stick to release its contents.

The two poems that follow come from *Five Indiscretions* (1985). Ríos calls his poem about the wrestler El Santo "one of my favorite poems in that book" and continues, "In Latin America, and in Mexico in particular, wrestlers have a recognized presence in the greater community."

**Before You Read**  *This chapter from Ríos's memoir,* Capirotada, *is deceptively simple. Ríos reflects on the difficulties that parents have in communicating with children and on the role that sheer luck plays in accidents occurring or not occurring. How would you explain to a child that it is acceptable to hit a piñata, even though you have previously told the child not to hit things? Is it possible for us to prepare, or position ourselves, to avoid accidents; or will accidents just happen or not happen, no matter what we do?*

# Breaking Piñatas
## Alberto Ríos

The day came when my son, Joaquín, was old enough to recognize a birthday, and that he could get some pretty good stuff out of his parents, out of his friends, and out of strangers, even, if he was smart enough. And we got him everything it takes—the cake, the decorations, the invitations, the loot bags for his miniature thug gang of elves, who were all catching on pretty fast.

We got him all this—and, the piñata. A fine, very large, turquoise and white and yellow Humpty Dumpty. My parents, actually, were the ones. They got him from across the line, Nogales, Mexico, and he was the real McCoy, this fine fellow, full of detail and energy. A Humpty among Humpties.

"I'm not going to hit it," he said.

We looked at him.

"You told me not to hit things."

We looked at each other. We had indeed said that to him, and more than once.

"But this is different, Joaquín," we said.

He burst into tears. "I'm not going to hit it," he said again.

There we all stood. The issue had come up before, and was always surprising. When he was a little younger, we had tried to keep guns away from him, until one day he approached us with the magnetic letter "L" in his hand, taken from the refrigerator. He held it just so, snuck up on us, and pointed.

"Bang," he said. "Bang, bang."

"We better get him a gun," I said. He had left us with no alternative.

So here we were again, confronting the issue of violence, and what were we telling him? It's okay, son. Go right ahead and beat the living daylights out of Humpty, and here's a beautiful bat to do it with. Try it, it's fun.

It's possible that might be a little confusing.

We finally reached a sort of compromise. We would keep Humpty safe and sound, and get him a Mickey Mouse that he and his friends could whack to pieces. Mickey, that was one thing. But Humpty, that was another. We couldn't explain it, and he couldn't explain it, but somehow things worked out. He didn't seem to mind taking a few swings at Mickey, I think maybe because he thought Mickey could take it. He had seen enough cartoons to know that. That mouse could bend and jump, and even if he got it, got it bad, he could "finger-snap" put himself back together. Everybody knew that.

But Humpty, Humpty was different. He was the real thing. In his story, things didn't turn out so well. Somewhere along the line, we had forgotten that—whatever "that" is. The moral or the message out of all this is not clear. It comes out of childhood, after all. It's not clear, but it is strong.

Don't hit, we told him, but showed him how to do it. Oh sure, we made him wear a blindfold, but then we cheered him on. I don't think I can figure it out any better than he could.

Once, at a piñata party in my neighborhood, a mother put a glass piggy bank into the piñata. I've never forgotten that. All the things that could have happened—glass splintering, all of us getting cut as we got down onto the ground with our hands and knees to grab the candy, the screaming.

I saw the thing come flying out when the piñata was finally broken. Nobody knew it was in there. It came flying out, and the moment was slow motion—the pig was moving in accident time. I watched it sail and arc and fall in a time so slow and rich that it still exists for me, right into a little boy's hands. Just like that. A glass piggy bank of terror, transformed into a moment incarnate, an unforgettable second, a smiling on that boy so big I thought its edges might swing past the edges of his face.

It was a moment full of all the things that could have happened, and what did. Piñatas have been like that for me. I shouldn't have been so surprised by my son's reaction. It's the only thing that does make sense.

**Before You Read** El Santo, the Mexican wrestler known for the silver mask that he reportedly wore "even when he slept," was so famous that during his long ring career he also starred in numerous action movies (with titles such as Santo vs. the Zombies) and in his own superhero comic book series that ran for thirty-five years. Celebrities like El Santo often gain a kind of immortality, remaining in the memories of their fans long after they die. As you read, consider why the speaker says that El Santo only "possibly" died. What makes El Santo a powerful figure even in death?

# On January 5, 1984, El Santo[1] the Wrestler Died, Possibly

## Alberto Ríos

The thing was, he could never be trusted.
He wore the silver mask even when he slept.
At his funeral as reported by all the Mexican news services
The pall bearers also put on their faces
5   Sequined masks to honor him, or so it was said.
The men in truth wore masks as much to hide from him
That he would not see who was putting him into the ground
And so get angry, get up, and come back after them
That way for which he was famous.
10  His partner el atómico pretended to think
There was no funeral at all.
He would have had to help el santo be angry
Come like the Samson running against the pillars
These men were, holding up the box
15  In which el santo was trapped;
Would have had to angle his head down, come at them
Mount them three men to a shoulder
As he ran through the middle, ducking under the casket
Bowling them down like all the other times
20  Giving el santo just a moment to breathe, get strong.
He will be missed
But one must say this in a whisper, and quickly.
One knows of the dead, of their polite habit of listening
Too much, believing what they hear, and then of their caring.

---

1. **El Santo** (ehl SAHN toh): "The Saint."

25  One knows of the dead, how it all builds up
    So that finally something must be said.
    One knows of the year in which the town of Guaymas²
    Had its first demonstration of a tape recorder.
    It confirmed only what was already known:
30  That people speak. And that the voice of the wind
    Captured finally, played back slowly
    Given its moment to say something of lasting importance
    Made only a complaint.
    If el santo were to hear of his being missed
35  He might get hold of the wind, this voice of the dead,
    And say too much, the way the best wrestlers do

---

2. **Guaymas** (GWAY mahs): town in northwestern Mexico.

         With all the yelling.
         So one will always be responsible enough only to whisper
         The best things about el santo
40       Out of concern for the crops and the sapling trees.
         This much was decided at the funeral.

         The decision to whisper was not too much.
         One had to be suspicious of this man with a mask
         Even as he reached out to shake your hand,
45       That you might be flung and bent around
         Knocked on the head and forced to say
         How glad you are to meet him, and his uncle;
         How suspicious that hand, which he always raised
         More slowly than a weightlifter's last possible push
50       As if he too were suspicious of you
         That you might at the last second
         Be the Blue Demon after all—*el demonio azul:*[3] ¡ahá!
              he recognizes you, ¡but too late! that you might
         In this last moment avoid his hand raised to shake
55       Hook the crook of your arm into his
         And flip him with a slam to a cement canvas.
         No, he could not be trusted
         And he could not trust you.
         In his last years very far from 1942
60       The year he gave his first bruise to another man
         One received as a greeting no hand from him any longer.
         A raised eyebrow, perhaps, *good morning to you,*
         Just visible through the mask on his morning walk.
         This was his greeting, one man to another, now.
65       But even then he could not be trusted
         Had not slipped with age even an inch:
         As he moved the hairy arm of his brow up and down
         Like a villain taking possession of the widow's house,
         If one quickly did not get out of his way—
70       Well, then, he kept it moving up and down, had gotten you
         Had made you imagine his eyebrow
         Making the sound of a referee's hand
         Slam beating the canvas ten times
         Telling you that you have lost.

---

3. *el demonio azul* (ehl  deh MOH nyoh  ah SOOL).

**Before You Read** In this poem, a boy named Florencio builds an "invisible wall" that shields him from the eyes of others and so allows him to make "ugly faces" without being seen. As you read, you may wonder if Florencio's wall—which is "Too beautiful to be described"—is an actual wall or an imaginary one. What do you think you would learn from living behind an "invisible" wall?

# The Lesson of Walls
## Alberto Ríos

    Florencio built a wall and told no one why.
    He was stubborn this way about things.
    Too beautiful to be described by the ill-educated
    tax assessor in this small but honorable town,
5   it was entered in no book and so did not exist
    in that way that other walls are known.
    Florencio stood behind his invisible wall
    and so quite reasonably was invisible himself
    and could do for the first time whatever he chose.
10  People came from the big cities on Sunday noons

       to see this thing that did not by its nature exist
       and Florencio, Florencio as he had always wanted
       since the early days of his troublesome schooling,
       made his five ugly faces at the faces of the people,
15     inverting his eyelids and pushing to the side his nose
       so as to look like the devil that children imagine,
       and he made sounds with his mouth to his pleasure.
       But through the years finally he grew
       bored of his invisible fame, and his mouth, or entirely
20     his face, became tired, so that it rested,
       let its weight fall, and it rolled over onto itself
       in its leisure making Florencio wrinkled and heavy.
       One morning he took a workman's hammer to his wall.
       People saw him again, and he found himself
25     drawing up his face, as one might pull up
       a stomach in front of a favorite aunt.
       He was young again, and unhappy, and happy.
       This business of the invisible,
       of a thing too beautiful for the weak
30     recreations of words and of penmanship,
       had taught Florencio who was a young fine horse of a boy
       again, why a man builds a common wall
       ugly, two bricks uneven, why he lets the paint chip.

# Gary Soto
b. 1952–    (Mexican American)

## Meet the Writer

Five years after **Gary Soto** was born in the San Joaquin Valley city of Fresno, California, his father died in a factory accident. This event affected Soto so deeply that he often refers to it in his writing. After several years, Soto's mother remarried, but the new husband was an alcoholic who had difficulty coping with the demands of everyday life. Soto yearned for the idyllic life of children he saw on television dramas, where there were no beatings or family arguments. As a below-average high school student, he was told that he would never amount to anything, and he imagined himself becoming a gardener or a farmworker.

Discovering contemporary poetry at Fresno City College changed Soto's view of the future. Edward Field and Pablo Neruda were his favorites. Although Soto's first poems were, according to him, awkward and filled with inflated language and ideas, he was determined to improve. He spent years perfecting his craft. Soto graduated with honors from California State University and received an advanced degree in creative writing at the University of California at Irvine. He published his poems in literary magazines and began his university teaching career. In 1977, he published *The Elements of San Joaquin,* a series of poems based on his often painful personal experiences. The poems also address events in the difficult lives of factory workers and farm laborers.

Despite often focusing on the Mexican American experience, Soto's work has a universal appeal. According to the scholar Raymund Paredes, "Soto establishes his acute sense of ethnicity and, simultaneously, his belief that certain emotions, values, and experiences transcend ethnic boundaries and allegiances."

Soto has also published books of poetry and fiction for young readers, including *A Fire in My Hands: A Book of Poems* (1990), in which he writes about everyday things. The celebration of the ordinary helps make his poetry immediately accessible to readers. In 1990, he published *Baseball in April,* a collection of stories about Chicano boys and girls growing up in California. It won an American Library Association Best Book for Young

Adults award. The book contains a charming but realistic story, "The No-Guitar Blues," that depicts a boy named Fausto, who finds a clever way to earn money for a guitar and learns a lesson in honesty. This story and others were anthologized in secondary school literature textbooks and extended Soto's audience. Soto has also published essays and novels, written a play called *Nerdlandia,* and made several short films. He has now left university teaching to write full time.

## Background

"The Mechanical Mind" comes from *Local News* (1993), a collection of Soto's short stories about growing up in a Mexican American neighborhood. This story showcases the humorous side of Soto's writing as he describes the attempts of a would-be mechanic to make some home repairs that will impress his parents.

The poem "Black Hair" evokes the vicarious thrill that the speaker felt when he was a boy as he watched baseball games from the bleachers. This poem uses the technique of *enjambment*—of continuing a thought from one line to the next instead of stopping or pausing with a period, dash, or comma. (Lines with this type of structure are known as run-on lines.) "History" comes from the final section of Soto's long poem *The Elements of San Joaquin.* Here the speaker focuses on personal memories that not only reflect social and economic conditions of Mexican Americans but also develop more universal themes.

**Before You Read** *Situational irony occurs when what actually happens is the opposite of what we expect. When a character encounters unexpected results in a humorous story, readers often laugh. This type of irony can also cause readers to question the author's tone, or attitude toward the character. For example, is Philip, the main character, being gently made fun of or being ridiculed? Is he being treated sympathetically or critically?*

# The Mechanical Mind
## Gary Soto

Philip Quintana discovered that he was mechanical on a hot summer day when he took a pair of pliers, climbed to the roof of his house with a boost from his younger sister, Leticia, and straightened the kinked tubing that fed water to their evaporator cooler. He opened the sides of the cooler and, peering in, studied the small greasy motor, its fan belt jumping violently as it turned the cagelike fan.

The pads were rotted, black as a diseased lung. They crumbled when he poked the pliers at them and gave off a musty smell from the years of water that had dribbled over them. Remembering the new pads stored in the garage, Philip tore the old ones out and, holding his breath, jumped off the roof. He landed with a groan but got up brushing grass from his palms. He fetched the new pads and, with the help once again of his sister, who complained that he was too heavy, Philip climbed to the roof.

"Higher, Leti," he yelled at his sister, who was trying to fling the new pads onto the roof. But Leticia was only seven and too weak to throw the pads high enough for Philip to catch them. Eventually a high school student riding by on his dirt bike stopped and flung the pads to the roof, and then Philip was able to get to work. And the work was easy. The pads were crisp as shredded wheat, and in a matter of minutes Philip, whistling away, was able to tuck them into the walls of the cooler.

"All right," he said, admiring his handiwork. He slapped his hands clean and jumped off the roof with the old pads, one in each hand. He heaved the pads into the alley and paraded into the house with his sister in tow.

"Smells good," Philip said, breathing in the smell of new cooler pads.

"Smells funny," his sister said. She stood under the vent that threw out the cool air. "It smells like when you sharpen pencils."

"Mom and Dad are gonna be surprised."

Their parents were at work, and because Philip was twelve and going into the seventh grade, he was expected to take care of his sister.

"Let's have lunch," Philip suggested. He washed his hands at the kitchen sink and made bologna-and-cheese sandwiches for his sister and for himself. They took their sandwiches, along with an orange soda to share, and sat at the kitchen table. Philip fed off his sandwich and the discovery that he was mechanically minded. Right then, as he ate, Philip got it into his head that he would look inside the telephone hanging on the wall. He ate quickly and then used a screwdriver to pop off the plastic front of the telephone.

"You're gonna get in trouble," Leticia said, her mouth full and her face greasy from the sandwich.

"No, I'm not," Philip replied. "If it breaks, I'll just fix it. I have a mechanical mind." He strummed the bunched strands of red and yellow wires, then put his ear to the receiver. The telephone still worked.

"See," he said when he dialed his best friend, Ricky, and got Ricky's mother, who answered, "*Bueno*." He hung up and said, "It ain't broke."

His curiosity satisfied, Philip replaced the face of the telephone and decided to open the back of the clock radio in his parents' bedroom. Ever since his father had knocked it over while putting a new light bulb in the lamp by the bed, the radio had hummed. Now Philip would see what was wrong. He unscrewed the back and lifted the top, discovering a simple network of circuits and wires. There were also clots of dust and a mysterious toothpick lodged inside. He blew away the dust and used the end of his T-shirt to clean the corners. He was surprised at the tiny puddles of solder and the fishline device that changed the stations. The humming miraculously stopped. Philip stood, hands on hips, feeling proud.

"See, it don't buzz no more," he said to his sister. Leticia lowered her ear to the radio. The buzzing had indeed stopped.

Perched on their parents' end table, along with the radio, was a bottle of moisturizing lotion with a pump. Philip pressed the pump, and a yellowish lotion oozed into his hand. He rubbed it into his face, some of it sticking to his eyelashes.

"The lotion works like this," Philip started. "You see the pump—it works like gravity, like when astronauts jump on the moon. You probably don't understand, Leti, because you're not mechanically minded."

Leticia looked at her brother with new respect. She had never heard talk like this. She pumped a dimple of lotion into one palm, pressed her hands together, and then rubbed it on her arms.

Next Philip unscrewed the hair dryer. He looked at the wires and the small motor encased in hard plastic. He explained to his awed sister that an electric fire was created in the motor and then air was trapped in a chamber that exploded every two or three seconds. "That's how your head heats up," he reasoned. He flicked on the hair dryer, and Leticia ran from the bathroom, her hands covering her head, screaming, "Don't burn my hair!"

Feeling more ambitious, Philip decided he would take apart the microwave oven. First he microwaved an ice cube and explained to Leticia that the waves were radar that could zap water from a stone.

"Go ahead and drink it," Philip dared Leticia as he shoved a cup of melted ice at her. Steam was rising from the near-boiling water.

"No way!" Leticia yelled. "And you better not mess with the microwave. Mom'll kill you."

But it was too late. Philip's screwdriver slipped and scraped off a piece of the imitation-wood facing. He decided to leave the microwave oven alone.

"Well, it was getting too old," he said. "Some of the radar leaked out and hurt the paint."

"Radar?" Leticia asked. "You're making this up."

"Radar heats the food," he said, feeling insulted that his mechanical mind was being doubted by a seven-year-old. "It's a proven fact. That's how astronauts heat up their grub in space."

Leticia looked up at her brother, again awed.

Then Philip remembered their television's lousy reception. He hurried to the living room with his screwdriver and studied the large, beast-like console, a gift from his grandmother, who had won it in a drawing at the bingo parlor. He turned it on and heard TV laughter as a clear picture came into view. A game show host was standing on his head.

"Is the TV upside down?" Leticia asked. Her mouth was stuffed with an Oreo cookie that blackened her front teeth.

"He's being stupid," Philip answered. "Leti, I'm going to climb the roof and adjust the antenna. I think that's the problem."

"I'm not going to help you up. You're too heavy."

"Just tell me when the picture is clear, OK?" he asked as he walked out the front door.

The afternoon heat created a mirage of water wavering on the street. On tiptoes, one hand cupped like a salute over his brow, Philip eyed the roof. The antenna, leaning slightly, stood right over the living room.

Using a ladder he had retrieved from behind the garage, Philip climbed onto the roof. He remembered his father saying that the television's reception could be adjusted by turning the antenna clockwise. Philip spit into his palms and turned the antenna, which bobbed softly as a tree branch.

"Is it better?" he yelled to Leticia.

"No," she yelled, her voice rising powerfully through the roof.

He turned it again and yelled, "How 'bout now?"

"No, it's really bad."

Sweating from the summer heat, Philip groaned and rotated the antenna, which began to shake and lean even more. "How 'bout now?"

"It's all weird."

Confused, Philip jumped off the roof. He was going to see for himself. He smashed a snail with the heel of one palm when he landed on the grass, but he didn't have time to get disgusted. It was time to put his mechanical mind to work. He went inside and saw that the television picture was a zigzag of colors. Philip watched the commercial. To him it looked like a woman was shampooing her hair with blue fire.

"It's makin' me sick," Leticia whined. She put her Oreo down on the coffee table and covered her mouth with both hands. She was getting ready to lose her sandwich and cookies—maybe even some of her breakfast.

Philip had to agree that the TV picture was sickening. He turned off the television, waited a few seconds, and then turned the set back on. The screen was still a zigzag of colors and long, frightful faces.

"Stupid thing," he scolded, pounding the television. The faces flickered but wouldn't fatten into regular human features. Philip wouldn't give up. He told Leticia, "I'm goin' to try again."

He climbed the ladder again but was having doubts. Maybe I'm not mechanically minded, he thought. He slipped on the roof and clutched at the grainy shingles so he wouldn't slide off. He got back to his feet, one knee bleeding, and leaned as he walked, as if he were trudging through a blizzard. He took the antenna in his hands and turned it clockwise, just as his father had explained.

"How is it now?" he yelled.

"I think the man is standing on his head again," Leticia yelled back.

"How 'bout now?"

"It's really bad."

"Now?"

"Everyone's orange."

Philip rotated the antenna until a clamp snapped and the antenna fell like a tree, striking the cooler and splitting the copper tubing he had repaired only an hour ago.

Philip's mouth fell open as he watched the water rush over the roof and off the eaves like a waterfall.

"It's working!" he heard his sister squeal. He could imagine her jumping up and down. "The TV is working. The guy is standing on his feet." His sister laughed and screamed through the roof, "Phil, you have a mechanical mind!"

**Before You Read** *In this poem, the speaker recalls what it was like to be an eight-year-old boy who idolizes a baseball player. What do you think the image of "black hair" might stand for, or symbolize?*

# Black Hair
## Gary Soto

At eight I was brilliant with my body.
In July, that ring of heat
We all jumped through, I sat in the bleachers
Of Romain Playground, in the lengthening
5   Shade that rose from our dirty feet.
The game before us was more than baseball.
It was a figure—Hector Moreno
Quick and hard with turned muscles,
His crouch the one I assumed before an altar
10  Of worn baseball cards, in my room.

I came here because I was Mexican, a stick
Of brown light in love with those
Who could do it—the triple and hard slide,
The gloves eating balls into double plays.
15  What could I do with 50 pounds, my shyness,
My black torch of hair, about to go out?
Father was dead, his face no longer
Hanging over the table or our sleep,
And mother was the terror of mouths
20  Twisting hurt by butter knives.

In the bleachers I was brilliant with my body,
Waving players in and stomping my feet,
Growing sweaty in the presence of white shirts.
I chewed sunflower seeds. I drank water
25  And bit my arm through the late innings.
When Hector lined balls into deep
Center, in my mind I rounded the bases
With him, my face flared, my hair lifting
Beautifully, because we were coming home
30  to the arms of brown people.

**Before You Read** *In this poem, the speaker's memories of his grandmother are a significant part of his personal history and reflect his cultural kinship with Mexican American experiences. As he describes his grandmother, he also suggests that we can have an inner life that we keep secret, even from family members, perhaps to spare them from our pain. What are the sources of the grandmother's grief?*

# History
## Gary Soto

Grandma lit the stove.
Morning sunlight
Lengthened in spears
Across the linoleum floor.
5   Wrapped in a shawl,
Her eyes small
With sleep,
She sliced papas,[1]
Pounded chiles[2]
10  With a stone
Brought from Guadalajara.[3]
        After
Grandpa left for work,
She hosed down
15  The walk her sons paved
And in the shade
Of a chinaberry,
Unearthed her
Secret cigar box
20  Of bright coins
And bills, counted them
In English,
Then in Spanish,
And buried them elsewhere.

25  Later, back
From the market,
Where no one saw her,
She pulled out
Pepper and beet, spines
30  Of asparagus
From her blouse,
Tiny chocolates

---

1. **papas** (PAH pahs): potatoes.
2. **chiles** (CHEE lehs): spicy red peppers.
3. **Guadalajara** (gwahd'l uh HAHR uh): capital of the state of Jalisco in west-central Mexico.

From under a paisley bandana,
And smiled.

35 That was the '50s,
And Grandma in her '50s,
A face streaked
From cutting grapes
And boxing plums.
40 I remember her insides
Were washed of tapeworm,
Her arms swelled into knobs
Of small growths—
Her second son
45 Dropped from a ladder
And was dust.
And yet I do not know
The sorrows
That sent her praying
50 In the dark of a closet,
The tear that fell

At night
When she touched
Loose skin
55 Of belly and breasts.
I do not know why
Her face shines
Or what goes beyond this shine,
Only the stories
60 That pulled her
From Taxco to San Joaquin,
Delano to Westside,[4]
The places
In which we all begin.

---

4. **Taxco** (TAHS koh) ... **Westside**: migrant workers come from towns such as Taxco in Mexico to work in the fields around San Joaquin, Delano, Westside, and other locations in the United States.

# Lorna Dee Cervantes

b. 1954 – (Mexican American/ Native American)

## Meet the Writer

Although **Lorna Dee Cervantes** has published only a few poetry collections, her work has brought solid critical acclaim. Her debut collection, *Emplumada,* won the American Book Award in 1982 and led critic Roberta Fernandez to call Cervantes "a poet who is on her way to becoming a major voice in American literature."

Cervantes is of Mexican and American Indian descent. Her parents required her to speak only English while she was growing up in California. Enamored at an early age with the world of books, she began reading works by Shakespeare, moved on to the Romantic poets, and was writing poetry by the age of eight. When she was a young adult, Cervantes became active in the Chicano and American Indian movements. At the same time she devoted herself to writing and publishing. She was editor and publisher of *Mango,* a literary review. Through Mango Publications, she published chapbooks of the works of Chicano writers. Currently, Cervantes is editor of the cross-cultural literary review *Red Dirt* and an associate professor of English at the University of Colorado.

Of all her contributions, however, Cervantes's poetry is the best known. In direct, precise language, she relates the complexities—political, social, and personal—of coming-of-age as a Chicana in the United States.

## Background

In 1974, Cervantes accompanied her brother to Mexico City to the *Quinto festival de los teatros chicanos.* Her brother was a member of a theater troupe from San Jose, and to expand their performance, the group asked Cervantes to read some of her poetry. Before an audience of thousands in an open-air venue, she read "Barco de refugiados" ("Refugee Ship"). This first public reading of her poetry led to the poem's publication in a Mexico City newspaper and in several journals and reviews.

**Before You Read**   *The speaker in this poem is returning to her childhood neighborhood. A freeway now runs through what was once a group of small homes with well-tended yards. In the abandoned lots below the lanes, some overgrown old gardens remain, and they offer evidence of the human history of the community. What significance do the gardens hold for the speaker? What do you think she hopes to find by returning to her old neighborhood?*

# Freeway 280
## Lorna Dee Cervantes

Las casitas[1] near the gray cannery,
nestled amid wild abrazos[2] of climbing roses
and man-high red geraniums
are gone now. The freeway conceals it
5   all beneath a raised scar.

But under the fake windsounds of the open lanes,
in the abandoned lots below, new grasses sprout,
wild mustard remembers, old gardens
come back stronger than they were,
10  trees have been left standing in their yards.
Albaricoqueros, cerezos, nogales . . .[3]
Viejitas[4] come here with paper bags to gather greens.
Espinaca, verdolagas, yerbabuena . . .[5]

---

1. **Las casitas** (lahs kah SEE tahs): the small houses.
2. **abrazos** (ah BRAH sohs): hugs; embraces.
3. **Albaricoqueros, cerezos, nogales** (ahl bah ree koh KEH rohs, seh REH sohs, noh GAH lehs): apricot trees, cherry trees, pecan trees.
4. **Viejitas** (vee eh HEE tahs): elderly ladies; dear old women.
5. **Espinaca, verdolagas, yerbabuena** (ehs pee NAH kah, vehr doh LAH gahs, yehr bah BWEH nah): spinach, purslane, peppermint.

I scramble over the wire fence
15　　that would have kept me out.
　　　Once, I wanted out, wanted the rigid lanes
　　　to take me to a place without sun,
　　　without the smell of tomatoes burning
　　　on swing shift in the greasy summer air.

20　　Maybe it's here
　　　en los campos extraños de esta ciudad[6]
　　　where I'll find it, that part of me
　　　mown under
　　　like a corpse
25　　or a loose seed.

---

6. **en los campos extraños de esta ciudad** (ehn lohs KAHM pohs ehx TRAH nyohs deh EHS tah syoo DAHD): in the strange fields of this city.

*Freeway Interchange* by Frank Romero
© Frank Romero. Courtesy of the artist.

**Before You Read**  *In just thirteen short lines, this poem captures the feeling of being caught between the two different worlds of Chicano culture and American culture. Read the poem once, and then read it a second time, noting the poet's use of similes and metaphors. What examples of figurative language do you find that give this poem its impact and richness?*

# Refugee Ship
## Lorna Dee Cervantes

Like wet cornstarch, I slide
past my grandmother's eyes. Bible
at her side, she removes her glasses.
The pudding thickens.

5   Mama raised me without language.
I'm orphaned from my Spanish name.
The words are foreign, stumbling
on my tongue. I see in the mirror
my reflection: bronzed skin, black hair.

10  I feel I am a captive
aboard the refugee ship.
The ship that will never dock.
*El barco que nunca atraca.*

**Before You Read**  In this poem, Cervantes shows both her political and her intellectual sides. Look for apparent contradictory statements, and contemplate the paradoxes these statements present. What is the speaker's political belief system? How do you think her politics have been shaped by her personal experiences?

# Poem for the Young White Man Who Asked Me How I, an Intelligent, Well-Read Person Could Believe in the War Between Races

## Lorna Dee Cervantes

In my land there are no distinctions.
The barbed wire politics of oppression
have been torn down long ago. The only reminder
of past battles, lost or won, is a slight
5   rutting in the fertile fields.

In my land
people write poems about love,
full of nothing but contented childlike syllables.
Everyone reads Russian short stories and weeps.
10  There are no boundaries.
There is no hunger, no
complicated famine or greed.

I am not a revolutionary.
I don't even like political poems.
15  Do you think I can believe in a war between races?
I can deny it. I can forget about it
when I'm safe,
living on my own continent of harmony
and home, but I am not
20  there.

I believe in revolution
because everywhere the crosses are burning,

sharp-shooting goose-steppers
   round every corner,
there are snipers in the schools . . .
25 (I know you don't believe this.
You think this is nothing
but faddish exaggeration. But they
are not shooting at you.)

I'm marked by the color of my skin.
30 The bullets are discrete and designed to kill slowly.
They are aiming at my children.
These are facts.
Let me show you my wounds: my stumbling mind, my
"excuse me" tongue, and this
35 nagging preoccupation
with the feeling of not being good enough.

These bullets bury deeper than logic.
Racism is not intellectual.
I can not reason these scars away.

40 Outside my door
there is a real enemy
who hates me.

I am a poet
who yearns to dance on rooftops,
45 to whisper delicate lines about joy
and the blessings of human understanding.
I try. I go to my land, my tower of words and
bolt the door, but the typewriter doesn't fade out
the sounds of blasting and muffled outrage.
50 My own days bring me slaps on the face.
Every day I am deluged with reminders
that this is not
my land

and this is my land.

55 I do not believe in the war between races

but in this country
there is war.

# Sandra Cisneros
b. 1954– (Chicana)

## Meet the Writer

Poet, fiction writer, teacher, and essayist **Sandra Cisneros** burst onto the literary scene in 1983 with the publication of *The House on Mango Street,* a work that has been widely celebrated for its fresh approach to issues such as cultural identification, self-discovery, and gender roles. The book, a loosely structured collection of vignettes sometimes referred to as "prose poetry," has defied classification. Whether it is considered a novel, a short story collection, or an autobiography, however, there is no denying the impact of *The House on Mango Street*. It received the American Book Award and the Before Columbus Foundation American Book Award, became a bestseller, has been reprinted numerous times, and has taken its place as required reading for courses in ethnic and gender studies.

*The House on Mango Street* follows the development of a girl named Esperanza as she navigates the conflicts associated with coming-of-age as a Mexican American female in a working-class Chicago neighborhood in the 1960s. In her unique lyrical style, Cisneros brings Esperanza and her cross-cultural world to light for the reader and explores the tensions that arise for young minority women who resist the limitations of traditional roles.

Cisneros's works are deeply influenced by the struggles of her childhood and adolescence. She was born into a lower-working-class family in Chicago in 1954. Her father was Mexican, and her mother was Chicana. As a result of her father's bouts with homesickness, the family traveled back and forth to Mexico frequently. They would end up in a different apartment in a different ghetto neighborhood each time they returned to Chicago, and thus Cisneros never felt settled as a child. The family did finally manage to buy a house, but a disappointed Cisneros found the home ugly and shabby. Her longing for a home she could be proud of surfaces in *The House on Mango Street.*

The only girl among seven siblings, Cisneros felt dominated by her brothers and father. Pressured to assume a traditional female role, she learned instead to make herself heard and to become independent. Her mother encouraged Cisneros by supporting her educational endeavors over her domestic ones and by repeatedly urging her to learn to take care of herself. It is no coincidence, then, that so many of Cisneros's heroines dream of self-sufficiency, economic independence, and freedom from the restraints of traditional gender-role expectations.

Although she is best known for *The House on Mango Street,* Cisneros has also published several other major works, including the poetry collections *My Wicked Wicked Ways* and *Loose Woman* and the short story collection *Woman Hollering Creek and Other Stories.* Her most recent full-length contribution is *Caramelo,* an autobiographical novel that took her nine years to write. In *Caramelo,* the narrator and protagonist, fourteen-year-old Lala, is traveling with her family by car from Chicago to her grandmother's house in Mexico City. In a rich narrative that alternates between past and present, Lala considers her family history and cultural heritage and attempts to reconcile them with her need to assert herself as an individual.

Cisneros's unique form of prose, which maintains both the musical qualities of poetry and the impact of fiction, has been lauded for its ability to transcend genre. Through her vivid language, lively and realistic bilingual dialogue, colorful characterizations, and descriptions of life in Latin American communities, Cisneros has met with both critical and popular success. In fact, this innovative writer is one of the most visible and influential Chicanas in mainstream American literature today.

## Background

The poems "Six Brothers" and "Traficante" are from the collection *My Wicked Wicked Ways.* Published in 1987, this collection of sixty poems is perhaps Cisneros's most widely read work in verse. The book contains four parts. In the first two, Cisneros describes, in radiant and precise language, the Latina community that has become such a part of her identity. The poems in the second two parts take on a more personal tone as the poet explores her relationships with men, reflecting on how she has treated the men in her life and how they have treated her.

**Before You Read** This poem is inspired by the fairy tale "The Six Swans" by the Brothers Grimm. In the tale, a spell cast on six brothers turns them all into swans. In order to restore the brothers to their human forms, their sister must keep a six-year vow of silence and weave six shirts out of thistle. When the brothers transform back into men, the youngest brother discovers he has a swan's wing instead of a left arm; his sister had woven all the shirts but had not completed the left sleeve of the final shirt.

Like many of Cisneros's poems, this one has an autobiographical element. Why do you think the poet compares her six brothers to the brothers in the fairy tale? What does this comparison reveal about her relationship with her brothers?

# Six Brothers
## Sandra Cisneros

*In Grimm's tale* The Six Swans *a sister keeps a six-year silence and weaves six thistle shirts to break the spell that has changed her brothers into swans. She weaves all but the left sleeve of the final shirt, and when the brothers are changed back into men, the youngest lacks only his left arm and has in its place a swan's wing.*

In Spanish our name means swan.
A great past—castles maybe
or a Sahara city,
but more likely
5   a name that stuck
to a barefoot boy
herding the dusty flock
down the bright road.

We'll never know.
10   Great-grandparents might
but family likes to keep to silence—
perhaps with reason
though we don't need far back to go.
On our father's side we have a cousin,
15   second, but cousin nonetheless,
who shot someone, his wife I think.
And on the other hand, there's
mother's brother who shot himself.

Then there's us—
20   seven ways to make the name or break it.
Our father has it planned:
oldest, you're doctor,
second, administration,
me, he shrugs, you should've been reporting weather,
25   next, musician,
athlete,
genius,

and youngest—well,
you'll take the business over.

30  You six a team
    keeping to the master plan,
    the lovely motion of tradition.
    Appearances are everything.
    We live for each other's expectations.
35  Brothers, it is so hard to keep up with you.
    I've got the bad blood in me I think,

the mad uncle, the bit of the bullet.

Ask me anything.
Six thistle shirts. Keep a vow of silence.
40  I'll do it. But I'm earthbound
    always in my admiration.
    My six brothers, graceful, strong.
    Except for you, little one-winged,
    finding it as difficult as me
45  to keep the good name clean.

**Before You Read** *Through figurative language that is at times startling, "Traficante" directly and mercilessly conveys the pain of a childhood trauma. As you read, notice the patterns of imagery; the figurative comparisons; and the bald, direct statements of actions. What effects do these techniques have on you as a reader? What emotions do they elicit, and why?*

# Traficante°

## Sandra Cisneros
*for Dennis*

Pink like a starfish's belly
or a newborn rat,
she hid the infected hand
for some time
5  before they noticed.
First the skin had been smooth
as the left hand.
Then the fence
had poked through,
10  a tiny slit, the mouth of a small fish.
A crispy scab had stitched it to a pucker
but this was picked on until the wound
turned a purple-pink
and gradually became swollen
15  and hurt to the touch.
She liked to draw the fat hand
into her sleeve,
keep it hiding there,
a fish in its cave.
20  Sometimes it would come out
and she would talk to it.

°**traficante** (trah fee KAHN teh): merchant; trader.

At school the teacher
pulled the hand out suddenly
and the child yelped.
25  The mother took her
to Traficante's Drugs
where the doctor had an office
behind the case of eyeglasses
all colors and different styles.
30  He asked to see the hand.
The fish poked out
from the cuff of a nubby sleeve,
darted back in, then was out again
and placed upon the table
35  beneath the bright lamp.
One finger pressed its side
and she whimpered.
The doctor took down from the shelf
the medical encyclopedia, vol. 2,
40  and holding her by the wrist
said turn around.
Mrs. Ortiz was having a prescription filled
for Reynaldo's fever and was asking
how much when the book came down.

# Rosario Morales
b. 1930–
# Aurora Levins Morales
b. 1954–   (Puerto Rican American)

## Meet the Writers

Writer, socialist, and antiwar activist **Rosario Morales** was born to Russian Jews who had immigrated to Puerto Rico. The family moved to New York when she was young. Morales and her husband lived for a while in Puerto Rico but eventually returned to the United States. In 1986, she published *Getting Home Alive,* a multigenre collection written in collaboration with her daughter.

The daughter in this team is **Aurora Levins Morales,** a poet and prose writer. Levins Morales moved to the United States with her parents when she was in her early teens. The family lived in urban Chicago and then in rural New Hampshire. In the late 1970s, Levins Morales moved to the San Francisco Bay area, where she was surrounded by political radicalism.

Levins Morales has been influenced by feminist writers such as Alice Walker and other important Latin American writers such as Pablo Neruda. With these writers and her Puerto Rican–Jewish heritage as guides, Levins Morales has used her poet's voice to bring the Latina experience to light and to explore her own identity as a woman. In addition to *Getting Home Alive,* she has published the collections *Remedios: Stories of Earth and Iron from the History of Puertorriquenas* and *Medicine Stories: History, Culture and the Politics of Integrity.*

## Background

*Getting Home Alive* is a collection of short stories, essays, poems, and journal entries unique for its dual voice. Both mother and daughter are passionate about social issues and serious about illuminating their personal histories. Their collaboration is a lyrical exploration of everything from grandmothers to religion and from civil rights to the meaning of "home."

**Before You Read** *Having a background of several diverse cultures has its challenges and rewards. In the following poem, repetition and sensory images are used to convey the sense of alienation, or not belonging, that can come from being an immigrant with roots in several countries. As you read, consider the other side of the coin—the vast traditions and experiences that serve to create a richly unique individual. Notice the change in the next-to-last stanza from the pronoun "I" to the pronoun "we." What is the significance of this shift?*

# Ending Poem
## Rosario Morales *and* Aurora Levins Morales

I am what I am.
*A child of the Americas.*
A light-skinned mestiza[1] of the Caribbean.
*A child of many diaspora,[2] born into this continent at a crossroads.*
5   I am Puerto Rican. I am U.S. American.
*I am New York Manhattan and the Bronx.*
A mountain-born, country-bred, homegrown jíbara[3] child,
*up from the shtetl,[4] a California Puerto Rican Jew.*
A product of the New York ghettos I have never known.
10  *I am an immigrant*
and the daughter and granddaughter of immigrants.
*We didn't know our forbears' names with a certainty.*
They aren't written anywhere.
*First names only, or mija, negra, ne, honey, sugar, dear.*

15  I come from the dirt where the cane was grown.
*My people didn't go to dinner parties. They weren't invited.*
I am caribeña,[5] island grown.

---

1. **mestiza:** a female of mixed race, especially a Latina with Spanish or Portuguese and American Indian ancestors.
2. **diaspora:** a scattering of people with the same origin or background; especially Jews.
3. **jíbara:** a peasant or farmer, especially one who is Puerto Rican.
4. **shtetl:** a type of Jewish community that formerly existed in eastern Europe or Russia.
5. **caribeña:** a female from the Caribbean islands.

*Spanish is in my flesh, ripples from my tongue, lodges in my hips,*
the language of garlic and mangoes.
20 *Boricua.[6] As Boricuas come from the isle of Manhattan.*
I am of latinoamerica, rooted in the history of my continent.
*I speak from that body. Just brown and pink and full of drums inside.*

I am not African.
*Africa waters the roots of my tree, but I cannot return.*

25 I am not Taína.[7]
*I am a late leaf of that ancient tree,*
and my roots reach into the soil of two Americas.
*Taíno is in me, but there is no way back.*

I am not European, though I have dreamt of those cities.
30 *Each plate is different,*
wood, clay, papier mâché, metal, basketry, a leaf, a coconut shell.
*Europe lives in me but I have no home there.*

The table has a cloth woven by one, dyed by another,
*embroidered by another still.*
35 I am a child of many mothers.
*They have kept it all going*
All the civilizations erected on their backs.
*All the dinner parties given with their labor.*

We are new.
40 *They gave us life, kept us going,*
brought us to where we are.
*Born at a crossroads.*
Come, lay that dishcloth down. Eat, dear, eat.
*History made us.*
45 We will not eat ourselves up inside anymore.

*And we are whole.*

---

6. **Boricua:** a female from Puerto Rico.
7. **Taína:** a female Taíno, peoples who originally inhabited the Caribbean islands.

# Martín Espada
b. 1957– (Puerto Rican American)

## Meet the Writer

**Martín Espada** (mahr TEEN ehs PAH dah), a professor in the Department of English at the University of Massachusetts in Amherst, has worked as an attorney, a gas station attendant, a bouncer, and a bindery worker in a printing plant. He says he discovered poetry in tenth grade. He and his classmates were assigned to produce an issue of a magazine. By the time the magazine reached him, all that was left for him to do was to write a poem. To avoid failing English again, Espada sat down and wrote a poem about rain, creating his first metaphor: "tiny silver hammers pounding the earth." He says, "I discovered something . . . that day. I discovered that I loved words. I loved slamming words into each other and watching them spin around the room."

Espada was born in Brooklyn, New York. Much of his writing is based on his Puerto Rican heritage and his work experiences. He writes about immigrants, fruit pickers, and cleaning crews—the downtrodden victims of oppression. Espada believes that art must reflect our efforts to obtain social and political justice.

## Background

Espada's first collection of poetry, *The Immigrant Iceboy's Bolero* (1982), was illustrated with photographs taken by his father, Frank Espada. His second collection, *Trumpets from the Island of Their Eviction,* appeared in 1987. In it, Espada's characters are cultural heroes who exemplify Puerto Ricans who have left their original land. *Imagine the Angels of Bread* (1996) won an American Book Award.

*Alabanza: New and Selected Poems, 1982–2002* was named an American Library Association Notable Book of the Year. The word *alabanza* means "praise" in Spanish. The poems in this collection celebrate persons and objects not often praised in literature, such as crusty rice and bindery workers. Espada's eighth collection of poetry, *The Republic of Poetry,* was published in 2006.

**Before You Read**   *The word* pegao *is the Puerto Rican Spanish word for "crusty rice at the bottom of the pot." How does Espada use humor to make a serious comment on the experience of Puerto Ricans?*

# Pegao
## Martín Espada

We Puerto Ricans say
that the hard rice
stuck to the bottom
of the pot
5   is a delicacy.
We scrape
with the spoon
like kitchen archaeologists.

Maybe it's the cost of rice.
10   Maybe we see the rice
stuck to the bottom
of the pot
as a metaphor.
Or maybe
15   we have learned to chew
the ow in pegao.

**Before You Read**   *In this poem, Espada draws on his experiences as a bindery worker in a printing plant. What does the poem suggest is the price paid for his success as a law student?*

# Who Burns for the Perfection of Paper
## Martín Espada

At sixteen, I worked after high school hours
at a printing plant
that manufactured legal pads:
Yellow paper
5   stacked seven feet high
and leaning
as I slipped cardboard

       between the pages,
       then brushed red glue
10    up and down the stack.
       No gloves: fingertips required
       for the perfection of paper,
       smoothing the exact rectangle.
       Sluggish by 9 P.M., the hands
15    would slide along suddenly sharp paper,
       and gather slits thinner than the crevices
       of the skin, hidden.
       Then the glue would sting,
       hands oozing
20    till both palms burned
       at the punchclock.

       Ten years later, in law school,
       I knew that every legal pad
       was glued with the sting of hidden cuts,
25    that every open lawbook
       was a pair of hands
       upturned and burning.

**Before You Read**   *The* guayabera, *which originated in Cuba, is a light sport shirt generally worn outside the pants. What conflicts does the speaker have with the teacher's request? What is the speaker's tone in this poem?*

# My Native Costume
## Martín Espada

When you come to visit,
said a teacher
from the suburban school,
don't forget to wear
5   your native costume.

But I'm a lawyer,
I said.
My native costume
is a pinstriped suit.

10   You know, the teacher said,
a Puerto Rican costume.

Like a guayabera? The shirt? I said.
But it's February.

The children want to see
15   a native costume,
the teacher said.

So I went
to the suburban school,
embroidered guayabera
20   short-sleeved shirt
over a turtleneck,
and said, Look kids,
cultural adaptation.

**Before You Read**  The colibrí, or hummingbird, is a sacred symbol to the Taíno people because the bird is a pollinator and symbolizes the rebirth of the Taíno nation. The poem is based on an actual experience Espada and his wife had on their honeymoon, when a frantic hummingbird trapped in a hallway tried to escape. To what does the author compare the hummingbird's ordeal? How might that comparison be related to the history of the region?

# Colibrí[1]
## Martín Espada

*for Katherine, one year later*

In Jayuya,[2]
the lizards scatter
like a fleet of green canoes
before the invader.
5   The Spanish conquered
with iron and words:
"Taíno" for the people who took life
from the plátanos in the trees,
those multiple green fingers
10  curling around unseen spears,
who left the rock carvings[3]
of eyes and mouths
in perfect circles of amazement.

So the hummingbird
15  was christened "colibrí."
Now the colibrí
darts and bangs
between the white walls
of the hacienda,
20  a racing Taíno heart
frantic as if hearing
the bellowing god of gunpowder
for the first time.

The colibrí
25  becomes pure stillness,
seized in the paralysis
of the prey,
when your hands
cup the bird
30  and lift him
through the red shutters
of the window,
where he disappears
into a paradise of sky,
35  a nightfall of singing frogs.

If only history
were like your hands.

---

1. **Colibrí** (coh lee BREE): a hummingbird.
2. **Jayuya:** the setting of a tourist attraction in Puerto Rico, once occupied by the Taíno people. It is known for its woodcarvers.
3. **rock carvings:** Among Puerto Rican tourist attractions is "La piedra escrita," a large stone in a river, which was carved by the Taíno people.

# Diana García
**b. 1960–**  (Mexican American)

## Meet the Writer

**Diana García** is not only a short story writer but also a distinguished poet, professor, and social activist. In all her roles, García shines as she gives a voice to the plight of less fortunate individuals and offers meaningful service to her community.

Perhaps García's most notable achievement is the American Book Award she won in 2001 for *When Living Was a Labor Camp,* a collection of poems telling the stories of migrant farmworkers, or *campesinos.* García, who was born in a migrant labor camp in the San Joaquin Valley of California, is close to the subject matter. The poems in the collection have gained critical acclaim for their bold use of sensory language and their ability to transport the reader into the lives of the workers. Commenting on how it felt to win the American Book Award, García said, "My first thought when my publisher called was a deep sense of gratitude that the plight of farm workers had been recognized. I keep getting this sense that the book won the award, not me, that the committee heard all the voices in the book."

A professor at California State University, Monterey Bay (CSUMB), García teaches creative writing and communications. Through the Service Learning Institute at CSUMB, she has been able to combine teaching and social activism. For instance, in one of her courses, students offered service to their local migrant communities and then wrote poetry relating to the effects of pesticide use on human health.

## Background

Mudflows are common in arid areas like deserts (where this story takes place); when hillsides become oversaturated with water, mudslides are almost inevitable in such areas. California, Diana García's home state, has suffered more than its share of devastating mudflows, even on the hillsides of large cities like Los Angeles. Mudflows can be dangerously fast, moving at thirty miles per hour. (Mudflows caused by volcanic eruptions have been measured at ninety miles per hour.)

This story involves a mudflow, but as you read, you'll note that *this* mudflow doesn't precisely follow scientific rules—or even the rules of logic.

**Before You Read**  The main character in this story is Amparo, a forty-five-year-old woman living in an abandoned old house in the middle of nowhere. With just two exceptions, the other characters with whom Amparo interacts are nonhuman entities—a mudflow, the house, the coyotes, the hills, and the sun. She speaks to these other "characters" and even seems to form a bond with a few of them.

As you read, consider Amparo's past, motivations, and state of mind. What do you think has led her to take up residence in this place and choose to stay? Why is she on disability income, and what might have happened to her son and ex-husband?

# The Flat of the Land

## Diana García

From the roof of her house, Amparo gauged the tilt of the old water tower with the name "Pixley" faintly outlined on the side. It was hard to say how long the tower would still be visible: another week or two, depending on the mud's flow. Not that a missing tower would make any difference in a place where the only off-ramp was at least five miles west and the combination store and restaurant with its dusty lunch counter was on the abandoned side of old Highway 99. Maybe the girl with the blonde hair and freckles who worked at the store or the girl's mother or grandmother would notice when Amparo stopped coming in for an occasional skinny hamburger and greasy fries.

The first time the mud caught Amparo's attention, it looked like a harmless bubble in the ground. It was an April morning, and she'd been hanging the wash out to dry on the clothesline behind her house. She had scarcely paid attention when the mud burped at her, distracted at the time by the breeze whipping the clothes on the line and thinking that the shadowy clouds overhead might contain some rain.

That had been almost six months ago. Amparo turned and studied the flat expanse to the east and the Sequoia foothills in the distance. At the point where the mud had first appeared, the bubble had grown to the size of a pond. Here the land sank into itself and followed the outline of some long-ago river, a few scattered cottonwoods the only clues to its crumbled banks. From this source, the mud had developed an easterly flow that skirted the stand of cottonwoods. Amparo wondered why the mud had left the trees untouched.

On the land next to hers, bulldozers had carved foundations for a style of house popular forty years earlier. From her roof, the excavations looked like archaeological digs. By the time Amparo moved here, no one was left who could tell her why the development had been abandoned. All that remained of the original site was the water tower and the water main to her house. The only other trace of water was the mud; how else would the mud keep rising and spreading the way it did?

When the dimple of mud turned into a smile and then a six-inch wide crevice that threatened to swallow her clothesline, Amparo began to sense a possible threat to her hideaway. Up until now, she had kept her brothers and parents at bay by giving them a Fresno post office address. She visited them as often as twice a month so that they wouldn't press her for more information about where or how she was living. They seemed satisfied knowing she was living alone and that her disability income was more than adequate for all her needs. She never talked about her son or her former husband, so they assumed she had laid those memories to rest. That damn mud, though, might spoil everything. At first she talked to it.

"What do you think you're doing? You have no business out here in this weather. The sun will bake you before the summer is over and then you'll have done all this work for nothing." When the sun didn't bake the oozing crack to a dry, light finish, she started asking, "Why don't you go downhill?"—indicating a direction opposite her house—"It's much easier than going uphill." The crack widened, its banks thickening and hardening, creating an impenetrable barrier within a few days' exposure to the sun.

Amparo trained herself not to think about the spreading mud. She listened to the Mexican stations on the radio. At night, she'd lie in bed and pretend the coyotes were talking to her instead of to the foothills and the jack rabbits. She'd answer, "Yes, manzanita[1] does make the best cover," and, "No, the easiest way to get yourself killed is expose yourself." She rarely turned the lights on after dark, afraid someone might see the glow and learn she had discovered the house.

The house was no secret, really. A developer had built the two-story structure as a marketing device and then abandoned it as too expensive: adobe walls like those of a Pueblo ruin and energy supplied by an underground cable and a solar-powered generator. At one time, someone else must have lived here. Perhaps it had been a retired construction worker, some laborer or cement finisher destined to end his days sweeping dust from the compacted dirt floors and enjoying the cool feel of the dark tan walls, secure in the knowledge that no one would look for him here—no former wives or children with grandchildren to bother him.

Now it was Amparo's house. She washed her clothes in a wringer-washer like the one her mother had taught her to use when she was a little girl, like the one she had used when her son was born, the one in which she had washed his diapers. She admired, as if they were someone else's, the bookshelves carved into the sixteen-inch-thick walls of the living room and bedroom. When she felt the need for exercise, she'd run up and down the steps to the second floor loft and master bedroom, chanting "upstairs and downstairs and in my lady's chamber." And, of course, there was the six-inch plumbing throughout, wide enough to handle anything, even a pot of scorched beans.

Not that she ate much these days. She still enjoyed her plain Cream of Wheat for breakfast every morning—her *atole*,[2] she called it. For lunch and light snacks she had learned to eat seasonally, buying all her produce at the roadside stands along old Highway 99. There were almonds and raisins year-round; strawberries, peaches, tomatoes, and peppers during the summer. By early May she was tired of apples and oranges but with June came early corn and sometimes a melon or two. Dinner was always corn tortillas, beans, and rice. She made a pot of beans and another of rice every Sunday. Sometimes she'd toss some bits of chicken or beef along with a handful of garbanzos, some chopped onion, and cilantro into the steaming

---

1. **manzanita** (man suh NEET uh): a shrub or small tree in the heath family, found in the western United States.

2. **atole** (ah TOH leh): thin porridge or drink made with corn flour.

rice. Her biggest craving was grease; once or twice a month she'd drive to Pixley for a hamburger and fries at the store's lunch counter.

The day the mud licked the left front tire of her old white Studebaker Lark station wagon, Amparo drove to the store for a "grease bomb"—that's what she called the hamburgers. It was the first official day of summer. By then, the mud-filled crevice was about twenty yards long, six inches wide, and about a foot-and-a-half deep. That day at the lunch counter she'd asked the young girl's mother, "Did they used to have a mud bath around here that you know of?"

"What do you mean, mud bath?" the woman had answered, poking a few loose strands of dark brown hair underneath one of the pink foam rollers on her head. At least the rollers worked better than the torn hair net the woman usually wore. "You mean the hot springs?"

Amparo checked her fries for stray hairs before she dipped them in ketchup. She knew about the dots on the map called Fountain Springs, California Hot Springs, and Miracle Springs. No water at any of them. "No, not water. Mud. Did they ever have mud baths over by the old water tower?" Amparo asked, trying not to sound too curious.

"No, no mud. This is a desert." The woman had a droning voice, like an old record player at slow speed. "The only water for mud would have to come from the creeks. We haven't had enough water for the creeks to run in almost ten years."

The woman's mother had interrupted, "The last time I saw the Chocolate River—that's the old riverbed over by your house—was when I was still a girl at home. That was about seventy years ago when the flash flood tore out the old road right after the war." Almost as an afterthought the old woman had added, "You know, a long time ago, when my grandmother's grandmother came here from Illinois, it was all tule[3] marshland like Three Rivers."

That was when Amparo began parking her Studebaker on the side of the house away from the cottonwoods.

After the mud ate the clothesline and then the smallest manzanita bush, the one farthest from the house, Amparo consoled herself with the thought that at least the muddy flow didn't interfere with her sewer line. By the Fourth of July, when the crevice reached a foot wide and the dried banks on each side made a slick sidewalk cooler than the surrounding earth, she had made some allowances for its existence. That night, she lit sparklers in the starlight. She jumped and danced from bank to bank, playing a cheery game, a combination of hopscotch and jump rope, remembering incantatory lyrics from first grade.

*Mother, Mother, I am sick.*
*Call the doctor, quick, quick, quick.*
*In comes the doctor, in comes the nurse,*
*In comes the lady with the alligator purse.*
*Out goes the doctor, out goes the nurse,*
*Out goes the lady with the alligator purse.*

In the morning, the crevice was fifty yards long—Amparo estimated this from the thirty-foot foundations on each side of her lot—and anywhere from three to four feet deep, depending on where she pushed an old mop handle into the ground. Much more than four feet deep and Amparo wouldn't have anything long enough to measure the depth. As it was, when she pushed the mop handle into the section closest to the biggest manzanita bush, her fingers could touch the slowly rising mud.

---

3. **tule** (TOO lee): a kind of marsh plant found in the southwestern United States.

It was such fine, clean mud—no worms or sharp rocks. "How would you like some roses, an old grandiflora, a wine- or cinnamon-scented bush? Would you like that? I could plant a row on each side of the front yard, use some of your mud for fertilizer. I bet you'd make good fertilizer?" This last a question. It was hard to say what the mud wanted.

On July 15, her forty-fifth birthday, Amparo washed her bathtub and sprayed it with rosewater. When the sun was at its highest, she started dragging buckets of warm mud to the tub, climbing the stairs to the master bathroom, careful not to slosh too much onto the floor. Not that it mattered. Once the mud set, it was hard to tell where the original dirt floor ended and the new layer of mud began.

Amparo patted the mud to remove any air pockets, then took off all her clothes. She combed her long, still mostly black hair until it sparked with static electricity. Carefully she packed mud into her hair, arranged the entire mass into a turban on top of her head. Then she delicately dipped her right toes into the mud. Thick, lukewarm liquid squeezed between her toes. She lowered herself into the tub and let the mud ooze above her knees, her belly button. Eyes closed, she finally sank to her chest and leaned her head against the back of the tub.

She thrilled to the sensation, like that of someone holding her without making contact. It was as if she had lost half her body weight. She felt an unnatural buoyancy, an inability to touch the very bottom of the tub. With smooth, even strokes, she massaged a thick layer of mud on her face and behind her ears.

She felt her skin tighten as the mud dried. When the mud grew cooler than her body, she pulled the plug and watched the mud make its way down the drain in small gulps. Then she padded downstairs, mud dribbling in small clumps wherever she stepped too hard.

Amparo sat outside in the late afternoon sun, her legs stretched in front of her, the heat baking her body mask to a glossy finish. She studied the effect in the hand mirror. As long as she kept her body perfectly still, she looked like an ancient statue. All the wrinkles were gone, the deep lines around her eyes and forehead, the cellulite. And her back pain was gone.

Amparo stretched from her waist to touch her toes. Where the mud started to crack, she carefully peeled it away, conscious of the adhesive-like grip that caused her skin to redden wherever there was too much hair. Her skin had the firm smoothness of a ripened peach fresh from the tree. The pores on her nose had disappeared and her hair shone in the sunlight. She remembered how Sammy, her ex-husband, used to tell her that the first time he spotted her running her old black German shepherd in the park, the sun made her black-brown hair look like a comet. "How perfectly you've caught me," she told the mud, its slick surface stamped with the lines of her body. That night she fed the mud her leftover beans and rice.

In early August she spotted a possible hairline crack just to the right of the main crevice. She brushed the line with a manzanita branch and it seemed to go away. It was hard to say. By late August, when the hairline crack had lengthened to form a thin leg to a V, she was sure. This leg was aimed at the opposite corner of her house, and like the first leg, it pointed in the same direction. "Ahh, you want the foothills," she whispered.

At first, the mud's flow was indiscernible unless she sat for several minutes, her eyes focused on a mark she'd scratch into the still-damp sides of the widening cracks. Another trick she used to measure the mud's movement was to make little paper boats from old Christmas wrapping paper and watch them gently float and bob on the barely moving surface. By early October the mud flow was obvious—a steady movement east despite the three-year drought.

When she first found the house three years ago, its biggest attraction had been the roof, the easy access along the molded staircase that climbed in profile up the east wall of her second-floor bedroom to the roof escape. Amparo had always thought she would like to live in a house with a hidden staircase to some underground study; now she knew that her real dream had always been of such a skylight escape. She enjoyed climbing the stairs in the morning, sliding the double-construction skylights open. She'd clamber over the lip of the stairs and eat her *atole* on the roof, watching the day take hold. It was as if the house had been designed just for her.

Now she made the roof her lookout post; the mud would need guidance. "Foothills to the east, say 15 miles, straight flat land, hardly any sage," she announced her first day on the job. She listened to the mud's distinctive sound. She could hear it humming and swallowing, no longer baffled by its inability to lay claim to the house. There were no windows or doors on the east side of the first floor of the house. The mud waited at the weep holes and joints, sensitive to the loosening of a corner as the house gave ground.

The coyotes' yips and cries grew more distinct. She counted how long it took their echoes to reach her, much as she would count the space between a thunderclap and a lightning flash. When they lurked too long she belittled them, smirking at their mangy coats, "Try a little mud in your fur. You'll kill a few fleas that way, I assure you," and "I once had a jacket with a red fox fur." She relented when they turned tail and skulked away. The next night she left a pile of freshly grilled chicken breasts seasoned with rosemary.

On the day of the harvest moon, Amparo drove to the Fruit Patch produce stand and bought the last of the zucchini, now over a foot long and four inches in diameter. She chose a pumpkin the size of her head, as well as a garland of dried red New Mexico chili pods and a selection of Indian corn tied with twine.

At sunset, Amparo climbed to the roof and arranged the offerings on favorite plates. She poured a mixture of *atole* topped with raisins and walnuts in a mixing bowl. When the moon was full overhead, she placed the plates and bowl in a star-shaped pattern, one for her head, the others for her hands and feet. Then she lay on the roof enjoying the cool breeze overhead.

To the mud she tossed an inconsequential aside. "Isn't it nice not to have to worry about cleaning and cooking and washing and worrying about someone all the time?" When the mud withdrew like a sulky child and refused to respond to her chatter, she confessed, "Yes, I give you credit for going uphill away from the riverbed. I never would have thought of that."

To the house she offered soothing counsel. "We'll ride it out together, the two of us. You'll see. I'll take good care of you." The mud hiccupped and poured a thick sheen over the lot. Amparo imagined how the land might have looked as an inland sea. "Just think of all that water." She felt the house shiver.

In Amparo's dreams that night, a stand of cottonwoods turned into a grove of ancient trees. Where a clothesline once twirled like a giant umbrella, clumps of tule rushes danced in the surge of a waxing moon. In the distance, the flat roof of a house bobbed above the flat of the land that stretched toward the foothills.

And as she slept, the mud came close and caressed the base of the house. It told of the excitement of heat lightning cast on the horizon on summer evenings; of the tenderness of misty sighs heaved from a roiled earth on snow-swept mornings; of a world best viewed from a height of 1500 feet.

In turn, the house recounted the thrill of water tumbling over a bed of smooth-ground gravel; of air so cold in autumn that spawning salmon gasped when they broke the surface.

House and mud lingered over shared secrets, reveling in this moment of discovery. The house openly admired the reflection of stars on the moist surface of the mud. In turn, the mud thrilled to the crusted surface of the house, each trowel-stroke another mystery to be explored.

In the predawn hours, Amparo awoke to the lurch of the house lifting and settling on a wide river of mud. House and mud paused as she clambered to the roof. They allowed her time to adjust her stance to the house's uncommon roll, then the house made a slow 180-degree turn from the old highway to the foothills.

Like a swimmer learning a new stroke, the house muscled through the mud, at first tentatively, then with increased fluidity. Loose pieces of masonry scattered as the house and mud picked up speed. The mud wash kicked up nearly one story high, flattening sage and manzanita.

"We're coming, we're coming, it won't be long before we're there," Amparo shouted to the hills. To the sun she complained, "We need some light over here. How do you expect us to see where we're going if you wait until six o'clock to get up?" To the house and mud she instructed, "Faster, go faster, we're almost there! Don't worry about me." As they drew closer, a cleft in the foothills parted, and house, mud, woman squeezed through in an eruption of closely contained forms, aiming for the tree-laced meadow above.

Through the temporary opening could be seen air so clear the sky looked like cut crystal, a passage so smooth that a traveler could press one hand against each side and never feel the moment of contact.

# Acknowledgments

For permission to reprint copyrighted material, grateful acknowledgment is made to the following sources:

**Isabel Allende:** From "Writing As an Act of Hope" by Isabel Allende from *Paths of Resistance: The Art and Craft of the Political Novel,* edited by William Zinsser. Copyright © 1989 by Isabel Allende. Published by Houghton Mifflin, 1989.

**Arte Público Press, University of Houston, Houston, TX:** "Emily Dickinson" (English and Spanish version) and "Mexico/México" (English and Spanish version) from *Palabras de Mediodía/Noon Words* by Lucha Corpi, translated by Catherine Rodríguez-Nieto. Copyright © 1980 by Lucha Corpi and Catherine Rodríguez-Nieto. "Niña" by Margarita Engle from *Short Fiction by Hispanic Writers of the United States,* edited by Nicolás Kanellos. Copyright © 1993 by Arte Público Press, University of Houston, Houston, TX. "Colibrí" by Martín Espada from *The Americas Review,* vol. 18, Summer 1990, no. 2. Copyright © 1990 by Martín Espada. "Birthday" by Dagoberto Gilb from *The Americas Review,* vol. 15, 1987, no. 2. Copyright © 1987 by Dagoberto Gilb. "Words and Palabras" by Rolando Hinojosa-Smith from *The Americas Review,* vol. 24, Fall/Winter 1996, nos. 3–4. Copyright © 1998 by Arte Público Press, University of Houston, Houston, TX. "In the Family" by María Elena Llano, translated by Beatriz Teleki from *Short Stories by Latin American Women: The Magic and the Real,* edited by Celia Correas de Zapata. Copyright © 1990 by Arte Público Press, University of Houston, Houston, TX. "Graduation Morning" and "Mi Madre" from *Chants* by Pat Mora. Copyright © 1984 by Pat Mora. "Arte Popular" from *Communion* by Pat Mora. Copyright © 1991 by Pat Mora. "Peruvian Child" from *My Own True Name: New and Selected Poems for Young Adults, 1984–1999* by Pat Mora. Copyright © 2000 by Pat Mora. "Breaking Piñatas" by Alberto Ríos from *The Americas Review,* vol. 24, Fall/Winter 1996, nos. 3–4. Copyright © 1998 by Arte Público Press, University of Houston, Houston, TX. "The Hammon and the Beans" from *The Hammon and the Beans and Other Stories* by Américo Paredes. Copyright © 1994 by Américo Paredes. "Coming Back from It," "Olivia," and "This Is What I Said" from *The Sadness of Days: Selected and New Poems* by Luis Omar Salinas. Copyright © 1987 by Luis Omar Salinas. "The Harvest" from *The Harvest: Short Stories* by Tomás Rivera, edited by Julián Olivares. Copyright © 1989 by Tomás Rivera Archives/Concepción Rivera.

**Atheneum, a division of Simon & Schuster Adult Publishing Group:** "Two Words" from *The Stories of Eva Luna* by Isabel Allende, translated by Margaret Sayers Peden. Copyright © 1998 by Isabel Allende; Translation copyright © 1991 by Macmillan Publishing Company. Pages 145–149 (retitled "The Creation of Humans") and excerpts from *Popol Vuh: The Mayan Book of the Dawn of Life* by Dennis Tedlock. Copyright © 1985, 1996 by Dennis Tedlock.

**Aunt Lute Books:** "To live in the Borderlands means you" from *Borderlands: La Frontera* by Gloria Anzaldúa. Copyright © 1987, 1999 by Gloria Anzaldúa. Copyright © 1999 by Karin Ikas.

**Susan Bergholz Literary Services, New York, NY:** "Washing the Windows" and "Woman's Work" from *Homecoming: New and Collected Poems* by Julia Alvarez. Copyright © 1984, 1996 by Julia Alvarez. Published by Plume, an imprint of Dutton Signet, a division of Penguin Group (USA), Inc. "Audition" from *The Other Side/El Otro Lado* by Julia Alvarez. Copyright © 1995 by Julia Alvarez. Published by Dutton, a division of Penguin Group (USA) Inc. From "El Doctor" and "My English" from *Something to Declare* by Julia Alvarez. Copyright © 1992, 1998 by Julia Alvarez. "A New Mexico Christmas" by Rudolfo Anaya from *The Anaya Reader.* Copyright © 1982 by Rudolfo Anaya. First published in the *Los Angeles Times,* 1982. From "Message from the Inca" from *The Anaya Reader* by Rudolfo Anaya. Copyright © 1995 by Rudolfo Anaya. All rights reserved. "Six Brothers" and "Traficante" from *My Wicked Wicked Ways* by Sandra Cisneros. Copyright © 1987 by Sandra Cisneros. First published by Third Woman Press, 1987.

**Bilingual Press/Editorial Bilingüe, Arizona State University, Tempe, Arizona:** "Golden Glass" by Alma Villanueva from *Hispanics in the U.S.: An Anthology of Creative Literature,* edited by Francisco Jimenez and Gary D. Keller. Copyright © 1982 by Bilingual Press/Editorial Bilingüe.

**Cecilia Burciaga:** Adaptation of "La Puerta" by José Antonio Burciaga. Copyright © 1992 by José Antonio Burciaga.

**Fray Angélico Chávez History Library, Palace of the Governors, Santa Fe, NM:** "Hunchback Madonna" from *New Mexico Triptych* by Fray Angélico Chávez. Copyright 1940 by Fray Angélico Chávez.

**Cinco Puntos Press:** "La Llorona: The Weeping Woman" (English version) from *La Llorona: The Weeping Woman* by Joe Hayes. Copyright © 2004 by Joe Hayes.

**Coffee House Press:** "Problems with Hurricanes" from *Red Beans* by Victor Hernández Cruz. Copyright © 1991 by Victor Hernández Cruz.

**Da Capo Press, a member of Perseus Books, L.L.C.:** "A Shot at It" from *When I Was Puerto Rican* by Esmeralda Santiago. Copyright © 1993 by Esmeralda Santiago.

**Duke University Press:** From Chapter XX from *The Discovery and Conquest of Peru: Chronicles of the New World Encounter* by Pedro de Cieza de Leon, edited and translated by Alexandra Parma Cook and David Noble Cook. Copyright © 1998 by Duke University Press.

**Farrar, Straus and Giroux, LLC:** "Horses" from *Extravagaria* by Pablo Neruda, translated by Alastair Reid. Copyright © 1975 by Farrar, Straus and Giroux, LLC. "Ode to My Suit" from *The Poetry of Pablo Neruda,* translated by Margaret Sayers Peden. Copyright © 2003 by Farrar, Straus and Giroux, LLC.

*Firebrand Books:* "Ending Poem" from *Getting Home Alive* by Aurora Levins Morales and Rosario Morales. Copyright © 1986 by Aurora Levins Morales and Rosario Morales.

*Folk Arte Gallery:* "La Ofrenda" as told by Francisco González Sol from *Cuentos de el Día de los Muertos: Day of the Dead Folk Tales,* translated by Colleen González. Copyright © 1997 by Salvador González and Nina Vivian Huryn.

*Professor Diana García:* "The Flat of the Land" by Diana García. Copyright © 1992 by Diana García.

*Harcourt, Inc.:* "The Mechanical Mind" from *Local News* by Gary Soto. Copyright © 1993 by Gary Soto.

*HarperCollins Publishers, Inc.:* "The Handsomest Drowned Man in the World" from *Leaf Storm and Other Stories* by Gabriel García Márquez. Copyright © 1971 by Gabriel García Márquez. "Mr. Mendelsohn" from *El Bronx Remembered: A Novella and Stories* by Nicholasa Mohr. Copyright © 1975 by Nicholasa Mohr.

*Harvard University Press, Cambridge, MA:* "Poem 7," "Poem 15," "Poem 22," "Poem 27," "Poem 29," and from "Reply to Sister Philothea" by Sor Juana Inés de la Cruz from *A Sor Juana Anthology,* translated by Alan S. Trueblood. Copyright © 1988 by the President and Fellows of Harvard College.

*Holmes & Meier Publishers, Inc.:* "The Two Princes" from *Major Poems: A Bilingual Edition* by José Martí, translated by Elinor Randall. Copyright © 1982 by Holmes & Meier Publishers, Inc.

*The Johns Hopkins Press:* "Serene Words" from *Selected Poems of Gabriela Mistral,* translated by Doris Dana. Copyright © 1971 by Doris Dana.

*International Publishers:* "Easy Job, Good Wages" from *A Puerto Rican in New York* by Jesús Colón. Copyright © 2000 by Jesús Colón.

*Museum of New Mexico Press:* "The Force of Luck" from *Cuentos: Tales from the Hispanic Southwest,* retold in English by Rudolfo A. Anaya. Copyright © 1980 by the Museum of New Mexico Press.

*New Directions Publishing Corporation:* "Accountability" and "Tomás Lucero" from *Black Mesa Poems* by Jimmy Santiago Baca. Copyright © 1989 by Jimmy Santiago Baca. "It Started" from *Immigrants in Our Own Land* by Jimmy Santiago Baca. Copyright © 1982 by Jimmy Santiago Baca. "The Face and the Wind" from *The Collected Poems of Octavio Paz,* translated by Eliot Weinberger. Copyright © 1971 by New Directions Publishing Corporation.

*Josephina Niggli Scholarship Fund, c/o Western Carolina University:* "The Ring of General Macías" by Josephina Niggli. Copyright 1943 by Josephina Niggli.

*The Nobel Foundation:* From "Towards the Splendid City" by Pablo Neruda from *Nobel Lectures, Literature 1968–1980.* Copyright © 1971 by The Nobel Foundation. From "In Search of the Present" by Octavio Paz from *Nobel Lectures, Literature 1981–1990,* translated by Anthony Stanton. Copyright © 1990 by The Nobel Foundation.

*North Point Press, a division of Farrar, Straus & Giroux, LLC:* "Up Among the Eagles" from *Open Door* by Luisa Valenzuela, translated by Margaret Sayers Peden. Copyright © 1976, 1978, 1988 by Luisa Valenzuela.

*W. W. Norton & Company, Inc.:* "My Native Costume," "Pegao," and "Who Burns for the Perfection of Paper" from *Alabanza: New and Selected Poems 1982–2002* by Martín Espada. Copyright © 2003 by Martín Espada.

*Orchard Books/Scholastic Inc.:* "An Hour with Abuelo" from *An Island Like You: Stories of the Barrio* by Judith Ortiz Cofer. Copyright © 1995 by Judith Ortiz Cofer. All rights reserved. "Confessions of a Non-Native Speaker" and "Picture of Whoopee" from *Call Me Maria* by Judith Ortiz Cofer. Copyright © 2004 by Judith Ortiz Cofer. All rights reserved.

*Oxford University Press, Inc.:* "Plague of Ants" by Fray Bartolomé de las Casas, translated by Sandra Ferdman from *The Oxford Book of Latin American Short Stories,* edited by Roberto González Echevarría. Copyright © 1997 by Oxford University Press, Inc.

*Pantheon Books, a division of Random House, Inc.:* "Continuity of Parks" and "House Taken Over" from *Blow-up and Other Stories* by Julio Cortázar. Copyright © 1963, 1967 by Random House, Inc.

*Penguin Books Ltd.:* From Preface from *A Short Account of the Destruction of the Indies* by Bartolomé de las Casas, translated by Nigel Griffin. Translation copyright © 1992 by Nigel Griffin.

*Alberto Ríos:* "The Lesson of Walls" and "On January 5, 1984, El Santo the Wrestler Died, Possibly" from *Five Indiscretions: A Book of Poems* by Alberto Ríos. Copyright © 1985 by Alberto Ríos. All rights reserved.

*Rosemont Publishing and Printing Corp.:* "Autumn Verses," "Lo Fatal," "Versos de Otoño," and "What Gets You" from *Selected Poems of Rubén Darío: A Bilingual Anthology,* translated by Alberto Acereda and Will Derusha. Copyright © 2001 by Rosemont Publishing and Printing Corp.

*Carmen Tafolla:* "marked" from *Sonnets to Human Beings and Other Selected Works* by Carmen Tafolla. Copyright © 1992 by Carmen Tafolla.

*University of New Mexico Press:* "My Wonder Horse" from *Tierra Amarilla* by Sabine R. Ulibarri. Translation copyright © 1971 by University of New Mexico Press.

*University of Pittsburgh Press:* "Freeway 280," "Poem for the Young White Man Who Asked Me How I, an Intelligent, Well-Read Person Could Believe in the War Between Races," and "Refugee Ship" from *Emplumada* by Lorna Dee Cervantes. Copyright © 1981 by Lorna Dee Cervantes. "Black Hair" from *Black Hair* by Gary Soto. Copyright © 1985 by Gary Soto. "History" from *The Elements of San Joaquin* by Gary Soto. Copyright © 1977 by Gary Soto.

**University of Texas Press:** "A Pact with the Devil" from *Confabulario and Other Inventions* by Juan José Arreola, translated by George D. Schade. Copyright © 1964 by Juan José Arreola. "A Canary's Ideas" from *The Devil's Church and Other Stories* by Joaquim Maria Machado de Assis. Translation copyright © 1977 by University of Texas Press. "The Ballad of Gregorio Cortez" from *With His Pistol in His Hand: A Border Ballad and Its Hero* by Américo Paredes. Copyright © 1958, 1986 by Américo Paredes. "The White Uniform" from "Viña: Three Beach Plays" by Sergio Vodánovic from *Voices of Change in the Spanish American Theater: An Anthology,* translated by William I. Oliver. Copyright © 1971 by William I. Oliver.

**University Press of Florida:** "What I Mean" from *Our Lives are Rivers* by Mark Smith-Soto. Copyright © 2003 by Mark Smith-Soto.

**VerbSap.com:** From Preface from "Interview: Margarita Engle" from *VerbSap: Concise Prose. Enough Said* Web site on April 27, 2006 at http://www.verbsap.com/2005june/interviewengle.html.

**Viking Penguin, an imprint of Penguin Group (USA) Inc.:** "The Other" from *Collected Fictions* by Jorge Luis Borges, translated by Andrew Hurley. Copyright © 1998 by Maria Kodama; translation copyright © 1998 by Penguin Putnam Inc.

**White Pine Press:** "The Turtle" from *The Stones of Chile* by Pablo Neruda, translated by Dennis Maloney. Copyright © 2003 by White Pine Press.

**Sources Cited:**

From "Jimmy Santiago Baca" from *Contemporary Authors Online,* 2006. Published by Gale Group, 2006.

From "Mora, Pat(ricia)" from *Major 21st-Century Writers,* Gale Group, 2005.

Quote about Alberto Ríos by Jose David Saldivar from *Dictionary of Literary Biography,* Gale Group.

From "An Interview with Alberto Ríos" by Tina Eliopulos from *Red Rock Review,* August 30, 1998.

Quote by Judith Hemschemeyer from review of *Our Lives Are Rivers* by Mark Smith-Soto. Published by University Press of Florida, 2003.

# Photo Credits

Page 4, ©Photodisc/Getty Images; 12, ©Bettmann/CORBIS; 14, North Wind Picture Archives; 18, Library of Congress; 27, ©Werner Forman/Art Resource, NY; 30, ©Werner Forman/Topham/The Image Works; 32, Art Resource, NY; 52, ©Lindsay Hebberd/CORBIS; 58, Courtesy of Photofest; 70, iStockphoto.com; 72, ©Bettmann/CORBIS; 74, ©Farrell Grehan/CORBIS; 75, Courtesy of The Hispanic Society of America, New York; 78, ©CORBIS; 79–80, iStockphoto.com; 81, Courtesy of the Consulate of Uruguay, NY; 83, iStockphoto.com; 90, iStockphoto.com; 92, ©PAL/Topham/The Image Works; 100, Keystone/Hulton Archive/Getty Images; 103, Lambert/Hulton Archive/Getty Images; 104, iStockphoto.com; 105–106, iStockphoto.com; 107, Steve Northup/Time & Life Pictures/Getty Images; 109, copyright ©Jean Paul Nacivet/eStock Photo. All Rights Reserved; 110, ©Sophie Bassouls/CORBIS SYGMA; 118. ©Ricky Davila/COVER/The Image Works; 121, Anthony H, Fisher/Indigo Arts Gallery, Philadelphia; 125, Courtesy Stephanie Franklin; 131, ©R. Grazioli/CORBIS SYGMA; 138, ©Nancy Crampton; 141, ©Christie's Images/CORBIS; 144, Arte Público Press–University of Houston, Reprinted with the permission from the publisher; 148, ©Isabella Stewart Gardner Museum, Boston, MA/Bridgeman Art Library; 163, Courtesy The University of Puerto Rico; 165, ©Bettmann/CORBIS; 166, 169, Courtesy of the Fray Angélico Chávez History Library. Palace of the Governors, Santa Fe, NM; 173, Courtesy Western Carolina University; 175, ©CORBIS; 186, Photograph by Tino Mauricio. Courtesy of the Nettie Lee Benson Latin American Collection, University of Texas Libraries, the University of Texas at Austin; 189, ©Christie's Images/SuperStock; 191, ©Cynthia Farah Haines; 195, Darrell Gulin/The Image Bank/Getty Images; 196, ©Cynthia Farah Haines; 202, ©2005 Chris Bell; 213, Arte Público Press–University of Houston, Reprinted with the permission from the publisher; 216, ©Brand X/SuperStock; 217, Steve Snowden/Getty Images Entertainment; 226. ©Danny Lehman/CORBIS; 229, Arte Público Press-University of Houston, Reprinted with the permission from the publisher; 232, Kajino/Orion Press/Jupiter Images; 233, ©Cynthia Farah Haines; 236, iStockphoto.com; 240, ©David H. Wells/CORBIS; 241, ©Cynthia Farah Haines; 243, ©David Muench/CORBIS; 244, ©Neil McAllister/Alamy; 245, ©David Young-Wolff/PhotoEdit; 246, ©Kelly-Mooney Photography/CORBIS; 247, Courtesy Alma Luz Villanueva; 250, ©Royalty-Free/CORBIS; 251, Arte Público Press-University of Houston, Reprinted with the permission from the publisher; 252, ©age fotostock/SuperStock; 253, ©Bettmann/CORBIS; 254, Bob Curtis; 258, Frank Cantor; 262, Austin Iglehart; 264, Photo by Christopher Felver; 265, ©Carl and Ann Purcell/CORBIS; 266, ©Dorothy Alexander; 271, ©Purestock/Alamy; 275, Steven Weinberg/Stone/Getty Images; 278, Tadashi Ono/Amana Images/Getty Images; 279, ©Danny Lehman/CORBIS; 281, ©Bret Brookshire; 283, iStockphoto.com; 285, courtesy of the author; 287, ©Tim Page/CORBIS; 291, courtesy of Jimmy Santiago Baca; 298, Rick O'Quinn; 301, Bruce Ayres/Stone/Getty Images; 305, ©Rosa Ibarra/Omni-Photo Communications; 308, iStockphoto.com; 309, Lupita Barron-Rios; 312, Digital Vision Ltd./SuperStock; 314, Everett Collection; 316, iStockphoto.com; 318, ©Carolyn Soto; 321, iStockphoto.com; 324, ©Tony Freeman/PhotoEdit; 325, Benelux Press/Index Stock Imagery/JupiterImages; 327, Arte Público Press-University of Houston. Reprinted with the permission from the publisher; 331–332, iStockphoto.com; 333, ©Cynthia Farah Haines; 336, iStockphoto.com; 338, ©Linda Haas; 341, AP Photo/Daily Hampshire Gazette/Kevin Gutting; 343, Nick Vedros & Associates/Stone/Getty Images; 344, ©Jeff Greenberg/Alamy; 345, iStockphoto.com; 346, photo by Michael R. McNew; 352, ©Gene Blevins/LA Daily News/CORBIS

# Index of Authors and Titles

*Accountability,* 297
Acereda, Alberto, 77, 79
Allende, Isabel, 144
*Alligator War, The,* 82
Alvarez, Julia, 266
Anaya, Rudolfo A., 42, 217
Anzaldúa, Gloria, 238
Arreola, Juan José, 118
*Arte Popular,* 246
*Audition,* 279
*Autumn Verses,* 79

Baca, Jimmy Santiago, 291
*Ballad of Gregorio Cortez, The,* 56
Bandelier, Fanny, 11
*Birthday,* 282
Blackburn, Paul, 112, 114
*Black Hair,* 324
Borges, Jorge Luis, 92
*Breaking Piñatas,* 311
Burciaga, José Antonio, 233

Cabeza de Vaca, Álvar Núñez, 9
*Call Me Maria,* from, 304, 307
*Canary's Ideas, A,* 68
Casas, Fray Bartolomé de las, 22
Cervantes, Lorna Dee, 327
Chávez, Fray Angélico, 166
Cisneros, Sandra, 333
Cofer, Judith Ortiz, 298
*Colibrí,* 345
Colón, Jesús, 163
*Coming Back from It,* 232
*Confessions of a Non-Native Speaker,* 307
*Continuity of Parks,* 112
Corpi, Lucha, 251
Cortázar, Julio, 110
*Creation of Humans, The* 28
Cruz, Sor Juana Inés de la, 32
Cruz, Victor Hernández, 264

Dana, Doris, 90
Darío, Rubén, 75

Derusha, Will, 77, 79
*Disillusionment,* 34

*Easy Job, Good Wages,* 164
*El Bronx Remembered,* from, 203
*El corrido de Gregorio Cortez,* 56
*El Doctor,* 268
*Elements of San Joaquin, The,* from, 325
*Emily Dickinson,* 253
*Emily Dickinson* (Spanish), 253
*Ending Poem,* 339
Engle, Margarita, 285
Espada, Martín, 341

*Fabio, what pretty women covet most,* 35
*Face and the Wind, The,* 109
Ferdman, Sandra, 23
*Flat of the Land, The,* 347
*Force of Luck, The,* 42
*Freeway 280,* 328

García, Diana, 346
García Márquez, Gabriel, 131
Gilb, Dagoberto, 281
*Golden Glass,* 248
*Graduation Morning,* 245

*Hammon and the Beans, The,* 187
*Handsomest Drowned Man in the World, The,* 133
*Harvest, The,* 214
Hayes, Joe, 49
Hinojosa-Smith, Rolando, 196
*History,* 325
*Horses,* 104
*Hour with Abuelo, An,* 300
*House Taken Over,* 114
*Hunchback Madonna,* 167
Hurley, Andrew, 94

*If men weighed the hazards of the sea,* 37

*In the Family,* 152
Ishimatsu, Lorie, 68
*Island Like You, An,* from, 300
*It Started,* 293

*Journey of Álvar Núñez Cabeza de Vaca, The,* from, 11

*La Llorona, the Weeping Woman,* 49
*La Ofrenda (The Offering),* 52
*La Puerta,* 234
*Lesson of Walls, The,* 316
Levins Morales, Aurora, 338
Livingston, Arthur, 82
Llano, María Elena, 151
*Local News,* from, 320
*Lo fatal,* 76
*Los dos príncipes,* 73

Machado de Assis, Joaquim Maria, 67
Maloney, Dennis, 106
*marked,* 290
Martí, José, 72
*Mechanical Mind, The,* 320
*Message from the Inca,* 218
*Mexico,* 252
*México,* 252
*Mi Madre,* 243
Mistral, Gabriela, 89
Mohr, Nicholasa, 202
Mora, Pat, 241
Morales, Rosario, 338
*Mr. Mendelsohn,* 203
*My English,* 273
*My Native Costume,* 344
*My Wonder Horse,* 192

Neruda, Pablo, 100
*New Mexico Christmas, A,* 224
Niggli, Josephina, 173
*Niña,* 286

*Ode to My Suit,* 102
Oliver, William I., 124
*Olivia,* 230

*On January 5, 1984, El Santo the Wrestler Died, Possibly,* 313
*Other, The,* 94

*Pact with the Devil, A,* 119
Paredes, Américo, 186
Paz, Octavio, 107
Peden, Margaret Sayers, 102, 139, 145
*Pegao,* 342
*Peruvian Child,* 244
*Picture of Whoopee,* 304
*Plague of Ants,* 23
*Poem for the Young White Man . . . ,* 331
*Popol Vuh,* from the, 28
*Problems with Hurricanes,* 265
*Puerto Rican in New York and Other Sketches, A,* from, 164

Quiroga, Horacio, 81

Rabassa, Gregory, 133
Randall, Elinor, 73
*Refugee Ship,* 330
Reid, Alastair, 104
*Reply to Sor Philothea,* from, 38

*Ring of General Macías, The,* 174
Ríos, Alberto, 309
Rivera, Tomás, 213

Salinas, Luis Omar, 229
Santiago, Esmeralda, 254
Schade, George D., 119
Schmitt, Jack, 68
*Serene Words,* 90
*Shot at It, A,* 255
*Six Brothers,* 335
Smith-Soto, Mark, 262
Sol, Francisco González, 52
*Something to Declare,* from, 268
Soto, Gary, 318
*Speaking to you, belovèd, this afternoon,* 35

Tafolla, Carmen, 289
Tedlock, Dennis, 28
Teleki, Beatriz, 152
*These lying pigments . . . ,* 36
*This Is What I Said,* 231
*To live in the Borderlands means you,* 239
*Tomás Lucero,* 295
*Traficante,* 337

Trueblood, Alan S., 34, 35, 36, 37, 38
*Turtle, The,* 106
*Two Princes, The,* 73
*Two Words,* 145

Ulibarrí, Sabine, 191
*Up Among the Eagles,* 139

Valenzuela, Luisa, 138
*Versos de otoño,* 78
Villanueva, Alma Luz, 247
Vodánovic, Sergio, 123

*Washing the Windows,* 277
Weinberger, Eliot, 109
*What Gets You,* 77
*What I Mean,* 263
*When I Was Puerto Rican,* from, 255
*White Uniform, The,* 124
*Who Burns for the Perfection of Paper,* 342
*Woman's Work,* 278
*Words and Palabras,* 197